the guide for
white women
who teach
black boys

To my wife, Laura Moore, my children, my family, and all of those who continue to work toward a society grounded in peace, equity, and justice for all, regardless of the boundaries placed on them.

—Eddie Moore Jr.

To Gertrude, Tetile, Evelyn, Thania, Sipho, and Sitetile. I am who I am because you are who you are.

—Ali Michael

To my parents, George and Marguerite Penick, for teaching me to believe in humanity; and to all of the students who crossed my path, from my high school students to my graduate students, who continue to convince me of the power of education.

—Marguerite W. Penick-Parks

the guide for white women who teach black boys

understanding

respecting

connecting

eddie moore jr.
ali michael
marguerite w. penick-parks

Forewords by Glenn E. Singleton and Heather Hackman

CORWIN

A SAGE Publishing Company

FOR INFORMATION:

Corwin

A SAGE Company

2455 Teller Road

Thousand Oaks, California 91320

(800) 233-9936

www.corwin.com

SAGE Publications Ltd.

1 Oliver's Yard

55 City Road

London EC1Y 1SP

United Kingdom

SAGE Publications India Pvt. Ltd.

B 1/I 1 Mohan Cooperative Industrial Area

Mathura Road, New Delhi 110 044

India

SAGE Publications Asia-Pacific Pte. Ltd.

3 Church Street

#10-04 Samsung Hub

Singapore 049483

Program Director: Dan Alpert

Associate Editor: Lucas Schleicher

Senior Editorial Assistant: Katie Crilley

Production Editor: Amy Schroller

Copy Editor: Jacqueline Tasch

Typesetter: C&M Digitals (P) Ltd.

Proofreader: Dennis Webb

Indexer: Sheila Bodell

Marketing Manager: Charline Maher

Printed in the United States of America

ISBN 978-1-5063-5168-1

This book is printed on acid-free paper.

SFI label applies to text stock

19 20 21 22 23 10 9 8 7 6 5 4

Contents

Note From the Publisher

The authors have provided access to video content made available to you through QR codes. To read a QR code, you must have a smartphone or tablet with a camera. We recommend that you download a QR code reader app that is made specifically for your phone or tablet brand. You may also access the videos at **http://resources.corwin.com/WWBBGuide**.

Forewords

Foreword 1

Glenn E. Singleton

Beginning in third grade, our class would travel downstairs to the basement Music Room of Baltimore City's Hilton Elementary School to learn from our beloved teacher, Mrs. Buckskin. This is when I truly learned to use my pipes. Somehow, belting out "To Be Young Gifted and Black," made me and most of my thirty-nine classmates come alive and enjoy choral music. I was in kindergarten when jazz vocalist and legend Nina Simone had released the song, which is still my favorite. And in fourth grade, I remember being quite sad to see Mrs. Buckskin depart Hilton; but I welcomed a younger, hipper, and dare I say prettier Mrs. Butler, who replaced our retiring idol in the underground chambers. She and her cultural music selections not only cemented my lifelong love for all things choral but also inspired my first crush on one of our esteemed educators! Such childish antics as well as profound connections and relationships were commonplace at my inner-city school.

Music class at Public School no. 21 is just one of many scholastic moments that illuminate what it was truly like to be a Black boy in a Baltimore city public elementary school in the late nineteen sixties to mid-seventies. Throw in daily, challenging phonics lessons and cursive writing drills facilitated by a "family" of about thirty Black teachers, each of whom I knew by sight, and eventually all of them by name, and what resulted was my effective schooling. Together, Hilton's faculty and staff expertly guided my academic and civic progress and were instrumental in supporting my high standing in our community. Whether they were boasting of my recent accomplishments to my mother in the grocery store on Saturday morning, driving me home after detention because I talked too much in class, or reporting my progress in a traditional "Back-to-School" parent-teacher conference, Hilton teachers were professionals with purpose that extended well beyond any district education policy, program, or practice. Certainly, we were the offspring of other people, but many of us got the feeling that our proud teachers held us to the same high standards of excellence to which they held their very own children, many of whom were simultaneously being educated in adjacent classrooms. Through fourth grade, the aforementioned model of teaching and learning captured the essence of my privileged, racially segregated, school narrative.

The summer before I entered fifth grade, our church and other community centers were abuzz with a story of White teachers coming to Hilton Elementary School, an innovative Baltimore response to court-ordered school desegregation. At that time, I was more interested in playing block ball, scully, and hopscotch in the alley or venturing on public transportation (my school bus since third grade) to the Druid Hill Park pool. Thus, I failed to capture how the essence of my family's conversations, related to this Baltimore answer to the famed 1954 *Brown v. Board of Education* decision, would greatly impact my inevitable "back-to-school" experience. Clear to me, however, was that few community elders seemed pleased with the idea of White teachers coming to our schools, or even fewer supported the firing of some legendary Black teachers. I vaguely recall overhearing family members comment about White Baltimore families' unwillingness to send their children to our beloved Hilton Elementary; they also noted that relatively few White students were being educated in Baltimore public schools, which reduced opportunities for displaced Black teachers. Given the intense racism that characterized 1970s' Baltimore, I imagine that even if our Black teachers had desired teaching positions in suburban Baltimore schools, those jobs still would not have been realistic options for them.

The famed yet flawed court-ordered racial desegregation law became real to me when my new fifth-grade teacher, Mrs. Fran Finnegan, a White woman, spent her first semester eliciting unsavory results and unanticipated consequences in Room 216. For the very first time in my life, I faced a nice teacher who was ill-equipped to meet my needs. When she entered a school full of Black children, Mrs. Finnegan, like the other White women teachers arriving at Hilton, came with limited racial consciousness, a singular pedagogical interpretation, and an unwillingness to implement culturally responsive lessons. Instead, she insisted that we learn and sing several cuts on the Simon and Garfunkel album, *Bridge Over Troubled Water*. To this day, I still chuckle at the singers' names and struggle to interpret the lyrics of "If I Could" (El Condor Pasa). Yet, Mrs. Finnegan's initial mission—to assist her students in understanding and embracing what was familiar and important to her—caused my fifth-grade year to become something short of a racial horror story. By the grace of God, my five previous years of preparation, the support of my family and community, and Mrs. Finnegan's courage and willingness to learn, grow, and stick it out with us, the glory was eventually ours!

Of course, Mrs. Finnegan wasn't to blame professionally. Nowhere in her preparation, experience, or studies had she been introduced to the essence—that is, the spirit, souls, and intellect—of Black children, our families, and community. Nor was it our fault that as fifth graders, we knew of and about White women only through "para-social" television relationships. Indeed, we acquainted ourselves with Mrs. Finnegan in the same way we would have reacted to Misses Brady, Partridge, Walton, Ingalls, Jetson, Flintstone, and Rubble, had they turned up in our classroom one fall morning. Thus, our relationship was imaginary and therefore dishonest from Day One. On her part, Mrs. Finnegan was a veteran, enthusiastic, suburban White woman who initially could not acknowledge her Black inexperience. On my part, I was one of forty Black children, at least half of us boys, who were already socialized never to honestly remind her of her White ways and never to discuss her Whiteness in public or within earshot of our former Black educators. This ingrained model of selective silence served only to exacerbate my interracial disharmony, tension, and distrust; this societal practice prompts feelings of unresolved trauma in me to this day.

With so many racial injustices wearing down our Black community in the Seventies, initially my family wondered why were we being dealt yet another slight. But after an extremely rocky start, miraculously it seemed, Mrs. Finnegan's will, skill, knowledge, and capacity to meet our needs greatly improved within months. She soon realized herself to be part of a community of awesome teachers, including Mrs. Butler, who took great care in selecting and teaching music. Mrs. Finnegan also effectively learned to engage our busy parents and weave our everyday life stories and experiences into math and science lessons. Mrs. Finnegan was the first of roughly one hundred ill-prepared White women teachers whom I would encounter along my own scholastic pathway from Hilton Public School 21 to The Park School, the University of Pennsylvania, and, finally, Stanford University. Sadly, only a handful of these White women became effective facilitators of my holistic Black male development in the way of Fran Finnegan. In fact, upon arriving at The Park School, a predominantly Jewish, independent day school, for seventh grade in the summer of 1976, I did not understand that my opportunities to learn from and with Black teachers would end completely and not resume until well into my college years. Even more challenging was that only a handful of the 98 percent White faculty at Park, ever rose to the level of Mrs. Finnegan's cultural fluency.

The still-wounded fifth-grade Glenn, some forty years later, still holds an almost photographic memory but has yet to fully discuss in print about what has happened to *US* in the hands of *THEM*. Thus, I initially struggled to participate in a project entitled, *The Guide for White Women Who Teach Black Boys*. A part of me still embraces interracial dishonesty and silence as a foolproof way of preserving the negative peace that Martin Luther King, Jr., described in his "Letter From a Birmingham Jail"—one that avoids discomfort and simultaneously robs students, in my image, of their freedom to learn. In the past, my near approaches to such honesty caused pain. My candid counternarrative has triggered tears among White women. The Black boys and young men who are their students have been further criminalized as scary, angry, or threatening. I'm left nothing short of indignant. If this is the effect, how can I support the cause?

Even if this book succeeded in not making Black boys and young men the problem in the readers' eyes, I still held doubt as to whether, barring exceptions, White women teachers would ever invest the prerequisite energy and time to understand the damaging aspects of their own Whiteness. I held doubt that they would embrace the innate beauty and brilliance of Black people—a prerequisite to becoming successful stewards of our learning. I doubted whether a new generation of willing White women could learn to purposefully love Black boys and young men and construct for them the appropriate physical, cultural, and intellectual environments in which they would authentically thrive and excel.

Upon further reflection though, I realized that this book represented an important opportunity: to establish the foundations for how White women can beat the overwhelming odds and become successful teachers of Black boys and young men. The extraordinary thinking of contributing authors, such as Dr. Jawanza Kunjufu, who writes on the critical nature of understanding Black boys' and young men's histories, is derived from decades of research and teaching experience. As a former Ivy League admissions director, I am particularly moved by Dr. Edward Smith's narrative regarding systemic low expectations for Black boys and young men, cautioning White women educators to guard against a propensity to "undermatch" these students in the college selection process. Within this volume, I have become acquainted with some of the revolutionary understandings successful White women teachers possess. Armed with this Guide's wisdom, indeed, they are exemplars of an uncommon love. They move out of the celebrated mainstream systems of educators who take the well-paved road to the White institutionally racist destruction of Black lives. They are champions of purposeful teaching, and they defy daily pressures to render their Black boys and young men students, "Beyond Love" (Duncan, 2002).

Such purpose for educating *all* children is how my mentor, Dr. Asa Hilliard, shaped my own personal and professional foundation, in which I proudly embrace as an honor and privilege the opportunity to educate Black children. Dr. Hilliard instilled in me the truth that "there are no pedagogical barriers . . . when willing teachers are prepared and made available to children" (Hilliard, 1995). In my own language, we as teachers of Black boys and young men need a deep sense of purpose imbued in our passion, practice, and persistence. From the moment I first sat at Dr. Hilliard's feet in a seminar on educating African American children in 1993, I was clear that my work was to convey to others, in a *Courageous Conversation*, the importance of educators touching the spirit of Black children as the primary learning and teaching strategy.

Rather than recounting the failures of countless White women teachers, subjecting them and me to new traumas, I prefer to highlight a few ways in which Fran Finnegan and Theresa Schwartz (Hilton Elementary), Jane Gutman and Rachelle Johnson (The Park School) as well as Carolyn Marvin (University of Pennsylvania) and Patricia Gumport (Stanford University) back in the day emerged as exceptions to the rule. I recognize these White women teachers among my all-time exceptional educators. Furthermore, as one who has spent three decades instructing White women teachers and developing them into culturally responsive, anti-racist educators, I will also draw insight from my better students, who purposefully transformed their racially unconscious and biased beliefs, behaviors, and practices in order to reach their "hardest to teach" students.

Aligning with this Guide's framework of *understanding, respecting, and connecting*, my professional offering to White women teachers who yearn to experience success with Black boys/young men is to develop an enhanced personal consciousness and literacy around the impact of race in their own lives. Such discovery will naturally lead to you professionally uncovering insights about the presence and role of whiteness on Black student achievement. As a way of doing this, I have supported countless teachers in becoming proficient practitioners of the Courageous Conversations About Race™ (CCAR) protocol (Singleton, 2015). CCAR offers tools for deepening our understanding of and expression about race and racism, allowing White women teachers to discover essential racial information about themselves, their students, and the systems in which they are called to interact. Furthermore, White women teachers who extend to their students the practice of using the Four Agreements, Six Conditions, and Compass of Courageous Conversation™ will unlock the unspoken or unexpanded racial narratives about themselves and the Black boys and young men in their care. It is precisely through voicing our unspoken truths that we gain critical racial understandings that the best White teachers of my time in school were left to simply figure out in silence on their own. Addressed directly to White women teachers who are reading this book: the following is just a brief overview of CCAR:

The Four Agreements of Courageous Conversation™ offer norms or rules for inter/intra-racial engagement. Accordingly, for you to achieve success teaching Black boys and young men, you must:

- Stay Engaged: Don't give up when it gets personal, difficult, or uncomfortable;

- Speak Your Truth: Even when you feel you may be exposing your racial ignorance;

- Experience Discomfort: Transforming beliefs will not come easily or painlessly; and

- Expect/Accept Non-Closure: Continuous learning requires you choose imperfection over inaction.

Just as there are conditions for successfully meeting students' developmental needs at the elementary, secondary, and higher education levels, generically speaking, there are also specific conditions for White women teachers to successfully establish at each of these junctures authentic and productive interracial relationships with their students who are Black boys and young men. Courageous Conversations™ instructs us to view three distinct phases of the effective interracial interaction, those being *Engaging, Sustaining,* and *Deepening.*

Before working to understand the racial, cultural, and gendered foundations at the intersections of being Black and male, you must first discern and examine your own individual and collective racial narratives. Identifying what it means to be White and female is a prerequisite to understanding how you view self and others. Whatever may be confusing or distorted in your own racial autobiography will certainly lead to a confused and distorted interpretation of a Black male's individual and collective perspective and reality. Simply put, to engage in a sound relationship with Black boys and young men, you must recognize the racial texture of your own history and contemporary experiences and pay the closest attention to the way in which Black boys and young men figure into such narratives.

Being willing and ready to embrace racial/cultural perspectives and experiences different than your own is another important condition that you must master to effectively reach and teach Black boys and young men. In terms of both race and gender, how we are treated by society and how we respond to that treatment can define the essence of who we are. How we appear racially impacts how we interact with society, which impacts how we behave and reason. You must not be confused by the fact that this U.S. society in general, and U.S. schools more specifically, have struggled to appreciate the image, gifts, and talents of Black boys and young men. This lack of appreciation can cause Black boys, from a very young age, to develop a survival response that includes donning a protective armor of sorts. A successful White woman teacher will need to penetrate this protective shell to engage with and educate Black boys and young men. Only when our unique Black male perspectives are welcome and understood can we be participants in authentic and meaningful relationships with White women teachers. Expect some anger, even rage, to surface. It is a natural response to racial injustice. Your job is not to minimize or quiet this pained voice, but rather to assist your Black boys and young men students in expressing it constructively in meaningful, relevant, and rigorous academic lessons and co-curricular activities.

A final and critical condition worth mentioning here is that effective White women teachers must constantly examine the presence and role of whiteness in their personal deportment, in their physical classroom environment, and in their curricular, instructional, and assessment practices. What I mean by whiteness is the reality of how existing dominant racial culture finds its way into the interaction of White women teachers and students who are Black boys and young men in three primary ways: color, culture, and consciousness. Specifically, from first sight, a teacher's white skin holds meaning for Black boys and young men students. It may not initially register as a positive attribute, and it may signal an impending negative experience. By the time we first attend school, research shows that many Black children have already had unfavorable, demeaning experiences with White people, leading to them developing feelings of holistic inferiority (Cross, 1991). Such feelings may cause Black boys and young men, especially, to be even less trusting of the unfamiliar White women's image and less likely to engage, perhaps presenting themselves as defensive or combative. Again, this might be the Black boys' or young men's way of protection, a reflexive response that can often be alarming and even frightening to a White woman teacher. To allay the hostilities or suspicions of the student, you must transcend your own fear in order to validate the student and the experiences that can cause Black boys and young men to be leery about White strangers. Developing understanding about and showing an interest in those things that are relevant to the Black boys and young men is one way that you can appear less threatening. How you respond in these circumstances gives some definition to their racial culture and consciousness. Unfortunately, many White women respond inappropriately to Black resistance to racial dominance by overpersonalizing the circumstance and further marginalizing racially targeted students. Such typically White attitudes, beliefs, and behaviors foster greater deterioration in the relationships between White women teachers and Black boys and young men.

Last, the Courageous Conversations™ Compass is a tool that you can use to broaden your responses while interacting with Black boys and young men. Generally, a singular reaction stemming from our own personal racial beliefs, thoughts, feelings, or acts causes us to miss opportunities for empathic engagement. The Compass not only helps you recognize the way in which you are approaching Black boys and young men, but enables you to identify the ways in which your students are approaching any given interaction. When you are practiced in "getting centered"— that is balancing your racial intellect—in interracial classroom interactions with

Black boys and young men, you can more quickly and precisely move to support your students' positioning, no matter how distinct or extreme their competing beliefs, feelings, thinking, and acting may be in the moment. In Compass language, for example, you might consider the following:

Believing: Teaching Black boys and young men is not simply a vocation but also a purpose. Thus you must determine what you want to teach Black boys and young men to know and be able to do and identify how such knowledge and abilities will enable them to be a force for racial justice in our world. Until such a belief is internalized, schools will continue to destroy Black boys and young men's spirit and promise. The stakes are high!

Feeling: Being overwhelmed, disillusioned, fearful, and fatigued are all emotions evoked by the extraordinary challenge you have undertaken in classroom experiences with Black boys and men. At the same time, when you experience success, you will evoke hopefulness, accomplishment, satisfaction, and humanness. Feel it all, every day.

Thinking: Because we have all grown up in a society that struggles to learn from Black men, even about the experience of being Black boys, you especially must recognize, examine, and understand how your own ingrained White terror, White fragility, and White-lashing—retaliating against people of color—yield scholastic conflict. How will you guard against these phenomena to develop the necessary knowledge, skills, and capacity to effectively teach Black boys and young men?

Acting: Recognizing you need help and that you can get better in this critical work is essential but insufficient. Proficiency in meeting the needs of Black boys and young men will take hard work. Improvement will result from taking bold, courageous action over time. You need to revisit this book, and many others on the topic, again and again. You must continue to look at your own racial attitudes, beliefs, and behaviors first, especially in those moments when your success seems most distant or impossible.

I am hopeful that my personal experience and professional insight invite and challenge readers to courageously immerse themselves in this important book. Stay engaged with authors Moore, Michael, Penick-Parks, through *The Guide for White Women Who Teach Black Boys*. Doing so will equip White women teachers with an organizing framework that masterfully supports them in effectively *understanding* themselves, *respecting* the constraints and narratives of Black boys and young men, and *connecting* with their families and communities. Welcome the discomfort you will inherently feel as expert authors challenge your own personal and societal beliefs about the educability of our most vulnerable students. Ward off desires you may have to reach conclusions or closure, but rather remain open to a practice of ever-evolving awareness and self-assessment. You now hold in your hands a resource which can enable you to change the scholastic trajectory of Black boys and young men of color, who currently suffer academically and politically in the hands of many White women teachers, so that they become scholars and citizens who are racially conscious and practiced in effective strategic resistance to internalized, interpersonal, and systemic racism.

I hope that you allow this book to empower you so that you can, in turn, empower Black boys and young men to act in strategic opposition to what their society's greatest institutions were designed to have them do—fail. Instead, you can empower our Black boys and young men to dream, develop, excel, achieve, thrive, and lead. You can educate them *To Be Young Gifted and Black*!

Foreword 2

Heather Hackman

I am deeply grateful for this book. Given the recent spate of highly visible murders of Black and Brown men, women, and trans* folks by police and other authorities, the concomitant rise of Black Lives Matter, the fevered anti-immigrant and xenophobic attitude enshrined in new federal policy, and the end of the post-racial mythos, I cannot think of a more important moment for a book on race in education, and in particular on what White women educators (and by extension, our entire society) can and should do for equity in education. Thus, a book that not only extols the importance of talking about race but also highlights one of this nation's most complicated racial relationships—that of White women* and Black boys/men*—is prescient and timely indeed. The editors and authors speak to the breadth and depth of this complex racial dynamic, while also deftly explicating a range of changes needed in U.S. preschool through twelfth-grade education and the preparation of those who teach there. In the process, the nature of the explosive racial chemistry in our education system as well as our whole society becomes clearer. I know many of the authors contributing to this book, and I am thankful that their voices—voices that ring of clarity, truth, purpose, and vision—have been brought together in such a powerful compendium. So, yes, I am grateful for this book, now more than ever, and for the contribution it will make toward lighting a path to our fullest humanity as educators and our best possible selves as a nation.

Anthologies such as this are never easy to compile. Myriad issues intersect when addressing the dynamics between White women educators and Black boys/young men. To help elaborate on these dynamics and place this book in a larger context, I want to emphasize three critical elements: the history surrounding the use of the "White woman/Black man" dynamic in perpetuating racism, the way gender socialization influences White women's understanding of their racial equity work in education, and the place this race/gender relationship has in U.S. education's maintenance of racial divisions and disparities. Certainly, a range of other areas is worthy of attention, but in my sixteen years of educating mostly White women preservice and inservice teachers (and administrators), the above three foci represent the largest gaps in this population's knowledge and skill base and therefore warrant particular mention.

First, a book of this nature cannot be fully understood without knowing the deeply fraught history between Black boys/men and White women in the United States. It was the British colonists who most robustly brought the laws of coverture from Europe to North America. Under these laws, women were the property of men, had no rights of their own, and were often considered biologically inferior to men. These same British colonists are responsible for the creation of racial categories that established Black people (and later other categories of People of Color/Native peoples) as property with no rights and deemed them a subspecies of humanity second to White, Christian, land-holding men. Both White women and Black men were placed in subordinate positions to White men, and yet both groups' dominant identities (White and male, respectively) were (and still are) insidiously used by White men to further the racial and gendered power divides in this country. Thus, we cannot talk about the relationship between White women educators and Black boys/young men in our schools as if it exists outside of history. One example is the long and painful dynamic of using White women and their socially constructed gender purity as the "reason" for enacting violence against Black men. Such violence existed in the institution of slavery, with Black men being punished if White women gave them attention; persisted in the period of Reconstruction with absurd laws dictating how Black men were allowed to engage with White women in public places; was writ large during Jim Crow, with any unfounded accusation by a White woman (or her patriarch) used to justify the lynching of Black men, and continues today in the minds of murderers like Dylan Roof in Charleston, South Carolina, who cited the age-old trope that "Black men are raping White women" as one of the many reasons he wanted to incite a race war. Forged from this history, the precarious dance that Black men are expected to enact with and around White women is rife with the silencing of Black men, the incessant suspicion of Black men, and violence toward (often leading to the death of) Black men. To be sure this is not "ancient history" as many of the White preservice students in my teacher preparation classes would like to think. Rather, it is alive and well in the most powerful institutions of this country, with preK–12 schools being no exception to that.

The research in this book citing the attitudes of fear that White women express toward the Black boys/young men in their classrooms is not merely the result of racial stereotyping. Rather, it is a treacherous product of the history of White women being repeatedly used as the fictitious target of "dangerous" Black men, thereby justifying the rage and violence of White men as they "protect" their women. Lacking a critical race lens, White women will have absorbed this age-old racist lie and then act it out in their classrooms *despite* their intention to teach all of their students well and even to support their Black boys/young men. As we see in various chapters of the book, no amount of "color blindness" or good intentions is sufficient to undo this centuries-old messaging. What is needed is the critical race frame that the authors and editors offer throughout this text. Nothing short of an explicit, consistent, and progressive understanding of race, and the role of the "White woman/Black man" dynamic in perpetuating it, will right the pernicious effect of this history. By dismantling society's long-standing notion that Black boys/young men are a "threat" to White women, we deal a blow to the racist structure of U.S education and lend substantial support to the creation of the racially just schools we all seek.

Developing a racial justice lens is, unfortunately, not enough to dissolve the influence of this intersectional dynamic. One would hope that the two major waves of feminism would have heralded a shift in the ways most White women perceive their gendered experience in education. The rise of feminist pedagogy and some changes around gendered language in U.S. education, for example, certainly suggest that some things have changed, and yet these movements have ultimately done little to create deep change around gender/race dynamics in U.S. education. To be sure, White women are less able to be used as the justification of violence toward Black men, but this strategy has been supplanted by an even more insidious "White liberal" and stereotypically gendered desire on the part of White women to "save People of Color" and especially Black boys/young men. Movies like *Dangerous Minds* and to a lesser extent *Freedom Writers,* as well as the profoundly classist and racist work of Ruby Payne, depict White women braving the scary ghettos to "help those poor kids" and especially to raise Black boys/young men from the "depths of hopelessness" and "place them on a path to success." In my many years in teacher preparation, I have seen far too many moments where the deeply rooted gender socialization of White, middle-class women (in combination with unquestioned racial stereotypes) has manifested in a profoundly condescending and deficit-based approach to racial issues in education. These White women assume that Black boys/young men are not succeeding because they come from broken homes, they have no role models, their communities do not care about education, and they have no internal resilience. And because their gendered social positioning dictates that women be "natural" caregivers, these well-meaning educators see it as their duty to rescue these troubled, "at risk," and potentially dangerous Black boys/young men. Unfortunately, these educators' good intentions are outweighed by the racist assumptions they make about these boys/young men; combined with the socially constructed gender expectations of caregiving, nurturing, and "saving" children, the end result is a focus on the individual student while the system responsible for the propagation of racism and racial marginalization in our schools goes completely unchecked and unchanged. As a result, some of the most troubling gatekeepers of the school-to-prison pipeline for Black boys/young men are not the overtly racist White teachers, but the well-meaning, badly educated White women caught in their gendered savior complexes and lacking the tools and information to interrupt the racist realities they themselves are unwittingly playing out in their classrooms.

The dynamics described above are compounded even further when conjoined with Christian hegemony, disability oppression, or LGBTQIA issues. In short, the "White savior" complex is exacerbated when combined with other forms of oppression and privilege. For example, when disability oppression combines with the racial and gender dynamics described above, it often results in the overdiagnosing of Black boys as having Emotional and Behavioral Disorder (EBD), Attention Deficit Disorder (ADD), or Attention Deficit and Hyperactivity Disorder (ADHD). Or, if these Black boys/young men are gay, bisexual, queer, or gender nonconforming, the combination of race and gender dynamics often buttresses homophobic notions of the students being "sick" and can elicit "solutions" such as counseling and even conversion therapy to "help" these Black boys/young men "out of their confusion." To be fair, while this book does have chapters that address intersectionality with respect to race, gender, LBGTQIA, and disability oppression, it simply does not have the space to explore these dynamics in depth. And while I am a strong proponent of intersectional education, organizing, and activism, I also know that White women have a long and unfortunate history of hiding behind their gender oppression as a means of avoiding responsibility for their racial privilege. I appreciate the editors' attention to this history (aka the first and second waves of mainstream feminism) and their steadfast commitment to a racial justice focus, while also respectfully acknowledging that a vast and complicated range of additional social justice dynamics is in play. It is a difficult tension to hold, and I believe the editors have attended to it well.

This then leads to my third point of emphasis: the responsibility of U.S. preK–12 and teacher education in the maintenance of this racialized dynamic. White women are not often playing this role by choice. Extensive research has shown that their preK–12 education and later their postsecondary education provided literally *nothing* to prepare them to do anything but play the role described above. If their educational lives had been filled with information about gender justice, feminism, the social construction of race and its role in buttressing racial oppression, and the realities of how racism in education works, many of these White women would be tireless champions of an education that is racially just. Ignorance of these key social justice issues, however, leaves many White women educators with no option but to repeat long-established patterns of racial oppression and internalized gender dynamics and thereby to maintain this system of racial marginalization for Black boys/young men in U.S. education. Teacher education is particularly culpable. Many teacher preparation programs "celebrate diversity" but stay silent with respect to racial equity issues, thus allowing Whiteness to remain at the center of the training of their educators. White women are the overwhelming majority of preK–6 teachers, and thanks to the dearth of attention to racial equity in this nation's teacher preparation programs, these teachers are laying a problematic and painful educational foundation for countless Black boys/young men in this country.

The writings in this book, however, help bridge the informational and experiential divides described above and, through both research and personal testimonial, offer a way to derail this long-standing pattern. The balance of theory and practice in this text is critical in shaping new and definitively different conversations in our schools and teacher education programs. I know that the parents and families of Students of Color and Native students have been sharing these insights for countless decades, and thus I am not pretending that the narratives from the White women in this book are unique. But there is often value in the "it takes one to know one" conversation, and thus there is certainly utility in White women sharing their critical insights and proffering new pedagogic and policy-based solutions. The tireless work and forthright commentary of the editors and contributors within this book provide an honest, hopeful, and tangible set of ideas and practices that I encourage anyone committed to racial justice in education to put into action. This nation has seen its share of painful and fraught racial moments; let us utilize this book and the many resources it offers as one tool among many in making our current highly racialized moment one of deep and lasting change.

*Note: Throughout this foreword, the reference to White women is specific to White, cisgender women, meaning women whose gender identity and presentation match the socialization they received as a result of their perceived biology at birth. The characterizations, therefore, do not include the experience of White transwomen, as those are likely even more complex, are outside the bounds of this book, and likely do not touch into the root dynamics this book is seeking to address. Similarly, the introduction focuses on the experiences of cisgender Black boys and men.

Acknowledgments

We have so many people to thank for their contributions to this incredible volume. Thank you to all of the chapter authors, vignette writers, and video interviewees who contributed their deep knowledge, broad experience, and uniquely personal stories with vulnerability, insight, brilliance, wit, authenticity, generosity, kindness, audacity, and beauty. This book is the powerful volume that it is because of their personal and professional commitment to creating work that is accessible, challenging, and relatable.

Thank you to all of the parents, teachers, and individual Black men and women who came to our workshops over the past four years, shared their stories and support, introduced new ideas and interpretations, and challenged our framework. This book is so much stronger because of those collaborative efforts to envision what *The Guide for White Women Who Teach Black Boys* should look like.

Thank you to the members of the Race Institute for K–12 Educators Advisory Board who gathered in the early years of this book's conception and contributed your ideas as members of the Black Boy Achievement Sub-Committee. This group includes: Dr. Frederick Bryant, Marissa Colston, Nora Durant, Kareem Goodwin, Dr. Barbara Moore-Williams, Dr. Howard Stevenson, Dr. Chezare Warren, and Toni Graves Williamson.

Thank you to all of the members of the Center for the Study of Race and Equity in Education at Penn, who supported the early vision of this book.

Thank you to Dr. Howard Stevenson, Brother Robb Carter, Brother Eric Grimes, and Dr. Lathardus Goggins II for Education 545: Psychoeducational Interactions with Black Males—the original guide for White women who teach Black boys. You taught the value of learning about Black boys as a broadly diverse group, with both individual and group-level concerns. Your four different approaches, as four Black men, were so instructive and powerful.

Thank you to Kendra Green, University of Wisconsin, Oshkosh, master's student, who worked tirelessly to keep us organized and on time with our deadlines.

Thank you to Nora Gross at PennGSE, who conducted and transcribed interviews for the film portion of this project.

Thank you to our publisher, Dan Alpert, for your courageous support of this powerful vision and for your labor and support on our film interviews. Thank you to our copyeditor Jacqueline Tasch, for your patience and expertise in editing this massive project.

Thank you to our families for reading drafts of our work, for supporting us in our travel, for reminding us why it's important for schools to be places where all children are seen and understood, and for loving us.

About the Authors

Ali Michael, Eddie Moore Jr., and Marguerite W. Penick-Parks

Our multiracial author team is held together with the magnetic energy that comes from honoring different—and sometimes opposite—polarities. We disagree; we have different assumptions; our styles clash. And we love each other. We love the electrical current that our differences spark; we honor our seemingly contradictory answers that together lead to complex, multifaceted solutions. We recognize that without each other we could not even ask these questions, much less answer them.

—**Eddie Moore Jr., Ali Michael, and
Marguerite W. Penick-Parks**

Eddie Moore Jr. has pursued and achieved success in academia, business, diversity, leadership, and community service. In 1996, he started America & MOORE, LLC [www.eddiemoorejr.com] to provide comprehensive diversity, privilege, and leadership trainings/workshops. Dr. Moore is recognized as one of the nation's top motivational speakers and educators, especially for his work with students K–16. Dr. Moore is the Founder/Program Director for the White Privilege Conference

(WPC) [www.whiteprivilegeconference.com]. Under the direction of Dr. Moore and his inclusive relationship model, the WPC has become one of the top national and international conferences for participants who want to move beyond dialogue and into action around issues of diversity, power, privilege, and leadership. Dr. Moore's interview with Wisconsin Public Radio won the 2015 Wisconsin Broadcasters Association's Best Interview in Medium Market Radio, First Place [http://www.wpr.org/shows/newsmakers-december-4-2014], and he is featured in the film "I'm not Racist . . . Am I?" In 2014 Dr. Moore founded The Privilege Institute, which engages people in research, education, action, and leadership through workshops, conferences, publications, and strategic partnerships and relationships. Dr. Moore is co-founder of the online journal, *Understanding and Dismantling Privilege,* and co-editor of *Everyday White People Confront Racial and Social Injustice: 15 Stories.*

Ali Michael, PhD, is the co-founder and director of the Race Institute for K–12 Educators, and the author of *Raising Race Questions: Whiteness, Inquiry, and Education,* winner of the 2017 Society of Professors of Education Outstanding Book Award. She is co-editor of the bestselling *Everyday White People Confront Racial and Social Injustice: 15 Stories* and sits on the editorial board of the journal *Whiteness and Education.* Dr. Michael teaches in the mid-career doctoral program at the University of Pennsylvania's Graduate School of Education, as well as the Graduate Counseling Program at Arcadia University. In the 2017–18 school year, she will hold the Davis Visiting Professorship at Ursinus College. Michael's article, *What Do White Children Need to Know About Race?,* co-authored with Dr. Eleonora Bartoli in *Independent Schools Magazine,* won the Association and Media Publishing Gold Award for Best Feature Article in 2014. She may be best known for her November 9, 2016, piece *What Do We Tell the Children?* on the *Huffington Post,* where she is a regular contributor. For more details see www.alimichael.org.

Marguerite W. Penick-Parks received her PhD from the University of Iowa in Curriculum and Instruction. Prior to attending graduate school, she worked as a high school teacher in an urban school in Kansas City, Kansas. Dr. Penick-Parks currently serves as Chair of Educational Leadership and Policy at the University of Wisconsin, Oshkosh. Her work centers on issues of power, privilege, and oppression in relationship to issues of curriculum with a special emphasis on the incorporation of quality literature in K–12 classrooms. She appears in the movie *Mirrors of Privilege: Making Whiteness Visible,* by the World Trust Organization. Her most recent work includes a joint article on creating safe spaces for discussing white privilege with preservice teachers and is a co-editor of *Everyday White People Confronting Racial and Social Injustice: 15 Stories,* with Eddie Moore Jr. and Ali Michael.

About the Contributors

Aaron Abram serves as the Civil Rights Compliance Coordinator in the Office of Equity and Affirmative Action at University of Wisconsin-Oshkosh. His work in developing and training young leaders and volunteers includes being a paraprofessional within the Minneapolis Public School District, Housing committee lead with the Minneapolis Youth Congress, and site liaison for the Boys of Hope program with the Power of People Leadership Institute. In pursuit of equity in policy, he has served as a Voting Rights Campaign Organizer with TakeAction Minnesota, North Minneapolis Organizer for a State Auditor campaign, and Policy Lead for a Minneapolis City Council Campaign. Aaron is an active member of Phi Beta Sigma Fraternity, Inc. and is a graduate of Morehouse College, where he received his BA in Political Science and also holds a Juris Doctorate from Ohio Northern University Claude W. Pettit College of Law.

Valerie Adams-Bass is an Assistant Professor of Youth and Social Innovation, a faculty affiliate of the Youth-Nex Center to Promote Effective Youth Development in the Curry School of Education at the University of Virginia, and a faculty affiliate of The Racial Empowerment Collaborative at the University of Pennsylvania's Graduate School of Education. Her research explores the relationships of racial socialization and racial identity with identity development processes and the social and the academic experiences of Black adolescents. Dr. Adams-Bass regularly trains youth development professionals to use culturally relevant practices when serving African American children and youth.

Jillian Best Adler has built her career on the belief that infants and young children are best served when they have healthy attachments with parents and educators who are knowledgeable, confident, and well supported. She earned her Master's degree in Child Development from the Erikson Institute in Chicago. As an Early Childhood Education Consultant with the Delaware Valley Association for the Education of Young Children, Jillian provides coaching and training to early childhood professionals in child care centers and preschools throughout the Philadelphia region.

Shemariah Arki identifies as an educator, an activist, and an organizer. She is an interdisciplinary scholar with expert knowledge and skills to develop, implement, facilitate, and evaluate curricula that promote institutional equity, communication, and access for traditionally marginalized students and families. As a master teacher and facilitator, she consults with a myriad of education-based organization around issues of process improvement with a goal of moving organizations from efficient to excellent. Currently a doctoral candidate in the College of Education at Northeastern University, her dissertation focuses on motherwork in the wake of #BlackLivesMatter.

Chris Avery is the Vice President of Programs for Steppingstone Scholars, a college access program in Philadelphia. He is a former teacher and administrator. He has worked with schools and school districts around the nation on creating safe and welcoming communities, particularly for boys of color. He is also a member of the National S.E.E.D. Project on Inclusive Curriculum.

April Baker-Bell is an assistant professor of language and literacy at Michigan State University. The primary goal of her professional work is to provide a pathway to cultural, linguistic, racial, and educational justice for Black students across K-U settings, and by extension, the Black community and other communities of color. In her research, Dr. Baker-Bell strives to present the fields in which she works guidance for rethinking the linguistic and racial deficit theories that underpin and shape our disciplinary discourses, pedagogical practices, and approaches to qualitative inquiry.

Keisha L. Bentley-Edwards is an Assistant Professor at Duke University's School of Medicine and the Associate Director of Research for the Cook Center for Social Equity. Dr. Bentley-Edwards is a developmental psychologist who studies how health, social, and educational outcomes are influenced by race-based experiences in the classroom and in the community. She has conducted seminars and lectures for teachers, students, and school leaders on identifying and managing racial stress in the classroom.

Amber Bryant is a third-year doctoral student at UNC Charlotte in the urban education and literacy program. She is a Detroit native and a graduate of the University of Michigan in Ann Arbor. After moving to North Carolina, she attended North Carolina State University where she received her MAT in Secondary English Education. She has taught in both Michigan and North Carolina. Her research interests are education and economics, emergency management in schools, and urban school environments.

Shaki Butler is a visionary, filmmaker, transformative learning educator, wife, mother, grandmother, and friend to many—is President and Founder of World Trust Educational Services, Inc. Through transformative education, rooted in love and justice, Dr. Butler produces films, curricula, workshops, and programs that are catalysts for institutional, structural, and cultural change. Shakti has produced four documentaries: *The Way Home, Mirrors of Privilege: Making Whiteness Visible, Light in the Shadows,* and *Cracking the Codes: The System of Racial Inequity.* World Trust's films have generated conversations—well over 23 million views through one clip alone.

Adrian Chandler has served on the Youth Action Board for the Annual White Privilege Conference (WPC) for the last three years. He has also assisted in facilitating racial literacy workshops with teens. His capstone high school project focuses on increasing racial literacy for teens and for high school educators.

Jennifer Chandler teaches and researches Organizational Leadership at Arizona State University. Dr. Chandler problematizes and examines dominant social norms perpetuated in groups. Her book, *Colluding, Colliding, and Contending with Norms of Whiteness* was published in 2016 by Information Age Publishing.

Becki Cohn-Vargas is the Director of Not In Our School (NIOS), part of a national project that creates films and resources, working with communities to combat hate, bullying, racism, Islamophobia, and homophobia. She has published articles, developed curriculum, produced films, and lead professional development at schools and universities across the United States. Dr. Cohn-Vargas co-authored "*Identity Safe Classrooms: Places to Belong and Learn,*" with Dr. Dorothy Steele. She spent over 35 years in public education, working for equity and social justice, as a teacher, principal, curriculum director, and superintendent.

Jabina G. Coleman is a Licensed Social Worker and International Board Certified Lactation Consultant who has dedicated the past decade of her life to serving women, children, and families. Jabina received her bachelor of science in biobehavioral health from the Pennsylvania State University. She later went on to earn a master's degree in social work from the University of Pennsylvania, School of Social Policy & Practice. Jabina has since become an International Board Certified Lactation Consultant and is the owner of LIFE House Lactation & Perinatal Services, LLC where she provides in-home lactation consultations, teaches breastfeeding and childbirth classes, and provides psychotherapy to parents experiencing perinatal mood and anxiety disorders. Jabina is also the co-founder of the Perinatal Mental Health Alliance for Women of Color, where the mission is to support professionals and communities of color who are dealing with the complications of perinatal mood disorders. Jabina is also the mother of two beautiful children.

Chonika Coleman-King is Assistant Professor of Urban-Multicultural Education at the University of Tennessee, Knoxville, where she prepares teacher interns to teach with an emphasis on social justice. Her research interests include the development of culturally responsive and anti-racist teachers, urban education, and the experiences of Black immigrant and Black American youth in U.S. schools. Dr. Coleman-King is the author of the book, *The (Re-)Making of a Black American: Tracing the Racial and Ethnic Socialization of Caribbean American Youth.*

Justin Coles is a fourth-year doctoral candidate in the Department of Teacher Education, Curriculum and Instruction at Michigan State University's College of Education. More specifically, his work is located in the Race, Culture, and Equity division, with a focus on Urban Education. Prior to his doctoral studies, Justin served as a middle school English teacher. He currently serves as a Research Associate at The University of Pennsylvania's Center for the Study of Race and Equity in Education.

Dion Crushshon is the Director of Global Programs at The Blake School in Minneapolis, where he has developed global programming for high school students for 10 years, in addition to serving as an academic administrator and teacher. Dion has also worked as a culturally-specific counselor/therapist for African-American men and conducted diversity and cultural competency workshops for educators and other helping professionals.

Phillipe Cunningham is an out and proud Black, queer and transmasculine educator, advocate, and policy nerd. Currently, he serves as the Senior Policy Advisor to Minneapolis Mayor Betsy Hodges for education, youth success, racial equity, and LGBTQ rights. Prior to his work in policy, Phillipe was a youth work professional for over ten years with experience ranging from afterschool program development to teaching special education in Chicago Public Schools. He is the chair of the City of Minneapolis' Transgender Equity Council, as well as the primary coordinator for the City of Minneapolis' My Brother's Keeper Initiative, work launched by President Barack Obama focused on improving the life outcomes for boys and men of color.

Krystal de'León has her Master's degree in Clinical Mental Health Counseling from the University of Wisconsin-Whitewater, and a Bachelor of Arts degree in Communications from the University of Wisconsin-Oshkosh. She practices using a client-centered approach to treat (childhood) trauma and uses a variety of techniques to provide culturally sensitive therapy.

Elizabeth Denevi is the Associate Director for Mid West Educational Collaborative, a non-profit agency that works with schools nationally to increase equity, promote diversity pedagogy, and implement strategic processes for growth and development. Prior to her work at Mid West Ed, Dr. Denevi served as both a classroom teacher and a senior administrator at several preK–12 schools.

Robin DiAngelo is a former Associate Professor of Education. Dr. DiAngelo has numerous publications and books on white racial identity and race relations. Her work on *White Fragility* has influenced the national dialogue on race and has been featured in Alternet, Salon, NPR, Slate, and Colorlines.

Ty-Ron Douglas is an Associate Professor in the Department of Educational Leadership and Policy Analysis Department at the University of Missouri. His research explores the intersections between identity, community/geopolitical space, and the socio-cultural foundations of leadership and education, with an emphasis on Black masculinity, spirituality, and community-based spaces (e.g., barbershops, churches, and sports venues). The author of *Border Crossing Brothas: Black Males Navigating Race, Place and Complex Space* and the recipient of an NCAA Innovations in Research and Practice Grant to study Black male student athletes, Dr. Douglas's work has also appeared in outlets such as *The Urban Review, Educational Studies, Teachers College Record,* and *Race, Ethnicity, and Education.* He can be reached at info@DrTyDouglas.com.

Diane Finnerty is the Assistant Provost for Faculty at the University of Iowa and holds an adjunct faculty appointment in the UI School of Social Work. Diane has over thirty years' experience as an organizational consultant and social justice educator. Her scholarly and educational work has focused on unconscious bias, white privilege in LGBT communities, critical cultural competence, (im)migration in the global economy, and effective alliance building.

Suzanne Fondrie received her Curriculum and Instruction PhD from the University of Wisconsin Madison and currently teaches children's literature and secondary English language arts courses at the University of Wisconsin Oshkosh, helping teacher candidates develop a diverse perspective on texts, students, and literacy. Dr. Fondrie engages with classroom issues by supervising clinical students and teacher candidates. Her research interests are children's literature, service-learning, and LGBTQ issues in education.

Donna Y. Ford is a Professor and Cornelius Vanderbilt Endowed Chair at Vanderbilt University. She is in the Department of Special Education. Dr. Ford's research and scholarship focus extensively on closing achievement and equity gaps, desegregating gifted education, and preparing educators to be culturally competent. She has written numerous books and hundreds of articles and chapters and has received several awards for her work.

Ty Gale (they/them) are a writer, musician, activist, and loudmouth living in St. Paul, Minnesota. They have brought their focus on accessible, professional communications and logistics to a variety of activistic and artistic organizations. Their extroversion and penchant for the melodramatic unsurprisingly led them to public speaking and performing arts, most recently as part of the all-trans indie pop band 4th Curtis. They are an executive board member at Transforming Families Minnesota, a regular workshop facilitator at events throughout the Twin Cities area, a co-founder of the trans youth leadership development program Gender Revolution 8, and an avid makeup enthusiast.

Frederick Gooding Jr. is an Assistant Professor within the Ethnic Studies Program at Northern Arizona University in Flagstaff, AZ. A trained historian, Dr. Gooding most effectively analyzes contemporary mainstream media with a careful eye for persistent patterns along racial lines that appear benign but indeed have problematic historical roots. Uncomfortable with the anti-intellectualist approach to hip hop within academia, Gooding has also fostered new learning opportunities for students and community members to appreciate the genius of hip hop through new courses, seminars and study tours abroad as far away as Australia and New Zealand. A developing scholar, Gooding's most well-known work thus far is *You Mean, There's RACE in My Movie? The Complete Guide to Understanding Race in Mainstream Hollywood* that critically analyzes the value and impact of contemporary racial imagery based upon historical narratives of sex, power, and violence.

Tarek C. Grantham is a professor in the Department of Educational Psychology at the University of Georgia. He teaches in the Gifted and Creative Education Program, primarily in the Diversity and Equity Strand. Dr. Grantham's research addresses the problem of underrepresentation among ethnic minority students, particularly Black males, in advanced programs. He currently serves as the Chair for the Special Populations Network of the National Association for Gifted Children.

Heather Hackman: After receiving her doctorate in Social Justice Education from the University of Massachusetts at Amherst, Dr. Heather Hackman served as an

Associate Professor in the Department of Human Relations and Multicultural Education at St. Cloud State University where she taught a range of courses on social justice issues in education to pre-service and in-service educators. In 2005, she founded Hackman Consulting Group, and in 2012 she resigned in order to consult and train full time in educational settings. She is a co-editor of the widely used *Readings for Diversity and Social Justice* and has published on a range of social justice issues in education.

Shaun R. Harper is a Professor and Executive Director of the Center for the Study of Race and Equity in Education at the University of Southern California. The Center is a member of the Seven Centers Consortium.

Frank Harris III is a Professor and Co-Director of Minority Male Community College Collaborative (M2C3) at San Diego State University. The Collaborative is a member of the Seven Centers Consortium.

Jack Hill is a facilitator, educator, writer, and child advocate. His articles and essays on education, race, and religion have appeared in the *Baltimore Sun*, *Black Issues Book Review*, *The Chicago Tribune*, *Urbanite Magazine*, and *The Afro- American Newspaper*. He has given a number of presentations, and workshops, locally and internationally, and has offered consultation to schools and organizations nation-wide in the areas of multicultural education, diversity, equity, social justice, and organizational culture. He is the current Dean of Multicultural Education and Student Affairs at Stanley British Primary School in Denver, Colorado.

Tyrone C. Howard is a Professor of Education and Director of the Black Male Institute at the University of California at Los Angeles. The Institute is a member of the Seven Centers Consortium.

Debby Irving brings to racial justice the perspective of working as a non-profit manager and classroom teacher for 25 years without understanding racism as systemic or her own whiteness as an obstacle to grappling with it. Author of *Waking Up White, and Finding Myself in the Story of Race*, Debby now devotes herself to working with people exploring the impact white skin can have on perception, problem solving, and creating equitable communities. A graduate of the Winsor School in Boston, she holds a BA from Kenyon College and an MBA from Simmons College.

Jerlando Jackson is the Vilas Distinguished Professor of Higher Education and Director of the Wisconsin's Equity and Inclusion Laboratory. The Laboratory is a member of the Seven Centers Consortium.

Charlotte E. Jacobs is currently an Associate Director of the Independent School Teaching Residency program at the University of Pennsylvania Graduate School of Education. Prior to her work in higher education, Dr. Jacobs taught 7th grade humanities at the University of Chicago Laboratory Schools in Chicago, IL, and was a faculty member of the NAIS Student Diversity Leadership Conference. Dr. Jacobs is also the Executive Director of Girls Justice League, a non-profit organization supporting the social, political, and economic rights of girls in Philadelphia (www.girlsjusticeleague.org). Dr. Jacobs' research interests focus on issues of identity development and gender in education concerning adolescent girls of color, teacher education and diversity, and youth participatory action research.

Brian Johnson is a career educator with 26 years of experience: 20 years as a public school Social Studies Teacher, 1 year as an Apprentice Principal of Instruction in an inner-city charter school, and 5 years as an independent school administrator. He currently serves as the Director of Admission, 1st-7th Grade and Diversity Director at The Philadelphia School. His experience in these distinctly different educational environments has given him a unique perspective when addressing equity and inclusion. Consulting, developing strategies to close the Achievement (Performance) Gap and ensuring the classrooms of his current school are truly equitable are a primary focus and passion for him. He is also the author of "A Look in the Mirror, One School's Study of Raced Based Achievement"—*Independent School Magazine*, Winter 2014.

Jawanza Kunjufu has been a consultant to school districts since 1974. A renowned author, Dr. Kunjufu's books include *Changing School Culture for Black Males; 100 Plus Educational Strategies to Teach Children of Color; Understanding Black Male Learning Styles; Reducing the Black Male Dropout Rate;* and others. His work is used in online courses nationwide. Kunjufu can be reached at customersvc@africanamericanimages.com.

Julie Landsman is the author of many articles and three books on education: *Basic Needs: A Year with Street Kids in a City School* (Milkweed Editions, 1993), *A White Teacher Talks About Race* (Rowman and Littlefield 2001), and *Growing Up White; a Veteran Teacher Reflects on Racism* (Rowman and Littlefield, 2008. Dr. Landsman is also the editor of many collections of essays stories and poems, the most recent being *Voices for Diversity and Social Justice, A Literary Education Reader,* with Paul Gorski and Rosanna Salcedo (Rowman and Littlefield, 2015), and *Talking About Race*, with Robert Simmons and Steven Grineski. She is a retired teacher from the Minneapolis public schools, consults, and teaches seminars on education, writing, race and culture. www.jlandsman.com.

Crystal T. Laura (crystaltlaura@gmail.com) is Associate Professor of Educational Leadership at Chicago State University and the author of the bestselling book *Being Bad: My Baby Brother and The School to Prison Pipeline* (Teachers College Press). Dr. Laura's research has focused on the social foundations of education, diversity and equity in schools, and building the capacity of teachers and school leaders to promote social justice. She conducts workshops across the U.S., and is a frequent presenter at the annual meeting of the American Educational Research Association, to which she has belonged since 2006.

Chance Lewis is the Carol Grotnes Belk Distinguished Professor of Urban Education and Director of The Urban Education Collaborative at the University of North Carolina at Charlotte. Dr. Lewis's research interests focus on the academic achievement of students of color, recruitment and retention of teachers of color, and promoting a high-quality diverse teaching force. He can be reached by e-mail at chance.lewis@uncc.edu or on the web at http://www.chancewlewis.com.

Sharoni Little, Educator-Activist, CEO, The Strategist Company, LLC is also an Associate Professor of Business Communication at the University of Southern California, and a Non-Profit Executive. Dr. Little's research centers on executive leadership, critical race, social justice, global communication, and academic success. She is completing her forthcoming books, *Diapers and Dissertations: Women Successfully Achieving the "Implausible"* (2018), and *Perpetual Surveillance: The Intense Scrutiny of Black Men* (2018). In addition to her scholarly and advisory efforts, she is an educational and social advocate who serves as an Executive Adviser for the Compton, California, My Brother's Keeper Initiative for boys and men of color, and sits on several organizational boards. While she values her role as a strategist, advocate, and scholar, Dr. Little's most cherished blessing is being the proud mother of twin sons, Jared and Jaren, who are the inspiration for her scholarly endeavors, including her TEDx talk, *The Gift of Corrective Lenses.*

Bryant T. Marks is an Associate Professor of Psychology and Director of the Program for Research on Black Male Achievement at Morehouse College. The Program is a member of the Seven Centers Consortium.

Russell Marsh has been a musician, educator, and consultant in the New York Metro area for over twenty years. He developed his passion for equity and inclusion work while teaching at his alma mater, St. Benedict's Prep in Newark, N.J. Currently, he is the Associate Director of Equity and Inclusion at a private school in New York City where, in addition to other responsibilities, he is charged to look at curriculum and the impact of curriculum on identity development.

John Marshall received his doctorate from Western Kentucky University. His research and work focus on equity, culturally responsive teaching, and student engagement. Dr. Marshall illuminates systemic racism and works to assure all students have access to rigorous classes, effective teachers, and opportunities. Even further, Marshall posits that the saving grace for American Education is predicated on those bold enough to challenge and change the system.

Christopher McGinley's perspectives on leadership and learning have been shaped significantly by the roles that he has played as a teacher, school principal, and school district superintendent. Dr. McGinley currently serves as coordinator for the Educational Leadership Program at Temple University where he holds the post of associate professor. From 2008 to 2014 he served as the Superintendent of Schools at the Lower Merion School District. He is also the former Executive Director of the Delaware County Intermediate Unit and former Superintendent for the District of Cheltenham Township.

Marie Michael is PK–12 Chair of Equity and Instruction at the Blake School where she provides visioning, strategic planning, and action steps to support the school in living its mission of equity and inclusion. She leads professional development, coaches faculty and administrators, develops and revises curriculum, and directs *PK-12 Cornerstone: An Alliance for Students and Families of Color.* She is also a member of Hackman Consulting Group (HCG), where she trains and coaches educators, leaders, community activists, and others committed to embodying racial equity and social justice in their lives and work. In all she does, Marie shares strategies to counteract the physiological effects of bias and oppression, so we can creatively embody the liberatory actions we need to individually and collectively transform ourselves, our systems, and our communities.

H. Richard Milner IV is Helen Faison Professor of Urban Education at the University of Pittsburgh. Dr. Milner's research, policy, and teaching interests concern urban teacher education, African American literature, and the social context of education. His most recent book, *Rac(e)ing to Class: Confronting Poverty and Race in Schools and Classrooms*, was published by Harvard Education Press in 2015. He can be reached at Rmilner@pitt.edu.

Barbara Moore-Williams is an education consultant with over forty years experience including teacher, coach/trainer, curriculum support person, and Director of Teacher Development in a large urban district. Dr. Moore-Williams currently conducts workshops and year-long training in cultural proficiency and the influence of race in teaching and learning. She has been an adjunct professor at Temple

University in the College of Education and Cheyney University as well as delivered seminars at the University of Pennsylvania, Drexel University, and Widener University. Her dissertation focused on academic achievement of African American adolescent males in an urban high school.

Carl Moore is currently the Assistant Chief Academic Officer at the University of the District of Columbia. Dr. Moore also serves as Certificate faculty in Temple University's Teaching in Higher Education Certificate program. He has dedicated his career to promoting inclusion and social justice in the classroom, across campuses and institutional level. As such, Dr. Moore is frequently an invited speaker and consultant on inclusion, leadership, and faculty development and teaching and learning related topics.

James L. Moore III Dr. Moore is the EHE Distinguished Professor of Urban Education and Executive Director of the Todd Anthony Bell National Resource Center on the African American Male at The Ohio State University. The Center is a member of the Seven Centers Consortium.

Vernā Myers, Esq., is Founder and President of The Vernā Myers Company. She is on a personal mission to disrupt the status quo, and she knows how to: she's lived it. Author of the best-selling books *Moving Diversity Forward: How to Move From Well-Meaning to Well-Doing* and *What If I Say the Wrong Thing? 25 Habits for Culturally Effective People*, Vernā has touched over 1,000,000 people through her speeches, appearances, and transformative message of power and possibility. For the last two decades, Vernā has worked to eradicate barriers of race, gender, ethnicity, and sexual orientation at elite international law firms, Wall Street powerhouses, and the 10,000 member Fire Department of New York, with the aim of establishing a new, more productive and just status quo.

Joseph Derrick Nelson, PhD, is a Visiting Assistant Professor of Educational Studies at Swarthmore College and a Senior Research Fellow with the Center for the Study of Boys' and Girls' Lives at the University of Pennsylvania. His scholarship to date has explored Black boys' identities and schooling during childhood and early adolescence. These empirical projects led to publications with *Harvard Educational Review, Teachers College Record, Culture, Society, and Masculinities*, and guest co-editing a special issue on boys' education with the *Journal of Boyhood Studies*. In his hometown of Milwaukee, Wisconsin, Dr. Nelson taught first grade for two years in a single-sex classroom for Black and Latino boys.

Sean Norman, undergraduate student majoring in Physical Education and Recreation at Gallaudet University anticipates graduation as of August 2017. Sean was born and raised in Harvey, Illinois, and became Deaf at the age of 2. Before Sean enrolled Gallaudet University, he majored in Deaf Education and worked with deaf and hard of hearing children and teenagers for 7 years as Teacher's Aids, Camp Director, and Sponsor Junior Illinois Association for the Deaf.

Omobolade Delano-Oriaran is an Associate Professor of Teacher Education at St. Norbert College, De Pere, Wisconsin. Her teaching and research focus on diversity and inclusion issues in schooling and society; authentic, critical, culturally-engaging service-learning; White teachers and diverse classrooms, closing the opportunity gap; multicultural education; and engaging African American students, families, and communities. Dr. Delano-Oriaran is the lead editor of two volumes on service-learning: *SAGE Sourcebook of Service-Learning and Civic Engagement,* and *Culturally Engaging Service-Learning with Diverse Communities.*

Marvin Pierre received his Masters in Education Administration and Supervision from the University of Houston. He currently serves as the Program Director of an alternative education program called 8 Million Stories. The program is designed to help students build meaningful relationships in their community, access a wide range of social services, develop critical life and job skills, continue their education, and secure meaningful employment. As a former school leader, Marvin is passionate about helping school districts and leaders develop a more restorative approach to student discipline, when working with young boys of color.

Luis Ponjuan is an Associate Professor at Texas A&M University and Co-Director of Project MALES and the Texas Education Consortium for Male Students of Color. The Consortium is a member of the Seven Centers Consortium.

Zeam Porter is a first year student at Macalester College in St. Paul, Minnesota. He is a youth advocate for Black and Trans students and served on many boards including Governor Mark Dayton's Technical Council Against Bullying, the youth board of directors for the organization The National Gender and Sexualities Alliance and is currently a member of The Transgender Law Center's TRUTH, a national council for trans youth doing media advocacy. He is also a co-founder and teacher for the program Gender Revolution 8, a leadership program for transgender and gender nonconforming youth through the nonprofit Minnesota Transgender Health Coalition.

Paul A. Robbins received his PhD in Educational Psychology from The University of Texas at Austin. His research interests include issues of identity, the academic impact of athletic participation, and the transmission and reception of academic messages. Prior to attending graduate school, Dr. Robbins taught high school mathematics in South Carolina.

Stefanie Rome is a doctoral student, graduate research assistant, and a Gus T. Ridgel Fellow at the University of Missouri-Columbia, where she is pursuing her PhD in Educational Leadership and Policy Analysis. Stefanie is the former Director of Curriculum and Professional Development for the National Urban Alliance for Effective Education. She has spent more than 20 years as a classroom teacher, teacher mentor instructional coach, and project director, committed to the creation of pedagogical spaces where student culture is honored and celebrated.

Victor Săenz is an Associate Professor at the University of Texas at Austin and Co-Director of Project MALES and the Texas Education Consortium for Male Students of Color. The Consortium is a member of the Seven Centers Consortium.

Eli Scearce is a furniture maker and woodshop teacher living and working in Philadelphia. She is the mother of two children whom she raises with her wife and partner of twenty three years. For the past eight years, Eli has immersed herself in multicultural studies and anti-racism work.

Darla Scott currently serves as an Assistant Professor in the School Psychology program at Bowie State University. Dr. Scott has over a decade of expertise in instructional design and delivery and conducted her doctoral dissertation on the utilization of culturally relevant pedagogy with African American students. Her research interests are focused on the development of educational equity through inclusive instructional strategies and she can be reached at dmscott@bowiestate.edu.

Michelle Trotman Scott is the College of Education Director of Graduate Studies and an associate professor at the University of West Georgia. She teaches in the Department of Literacy and Special Education. Dr. Trotman Scott's research interests include special education overrepresentation, gifted education underrepresentation, twice exceptional, culturally responsive instruction, and family involvement. She has authored several articles, chapters, and books.

Glenn E. Singleton has devoted over thirty years to constructing racial equity worldwide and developing leaders to do the same. As President and Founder of Pacific Educational Group, Inc. (PEG), Singleton has created an agency that has developed racially conscious leaders in a variety of sectors: education, government, business, law enforcement, and community organizing among them. He is the author of *Courageous Conversations About Race: A Field Guide for Achieving Equity in Schools* (2006), a protocol for sustained, deep interracial dialog, and the creator of Beyond Diversity™, the curriculum that has taught hundreds of thousands of people how to use it. He is a graduate of the University of Pennsylvania (BA) and Stanford University (MA) and the recipient of The 100 Black Men of the Bay Area Community Service Award in 2015 and The Eugene T. Carothers Human Relations Award in 2003.

Solomon Smart is a fourth-grade chess master and power forward basketball player at Greenview Upper Elementary School. Solomon loves math and science and wants to be a pilot. His hobbies are cooking and art. In his spare time, Solomon can be found reading *Harry Potter* or hanging out with his little brother Malcolm as they help their mom *agitate, educate, and organize* in the community.

Edward J. Smith is a PhD candidate at the University of Pennsylvania's Graduate School of Education. His research focuses on building and sustaining education attainment efforts in metropolitan areas, with a particular emphasis on better understanding the effects of municipal, institutional, and community practices and policies on educational outcomes. Ed earned his bachelor's degree in Economics and master's degree in College Student Affairs from The Pennsylvania State University.

Leann V. Smith is a doctoral candidate of the University of Texas at Austin's School Psychology Program and a current doctoral intern at the Momentous Institute in Dallas, TX. Her research examines cultural and contextual factors of Black youths' academic achievement and prosocial development. As a school psychologist, Leann has had experience working directly within the school system helping teachers and administrators attend to the unique needs of children, particularly those with diverse backgrounds, while utilizing an asset-oriented and culturally sensitive lens.

Erica Snowden has been an educator for 13 years within the Friends Schools network. Currently, she is the Lower School Dean and Learning Support Specialist at Greene Street Friends School in Philadelphia. She serves as the Diversity Clerk; promoting social justice and race-based conversations within affinity groups. An alumna of the Graduate School of Education at the University of Pennsylvania, she is also a presenter at the Ethnography Conference.

Deitra Spence is an educational consultant with over 35 years of experience as a teacher, administrator, and adjunct professor in a variety of urban, rural, and suburban school settings. As an educational consultant, Dr. Spence participates in curriculum audits, coaches principals, mentors aspiring administrators, and provides professional development for K–12 teachers and administrators. Her dissertation findings focused on the pedagogical strategies used by White teachers that were most effective with their African-American middle school students.

Howard Stevenson is the Constance Clayton Professor of Urban Education, Professor of Africana Studies in the Human Development Division of the Graduate School of Education at the University of Pennsylvania. Dr. Stevenson is also the Executive Director of the Racial Empowerment Collaborative (REC), a research, program development, and training center that brings together community leaders, researchers, authority figures, families, and youth to study and promote racial literacy and health in schools and neighborhoods. His research publications and clinical work involve developing culturally relevant "in-the-moment" strengths-based measures and therapeutic interventions that teach emotional and racial literacy skills to families and youth.

David Stills currently teaches 4th/5th grade at The Philadelphia School. He began his teaching career 6 years ago and is a certified Montessori educator. David believes that learning and growth have their own intrinsic value and reward, and that on some level, we all crave opportunities to witness our most-empowered selves influencing our environments and our learning process. This drive to move forward is what every educator is depending on and what every budding activist recognizes as a part of the human experience. Prior to teaching, David used his voice to reach people in a different way; he was a professional singer. Although it's been a while since he sang full-time, David still writes and performs music with an encouraging message, and often draws inspiration from his amazing wife and two beautiful children.

Orinthia Swindell has had a lifelong passion for learning and teaching others about equity and inclusion work. She has served as an early childhood educator for over twenty years, currently serves as the Director of Equity and Inclusion at an independent school in her hometown, Brooklyn, New York, in addition to her role as an independent consultant. Orinthia has facilitated numerous workshops and presentations, presented at national conferences and has been a guest speaker at teacher preparation programs. One of her most esteemed accomplishments is being the mother of two amazing black young men.

Benny Vásquez describes himself as a lifelong learner and a seeker of justice. A native of Brooklyn, he graduated from Wesleyan University with a BA in African

American Studies and Sociology, then completed his master's in curriculum and teaching from Columbia University and then an MPA at New York University. Benny is the co-executive director of Border Crossers, a national organization that is committed to dismantling racism in K–12 educational organizations. He is also an independent diversity and equity consultant and is working with various schools/organizations across the country in fulfilling their mission to create inclusive communities that value race, gender, sexual orientation, and all the other identities that make us whole. Benny has always had a strong passion for social justice, education reform, and anti-racism work within educational settings and lives and breathes in the intersectionality of his work.

Chezare A. Warren is an Assistant Professor in the Department of Teacher Education, affiliate faculty in Mathematics Education, and core faculty in African American and African Studies at Michigan State University (MSU). Dr. Warren's research interests include urban (teacher) education, culturally responsive teaching, and critical race theory in education. His award-winning research has been published in several peer-reviewed journal outlets including *Urban Education, Teachers College Record, Race, Ethnicity, and Education,* and the *Journal of Negro Education.* He is co-editor of *White Women's Work: Examining the Intersectionality of Teaching, Identity, and Race* (Information Age Publishing, 2017) and the author of *Urban Preparation: Young Black Men Moving from Chicago's South Side to Success in Higher Education* (Harvard Education Press, 2017).

Jamie Washington serves as the President and Founder of the Washington Consulting Group (WCG), a Multicultural Organizational Development Firm out of Baltimore, MD. In October of 2015, WCG was named by *The Economist* as one of the Top 10 Global Diversity Consultants in the world, and one of two selected from the U.S. Rev. Dr. Washington has served as an educator, administrator, and consultant in higher education for over 32 years. Rev. Dr. Washington also serves as the President and a Founder of the Social Justice Training Institute. He was recently elected as the Vice President and President Elect of the ACPA (College Student Educators International).

Olugbala Williams is an elementary educator with over 20 years experience. Currently, he is also a Diversity Coordinator at a private school in Brooklyn. In addition to teaching, he conducts diversity workshops, mentors nascent teachers, and helps shape curriculums that are inclusive and develop strong identities. Mr. Williams is passionate about anti-racist work and related ideologies and strives to create a harmony in schools that respects and acknowledges all individuals and the many ways they identify.

Toni Graves Williamson is currently serving as the Assistant Head of School for Equity and Inclusion at Abington Friends School in suburban Philadelphia. She is a founding faculty member of the National Diversity Practitioners Institute and co-founded the Mid-Atlantic Region Diversity Conference. Toni conducts diversity climate studies and trains educators in cultural competency and institutional strategic planning as a principal consultant for The Glasgow Group. In addition, as a longtime Friends schools educator, Toni provides professional development opportunities for Quaker schools through a partnership with the Friends Council on Education.

J. Luke Wood is an Associate Professor and Co-Director of Minority Male Community College Collaborative (M2C3) at San Diego State University. The Collaborative is a member of the Seven Centers Consortium.

Brian L. Wright is an assistant professor of early childhood education at the University of Memphis. His research focuses on high-achieving African American males in urban schools preK–12, racial-ethnic identity development of boys and young men of color, African American males as early childhood teachers, and teacher identity development. Dr. Wright has published several articles and book chapters.

Deneen R. Young is a health advocate, motivational speaker, lifestyle coach, certified spin instructor, certified participant indoor row instructor, and an entrepreneur of YoungLife Coach ~ Beyond Fit. Young has worked in an independent school for 15 years administratively as well as several roles within the school community. Married for 26 years and counts it all joy to be blessed with two children ages 16 and 21. Deneen loves to write, educate, advocate, and inspire others to be their best self inside and out.

Introduction

Welcome to *The Guide for White Women Who Teach Black Boys*

**Ali Michael, Eddie Moore Jr.,
Marguerite W. Penick-Parks
with contributions from Edward J. Smith**

Welcome to *The Guide for White Women Who Teach Black Boys*. Some readers may be wondering where in the world this title comes from and what this book can do for you. Others may be wondering if there really is a difference between teaching Black boys and teaching White boys. Or girls, for that matter. There may be a question about the use of the term *boys* instead of *males* or *men*. Some readers may feel attacked. To teachers, the title may suggest they need a guide to do what they already do. We will answer all of these questions in turn because each question, concern, or trepidation that arises as you read this book will be critical to furthering and engaging in the conversation about White teachers and Black boys that usually goes unmentioned.

Teachers, like students, enter the classroom every September with hope for positive outcomes, but despite good intentions, the statistics hold that Black boys are underperforming in K–12 schools in the United States. *The Guide* does not set out to blame White women or Black boys for the current state of education. It instead takes a look at the reality of our current educational system. We believe that with the right tools, many teachers will be able to build classrooms and schools that recognize and honor the brilliance of Black boys, their potential for excellence, and their capacity to produce and create. We have witnessed eager, fierce, and courageous teachers who are ready to work toward this vision. But we can't change the direction of the structure if we don't understand the reality. We want to paint the truth about the current state of White women and Black boys in education and to offer new ways of seeing, hearing, and understanding those statistics. We want to offer new ways to move forward.

The Truth About Black Boys and White Women . . . in Statistics

The following few paragraphs tell the truth, the whole truth, and nothing but the truth (so help us!) about what is currently going on with White women and Black boys in education.

White women comprise a majority of the public-school teaching workforce, while Black males are one of the lowest demographic groups in academic achievement across a number of important learning and developmental metrics. White teachers (of all gender identities) comprise 82.7 percent of teachers in all public schools; 70 percent of teachers at all charter schools; 79.2 percent of teachers in schools with over 1,000 students; and 63 percent of teachers at schools in which at least 75 percent of students are approved for free or reduced lunch (Goldring, Gray, & Bitterman, 2013). In addition, women (of all racial backgrounds) comprise approximately 74 percent of all public-school educators (e.g., school leaders, teachers, education practitioners), and comprise 76.1 percent of the public-school teaching workforce in all public schools (Goldring et al., 2013). Very few reports filter for "White women" as a category, but estimates suggest that 62 percent of all U.S. educators are White women (Toldson, 2012).

The inequalities Black boys experience in educational environments manifest themselves very early and, if unaddressed, are compounded during middle school and secondary school experiences. Negative perceptions of Black boys begin as early as kindergarten, and their behaviors are often "adultified" during later stages of childhood (i.e., "their transgressions are made to take on a sinister, intentional, fully conscious tone that is stripped of any element of childish naiveté") (Ferguson, 2000, p. 83). These constructions often lead to the maintenance of classroom and campus management practices that have harmful effects on Black boys. Very rarely do teachers engage in professional development activities that focus on the racialized aspects of their students' experiences—and the impact on their academic identity and performance.

While disparities in academic achievement along racial and ethnic lines have narrowed since the early 1970s, significant discrepancies remain at all grade levels and in all subject areas. For example, at all testing levels, Black boys are predicted to score among the lowest on both reading and math portions of the National Assessment of Educational Progress (Kena et al., 2015). Moreover, Black boys continue to be largely underrepresented in gifted programs or honors and advanced placement courses (Schott Foundation, 2010). Finally, Black boys remain among the least likely to graduate from high school within four years. In some urban public school districts, for example, four-year graduation rates for Black boys remain between 25 and 45 percent (Schott Foundation, 2010).

Even as we present these statistics, we want to provide a reminder of what statistics are. They are a mathematical picture of a system. They do not describe any one person or any one school. For all the negative statistics we have about Black boys, we also know that there are almost two million (1,909,900) Black men in the United States who hold a four-year college degree (*The Journal of Blacks in Higher Education* (JBHE), 2017). And while that rate of college attainment for Black men is lower than any other demographic, that number of Black men college graduates is much higher than the popular media suggest. It is also greater than the number of Black men in prison, which is not obvious from most public depictions of Black men. We know that 409,000 Black men have master's degrees, and 71,000 Black men have PhDs (JBHE, 2017). We also know countless Black men whose lives straddled the statistics, such as Dr. Frederick Bryant,[1] co-founder of the Race Institute for K–12 Educators, who dropped out of high school at sixteen and went on to get his GED and later, a BS, MA, and a PhD in group dynamics.

We hope to reframe a fundamental assumption about the statistics on Black boys: these statistics are not about the failure of Black boys. But neither are these statistics about the failure of White women teachers. These statistics are indicators of the success and failure of an education system in which White women teachers, many of whom may have very little exposure to Black people outside of school, are responsible for the education of a population of children they have never been taught to teach. We have been producing these statistics for years and giving teachers the same tools to try to turn them around. With this guide, we offer something different.

The data on school discipline also support the need for a deeper understanding of the relationships between Black boys and their educators. Black boys are placed in special education, suspended, and expelled in higher numbers than their same-gender White and Latino peers. According to the U.S. Department of Education's Office for Civil Rights (2014; based on survey year 2011–2012), Black boys were 15.8 percent of the total public school male enrollment,[2] but represented 35.4 percent

---

[1] Before his untimely death in 2016, Frederick Bryant acted as a thought partner and member of the support team for this book.

[2] Public school male students overall and by race/ethnicity, students with disabilities served under IDEA and those served solely under Section 504, and students who are English language learners, by state: School Year 2011–12. For more information, visit www.ocrdata.ed.gov.

of all boys receiving one or more out-of-school suspension.[3] Furthermore, Black boys have the highest rate of placement in juvenile or residential facilities (733 for every 100,000 students), much higher than their same-race female counterparts (101/100,000) and same-gender, racial counterparts (White males, 153/100,000 and Latino males, 312/100,000, Kena et al, 2015). Taken together, these trends provide clear reminders of the urgent need for inquiry and interventions to examine the factors and interactions shaping Black male educational experiences.

One unique aspect of this book is the video links provided in the book via QR Codes, which will take you to interviews we conducted with Black males and White women teachers about their experiences of the White woman teacher-Black boy student relationship. Among both groups we interviewed, the most critical issue seemed to be fear. Both Black men and White women have fears: fear of each other, fear of one another's communities, fear of opportunities, fear of a lack of opportunities, and a fear of understanding. Fear. On both sides, it's not excitement, not anticipation, but fear. What an uncomfortable common ground on which to begin a relationship. Some teachers deny this. They say, "I'm not afraid of *my* Black students. But if I see a Black teen in the streets and his pants are sagging and his hat's on backward, then I'm going to be afraid." We believe White fear is killing Black men in this country, and it is this same fear that's failing Black boys in the classroom. It is this very fear we want to address. As Derrick Swanigan said in our interviews, "If you are afraid of my community, you are afraid of me."

The Guide did not evolve because we thought White women were bad people or bad teachers. *The Guide* arose because we realize that many White people struggle to understand race and the impact it has on the lives of students of color. Racial competence is not taught in most White families or in schools of education. Dr. Howard Stevenson, a professor of psychology at Penn's Graduate School of Education, suggests that racial stress—such as the kind that people encounter when they think about the role of race or racism in their teaching relationships—is not a matter of character, as it is so often made out to be. It's not about what kind of person you are. Rather, says Stevenson, it is a matter of competence (personal communication, 2013). In other words, if conversations about race—or even books about race—stress you out, that is not a sign you are racist. It is a sign you may lack the skills and competencies to engage in the conversation. It means you need to acquire a skill set you do not currently have—but it is one you can gain. In fact, it is one all educators must have. The corollary to this idea is that a teacher may be a very good person and still lack

---

[3] Number and percentage of public school male students with and without disabilities receiving one or more out-of-school suspension by race/ethnicity, by state: School Year 2011–12. For more information visit www.ocrdata.ed.gov.

racial competence. Being a good person is an important starting point—in fact, we assume most teachers are good people who want the best for their students—but being a good person does not mean one automatically has the skills of racial competence. Stevenson explains this another way: "If you are becoming a nurse and you're afraid to give an injection, that's okay. Fear is a normal human emotion. But if you don't acquire the skill to get over your fear, if you don't learn to give an injection, you can't become a nurse" (personal communication, 2013). Similarly, if you are a teacher who lacks racial competence, a teacher who is afraid of talking about race, or who is afraid of Black communities, that is okay; fear is a normal human emotion. And these are skills you can learn. But getting over that fear, and learning about race, are prerequisites for effective teaching of Black boys.

The Guide for White Women Who Teach Black Boys was written with the belief that these fears can be overcome and that our educational system can be transformed if educators are engaged in active personal and professional reflection on systemic issues, from teacher training to classroom practices to materials that privilege White students and inherently biased assessments. Working together is the only way to create change within a system built on the historical ideology that White is right and Black is wrong. This work is imperative if we are going to change outcomes for Black boys.

Another unique aspect of the guide is that it requires the reader to work through activities that may challenge them. We ask you to honestly reflect on who you are, where you come from, and what your role is in perpetuating a society that privileges White people, White ways of knowing, and White ways of "doing school." We ask teachers to consider their role in perpetuating an educational system designed around the educational needs of White people, a system that was designed to keep Black boys out. *The Guide* provides White teachers opportunities for personal growth as educators and for development of skills that support the academic achievement of their Black boy students. In a unique combination of both personal and professional introspective work, *The Guide* takes readers through academic work by experts, stories by educators and students, and videos that will help personalize the educational lives of Black boys.

If we can do this, if we can fix education so that Black boys show up at schools in the wholeness of their selves, so that Black boys feel a sense of belonging, nurturance, challenge, and love at school, so that Black boys grow up to live full lives with meaningful work and a sound educational foundation, it will be because White women made it happen. If we don't, it will be because White women didn't make it happen. Either way, White women are in the driver's seat in the classroom in America. We don't have an option here. White women have to do this work.

"Why Do You Need a Guide to Teaching Black Boys? Can't You Just Love Them?"

This question was asked in the very first workshop conducted with this guide. It gave the room and the presenters pause—why *do* we need a guide to teaching Black boys? What is so different about teaching Black boys that a teacher can't just do the same thing she does with other students? Why is loving African American children any different from loving all children, and isn't loving enough? The question asked was grounded in the idea that successful teachers simply must love their students and the rest will follow. As we struggled with this question, we came to two answers.

First, loving Black boys is not a straightforward enterprise. As a group, Black boys and men are stereotyped to be dangerous, lazy, dishonest, violent, athletic, and unintelligent (Harper, 2015). The images of Blackness are so distorted that very few people who grow up in U.S. society—including Black boys themselves—can simply love them without first dealing with the stereotypes, the misinformation, and the lies we have been taught about Black boys.

Second, we had to ask ourselves: Is "loving" one's students even the goal? Isn't the goal academic achievement, access to an equal education, closing of the opportunity gap? Isn't giving Black boys the tools they need to participate equally in society the best form of "loving" a teacher can give?

If academic achievement is the end goal, educators need to examine current educational systems, which too often evaluate performance based on the degree of assimilation to White ways of being, as opposed to valuing individual differences, strengths, and possibilities. We need to recognize that the current assimilationist model is a *privilege system,* built by and for the success of mainstream middle-class White people without consideration for the needs and circumstances of people of color and the working poor.

Why Do We Write Only About White Women and Black Boys?

One of the principles of universal design (Burgstahler, 2015) is that when you design for a small subpopulation, the specificity and practicality of that design often scales up to more effective practices for the general population as well. Gender scholars find this with teaching methods that are effective for boys. In searching for ways to better serve boys who were restless and seemingly uncooperative in school in comparison to their more compliant girl counterparts, teachers and researchers developed active learning strategies to accommodate learning needs of boys. But when these strategies are implemented, teachers tend to find that they are more effective for girls as well (Kimmel, 2000). The girls' previous compliance suggested that the old strategies were working for them, when actually, girls also learn better when they are actively engaged. This would never have been discovered, however, if we did not isolate the one gender demographic for whom education was not working.

When we look at the problems we have with race and education in the United States, we believe we will get closer to finding a solution if we can do two things in our analysis. The first, based on this principle of universal design, is to look specifically at the different issues that affect one particular subgroup. While what we learn won't necessarily be generalizable to Asian American, Latino, American Indian, White, or even Black girl students, the awareness that readers take away about the impact of racialization, our racially inequitable history, a racially segregated school system, and the predominance of Whiteness in education may help readers think differently about those subgroups as well. The second is to look critically at Whiteness. So often, when we write or talk about race in education, the discussion focuses squarely on the outcomes of students of color. But when we step back to see that most of our teachers are White, most administrators are White, most educational policymakers are White, most curriculum writers are White, and most teacher educators are White—then we get a much clearer picture of race in education. If we want to know about race and education in the United States, we will get closer to a deep and nuanced understanding if we look closely at White women teachers and one particular subgroup of students of color. Hence, *The Guide for White Women Who Teach Black Boys.*

Why do we write about *Black boys,* rather than *Black men* or *Black males*? We have heard this question a lot, and we acknowledge that the term doesn't exactly roll off the tongue. We acknowledge the problematic history of calling Black men "boys," a practice that has been used to denigrate and humiliate Black men who were fathers and grandfathers. But we write about boys because we want to emphasize that children who are 18 and younger are still children. They are not men. The police treat them like men. The courts treat them like men. Many adults fear them like adult men. Teachers often expect them to have skills of code switching and racial border crossing that most adults do not have. We want to remind ourselves and others that Blacks boys in K–12 educational spaces are boys—not men. But why not use the term *males*? We chose not to use the term *Black males* because it is most regularly used in the media and in social science in ways that turn individual children into a clinical, statistical category, which can be dehumanizing and minimizing. We are talking about children, from preschool to twelfth grade. They are still young, they still need our guidance and our support, and they need us to be the adults so that they can do the growing and learning that they need to do.

In addressing the experiences of Black boys, we have tried to represent them in the diverse complexity of their intersectional identities. While the population of Black boys in our K–12 schools is infinitely diverse—and we cannot possibly cover all the different combinations of identities here—we have tried not to portray Black boys as a monolith. In this book, you will hear stories of Black boys who are deaf, gay, trans, hetero, wealthy, poor, and cis. You will hear from Black men who are opera lovers, filmmakers, football coaches, world travelers, school superintendents, professors, and teachers.

What about Black girls? Black girl students face many of the same issues that Black boys face: a curriculum and book selection that doesn't reflect their reality, implicit bias on the part of teachers and others, a racialized history that limited their (and their ancestors') access to resources, jobs, and education. But Black girls—and the issues they face in education—are also unique in important ways. At the end of the book, we have an "outtro" written by womanist scholar Charlotte Jacobs, PhD, in which she explains some of the ways the lessons of this book could be applied to the education of Black girls, as well as the valuable ways that the issues that impact Black girls are different from those that impact Black boys.

OUR CONCEPT AND GOALS

From its earliest conception, this book has been oriented toward an audience of White women teachers. Every chapter, as you will see, addresses White women teachers, and all our ideas are built around the particular relationship between White women teachers and Black boy students. But as we have promoted the book around the country, we found ourselves realizing that many people besides White women want to use this as a resource. And as the book has come to completion, we have realized that these resources could be useful to many different types of readers. In developing a project that has a specific mission—White women, Black boys—we have created something that will likely be applicable for all. We hope that, whatever your race or gender identity, this book has value for you in your life and work. Whenever possible, we try to address the reader as "readers", rather than as "White women." The exception to this is within the individual chapters, some of which are written directly to White women teachers.

This book includes chapters by authors with a wide variety of experiences. Some are teachers, some are parents, some are educational experts, administrators, and teacher educators. Some authors approach their writing from personal experience, and others base their chapters on research—their own and others'. The authors are Black, White, Latino, biracial and multiracial, transgender and cisgender, women and men, gay and straight. The more than forty chapters that comprise this book present a broad array of voices and approaches to this topic that are deeply personal, as well as institutional and systemic.

You may notice an inconsistency in the approach that authors take to capitalizing the terms "Black" and "White" and "People of Color." As an editorial team, we prefer to let individual authors choose the system of capitalization that works for them, in spite of the inconsistency that creates in the book as a whole. There are many different considerations to make when deciding whether and when to capitalize. We capitalize "Black" and "White" in the introduction and in the passages between chapters to emphasize that these are not literal colors, but figurative, constructed, social and racial categories that are also political, sometimes legislated categories. We use the term *Black* rather than *African American* to be inclusive of our African immigrants and Caribbean students who do not identify as African American, even as we realize that issues of race and racism may affect them differently from their African American counterparts.

We use the term *White* rather than *Caucasian* because it is more accurately descriptive of European-descended, light-skinned people in the United States. The term *Caucasian* may feel to many like a more politically correct expression of Whiteness, but it is both geographically inaccurate and historically uncommon. Many of the laws that privileged Whiteness throughout U.S. history referred to "White people" (Lopez, 2006); it is not a new term.

Finally, we use the terms *Black* and *White* because these are salient racial categories today and have been throughout history. As the pages of this book can attest, they have significant consequences and ramifications for the lives of people who are labeled Black or White and who have family and ancestors who were labeled Black or White. These racial categories are not biological. They are socially constructed categories. Having brown skin or having peachy skin is biological, often inherited from birth parents and shared with siblings, although not always. But the meaning we give to that skin color (the access, the privileges, the resources, the right to vote or restriction against voting, the union membership or exclusion, for example)— the meaning of what you can get or cannot get because of that skin color—all of that is socially constructed. Race is based on biological features, but race is a fiction that we tell ourselves to convince ourselves that we are more different than we really are. And yet, the fact that race is a fiction does not mean that we don't have to deal with it. It has real and powerful consequences for our lives.

Throughout the book, when we refer to ourselves as "we," we are writing as a multiracial, crossgender writing team: Eddie Moore Jr., Ali Michael, and Marguerite W. Penick-Parks. Except for chapters and vignettes that are attributed to specific authors, we are the writing and editorial team responsible for all the content in this book.

The Framework

In 1996, co-editor Eddie Moore Jr., founded the national White Privilege Conference based on the idea that "equity and justice through self and social transformation" are the hallmarks of change. *The Guide for White Women Who Teach Black Boys* is grounded in the same conceptual framework as the White Privilege Conference: **U**nderstanding, **R**especting, and **C**onnecting. These three key actions guide the work: Through **U**nderstanding self and students, **R**especting individuality and differences, and **C**onnecting through the mutual goal of a quality education, White women and Black boys can come together for academic excellence, academic achievement, and personal and professional growth. This guide will help readers move beyond fear to understanding, respecting, and connecting.

Understanding

PART 1: EXPLORING THE SELF

The Guide for White Women Who Teach Black Boys is not solely a guide to understanding Black boys. It is as much—if not more so—a guide to understanding what it means to be a White woman. This guide aims to help White women teachers better understand the racialized, historical, and political relationship between White women and Black boys, to be conscious of the raced and gendered aspects of their relationships with Black boy students, as well as the raced and gendered aspects of their own experiences and those of the Black boys they teach. This section supports White women teachers, some of whom may never have thought about themselves as White before, to understand the ways they have been positioned in terms of race and gender—even without their knowledge or consent. Because many Black boys go through K–12 education without ever having teachers who are not White women, White women must have an understanding of self as well as an understanding of the experiences of Black boys in their classrooms.

PART 2: UNDERSTANDING THE CONSTRAINTS AND CHALLENGING THE NARRATIVES ABOUT WHO BLACK BOYS ARE AND WHO WHITE WOMEN CAN BE

Part 2 is about the narratives and common tropes that play almost as big a role in the relationship between White women and Black boys as the individual actors themselves. These narratives come from the media and then get perpetuated in teacher lounge conversations and in individual personal fears. They teach us to see Black boys as athletes and musicians at best, but not as scholars, scientists, mathematicians, and creative writers. These chapters will address those common tropes and demonstrate ways these rote narratives constrict the possibilities of authentic connection. White women will be encouraged to wrestle with the question that one Black man asked in our interviews, "Why are people afraid of us?" and to strategize ways to challenge these common narratives and tropes on multiple levels: in society at large, while consuming media, when you find them in your head, when you hear them in your school, and when you see your students have internalized them.

RESPECTING

PART 3: RESPECTING THE BROAD DIVERSITY OF BLACK BOYS' EXPERIENCES AND IDENTITIES

Part 3 addresses issues that are specific to Black boys, either because they are Black or because they are boys, or both. This section illustrates the broad heterogeneity of Black boys, even as we focus on Black boys as a group that has particular needs and a different social positioning than their Asian, Latino, Native American, multiracial, and White male peers, as well as their female peers of all racial backgrounds.

PART 4: RELATIONSHIPS WITH PARENTS, COLLEAGUES, AND COMMUNITY

Part 4 addresses the need to build relationships between White women teachers and Black boys and their families, as well as strategies for doing so. It emphasizes the importance of teachers working together with families and communities to create structures of safety and support to hold onto Black boys as they grow up in a society that so greatly misunderstands them. This section includes chapters on giving feedback to and receiving feedback from Black students and their families, as well as a larger section on relationships with families. It also discusses how teachers can teach to the *boy* in their boys, which means not holding them to behavioral expectations normed on girl students.

CONNECTING

PART 5: CONNECTING STUDENT SUCCESS AND FAILURE TO SCHOOL STRUCTURES AND CLASSROOM STRATEGIES

Parts 5 and 6 are about the ways that both school success and school failure are mutually constructed by teachers and students in interaction with school and state policies. It is meant to examine the ways in which teacher actions shape student responses. The goal is to examine the context in which misbehavior and failure occur in order to help teachers understand the ways in which student failure is often a consequence of a group dynamic, rather than an individual failing. This section examines how power struggles between teachers and students play out, why teachers need to be the responsible adult who takes the lead in de-escalating such struggles, and strategies for doing so.

PART 6: CONNECTING STUDENT SUCCESS TO SCHOOL STRUCTURES AND CLASSROOM STRATEGIES

Part 6 is the toolbox for teachers. It is a compilation of chapters written by visionary educators, who have designed and implemented programming that works for Black boys. While strategies and tools have been distributed throughout the book, this part focuses almost exclusively on actions that teachers can take in their classrooms to improve outcomes for Black boys.

If you are doing this work well, these are some of the outcomes you can expect to see:

- An increased awareness of yourself and of the ways that your race and gender impact you and your relationships

- A new lens for seeing Black boys more clearly as a group, and as individuals

- A capacity to understand specific issues that Black boys and their families might contend with

- Better relationships between you and your Black boy students, including more open communication

- Better communication with the families of the Black boys in your class

- Better relationships between the Black boys in your class and the students of other races

- Higher levels of engagement from the Black boys in your class

- Higher levels of achievement from the Black boys in your class

CONCLUSION

Schools that fail Black boys are not extraordinary. In fact, schools that fail Black boys are, in essence, doing what they were built to do. Schools in the United States were built by White people for the advancement and education of White people. For Black people in the United States, getting an education has historically been an illicit activity rife with danger, personal risk, and structural barriers. When schools fail Black boys, it's because they are *doing school* the way that school has always been done. It may be the only way schools know how. And yet, if we want to shift outcomes for Black boys, we need to create different ways to *do school* that acknowledge this history and that work for the vast majority of Black boys. *That* would be extraordinary.

UNDERSTANDING

Understanding Whiteness in education is key to understanding Blackness in education. It has been said that the first rule of multiculturalism is understanding one's own culture. Whiteness is not often seen as a culture. It is more often seen—especially by White people—as invisible, or as the norm (Sue, 2006). But Whiteness is just as much a part of the racial hierarchy—and every racial problem—as any other racial group in the United States. So if we believe that Blackness matters in our teaching relationships—Whiteness must matter, too.

PART 1
EXPLORING THE SELF

In Part 1, *The Guide* examines the selves that White women and Black boys bring to their school interactions. White women, who have spent years trying to figure it out, will explain how Whiteness matters in their relationships with students. Each of them writes with humor and humility, in a way that makes their experiences painfully relatable. In Chapter 1, Debby Irving writes about her mistaken assumption that because she is White, she thought she knew how to connect with Black students, perhaps even to "save" Black students. It wasn't until many years later that she realized this superiority complex was an impediment to connecting with Black students and families. This chapter will be followed by the first of many vignettes, this one by renowned psychologist Dr. Howard Stevenson. Stevenson writes about his middle school experience when a White teacher put her job on the line to centralize (rather than sideline) the lives and experiences of Black students in her classroom.

Chapters 2 and 3 orient us to the state of White women and Black boys in education. Julie Landsman gives us a demographic profile of White women teachers and then shares common group-level behaviors that White women teachers tend to demonstrate. You may notice some of these group-level behaviors in some of the personal narratives of other authors in this section. In Chapter 3, the researcher from the Seven Centers Consortium shares a demographic picture of who Black boys are. Those broad and global chapters will be followed by a vignette by Solomon Smart, a 10-year-old Black boy, who wrote a short letter to White teachers to share some of his experiences of school.

In Chapter 4, Dr. Diane Finnerty lays out all of the research relevant to unconscious bias in schools. She puts it together in a way that leaves little doubt that unconscious bias is at work in the relationship between White women and Black students and that an awareness of this bias could change what we do in schools. In Chapter 5, John Marshall, chief equity officer for the Jefferson County Public

Schools in Kentucky, affirms this perspective, writing about how he has seen this very dynamic play out among the White teachers with whom he has worked. In Chapter 6, Ali Michael describes White racial identity development: the idea that as White people learn more about racism, they go through different psychological phases of processing the feelings and information related to that learning. This chapter will likely help White readers navigate their own emotions as they read this book. In Chapter 7, Dr. Elizabeth Denevi reframes one of the scariest things that can happen to a White teacher—being called a racist—and asks, "What if that were the beginning of the conversation, rather than the end?" And finally, Dr. Robin DiAngelo, the researcher who first developed the concept of "white fragility," closes out this section by describing patterns that manifest in the lives of many White people, patterns that leave them, by virtue of their socialization, ill-equipped to be teachers of Black boys.

Debby Irving is a down-to-earth White woman whose wit, self-reflectiveness and willingness to be vulnerable help White teachers across the country as they seek a way in to conversations about race. She doesn't mince words, she speaks truth, and yet she doesn't position herself as better than anyone else because of what she has learned. In this chapter she shares stories from her very early teaching career, and her realization that teaching Black boys was going to require that she know a lot more—especially about herself—if she was going to be effective.

CHAPTER 1

Ready to Make a Difference, the Old-Fashioned Way

Debby Irving

Virtuous. Enthusiastic. Ready. If I had to pick three words to characterize the feelings I had when I chose to become a teacher in the Cambridge Public Schools, these would be the words.

After a number of years with two children in the Cambridge school system, its everyday happenings had become central to my life. The school community sparked curiosity and energy in me. I couldn't seem to get enough of it. What drew me to this district rather than schools in general was the level of racial integration. Raised in an affluent white suburb, I didn't want for my children the kind of racial or class isolation that I'd found so limiting in my own childhood. The racial diversity in the Cambridge schools intrigued me and drew me closer.

One cold December morning as I left my daughters' school, I stopped in my tracks with the thought, "I wish I were a teacher." Then, in mid-stride, it occurred to me, "Mid-life career change is a thing. I wonder what it would take to change careers?" One month later, I found myself as a teaching assistant at my daughters' school, one of the city's most successful and cherished elementary schools. My idea was to test the teaching waters before committing to the graduate education I'd need to qualify as a lead teacher.

As my start day neared, I imagined "My love of kids makes me a natural," and "I'll be able to make a real difference!" What I didn't yet know was that although I was a "natural" with children who looked like me, this didn't translate as I thought it would with children who did not look like me. I didn't understand that loving kids would not be nearly enough and that my ideas about "making a difference" smacked of historical patterns about "saving" and "helping" and "fixing" that held in place the very issues I envisioned conquering. My sense of entitlement to help, and my assumption that I was equipped to do so, were manifestations of my lack of cultural competence. Although cultural competence wasn't even a term in my white world, deep-seated ideas about being competent just by being white were.

I entered teaching fancying myself colorblind, and therefore able to love and teach each student equally. The truth, however, is that I did see color. In fact, race was very much on my mind. Despite a universally loved staff deeply committed to serving *all* children, I'd observed stark racial patterns emerge year after year at my daughters' school. White parents flocked to school events, sat on various committees, and occupied the room-parent positions. Integrated kindergarteners who'd once held hands and bounced gleefully through school hallways slowly but surely got racially segregated into hierarchical reading and math groups. While my daughters' friend groups grew whiter over the year, once-bright-eyed black and brown five-year-olds grew to ten-year-olds whose downcast eyes avoided mine. The principal's bench, where recalcitrant students awaited their fate, disproportionately housed angry- or despondent-looking black boys. Meanwhile, the white kids disproportionally maintained their youthful exuberance while advancing through reading and math levels and assuming leadership roles in the school.

These racial observations mixed and mingled with subconscious racial ideas I'd unknowingly absorbed in childhood. In my 1960s suburban life, white was my normal, the entirety of my visual backdrop. Immersed in a world of white families, white teachers, white books and TV characters, white presidents, white doctors, white dolls, whiteness became so normal as to be invisible. Although I consciously noticed race only when a person of color appeared, the reality is I subconsciously noticed whiteness every minute of every day. Far from benign, my racial observations packed unspoken ideas about inherent human difference along skin color lines. Without knowing it, my childhood belief system developed around a complex, better-than/worse-than value scheme in which white people were smarter, more responsible, harder-working, safer, and superior human beings.

So when I thought to myself, "I'll be able to make a difference," it's pretty clear who I had in mind. I wasn't going into teaching to "make a difference" for the white kids. And I was far from colorblind. My unspoken assumption was that I, as the mother of two high-achieving white kids, had what it took to "help" the black and brown kids. The tragedy here is that despite my best intentions, without knowing my own racial history or culture, I was destined to undermine the success of the very students I most wanted to "help."

A crucial aspect of dominant white culture was, and continues to be, an unspoken agreement that black people are not just "non-white others;" black people are "troubled others," and these troubles are somehow self-inflicted and/or biologically based. Integral to this silent narrative is a ubiquitous freedom-and-equality narrative: "Life, liberty, justice for all," "level playing field," and "land of the free." Language like this exalts U.S. ideals while ignoring U.S. discriminatory policies and practices. This skewed messaging allowed me to quietly buy into distorted ideas about black people as less-than and go on to use these ideas to explain away not only the divergent educational outcomes and parent engagement I observed at school, but also the black/white wealth gap and those scary "inner city" neighborhoods. My hushed explanations included thoughts like "they must not care about education," "they don't know how to make and save money," and "they have no regard for personal property." Having grown up in a white world where a white-authored history and version of current events shaped my worldview, I was oblivious to the way black people told their own history. White history and narratives saturated not only my formal education but also information I soaked up through the media and my own white family's stories. Amid this onslaught of one-sided history rumbled the unspoken understanding that talking about race was rude.

In that information void, I remained unaware that from the get-go, U.S. public and private programs and policies have disproportionally diverted resources toward white people, economically castrating communities of color, and then blaming them for their circumstances. Without knowing U.S. racial history, I couldn't consider the kind of frustration and anger it might engender, which further undermined my aspirations to be that awesome, loving, colorblind, pied piper of a teacher I imagined I would be. Not only did I subconsciously judge people of color for their circumstances, I judged their attitudes and behaviors. I cannot stress enough how deep beneath the surface of my consciousness this was. Nor can I stress how damaging and perverse a mindset it is, because really, my approach to making a difference was not about discovering policies and practices that were differentially impacting students along color lines; rather, my approach was rooted in wanting to teach "those" kids to have more "appropriate" attitudes and behaviors. I wanted to teach them to think and act more like me, to be more white.

I had no idea of the history I was repeating. Although consciously I scoffed at historical phrases such as "taming the heathens" and "civilizing the savages," subconsciously I was trapped in exactly that mindset. Beneath my colorblind fantasy, I was deeply invested in the white way as the right way. What's more, I'd bought into ideas about women being the cultural torchbearers, both in the family and in society at large.

SOURCE: Library of Congress. http://www.loc.gov/pictures/resource/ppmsca.09855/

Without conscious memory of seeing the painting *American Progress*, depicting a white woman floating over the western plains, a bible tucked under her arm, I essentially swallowed whole the narrative she conveyed: the white woman's role was to model how to be good, right, moral, and compliant. Choosing a career first in nonprofit management and later in elementary education fit right into the historically accepted role of white women doing society's "helping" and "fixing" charity work for the destitute and the young. And, like past tamers and civilizers, my actions would mostly make me feel good about myself while disempowering those on whom I imposed my ill-conceived ideas about right and wrong.

As I entered the classroom with these unexamined ideas, I unknowingly fueled the very racial divide I imagined I would bridge. I congratulated black and brown students for simply completing an assignment while pushing white students to make corrections. I worked closely with black and brown students to adhere to rules yet excused white students' rule-breaking with thoughts like, "gotta love her confidence" or "what spunk!" I bonded with the white parents who showed up at drop-off and parent-teacher conferences yet did little to connect with the parents of color who showed up less often, assuming their lack of engagement was due to external challenges such as work or transportation.

A key question I never asked myself was this: Is there anything about me that contributes to the outcome that parents or students of color engage more or less? What I didn't know was that the sight of white me could trigger historical feelings of mistrust and trauma for people of color. Nor did I understand that my cultural values around punctuality, efficiency, and independence were not similarly valued in all cultures. While I saw punctuality as a mark of ethical behavior, for instance, Black families may have seen my emphasis on punctuality as an indication that I value time more than I value human beings or relationships. By perceiving emotional restraint and conflict avoidance as a sign of good character combined with good rearing, I evaluated anger and agitation as character flaws combined with poor parenting, never as valuable feedback directed at me. Because my culture taught me to look for deficits in others, not to reflect on myself, I gathered evidence in support of black people's shortcomings, while never questioning my own.

Take Rosie, a first-generation Haitian girl I spent a year "helping" with all my white might. Rosie had a pattern of getting up in the middle of an assignment and walking to a classmate's desk. With the best of intentions, my white colleagues and I believed this was a serious self-control issue and created a behavior plan that offered the incentive of earning stars by staying in her seat. My job was to implement it. Her response to my daily interceptions was to look devastated, return to her seat, and put her head on her desk, crushed that she'd failed again and too disheartened to focus on her schoolwork. For eight months, I blamed noncompliance as the source of her behavioral and academic troubles. Not once did I consider how my white cultural expectations could be playing a role.

Toward the end of the school year, a course I was taking helped me to wonder if a culture clash might be in play. As I learned that Haitian culture values group functionality over individual achievement, I began to get in touch with my own socialization around individualism and the lens it had given me in judging Rosie's behavior. One day, after watching Rosie get up in the middle of a math problem, I refrained from intercepting her. Free from my demands, she walked to a classmate's desk across the room and began rubbing her back. When I checked in with her later, she told me how she'd heard Kendall (who is white) crying. I'd been closer to Kendall's desk and not heard a thing. This hit me like a thunderbolt. Rosie's connectedness and compassion put into relief my lack of both. Did I have something to learn from Rosie and her culture?

As the course pushed me to consider how different cultures develop different sides of our human capacities, I wondered what sensibilities and impulses I might have developed in my culture. As I reconsidered the pity I'd felt when I learned Rosie shared a bed with five siblings and cousins, I reimagined the human connectedness she would also develop from that experience. I rethought the insistence I'd had years earlier that my daughters "have their own space," each with her own bedroom. Had I set my own children up to thrive in the culture of individualism at the expense of human connectedness? Had my own lifetime of individual orientation left me communally challenged?

One manifestation of my lack of connectedness was the way I engaged with the idea of diversity. I was drawn to racially integrated communities because they felt exciting *to me*. A more connected, culturally aware person might have wondered: How does this community feel having me become a part of it?

If I could redo one part of my life, I would have become more culturally aware and competent before entering the classroom. Without either quality, I stepped into the role of educator with the only cultural training I'd had, the one centered on white, patriarchal cultural norms and social roles. Although I'd experienced the oppressiveness of men dictating what was best for me, thinking less of my abilities, and labeling me too emotional as a woman, I turned around and imposed these very tendencies on students and families of color. My own ignorance about my culture both obfuscated my capacity to look for value in other cultures and allowed me to impose mine.

Reminding myself that I did not invent America's racial caste system has helped me move quickly through feelings of guilt and defensiveness and onto the more productive feelings of mutual responsibility. Connecting with people and ideas with fearless vulnerability and humble curiosity has been the hardest and most rewarding endeavor of my life. How I wish I'd had the opportunity to cultivate this human capacity earlier. What I would give to turn back the clock and have decades of racial consciousness ahead of me. May young educators continue to unearth and expose the toxic ideology that reproduces racial inequity every day and leave the old-fashioned ways of denial and dominance where they belong, in the past.

■ ■ Engaging the Mind ★ Taking Action ★ Inspiring Excellence
Assessing Your Exposure

1) STEREOTYPES

Write

Set a timer for six minutes. During these six minutes, write every stereotype you've ever heard about each of the following groups. Keep going even if you think you're done, even if it means repeating what you've written.

Jews

Muslims

African Americans

Latinx

Native Americans

Asian Americans

Reflect:

> Are you surprised by what your mind holds?
>
> Can you trace where you learned these stereotypes?
>
> How do you think these ideas influence you?

2) SOCIAL ROLES

What gender roles were you exposed to in your childhood?

- Who worked in what kinds of jobs?
- Who were the primary caretakers in your home and the homes of extended family and friends?
- Who prepared meals?
- Who stayed home to take care of sick children?
- What were the genders of your childhood teachers?

What patterns do you notice?

What racial roles were you exposed to in your childhood? Write racial background next to each of the following:

- Family authority figures
- School teachers, principals, directors
- Extracurricular teachers, coaches, trainers
- Pediatrician, dentist, other medical caregivers
- Your five closest friends' parents

What percentage of your childhood authority figures were white? How might this influence your ideas about leadership along racial lines?

3) CULTURAL NORMS

Which of these messages did you hear inside and/or outside your home?

- Don't rock the boat.
- If you don't have anything nice to say, don't say anything at all.
- Never discuss politics or religion in polite company.

How did your family navigate conflict?

- We didn't. We avoided it.
- Shouting and disagreeing
- Silent anger and passive-aggressive behaviors
- Courageous conversations and reconciliation that resulted in increased connection

What messages did you receive about emotions and emotionally charged behaviors?

- Crying
- Anger
- Shouting
- Disagreement

What's your friend and family conversational culture?

- When you think about sharing the name of this book with your closest friends and family, what feelings arise?
- What reactions do you anticipate from these important people in your life?
- What might be the consequences of sharing parts of this book with them?
- What might be the consequences of not sharing parts of this book with them?

As *Debby writes in her chapter, she was not socialized to recognize or talk about race, or even to see racism. And while this is not the experience of all White people, or all White teachers, we know from the research on White racial socialization (Hamm, 2006; Bartoli et al., 2016) that many White people are taught to ignore race, to be colorblind, to see all their students as the same. Rarely are White teachers asked—or given the opportunity—to examine their own racial background as teachers. And yet teachers' inability to recognize their own racialized assumptions and behavior impact the classroom and their practices. The chapters in this section, we hope, will help White teachers recognize this socialization in themselves—to the extent that it is there—and see the damage that it does in a classroom with Black boys. The following vignette by Howard Stevenson demonstrates what it looks like when a White teacher is absolutely color-conscious in her teaching. Howard's drama teacher took so seriously the task of centralizing the lives and experiences of Black students that she risked her job to do so. And in so doing, she demonstrated that teaching Black boys well doesn't just mean changing the curriculum and reducing one's bias, it may also mean standing up to the community, to administrators, and to other teachers who believe (maybe even unconsciously) that Black students belong on the sidelines and periphery of our communities.*

Vignette: Raisins in the Sun: White Teacher as a Force of Nature Buffering the Radiation of Racial Retaliation

Howard Stevenson

White teacher. Enthusiastic in body, mind, and spirit. In the subtlest of forms, a force of nature, she was. Energetic and relentless. A thirst for justice in every bone of her theatrical body—theater arts to be specific. Harriet Jeglum, a name made for drama, introduced me and many of my tenth-grade teenage friends at Cape Henlopen High School to the word *thespian*. I joined as soon as I knew that thespian meant "serious actor." A club. A gang. A gang of actors who could change the world, we were. She was the ringleader and a delightful one at that—one many of us were more than happy to shapeshift ourselves and follow. She brought fun and life back to education. I remember her and regret that I have taken so long to remember her in print. It has been forty years since she carried the weight of racial discord, meant for me, so I could be in the center of the pedagogy we call school.

I've had many white teachers over the years. Mrs. Bounds, who was wonderful in second grade and who told my mother I would be somebody special. And then there was Mrs. Rust, who submitted my fourth-grade article on sea horses to the Sussex County newspaper, putting me on blast, famous for all who dared to question my professorial talents. And who could forget Ms. Phillips, who on the first day of geometry class called me a nigger and told me I'd never amount to anything including failing the snap-quiz she was passing out. I got a B in that class because I hated her and she hated me. There was the crush I had on both Ms. Yancy and the algebra taught in eighth and ninth grades: my favorite subject, my favorite teacher, my first favorite dream life. Still, while all my white teachers varied in their influence on my development as a student learner, one changed the ground upon which I could question learning at its core.

Few white teachers I've had in my life could fathom the seriousness of the role or the importance of exercising their professional passion as a calling. In the Fall of 1976, Ms. Jeglum decided to do something never ever done before in the history of Cape Henlopen High or lower Delaware, I daresay. Every year, the responsibility of choosing the school play fell on her.

Choosing the senior play was no small feat. In southern Delaware and in many high school theaters across this country in 1976, theater directors were beholden and even smitten by the plays of their cultural upbringing, popular cultural expression, and social whiteness of that time. Nostalgia for the good ole' days waxed heavy then, and the most common plays of record would be *Oklahoma* or *Hello, Dolly!* Musicals filled theaters with joy and happy times to distract us all from this country's political turmoil and racial woes. Unfortunately, very few parts in these plays were written with Black teenage boys in mind, except lifting things and getting shot.

The senior play was the event of the year, the character statement of the school's potential, hope, and energy. The play represented all that we as a school could be and become, and it didn't matter if you weren't in the performance. The play represented you whether you were a student, a teacher, family, or the maintenance worker. Ms. Jeglum alone could choose the play, and we had to contort ourselves into the characters of that choice and stake out multiple identity possibilities.

Needless to say, I was as shocked as any student, any teacher, any family, or maintenance worker when she chose *Raisin in the Sun*. Was I dreaming? Was she high? Was I in Delaware? *Raisin in the Sun*? Yes, oh my God, damn straight. What-the-? So many emotions and so much disagreement erupted in our school. There are only two white parts in Lorraine Hansberry's wonderful script about a Black family living in Chicago and trying to make a future for themselves, and they were the bad guys.

We all tried out for the performance. Some were happy to be stagehands. My brother Bryan won the role of Walter and was masterful. Pearlina Waples played Mama with soulful gusto. I won the role of Willie Bobo because I could whine pitifully with the best of men who lose the family's only resource for a financially stable future. (To be honest, loud and pitifully regretful whining is universally annoying and requires no particular acting talent). You couldn't tell us *nothin'!* Not only did I not have to take a rocket ship into outer space to create a black identity from a white protagonist in the senior play, I was in it, and it was about me. I was in the center of the pedagogy. My people were in the center. My culture was in the center. Our language, our loss, our style, our anger. Protagonist didn't matter. Antagonist didn't matter. We all were heroes and heroines. We were not toting bales of cotton. We were thespians!

But, boy, the proverbial thespian shit hit the fan. Ms. Jeglum had to deal with the chorus of angry voices from White students, teachers, families, and maintenance workers about her decision. The onslaught of whiteness retaliation was her weight to carry. How could she? What was she doing? Was she high? No, she was not high. She might have been irresistible and immovable, but she was not high. Since she had arrived, Ms. Jeglum had been a social irritant in action through acting, not just words. She hadn't changed her views, stripes, or values. She didn't waste time just talking. She made school joyous again. The senior play was just the icing on the cake, the lemonade from the lemons, the tip of an iceberg I would represent for years to come.

Ms. Jeglum carried an unusually troublesome and ignoble burden. Yet, she protected us from that drama, and while compromise forced her to decide to have two senior plays that year—*Raisin in the Sun* and *Hello, Dolly!*, the racial blindness shipwreck had already taken place. There was no stopping us. We sold out the first showing so that a second show had to be scheduled. Our people, understanding the importance of this event, showed up in their Sunday best!

All students want their teachers to stand up for them, but black and brown students need them to stand up against the rejection that suggests we have no right to be in the center of the pedagogy. Not as a visitor. Not as a grateful orphan. But as the brightly shining stars we are. Like ozone protects us from the sun's radiation or a starship shields us from enemy photon torpedoes or a dam holds back the flood of racial retaliation. Placing us in the center with *Raisin* was noble enough. But buffering us from the retaliation was as honorable a gift as any teacher could give to Black and Brown students in the 1970s or the 1870s. It was more influential than a compliment or a nasty slur; more stimulating than being published or having a schoolboy crush; more powerful than talking about social justice. What white teachers need to know is that you must sacrifice your comfort if you want to be the tip of the iceberg.

A force of nature she was, we were, I am.

The following two chapters—"The State of the White Woman Teacher" by Julie Landsman and "Advancing the Success of Boys and Men of Color" by The Seven Centers—are intended to give you a global portrait of who White women and Black boys are in schools today. We have been careful—in these two chapters and in the rest of the book—to present statistics in a way that does not paint Black boys or their families and communities with a deficit lens. When we look at the state of education today, we want to see all the assets that Black boys, their families, and communities bring to their schools and to recognize that many of the failures we see are failures of a system. These two chapters are meant to provide readers with a picture of that system, a system which encompasses all the individual stories of triumph, challenge, loss, and struggle portrayed in greater personalized detail throughout the book. Julie Landsman, a former English teacher and a nationally renowned teacher-educator, gives both quantitative data on the demographics of White women teachers and qualitative data on common patterns that White women exhibit. The subsequent chapter, by The Seven Centers, gives us a sense of who Black boys are as a collective and how their experiences vary in smaller subgroups.

CHAPTER 2

The State of the White Woman Teacher

Julie Landsman

Willie Gates, who was in [Abdul] Wright's seventh- and eighth-grade classes, cheered for the man he considers a 'brother figure' during the ceremony. Wright is Minnesota's first African American Teacher of the Year.

"When he talks to us, we just think of him as one of us," Gates said. "With the lack of father figures and brother figures in the community, and having a teacher like him . . . that connection is a beautiful thing. It's something you can't put your finger on." Gates described Wright's teaching approach as energetic and engaging. (Zamora, 2016, A Brother Figure section, para. 3)

Willie Gates's words, quoted here, demonstrate how important it is for Black male students to have contact, connection, and instruction from African American men. Their presence in schools and classrooms is essential. The statistics, however, are discouraging. Numbers from a 2011–2012 report show that 82 percent of teachers were non-Hispanic White, 7 percent were non-Hispanic Black, and 8 percent were Hispanic. Overall, schools had a larger percentage of female teachers—76 percent—than male teachers—24 percent. The average age of public school teachers was 43 years. In primary schools, 89 percent of teachers were female. In high school, this drops to 58% (Albert Shanker Institute, 2014).

Add to these numbers the fact that White women, who dominate the profession, are staying longer, while teachers of color are leaving in larger numbers (Broughman, Goldring, Gray, & Bitterman, 2013, p. 3). The average White women teachers have fourteen years of experience or more, their pay averaging $53,000 per year (Broughman et al., 2013, p. 3). They are also more religious than their nonteaching counterparts and are more likely to attend church more often.

These numbers present a sketch of White women in teaching: They are the majority of adults in a rapidly growing multicultural and multireligious demographic pool of students. They are more likely to be Christian and middle class, given their salaries and longevity. U.S. church membership is one of the most segregated groups. White women, thus, may be at a disadvantage in teaching a population whose religious backgrounds or church services are varied and unfamiliar to her.

None of these factors determine how an individual White woman will relate to her students. Activist and anti-racist White female teachers are doing remarkable work with Black male students. Yet it is important to look at demographics to find clues to what might be causing the mismatch between Black males and their White women teachers.

When I started teaching, I reflected this demographic: White, middle class, and raised as a Christian, I had attended all-White schools and religious services. I brought with me many of the assumptions about race and culture that a large percentage of white teachers have. Going beyond pure demographics, these ideas may help explain the disconnect between White teachers and Black students.

The consequences of this disconnect are shown in a study by Nicholas Papageorge at Johns Hopkins University and his colleagues:

> White and other non-black teachers were 12 percentage points more likely than black teachers to predict black students wouldn't finish high school. They also found that Black female teachers are significantly more optimistic about the ability of black boys to complete high school than teachers of any other demographic group. They were 20 percent less likely than white teachers to predict their student wouldn't graduate high school and 30% less likely to say that than were black male teachers. For Black students, particularly black boys, having a non-black teacher in a 10th grade subject made them less likely to pursue that subject by enrolling in similar classes. (Papageorge, Gershenson, & Holt, 2016, p. 222)

I came to Minneapolis public schools with certain assumptions about Black males. While I had been active in the civil rights movement and had a background of close relationships working with African American men and women, I had not examined my own whiteness. While the numbers in many studies include White male teachers, we must still consider that White *females* and their attitudes are in the majority in U.S. schools. It is often common for a sixth-grade Black male student to have experienced his entire school career of seven years without seeing a Black teacher, male or female, in front of the class. And given the percentages, he will probably be taught by White female teachers up until high school.

For Black males especially, this is critical: Rarely do they see before them any males and even fewer African Americans during their highly formative years. There are White educators who declare we live in a "colorblind" world. To them the lack of Black teachers is not seen as problem. However, the opportunity gap between Black and White students—the lower graduation rates, higher suspension rates, and the high rates of referral to Special Education for Black boys, accompanied by the lower rates of their referrals to gifted programs and resources—proves beyond a doubt that we do not live in a colorblind world. Rather we live and teach in a world that perceives its Black male students as less intelligent and with less potential for success than those who are White. I was naive for my first years of teaching and wanted to believe I should teach without seeing color. After my years working for voting rights, I knew this was not true. Still I clung to the belief we were all alike.

What does gender have to do with this picture? What is the dynamic, what are the expectations, reactions, and implicit biases that White women bring that influence the success or failure of Black male students? How well-prepared are White women to understand their students? What myths about Black males have they absorbed that hinder them from connecting with their students? And finally, what can be done to bridge this gap between teachers and those who sit before them? I had no training in White privilege in all my twenty-five years of teaching in city schools. What I learned I learned on my own, in summers, at conferences I chose to attend. Many White women teachers arrive in U.S. classrooms, even now, years later, with the same lack of awareness.

The following is not an attempt to generalize about a whole group of people based on their gender or race. We know that backgrounds, histories, families, economic status, and personal morality have much to do with how people function in the world. What I offer here is a set of constructs and commonalities that White female teachers often bring to their work, in different contexts. Given that as Whites, they come to the teaching profession with ingrained and implicit bias simply because they live in a White supremacist country, their Whiteness impacts their classrooms, and especially those Black males who exist in their space for the school year. This information is intended not to blame, but to explore how this situation in public education came about and what part gender plays in it as well as race. White males have similar barriers and problems in teaching Black males. However, their gender can be a positive connection with boys and youth in their care. It is White females who have a more complicated and fraught history and experience in schools, and so it is necessary to examine this situation.

I started teaching in a city school in a program for students who were kicked out of their regular home school and sent to a special site. I taught those who were in seventh and eighth grade and could not read. Instead of being surprised and disturbed by the preponderance of Black males in that program—80 percent—I did not question it. I assumed these Black boys were there because of their behavior or their learning disability. I did not think, in those first years, about how my Whiteness might affect my ability to connect with them. Luckily, I had learned to be a warm demander.

The mode of the *warm demander* is one proven to be effective with Black students (Carpenter-Ford & Sassi, 2014, p. 43). If White female teachers, because of bias or lack of training in cultural competence or in identity development, neither possess warmth nor demand high expectations of their Black male students, we are left with a crucial mismatch between students and what they need from their White teachers. Jose Vilson, author of *This Is Not a Test*, said that he has found "that the female teachers in his school who exude warmth tend to have more success than those who practice strict disciplinary procedures" (as cited in Pica, 2014, para. 6).

Baruti Kafele, author of *Motivating Black Males to Achieve in School and in Life*, says about student perceptions of their teachers:

> All they want to know is that the teacher cares about them. If you can convince a black male student that 'you're in this thing for the long haul; you're not going to give up on him; your expectations for him are sky-high; and you're going to maintain those expectations, no matter what the challenges are, that student is going to embrace you regardless of whether or not you're African American" (as cited in Pica, 2016, para. 7).

But what if White teachers, because of unexamined biases, do not care for their students? What if they provide the demands without the warmth? What if they are in teaching to "fix," "mend," or "save" their Black males—roles that many women are educated to fill—instead of insisting they do their best, holding high expectations for them, and believing they can achieve great things? They may be warm without the necessary demands. They may demand without any sense of caring or warmth. Yet many White female teachers have not been raised or trained or encouraged to have both.

I had warmth toward all children early in my life. I had that down. I did not know, however, how to demand great things from students when I started my job in

Minneapolis. I had not learned to provide explicit and affirmative expectations for each young man who came into the program. At that point, I am not sure I believed they could succeed.

The backgrounds of White women, the interactions they have with Black males, and their awareness of Whiteness and its advantages as well as their own White racial identity can make the difference between a White female teacher who can reach and encourage her Black male students and one who fails them. If they are aware of their privilege and its profound implications and, at the same time, of their students' Black culture—their history, their cultural styles, their experience of education—White women can teach African American males. They cannot *be* Black. They cannot change their past, their lack of knowledge, their upbringing. I knew something about Black history and culture when I began my career; yet not enough, not nearly enough. I was often uncomfortable talking about race with Black men and women. Yet, I did learn to remove barriers that prevented me from connecting with Black male students. This came from the guidance, work, and friendships I developed on the job and in the neighborhood.

Some White women do not come with the same barriers I did, some come with a few, some with many. These barriers apply to White males as well. Women, however, have their own response to students that can be influenced by gender.

BARRIERS WHITE WOMEN TEACHERS MUST OVERCOME

Lack of friends, peers, and teachers in the African American community. Many White women come to teaching in inclusive and diverse schools without having experience in day-to-day interactions with Black people. They may arrive at a school without the ease that accompanies regular conversation, community gatherings, even church services with Black adults and children. Often, because of the segregation in the United States, they never went to school with children of color. Early on in my work both in community organizing and education, I envied those White women who grew up in integrated neighborhoods. They seemed to come to teaching with a confidence in their ability to reach Black males that I lacked.

Attitudes and stereotypes. White women come with what they have learned at home, in the media, and at school: in the history they have read, the literature they were assigned. While some White women may come from homes where they were encouraged to look at issues of social justice and equity, and others may even have been raised with Black males as brothers, many come with negative stereotypes of Black males. These might include seeing them as angry, poor, irresponsible, or even dangerous.

Along with these stereotypes, myths, and attitudes is the belief that somehow all Black males are alike while Whites are individuals. Thus, White teachers lump their Black male students into a group, while seeing White students as separate and complicated individuals. They do not recognize each Black child's unique qualities, needs, and cultural strengths. I was fortunate in my first year of teaching students of color to have colleagues and staff who pointed out to me occasions when I did not see my Black students in all their differences from each other.

Lack of awareness of Whiteness. The day-by-day bombardment of biased statements, media portrayals, and family or peer perceptions is often combined with a lack of understanding about their own Whiteness on the part of White females. They see race as something "those others" have. To them, Whiteness is the norm. This thinking is the result of a lack of training, a lack of in-depth exploration of the social construction of race, and the influence of culture in all our lives. In their interactions with parents and students, White women teachers do not always factor in their own Whiteness as part of the dynamic. This was the case for me. After training in identity development and systemic racism, all in the first two years of my twenty-five-year career in city schools, I have been able to lower this barrier and teach with an entirely different perspective. I was lucky.

Belief in their understanding of racism based on gender-related experiences. Many White women feel they automatically understand the power of racism simply because as females, they experience sexism. This prevents them from understanding racism in all its institutional and societal—as well as historical—power. When their Black sisters confront them with their own different lives as women because of racism, White women are surprised. It took some very frank and painful conversations for me to stop equating my experience with sexism with my friends' and colleagues' experiences with racism. White women do well when they listen.

Assumptions about "good" student behavior. White women come to their classrooms with an image of what a well-behaved classroom looks like. This comes from being taught in classrooms that were governed by a system that has been instituted by Whites over the centuries. The "good" classroom is one that involves silence, individual work time, controlled discussion, little movement, and raised hands before speaking. The "good" classroom rarely involves storytelling or loud conversations, even interruptions. White women try to create a replica of how they were taught. Thus, their classrooms may be places of restriction and frustration. After my own experience of White boarding schools and a women's college, I had to unlearn the definition of what a good classroom could be. Many White women are changing this pedagogy, creating social justice curricula and collaborative student interactions no matter what kind of education they had themselves. They allow for warmth to radiate around their room, humor to have its place, and student input to drive decisions about what they teach.

Belief in colorblindness. Rather than recognize the historical weight of a country that oppresses people of color or the power of institutional racism that powers the U.S. educational system, many White women teachers, along with their White male counterparts, claim that they do not "see color" at all. They deny difference. This is how they were taught in their homes or colleges or in their training. If we are all alike, then if failure happens, it must mean the child is deficient, the home is deficient. If we don't look at the power of racism, we can focus on perceived deficits in the children. Without seeing the cultural beauty of classrooms vibrant with children who bring rich values and content, concerns, and hopes from their communities, White female teachers do not connect. The warmth of the *warm demander* will not be present.

Fear of Black males. White women who fear Black men also fear Black male students. This truth has emerged in interviews and discussions with teachers who admit to this fear (Woods, 2010, p. 85–137). If you fear something, you work to control it, to limit it, to regiment it, to avoid it. This background creates the believers in "tough" discipline policies, "no excuses" regimens, rote lesson plans, drill, and repetition. These regimented classrooms, with little room for play or creativity, music, art, or even critical thinking, are most often found in schools where the student population is heavily African American. I was fortunate enough to have supportive Black and White administrators who encouraged me to explore ways to connect and challenge students that did not require fear-based control measures. I know I came with an ingrained fear of Black men. Yet, this dissolved quickly in my first years.

White women who do not fear their students have open, provocative, stimulating, and demanding classrooms. This seems so simple, yet it can be difficult for some White women teachers to achieve due to a fear ingrained in them from their earliest years.

Lack of preparation in cultural and racial understanding. U.S. colleges and universities are all over the map in how they prepare young adults to teach in both public and private schools. Some require one week in one semester devoted to identity development, antiracism, and cultural competence. Some barely mention it at all. Without in-depth self-reflection and dialogue around race, Whiteness, cultural competence, White supremacy, and Black history, White female teachers find themselves lost in classrooms with many students who do not look like them. They come without the knowledge and understanding they so desperately need. They do not recognize their lens, the lens they were raised to use to see the world. Their teachers' lack of exposure to White activist and social justice education damages the Black males who sit in their classrooms, and this lack is caused by the institutions that train these White women, (and men) to be teachers now, in the twenty-first century.

I knew nothing of White privilege from my college or graduate coursework in education. I had to learn it through connections at work. I had to make mistakes, say the wrong thing to parents, use the wrong words—and get feedback—to learn how to see the world with a lens that took in the world of color. It was not until I read Peggy McIntosh's work that I even began to explore this idea and how I played a part in White supremacy. Attending the White Privilege Conference ten years into my career, I understood how much deeper I needed to go to be an effective teacher.

Deficit perspective/savior mentality. Many White female teachers come from suburban or rural homes to teach in urban schools. Their Black students often come from segregated neighborhoods, many living in homes of the working poor. Unfortunately, White women teachers may believe that the students, their parents, and the neighborhoods are utterly bereft of strengths and brilliance. These teachers have not been taught to see the resilience, the creativity, and the courage of the families that surround their school. The White female teacher's lens might mean that she constantly refers to her class as "those poor kids" from "homes that lack everything kids need." Her goal becomes to "save" them from their own community. Her connection to the storekeepers, the preachers, the artists, and the parents in the blocks surrounding her school may reflect condescension, pity, and fear. Those who have lived and grown in these communities, White or Black, perceive the strengths and possibilities in the adults and kids who live in neighborhoods nearby. Early work with colleagues who are African American helped me shift from a stance of wanting to "fix" my students to one of recognizing their power and strength. Again, I was lucky.

Individualism vs. collaboration, competition vs. cooperation. Because she believes in the power and responsibility of the *individual*, contrasted with the cooperative or the communal, a White female teacher may not be equipped to run a class based on the collaborative and cooperative pedagogy so many Black Male students need. Because she believes in a system that rates children on their individual test scores, or in–seat behavior, or work produced solely on their own, she cannot see any way to structure her classroom other than in rows of individual children, relegated to their desks. The White women teachers who are successful with Black Males allow for vigorous discussion, group activities, movement, music, and laughter as part of their pedagogy. I had to learn that noise in my classroom was acceptable, that it meant students were collaborating on a project or question. This was not easy for me; I had been used to silence or quiet much of my educational career. It takes work to undo limitations in our vision of the "good" class. I had to work hard.

Belief that "expertness" resides in the teacher, not among students, parents, colleagues. White women have seen themselves reflected in front of the classroom all their lives. Thus, some begin their teaching career believing that all expertise must reside in them as the teacher. After all, education has been successful for them. They have done well under the guidance of White female teachers. They can be reluctant to surrender such expertise to others: the students, the communities, or even their colleagues of color. One of the most liberating times in my career was when I realized the students had as much knowledge as I did and were willing to use it, to tell their stories, to explore issues of concern. It took the burden off me to have to be right, to be in charge all the time. I learned to challenge and expect greatness from students including from their work on projects that sprang from their own strengths, their own history. The barrier of having to *know it all*, can prevent White women from opening up to the knowledge that resides in so many around them.

Gender preferences. Because she has been educated in a White women's school system, and has been reinforced in polite, decorous, quiet, and passive ways of interacting, White women teachers often believe that such behavior is best for all students, including the Black males. Yet, most students want to move, to sing, or to argue. They are full of life. A White woman may see these behaviors as problematic, even though she might have wanted to behave in such a way herself. Her gender has often defined her behavior as acceptable if she is quiet and reserved, works well on her own, and rarely talks back.

White women have been denied ways of behaving and being in the world that they in turn deny to Black males. Their bias, often unconscious, and their White suprem-acist upbringing, combined with their own history of gender restrictions, create a mix that can be detrimental to Black male students more than any other group. Racism combined with White gender identity is a combination that is bound to affect Black boys in great numbers. I know that I came from a very restricted family and school life. It took patience and a lot of listening and asking for help to get me to understand not only how I had been denied experiences as a child and young woman, but also how this affected my classroom. Once I recognized all of this, my class became a place of activity.

There are many amazing White female teachers. They have done the work of dis-mantling the barriers discussed here. Because they believe in the potential of all their students, seeing Black male brilliance clearly before them, they demand exceptional work. Because they care and feel a connection to their Black male students as complex human beings with varied upbringing and quirks of personality, they generate a warmth and delight while raising expectations.

POSSIBILITIES FOR OUR FUTURE

Need for Black males. Students need to see before them those who look like them, who speak in similar rhythms and accents, and who are making a way in the world. Black male students rarely get this chance. Minneapolis Public Schools is now putting in place Black male classes for middle and high school students. These classes meet an hour a day and are taught by Black men from the communities surrounding the schools. These Black men provide mentors for the students, teach Black history and culture, and create a space to talk, respond, question, and dialogue together. These classes are designed to include high expectations combined with a refusal to give up on any individual in the room. They are run by warm demanders.

Such programs can have an impact on the future of Black male success in education. *It is up to White women teachers to support such programs and provide any logistical help getting the courses off the ground.* In alliances, White Women can find ways to connect.

Need for change in training teachers. It may seem repetitive to say that we need much more training in our schools of education. It may feel like a worn-out tune we keep playing without getting any response. What White women need before they enter classrooms is a year-long exploration of identity, White supremacy, White privilege, and institutional racism. They need a thorough grounding in institutional racism *in education* to be specific. A second year could be spent developing ideas for classrooms that address the needs of Black males and others, using pedagogies that emphasize cultural strengths, are project based, and are connected to student concerns and to the neighborhoods in which students live.

Understanding community. Christopher Emdin (2016), in his book *For White Folks Who Teach in the Hood and the Rest of Y'all Too,* describes the way his teaching changed when he began to look carefully at the neighborhood in the Bronx where he was teaching. He spends much of the book talking about church, barbershop and hip hop/rap as ways of communication that resonate with Black males in his school. This book could change the way White Women teach, the way schools are run, the way students are motivated and classes are structured. By connecting with communities, each complex in its own unique way, teachers can find methods to use what they learn from these communities in creating a curriculum that engages students. This may sound simplistic, yet it is not. It is at the heart of respect for Black males, at the heart of meeting their needs as students. If I had had this book from the beginning of my teaching career, I believe I would have been a much finer teacher. I was lucky to have colleagues who trained me to become the teacher I am.

These ideas—such as including community engagement, fostering connection, understanding the learning that goes on amid noise and movement, and using call and response—are essentially redefining what it means to be a "good" student and what it means to be a good teacher. This is possible when White teachers are willing and are supported to make changes in their perceptions and their beliefs about all those who come into their classrooms. It will not happen unless White women are supported in the work of undoing racist thinking and gendered definitions of what it means to be a good student. It requires resources devoted to teacher education, in-school training, and administrative support for those White women who are doing the hard work of radical change in education.

Yet it can be done. When asked if White educators can successfully teach Black boys, Baruti Kafele responded, "Emphatically, absolutely. Is it easy? No. It may not be easy, but it is time" (as cited in Pica, 2016, para. 1–2).

■ ■ Engaging the Mind ★ Taking Action ★ Inspiring Excellence
I Am From

One of the most powerful activities is to have students write a list-poem of I AM FROM statements. This is a way to build community, to listen to students, and to have students listen to each other.

1. Read an example of an I AM FROM poem you can find online or in the book, *Reading, Writing, and Rising Up* by Linda Christensen (2000, p. 18), or list or create one of your own as an example:

    I am from apples in the fall.

    I am from Christmas with my son and grandson in New York where we sing Hannukah songs and carols all together.

    I am from skating up at Three Ponds in Connecticut when I was small and playing "Crack the Whip" and spinning into the woods.

    I am from church services.

    I am from an all-White life in an all-White suburb growing up, to where I am today, in a city neighborhood made up of forty-three different cultures and colors.

2. Tell your students: Here is a list of things you might want to choose

from for your list. You do not have to include something from each category, and you may add ideas from your own life, like song lyrics or clothing styles.

You might want to think about:

Items found in your home

Items found in your yard

Items found in your neighborhood

Names of relatives

Sayings

Names of food dishes

Names of places you keep memories

Common greetings

Toys

Jewelry

Good luck emblems

Celebrations

Holidays

3. Have students go around, one at a time, and read from their list. Read from your own.

Here's a student example by David Onabanjo, Grade 8:

I'm from hearing "you'll be old enough to help next year,"

for five years.

I'm from rusty, old, gray hydrants

spitting out water in summer,

from knowing two ways to the library, to avoid that

hooded guy with a blank stare and baggy jeans.

I'm from if you sow only a few groundnuts, you won't

reap a plentiful harvest.

I'm from "Edo o loropin," Yoruba for

"No condition is permanent."

4. You can make a class *I Am From* poem with lines from the poems of each member of the class. This is the beginning of creating community. I have done this with students from first through twelfth grade.

5. Add to the lists as the year goes on. Tell students that it is a work in progress and that at the end of the year you will celebrate where everyone has come from.

CHAPTER 3

Advancing the Success of Boys and Men of Color

The Seven Centers

The Seven Centers is a consortium of research units that have collectively committed to doing research on boys and men of color. The Center for the Study of Race and Equity in Education at the University of Pennsylvania was led by Shaun R. Harper. The Minority Male Community College Collaborative at San Diego State University is co-led by Frank Harris III and J. Luke Wood. The Morehouse Research Institute at Morehouse College is led by Bryant T. Marks. The Project MALES and the Texas Education Consortium for Male Students of Color at the University of Texas at Austin is co-led by Victor Sǎenz and Luis Ponjuan. The Todd Anthony Bell National Resource Center on the African American Male at The Ohio State University is led by James L. Moore III. The Black Male Institute at the University of California, Los Angeles is led by Tyrone C. Howard. The Wisconsin's Equity and Inclusion Laboratory at the University of Wisconsin-Madison is led by Jerlando Jackson.

On February 27, 2014, President Barack Obama announced a new national initiative called My Brother's Keeper (MBK), which proposed to "address persistent opportunity gaps faced by boys and young men of color" (White House, 2014, para 1).

Evidence has mounted demonstrating how critical education is for success in today's American economy, yet too many males of color are not experiencing optimal outcomes at the elementary, secondary, and postsecondary levels. It is also widely understood that meager educational outcomes hinder the potential for future life successes. With these facts in mind, MBK proposed to concentrate on improving school readiness for early childhood education, grade-level reading proficiency, and rates of high school graduation, college-going, and completion of postsecondary education and training. By concentrating on the aforementioned areas, MBK stands to measurably improve the quality of life for males of color.

Institutions across the United States and throughout the educational pipeline (e.g., elementary, secondary, and postsecondary) have been confronted with innumerable challenges achieving parity in educating males of color compared to their White and Asian male counterparts. For example, only 18 percent of Black male youths are proficient in fourth-grade mathematics compared to 55 percent and 64 percent for their White and Asian peers, and 27 percent and 28 percent for Native American and Latino male youths. Similar trends are also evident in eighth grade mathematics, where only 13% and 21% of Black and Latino young men are at proficiency or above, respectively. Moreover, these educational disparities are evident in other key subject areas, including reading (National Assessment of Educational Progress, 2013).

Challenges experienced in the early education stages intensify over time, as evidenced by national high school graduation rates for men of color. According to the Schott Foundation (2012), Black and Latino males graduate from high school at significantly lower rates than their White peers. The four-year graduation rates for Black and Latino males are 52 percent and 58 percent, respectively, and 78 percent for White males. More revealing are the differences across states. For example, in the District of Columbia, only 38 percent of Black males and 46 percent of Latino males graduate from high school. In New York, only 37 percent of Black and Latino males graduate. Other states—including South Carolina, Mississippi, Michigan, Georgia, Florida, Delaware, Alabama, Colorado, and Connecticut—also have graduation rates below 60 percent for Black and Latino males.

For men of color, these negative trends persist at the postsecondary educational level. At four-year colleges, only 33.2 percent of Black males and 44.8 percent of Latino males earn a bachelor's degree within six years—rates strikingly lower than those of their White (57.1 percent) and Asian (64.2 percent) peers (Digest of Education Statistics, 2012). At two-year colleges, only 32.1 percent of Black males and 30.2 percent of Latino males earn a certificate or degree or transfer to a four-year institution within six years; compared to 39.8 percent for White males and 43.4 percent for Asian males (U.S. Department of Education, 2009).

TABLE 3.1 Percentage of boys at proficient or above by grade and subject, 2013

	FOURTH GRADE	ALASKA	HAWAII	EIGHTH GRADE
	MATHEMATICS	MATHEMATICS	READING	READING
White	55	45	41	38
Black	18	13	14	12
Hispanic	28	21	18	17
Asian	64	59	47	43
Native American	27	23	20	16

SOURCE: NAEP (2013).

Although often characterized as an at-risk population, boys and men of color possess the intellectual capacity to excel in preK–12 schools and postsecondary contexts when educational policies and practices support their success. Collectively, the contributors to this chapter[1] believe that "every system is perfectly designed to achieve the results it gets" (quote attributed to W. Edward Deming and Paul Batalden). Thus, the existing educational policies and practices that routinely fail to produce positive results for boys and men of color demand scrutiny. MBK represents a major undertaking in that it seeks to diagnose the pitfalls that plague educational achievement among males of color and to comprehensively catalog proven solutions to the problem. This chapter aims to contribute to this effort by proposing specific educational policies and practices to be implemented at the federal level to improve outcomes for boys and men of color at every junction of their education.

The following recommendations are divided into three sections. The first section focuses on educational pipeline recommendations, including policy interventions spanning preschool to doctoral education. The second section focuses specifically on preK–12 policy recommendations, and the last section focuses on postsecondary education policy recommendations, with major emphases on two-year and four-year colleges and universities. The recommendations offered below were derived from internationally and nationally recognized researchers who are leaders of major research centers throughout the United States. These include: The Center for the Study of Race and Equity in Education (University of Pennsylvania), Minority Male Community College Collaborative (San Diego State University), Morehouse

---

[1] The chapter was initially published as a report by the Seven Centers, it is has been slightly modified for use in this publication.

Research Institute (Morehouse College), Project MALES and the Texas Education Consortium for Male Students of Color (University of Texas at Austin), Todd Anthony Bell National Resource Center on the African American Male (The Ohio State University), Black Male Institute (University of California, Los Angeles), and Wisconsin's Equity and Inclusion Laboratory (University of Wisconsin-Madison). These researchers have rigorously studied factors that influence educational, social, and occupational opportunities for boys and young men of color. To this end, this chapter reflects their collective ideas, perspectives, and recommendations.

PIPELINE RECOMMENDATIONS

CREATE A NATIONAL CLEARINGHOUSE ON EXEMPLARY STUDIES, PRACTICES, AND POLICIES ON MALES OF COLOR IN EDUCATION

Over the past several decades, practitioners have increasingly recognized the need for greater support of boys and men of color in education through established programs, conferences, symposia, and initiatives designed to improve outcomes throughout the pipeline. Likewise, these intensified efforts have been mirrored in the scholarly community, resulting in the establishment of centers, peer-reviewed journals, and academic conferences focused on issues relevant to males of color in education. These combined efforts have produced effective policies at various levels of governance (i.e., school, district, state, national), as well as innovative practices (e.g., teaching strategies, counseling techniques, evaluation standards) and tools for research, assessment, and evaluation that can inform educational interventions for boys and men of color. However, access to and awareness of these newly developed resources is currently limited; no centralized location exists where such information is maintained, organized, and disseminated. A national clearinghouse or repository featuring exemplary studies, practices, and policies focused on males of color in education would help meet this need. The U.S. Department of Education's Institute of Education Sciences houses the *What Works Clearinghouse*, which features information on effective interventions for the general student population. A similar clearinghouse on educational interventions focused on boys and men of color in education should also be established as either a stand-alone entity or as a combined endeavor with the existing clearinghouse. Promising practices, studies, and policies featured in the repository should be subject to a rigorous review process by a board with extensive research experience and expertise on males of color.

IMPLEMENT A NATIONAL CENTER FOR EDUCATION STATISTICS (NCES) DATASET THAT TRACKS MALES OF COLOR ACROSS PREK–12 AND POSTSECONDARY EDUCATION

Social and behavioral science research continues to affirm that even as many boys and men of color successfully navigate preK–12 and postsecondary educational systems, some continue to face distinct barriers throughout the educational pipeline. These challenges may include but are not limited to poverty, access, single-parent households, and negative stereotypes. A national database (implemented through NCES) could track individuals in the pipeline and identify indicators of their past, current, and future educational status. An NCES data-tracking system would provide insight into enrollment, retention, and graduation trends throughout the educational pipeline, helping to optimize institutional success in society's high-skilled labor economy. The dataset should yield information on undergraduate participation, engagement at the graduate level, and detailed employment plans of boys and men of color. Because NCES currently records demographic information and associated behaviors that impact achievement, persistence, and outcomes in education, a tracking system devoted to this particular population would inform and embolden innovative high-tech educational policy and practice that intentionally and holistically serves this population. This evidence-based practice, rooted in accurate record keeping, would help identify emerging trends in educational progress and enable researchers to identify challenges and opportunities related to educational achievement. These efforts would facilitate research with significant implications for today's preK–16 educational systems and the broader twenty-first-century workforce.

REFINE ETHNIC CLASSIFICATIONS COLLECTED BY THE U.S. DEPARTMENT OF EDUCATION TO BETTER ACCOUNT FOR WITHIN-GROUP DIFFERENCES

The racial classifications currently collected by the U.S. Department of Education are in desperate need of refinement. For example, the National Assessment of Educational Progress (NAEP) reports racial demographic data in six categories: White, Black, Hispanic, Asian/Pacific Islander, American Indian/Alaskan Native, and two or more races. Particularly troubling are the categories for Hispanic and Asian/Pacific Islander students. Unfortunately, these data hide critical disparities across subpopulations that may otherwise heighten the need for subgroup-specific interventions. For example, Asian/Pacific Islander data currently conceal deleterious outcomes for Pacific Islander and Southeast Asian men (e.g., Hmong, Laotian, Cambodian, and Vietnamese), who have academic experiences and outcomes on par with those of other underserved men of color. As a result, it is recommended that a more expansive classification formula be used, including categories such as: Asian American, Southeast Asian, South Asian (e.g., Indian, Pakistani, Sri-Lankan), Pacific Islander, and Filipino. Similar problems are evident with respect to the Hispanic classification, which may mask the needs of the large percentage of students of Mexican/Mexican-American descent, particularly in the Southwest. At a minimum, the Hispanic category should be divided into two groups: Mexican/Mexican American and Latino (excluding Mexican heritage).

MANDATE THAT INSTITUTIONS CREATE EQUITY
PLANS TO IMPROVE SUCCESS OF BOYS OF COLOR

Using quantitative and qualitative data derived from periodic self-studies and external evaluations, school districts, colleges, and universities should be required to create equity plans for promoting student success. Equity plans should identify areas for intervention derived from regular analyses of experience and outcome disparities. Plans should identify goals for student access, retention, and completion for student populations in general and by race/ethnicity within gender. Equity plan goals should be accompanied by clearly specified outcomes and resultant courses of action focused on building institutional capacity to better serve student populations, particularly boys and men of color. The plans should also address resourcing strategies and methods for evaluating the success of planned interventions, with benchmarks and mechanisms to monitor performance. All plans should be submitted to the Department of Education for review every two years, with an accountability infrastructure in place to ensure that identified courses of action and evaluation of these actions are performed. Moreover, equity plans should be publicly shared documents that are available and accessible to prospective students and their families.

FACILITATE CURRICULAR
PARTNERSHIPS ACROSS THE PIPELINE

Currently, a lack of alignment and collaboration across successive levels of the pipeline may hinder efforts to effectively serve challenging student populations. Courses taken in high school may not necessarily prepare students for college-level coursework. Similarly, in many locales, community college coursework will enable a student to transfer; however, due to a misalignment in course learning outcomes, transfer students may have to obtain substantially more academic credits than would be expected, had they attended a four-year institution. To address these concerns, the federal government should require school districts, community colleges, and public four-year institutions to partner in designing curricula that create seamless pathways for students to matriculate across each sector. These partnerships should focus specifically on ensuring that students meet academic expectations at each successive level of schooling, adequately covering foundational content at each stage, and particularly prioritizing English and mathematics skills. By providing enhanced opportunities for information and resource sharing, pipeline partnerships are a key strategy for improving outcomes for historically underrepresented boys and men of color. Via partnerships, educators can identify common exit points in the educational pipeline where attrition among boys and men of color frequently occur. Institutions can then work collaboratively to reduce attrition at those junctures. The federal government can facilitate such partnerships by incentivizing collaborations across institutional types. Given the unique needs of pipeline collaborations across the region, federal grant monies can be directed to state governments to support the implementation of partnership structures.

IMPLEMENT INTERVENTIONS TO ENSURE THIRD- AND FOURTH-GRADE-LEVEL PROFICIENCY IN LITERACY FOR MALES OF COLOR

Literacy matters. The third- and fourth-grade marker is a foundational point in students' academic careers that has direct implications for future achievement. Outcome data presented in Table 3.1 of this report revealed that only 14 percent of Black and 18 percent of Latino males are proficient in reading by fourth grade, while rates for their White peers are 2.5 to 3 times higher (NAEP, 2013). Unfortunately, the longer males of color remain in school, the wider the literacy gap grows. Moreover, students who are not reading at grade level by the time they enter fourth grade are less likely to ever reach grade-level proficiency in reading, are more likely to be referred to special education, and are more likely to drop out of school. Given the importance of early grade-level reading proficiency, schools should provide specific interventions aimed toward students who are not demonstrating reading proficiency by third grade. These interventions should include supplemental learning opportunities with an intense literacy focus in the form of afterschool programs, summer school, literacy sessions, or Saturday academies. School districts and state departments of education should provide incentives for literacy teachers and instructional coaches to participate in such programs, which have advanced in recent years to include rigorous, culturally relevant frameworks that offer promise for diverse student populations, including males of color. Literacy has a direct impact on school outcomes and life chances. School districts should invest considerable financial and human resources to the development of appropriate structures and systems to prevent disproportionate numbers of boys of color from leaving third grade and entering fourth grade without the requisite skills needed to be successful in school and beyond.

ADOPT DATA TRACKING SYSTEMS AND SCORECARDS TO IDENTIFY SCHOOLS WITH DISPROPORTIONATELY HIGH SUSPENSION AND SPECIAL EDUCATION PLACEMENT RATES

Black and Latino male students are most likely to be suspended and expelled in preK–12 schools. They also tend to be grossly overrepresented in special education and underrepresented in gifted and talented programs and other accelerated learning programs. As a preventative measure, school districts should be required to adopt data systems that track the classrooms, teachers, and schools where levels of suspension are significantly higher. School districts and state departments of education should also be required to investigate whether their current policies contribute to "student push out" becoming commonplace. For example, the Los Angeles Unified School District recently dismantled their "willful defiance" policy, which led to large numbers of Black and Latino males being suspended for extended periods of time. Thus, it is imperative for all school districts to evaluate their current policies and practices to identify those that may be inappropriately used as a conduit for the removal of groups of students from learning communities in schools. It is also recommended that school districts consider the development and implementation of equity scorecards (see Harris, Bensimon, & Bishop, 2010, for example), which would spotlight schools for their success in identifying strategies and pedagogical practices to keep boys of color in the classroom. These scorecards could also include suspension and special education placement data for students, disaggregated by race within gender and socioeconomic categories.

FOCUS ON INCREASING MEN OF COLOR TEACHERS AND PRINCIPALS

There is growing concern that the current pool of school teachers and administrators does not mirror the growing racial/ethnic diversity of students. Despite promising programs (e.g., Call Me Mister program at Clemson University) focused on encouraging male college students of color to pursue teaching careers, colleges of education across the nation should do more to attract larger numbers of male students to teaching professions. Young men of color in high school require a critical mass of men of color teachers as positive male role models and mentors to better understand their own identities and to develop plans for college enrollment. Through unique partnerships between local high schools, colleges of education, and other institutions of higher education, potential male teachers of color can learn about the dire need to diversify the teaching profession, consider the benefits of becoming a teacher, and set long-term career goals to advance into educational administration. The federal government, via the Department of Education and the National Science Foundation, should implement demonstration grants that focus on bolstering the pipeline of men of color entering the teaching profession.

TIGHTEN ACCREDITATION AND STATE CERTIFICATION STANDARDS FOR TEACHER EDUCATION AND COUNSELOR EDUCATION PROGRAMS

Many educational problems that disproportionately affect young men of color (e.g., higher rates of suspension and expulsion) are attributable to a lack of substantive engagement of these issues in the curricula of programs that prepare teachers for preK–12 schools. The overwhelming majority of preservice teachers in the United States are White women. Teacher preparation programs do not devote enough of their curricula to enhancing the cultural competence of aspiring education professionals. Likewise, most academic training programs that prepare future guidance counselors provide too few courses on race and diversity, and they do not adequately prepare guidance counselors for the complexities of counseling in minimally resourced high schools that enroll students largely from low-income families. In addition, many counselor education programs include just one course on counseling high school students and their families on the vast landscape of postsecondary options. Given these deficits, these programs and the educators they prepare for careers in preK–12 schools warrant more rigorous accreditation and state certification standards. Accreditors and state licensing entities should demand greater evidence of efforts to vigorously engage aspiring professionals in meaningfully complex exercises that awaken and disrupt their assumptions about students and communities of color. Current state policies and certification standards do too little to ensure that highly qualified teachers and counseling professionals are prepared to effectively educate young men of color and other diverse student populations and families.

PreK–12 Recommendations

IMPLEMENT SUSTAINED PROFESSIONAL DEVELOPMENT STRUCTURES FOR EFFECTIVELY WORKING WITH BOYS OF COLOR

Students of color are disproportionately concentrated in schools with underqualified and less experienced teachers. In contrast, certified teachers with greater levels of experience are more likely to teach in predominantly White and affluent schools. The limited number of qualified teachers who do teach in majority-minority schools are retained at lower rates, and they often transition to schools with greater resources that can provide enhanced job security. Given these dynamics, the least capable teachers too often teach students that demand the most qualified teachers. In addition to these challenges, preK–12 educators tend to be disproportionately White and female, people who often struggle to connect with young boys of color personally and pedagogically. These teachers may inadvertently perpetuate social messages that school is not a domain suited for boys of color. A professional development infrastructure is needed to train teachers to work more effectively with boys of color. Districts and departments of education should be mandated to develop sustained professional development structures that assist practitioners in developing the knowledge, skills, and dispositions to effectively work with boys of color. Professional development activities should focus on the practical implementation of promising practices that enable teachers to better understand, work with, and support boys of color.

DEVELOP HIGH SCHOOL POLICIES AND PRACTICES THAT IMPROVE MALE OF COLOR PARTICIPATION IN ADVANCED ACADEMIC PROGRAMS

Extant research highlights the benefits that accrue to high school students who enroll in college preparatory coursework. However, national data reveal that few high school males of color enroll and complete dual-enrollment college courses, Advanced Placement (AP) courses, honors courses, International Baccalaureate (IB) courses, and other types of college preparatory courses. Ample evidence has shown that students who engage in college preparatory coursework are more likely to enroll in college and to navigate the transition to college more smoothly; they are better prepared for academic expectations in college. While many high schools offer advanced coursework, high schools need to do more to encourage historically underrepresented students (particularly male students of color) to enroll in these courses. One strategy is to mandate reporting of completion rates and access ratios to advanced coursework, disaggregated by race/ethnicity within gender. Schools with enrollment in advanced coursework that fall below a specified threshold proportionate to their overall demographics should be identified for program improvement. For some male students of color, their participation in these types of academic courses may serve as a catalyst for their improved academic motivation to attend and succeed in college.

Postsecondary Recommendations

REQUIRE ALL INSTITUTIONS TO IMPLEMENT AN INSTITUTIONAL-LEVEL EARLY ALERT SYSTEM

Many colleges and universities have support services (e.g., academic advising, counseling, tutoring, financial aid, etc.) that can curb challenges that inhibit student success in college. However, few institutions have mechanisms in place that can readily connect these resources to students when they are needed. Early alert systems have been identified as an important strategy to remedy this problem. These systems enable college personnel to identify and intervene with students who demonstrate warning patterns (e.g., low test scores, absenteeism, missing assignments) associated with premature school departure. In optimal circumstances, early alert systems detect concerns *early* in an academic semester/quarter, allowing time for appropriate interventions to occur before final course marks are significantly impacted. For instance, if a student misses several classes in a row, an automatic alert would be generated as soon as attendance records are updated by faculty members. In these cases, students would receive electronic communications informing them that they are required to meet with an intervention specialist (e.g., academic adviser or college counselor) immediately. If students fail to report to the intervention specialist by the specified timeframe, a follow-up is made by telephone. The specialists work individually with students to identify the root cause(s) of the challenges they face (e.g., academic, personal, institutional), providing guidance and referrals to key campus resources that can assist students. Unfortunately, early alert systems are almost uniformly underutilized and targeted primarily toward students in select areas (e.g., small retention programs, athletics). The federal government should require all Title IV degree-granting institutions to implement institutional-level early alert systems with associated standards of practice. Moreover, mandated training should be routinized to facilitate better utilization of the early alert system among campus personnel who provide and respond to referrals.

DISAGGREGATE STUDENT RIGHT-TO-KNOW DATA BY RACE/ETHNICITY WITHIN GENDER

In November 1990, Congress passed the Student Right-to-Know and Campus Security Act, requiring all Title IV institutions to disclose completion and graduation rates for current and prospective students. Specifically, colleges and universities must report completion and graduation rates for certificate- or degree-seeking full-time students. Student Right-to-Know data are essential for enabling the public to hold institutions of higher education accountable for student outcomes and allowing prospective students to make more informed decisions about where to attend college. However, the aggregate data mask disparities across racial/ethnic and gender groups, particularly among men of color. For that reason, Student Right-to-Know data should be disaggregated by race/ethnicity within gender. For Title IV institutions, disaggregated data by race and gender are already available for student athletes (per the Student Athlete Right-to-Know). Data for the general student population should be similarly available. This approach would provide prospective students and the general public a more nuanced understanding of how colleges and universities foster differential outcomes by student backgrounds. The act is flawed in that it focuses specifically on full-time students—even as men of color overwhelmingly attend institutions such as community colleges and for-profit colleges part-time. Thus, the law could be strengthened by specifying that rates for part-time students also be reported. Altogether, these revisions to the act would assuredly stand to benefit men and other subgroups experiencing deleterious outcomes.

MANDATE THAT INSTITUTIONS CONDUCT A
SELF-STUDY OF STUDENT EXPERIENCES AND OUTCOMES
WITH DATA DISAGGREGATED BY RACE WITHIN GENDER

Federal agencies already require that all institutions of higher education track the academic achievement and graduation rates of their students. However, many institutions have a limited understanding of specific personal (e.g., socioeconomic status, work ethic, self-efficacy), in-college (e.g., student leadership, joining a fraternity, studying abroad), and institutional factors (e.g., freshmen orientation, number of required years of on-campus living, advisement system) that foster success. While analyses of national datasets of college students can yield interesting results regarding predictive factors, these studies should serve as a guide rather than a prescription of colleges and universities. National studies include a diverse set of schools and often aggregate data may mask wide variation within the dataset. For instance, the impact of living on campus in rural Iowa may differ from the impact of living on campus in Washington, DC. It is imperative that each institution understand the impact of various factors on its campus. Furthermore, many institutions do not consider the extent to which factors that foster college success vary by race and gender. Institutions of higher learning should examine these factors specifically among segments of the student body that do not reach their full academic potential. According to national statistics, males of color, often Black and Latino males, are not performing as well as members of other racial/gender groups despite the potential to do so. If institutions truly wish to understand and facilitate the success of all their students, then they have a moral obligation to investigate and scale up what works for males of color and scale down what does not. Regular self-studies should be conducted that document student experiences and outcomes with data disaggregated by race within gender. Whenever possible, this assessment should incorporate a combination of research methods (e.g., surveys, focus groups, archival research, and interviews) that allow for the authentic voices of males of color to be heard. The use of mixed methods will also add confidence to the results. Ultimately, high-quality self-studies allow institutions to improve their selection and support of males of color; therefore, these practices should be integral to the operations of institutions of higher learning.

REQUIRE FEDERALLY DESIGNATED MINORITY-SERVING
INSTITUTIONS TO INCLUDE "SERVING HISTORICALLY
UNDERSERVED STUDENTS" IN THEIR STRATEGIC PLAN
WITH STATED STUDENT SUCCESS GOALS

Many postsecondary male students of color are enrolled in minority-serving institutions (MSIs). Some of these institutions, namely tribal colleges and historically

Black colleges and universities (HBCUs), have historically maintained a mission to specifically serve populations of color. However, a large contingent of MSIs receive that designation based solely on the percentage of their respective student populations who are students of color. The MSI designation allows institutions to qualify for federal grants as Hispanic Serving Institutions (HSIs), Asian American and Native American Pacific Islander Service Institutions (AANAPISIs), and predominantly Black institutions (PBIs). The scholarly community has leveled criticism that some of these institutions are minority enrolling, but not necessarily minority serving. Specifically, some MSIs have striking outcome gaps for students of color and, in particular, for men of color. These outcome gaps raise concerns about whether funding from the federal government intended to serve historically underrepresented students in these institutions actually reach the intended student populations. In light of these concerns, the federal government should require that all federally designated MSIs include the statement "serving historically underserved students" or similar phrases (e.g., "serving men of color," "serving Latino students," "serving Asian Americans") in their strategic plan. Moreover, the federal designation should also require institutions to set specific student success goals and associated benchmarks for achievement within their strategic plans, along with mechanisms to monitor performance toward identified targets. These modifications will help ensure that institutions with an MSI designation are actually serving the needs of the student populations they are designed to support.

Conclusion

Providing boys and men of color with viable educational advancement opportunities is a matter of both social and economic importance. For many young men of color, earning a college degree can change the course of their lives and the generations that follow. The policy recommendations proposed herein are reflective of the innovative and collaborative efforts that must be taken across the preK–20 pipeline to redress the inequities that have hampered educational opportunities—and ultimately life opportunities—for boys and men of color.

While these efforts aim specifically to improve educational outcomes for boys and men of color, it should be noted that these recommendations also stand to positively impact outcomes for other underrepresented and underserved students. Moreover, the proposed recommendations do not focus solely on remediating student deficits, but instead address institutional and systemic problems that enable outcome disparities to persist. To this end, it is essential to build on the capacity and effectiveness of educators who have a direct impact on the experiences of boys and men of color within schools and classrooms. Likewise, decision making and practice at all levels should be informed by data and knowledge derived from rigorous research and assessment. Finally, given the complexity of challenges facing males of color, and the interdependent nature of social and educational systems, efforts to improve educational outcomes for boys and men of color must be collaborative, entailing sustained partnerships with school districts, community partners, researchers, colleges and universities, policymakers, and other key stakeholders. Readers are encouraged to read the full report at (http://weilab.wceruw.org/CBCFALC/Boys%20and%20 Men%20of%20Color%20Policy%20Brief.pdf).

Having read through the data on the "state" of the White woman teacher and Black boy student, we want to give you a chance to hear from a Black boy who is in school right now, ten-year-old Solomon Smart.

Vignette: Two Black Boys

Solomon Smart

"Boys, for the tenth time, stop horsing around and sit down!"

Dear white teacher, I really like school and I am happy to come here every day. Sometimes I get too excited to see and talk to my friends that I don't always listen. Please be patient with us. We are good kids and want to obey the rules. We are also boys and it's hard for us to sit in this room all day without goofing off. We want to learn. Please help us.

"Can you please get your mother to sign this sheet? I can't give you full credit until your mother signs your packet."

Dear white teacher, I'm sorry my mom hasn't been signing my homework packet. She is really tired from working a lot. I try to make sure to help my brother and do my homework. Sometimes my grandmother or my dad can sign, if they come over. Sometimes when I wake my mother before she's up, I'll get in trouble and she will get mad at my brother and me.

White Teacher: **"In 1492, Christopher Columbus sailed the ocean blue . . . "**

Me: (*raises hand*) **"If there were people already here, why does it say he *discovered* America? Weren't the Native Americans here?"**

White Teacher: (*sighs and shakes head disapprovingly*) **Well, yes, of course they were here. Our book tells us that they were and also that Columbus helped to discover America by bringing everyone together.**

Dear White teacher, I asked this question because my dad told me to. He told me about a thing called the Trail of Tears where Native Americans were forced to move away because the White people with Christopher Columbus wanted to live where they were living. I have friends that have had to move and no one likes it because it's a lot of work and you miss a lot of memories you made there.

—Solomon, 10 years old

The following chapter by Diane Finnerty lays out the research on unconscious bias as it plays out between White women teachers and Black boys. There are so many compelling reasons to "know thyself," but few people lay it all out quite like Finnerty. This chapter demonstrates beyond any doubt that most people have racial bias, that the bias is usually unconscious, and that when people in power exercise their power with no awareness of that bias, it can have disastrous, sometimes deadly consequences. Finnerty describes not only the most relevant studies on bias in education but also the educational statistics that bear out the presence of bias in the system.

Understanding Unconscious Bias as One More Tool in the Committed White Teacher's Equity Toolkit

Diane Finnerty

What if, in spite of good intentions and explicit statements supportive of diversity, you learn that you are susceptible to treating Black children more negatively than White children? Learning more about unconscious bias and its influence on our behaviors can be a useful tool in understanding how "good" people may still be contributing to racially disparate treatment.

Unconscious bias refers to attitudes or stereotypes that affect our understanding, actions, and decisions in an unconscious manner (Staats, 2015). Unconscious bias is different than conscious or explicit bias in that a person often does not endorse the bias and may, in fact, hold beliefs starkly in contrast. For example, a White teacher may serve on a school diversity committee because she is committed to racial equity, but she may still harbor unexplored, unconscious biases that cause her to mete out more punitive discipline to Black children than to White children engaged in similar behaviors.

Unconscious bias grows out of everyday functions of human cognition. The human brain receives over eleven million bits of information per second, but it is only able to process consciously about forty bits per second of what it receives, leaving us "99.999996% unconscious" (Comaford, 2016). To function efficiently, our brains create "mental shortcuts" to automatically sort specific details about objects, people, events, places, and so on into broader categories (Kang, 2009). For example, if I see a flat surface held up by four wooden columns, I automatically categorize it as a "table" and make decisions about how to interact with it without spending excessive energy looking at every detail of the object's design.

Categorization is a necessary part of human cognition, but it can go too far when we sort humans into categories and use preconceived ideas or implicit associations in our interactions. For example, when school-age children were asked to "draw a scientist," 92 percent of boys and 86 percent of girls drew a male scientist and almost 99 percent of the children depicted the scientist's race as white (Fort & Varney, 1989). This kind of stereotype about a category of people unconsciously influences our expectations of members of that group—positively or negatively—and causes us to more critically regard someone who is incongruent with our expectations (e.g., a Black female scientist). Studies have shown that unconscious bias is more predictive of a person's behaviors than their expressed beliefs. Unconscious bias has been identified in men and women across all racial and ethnic groups, sexualities, and other social groups. Although levels of bias may differ among individuals, no one is immune.

EXAMPLES OF UNCONSCIOUS BIAS IN EDUCATION

Walter Gillam, a scholar who studies implicit bias in preschool settings, asserts that "implicit bias is like the wind—you can't see it, but you can sure see its effects" (Toppo, 2016). The following studies identify the potential effects of unconscious bias when White teachers interact with Black boys.

Expectations of classroom behavior. In a recent study, early childhood teachers were asked to watch video clips of four preschool children—a Black boy, Black girl, White boy, and White girl—engaged in typical preschool classroom activities. The teachers were told to look for "challenging behaviors" (even though no such behaviors were in the video), and their gaze while watching the video was monitored using eye-tracking equipment. The study showed that when expecting to find "challenging behaviors," the teachers watched the Black boys 42 percent of the time, more than any of the other children (Gillam, Maupin,

Reyes, Accavitti, & Shic, 2016). This may in part explain why Black children represent 18 percent of national preschool enrollment but 42 percent of preschool children who are suspended and 48 percent of those suspended more than once (US DOE OCR, 2014).

Perceptions of hostility and violence. In another study, subjects were shown a photo of a gun or a toy and asked to categorize the objects quickly and accurately by pressing a computer key (i.e., press one key if the image is a gun and a different key if it is a toy). The images of the gun or toy were shown immediately after the subjects were briefly shown a photo of either a Black or a White five-year-old boy. After seeing the brief image of a Black boy, the subjects more quickly and accurately identified the gun as a gun and more frequently mistook the toy for a gun. Conversely, after seeing a White child's face, the subjects more frequently mistakenly categorized the gun as a toy but accurately identified the toy as a toy (Todd, Thiem, & Neel, 2016). In a related experiment, subjects more quickly and accurately categorized "threatening" words (e.g., violent, dangerous, hostile, aggressive, criminal, threatening) and miscategorized "safe" words (e.g., innocent, harmless, friendly, trustworthy, peaceful, safe) after seeing the image of a Black child (Todd et al., 2016).

Previous studies have shown that Black men are perceived as more hostile (Devine, 1989), uncooperative (Greene et al., 2007), criminal (Dixon & Linz, 2000), and athletic (Biernat & Manis, 1994) than White men. Todd et al. (2016) conducted several tests to see if a different outcome could be reached when testing perceptions of Black *children* rather than Black adults. In other words, do Black boys receive the benefit of presumed innocence typically afforded children in our society? The studies showed that this was not the case.

Assumptions of innocence and accountability. Studies have shown that Black boys are generally perceived as older than their White peers, with an average overestimation of 4.5 years (i.e., a nine-year-old is perceived and treated as a teenager; a fourteen-year old as an adult) (Goff et al., 2014). This assumption of adulthood can result in Black boys being held more accountable for their actions and more severely punished than White boys whose same behaviors might be more readily attributed to "youthful indiscretions" in need of a developmentally appropriate, rather than punitive intervention (Goff et al., 2014). This may be in part why Black children are eighteen times more likely than White children to be sentenced as adults in criminal justice courts and represent 58 percent of children sentenced to adult incarceration facilities (Poe-Yamagata & Jones, 2007, as cited in Goff et al., 2014). Research further suggests that teachers and school administrators often choose more severe punishment for Black students who commit a relatively minor offense than for White students for the same offense (Rudd, 2014).

Expectations of intelligence and academic performance. In a study assessing bias and expectations of intelligence, senior attorneys were asked to evaluate the writing competencies of a young attorney (Reeves, 2014). The senior attorneys were given legal memos written by someone identified as "Thomas Meyer," a third-year associate and graduate from New York University (NYU). Twenty-two errors were imbedded in each memo (e.g., spelling, grammar, facts, technical writing errors), but they were otherwise identical except that "Thomas Meyer" was randomly identified as either African American or White. On a scale of 1 to 5 (5 being excellent), the memo written by the White Thomas Meyer received an average of 4.1 points for overall quality, compared to an average of 3.2 points for the Black Thomas Meyer; 2.9 of the 7 imbedded spelling errors were found in the White author's memo, while 5.8 out of 7 were found in the Black author's memo. Furthermore, the White author received encouraging, strength-based comments such as "generally good writer, but needs to work on," "has potential," and "good analytical skills." The Black author received negative, deficit-based comments such as "needs lots of work," "average at best," and "can't believe he went to NYU." Unconscious bias predisposes us to see what we expect to see, rather than what is objectively in front of our eyes.

Another study showed that teachers perceived students who displayed a "Black walking style" as having lower academic achievement, being highly aggressive, and being more likely to need special education services (Neal et al., 2003, as cited in Rudd, 2014). Much attention has been paid to the Pygmalion effect, which shows how teacher expectations influence a student's performance, and also to stereotype threat (Steele & Aronson, 1995), in which a student perceives and internalizes negative stereotypes about his/her social identities, which can then induce anxiety and decrease academic performance. Unconscious bias can manifest in verbal and nonverbal behaviors that communicate lowered expectations and decreased warmth, such as reduced eye contact, shortened interactions, and heightened anxiety during interactions.

Microaggressions. Microaggressions, or "brief, everyday exchanges that send denigrating messages to certain individuals because of their group membership" (Sue et al., 2007), can arise as a result of unconscious bias. For example, saying that a Black student is from a "good" family may imply that the alternative was anticipated. Calling one Black student by another Black student's name (e.g., LaToya for LaTasha) may signal that the students reside in a similar category in your mind, rather than as unique individuals.

Implicit bias is like a habit that can be changed through a combination of efforts. Our biases have been formed over a lifetime and efforts to change should be viewed as life-long, as well. Here are a few strategies to get us started.

1) Clarify your motivation. Studies have shown that having a professional commitment to equality without also having a personal one has a limited effect on decreasing implicit racial bias (Rachlinski & Johnson, 2009). Examine why reducing the impact of bias in your interactions is "personal" to you. Write down your motivation, share the document with a colleague, post it somewhere, and revisit it regularly.

2) Increase your self-awareness. Explore your implicit biases by taking one or more of the race-related Implicit Association Tests (IAT) via the Project Implicit® online test site hosted by Harvard University (www .projectimplicit.org). Knowing what is in your own mind is an important first step to decreasing its influence on your behaviors.

3) Create new thought patterns. Although we can't go back and change our childhood socialization,

we can continue to create new associations in our minds. Surround yourself with people who exemplify ideals counter to your stereotypes (e.g., images of Black scholars and artists). Seek out media outlets led by and for people of color to reduce the reinforcement of stereotypes perpetuated by mainstream media (e.g., overrepresentation of Blacks as criminals). Develop authentic relationships with people of different racial/ethnic backgrounds who hold equal status to you (e.g., not only with the children or families in your school over whom you hold power). Studies have shown that deep friendships, especially romantic relationships, with someone of a different race assist in developing deeper empathy and increase a person's ability to take the perspective of people who are different (Todd, Bodenhausen, Richeson, & Galinsky, 2011).

4) Increase your "bias literacy" and engage in reflective practice. Learn more about how unconscious bias might influence teachers' behaviors. Create a group to engage in reflective practice through discussions of readings. Videotape classroom teaching, and use case studies to understand how/if

(Continued)

(Continued)

patterns exist in your classroom and school. The group could pay particular attention to the micro- and macro-practices that may result in disparate outcomes reported at your school (e.g., suspensions, access to advanced placement classes, graduation rates). Consciously monitoring the influence of bias in everyday decision-making has been shown to decrease its impact.

5) Be a change agent in your school and profession. Changing ourselves as individuals is important, but if we don't change the systems that perpetuate bias then we've done little to tackle the problem. Educate yourself and others on unconscious bias in hiring and advocate for hiring more staff and faculty of color; serve on a curriculum committee and ensure that the curriculum teaches about the greatness of all racial/ethnic groups; develop authentic relationships with colleagues of color to hear about their experiences and work together to change your institution.

6) Last, but certainly not least, take care of yourself: Research has shown that we are most prone to biased decision-making when we are tired, rushed, or otherwise cognitively burdened. Teachers too often work in underresourced, overly monitored environments where these conditions might occur. By taking care of yourself, you will be able to be more mindful about your behaviors and behaviors of others.

As a teacher, you have one of the most profound opportunities to make a difference, for the positive or negative, in a child's life. Addressing unconscious bias won't fix everything that hinders students' success in our society, but it will provide tools to create more equitable and inclusive classrooms. It will also strengthen our individual and collective abilities to form more authentic multiracial relationships with colleagues and families to work together to forge a more just educational system for all.

The following piece by John Marshall implores White women to know themselves before they try to understand Black boys. Dr. Marshall, the chief equity officer for Jefferson County Public Schools in Louisville, Kentucky, has created systemic change that has raised the number of Black students in advanced placement classes throughout his district. However, when asked to write a chapter for The Guide, he chose to write about the importance of White women understanding their own identity because of how foundational that knowledge is to any lasting change within any system. Notice any feelings that come up as you read this chapter. It may be different to hear this message from a Black man rather than a White woman. Debby Irving and John Marshall have distinctly different styles. But the message is the same. Our work, as readers, is to learn to listen—and to hear—from many different voices. And in particular, our work, regardless of our racial background or gender identity, is to hear and understand the words that Black boys, Black men, and the families of Black boys are trying to tell us.

CHAPTER 5

White Female Teachers and Black Boys

Right Teachers and (Mis)Understood Boys

John Marshall

It is abundantly clear that there continues to be a need to focus on the exclusion and underestimation of black boys in the American school system. While there have been many efforts throughout the nation (some successful) to address and readjust the image many [white] teachers have of black boys, data say that much more needs to happen in the schoolhouse if America is to improve the academic outcomes for our black boys. Even further, we must continue to set high expectations not just for students, but for the teachers who have agreed to teach [black] boys.

This article is steeped in the notion that [black] students are very capable of learning at a high level. Research has proven repeatedly that the learning styles of [black] students are an asset and that there is brilliance, ambition, and boundless potential in our [black] boys. Calling on the work of Lee (2005), we see that in schools throughout the nation, [black] boys are performing outstandingly well. To be clear, not all [black] boys are failing, getting suspended, and/or dropping out. Nor are all [white] teachers ineffectively including and educating [black] boys. Thousands of [black] boys are excelling in school and serve as proof that [black] boys—and how they succeed in school—cannot be discussed in a monolithic manner. Consequently, one cannot assert that no [white] teachers are reaching and teaching [black] boys. To do so would be to simplify the complexity of racism, sound pedagogy, teacher authenticity, and gender. We must keep the problems facing [black] boys and [white] teachers teaching them in proportion. Sensationalizing the situation and promulgating inaccuracies adds to the demolition of [black] boys and mutes the culturally responsive teaching that some [white] teachers effectively employ every day.

Be that as it may, Gilliam (1982) suggests that many black boys in schools are getting the message that they must "be two times better than white counterparts just to get half of what white people have." What then often transpires is black males come to school believing that they will not be able to succeed unless they accomplish feats that are almost impossible. In turn, such a sentiment can often manifest itself in the outputs and actions of whites, which in turn becomes negatively internalized to the [black] boy who wants to succeed. Fordham and Ogbu (1986) posit that black boys receive mixed messages about classroom inclusion and are relegated to a level of dissonance that stunts the obtainable level of achievement that they want and that the white teacher is supposed to facilitate. Even further, a question still begs to be answered: Can [most or any] white teachers successfully teach black boys?

Far too often, when researchers and practitioners talk about teaching and learning, the discourse is partisan and dismissive of the teacher's role. [White] teachers should be allowed, mandated, and trained to investigate and discern the impact of their own cultural references, preferences, and biases play on the behavior and reaction of [black] boys in the classroom. The personal assumptions and knowledge that [white] teachers share must be weighed as a portion of the learning or lack thereof that we see in [black] boys. The teacher must continue to be willing also to be the learner if [black] boys are to learn. It is in such willingness and continuation(s) that we will then see transformative education. Such a transformation morphs the [white] educator into a symbiotic relationship of (cultural knowledge) educating betwixt the [black] boy and the teacher.

We must examine the pedagogical and cultural orientations of many white teachers. Many white teachers are entering classrooms, particularly urban schools, with little to no understanding or training in culturally responsive teaching, macroaggressions, and/or implicit bias. In that same vein, many white teachers were raised in a culture that offered little to no interaction with [black] boys from the urban core. Delpit (1988) has described the complexity of the teacher and [black] student relationship as a "culture of power." Nestled inside this culture of power is the teacher, who sometimes has unchecked and unknown power, and the [black] student, who is often left with no choice but to submit to the power or be suspended from the power source that is believed to be the route to achievement.

Those wielding this power are also privileged to ignore their power and/or not share that power with [black] students. This leaves a vacuum in the classroom that is sometimes filled with resentment and confusion from both the teacher and the [black] student. To be clear, if a [black] student does not know how to navigate through the labyrinths of the school system, the [black] boy may forever feel hopeless and helpless. If a [white] teacher is ignorant of the power she has, she may find herself (sub)consciously retreating from believing that the failure of the black boys sits partially with her. Such a gargantuan cultural collision is where some [black] boys become misguided and white teachers become misinformed.

In regard to this hoarding of power, which I will call "pedagogical power hoarding," we know that some practices of teaching and learning often marginalize [black] boys. As the power source [i.e., White teachers] attempts to make teaching efficacious, the tidal wave of power inherently dams efficacy due to the fact that many [white] teachers do not have the knapsack of tools or personal exposure to infuse any other culture or differences into what they are teaching. The marrow of education is to liberate both the teacher and the student. Black boys are often hard-pressed to find such academic liberation, especially when the teacher collides with the ways in which [black] boys learn, as well as with the rich cultural knowledge they have received from places other than the schoolhouse.

If [white] teachers do not recognize their privilege, societal positionality, and the systemic prejudices that are omnipresent in all institutions, the question—can white teachers teach black boys—is even more difficult to answer. Prior to asking that question, one must first ask: considering the systemic inequities and unearned power afforded to [white] teachers, do white teachers have to teach [black] students at all? One may contend that teachers are expected to teach all students who enter their classroom. On the surface, I wholly agree with that retort; however, it is abundantly clear to me that more than a few teachers "give it all they have every day" and that is nowhere near enough. [White] teachers have their unshared, unearned, and (maybe) unrecognized power, while [black] boys in their classroom are in a maze of misunderstanding and miseducation.

Slaughter-Defoe and Carlson's (1996) research illuminates the significant role that teachers play in student growth or the lack thereof. They focused on student voices and provided a narrative that Howard (2001) posits is often missing in addressing school improvement. In turn, it is evident that perceptions that both [black] boys and [white] teachers have of one another are often wrong. The student voices project, a professional development offering for teachers and administrators, records [black] boys responding to questions that focus on their understanding, feelings, and outlooks of school. The voices are then played in staff meetings or during trainings to evoke conversation and introspection from the teachers. This project, done in Jefferson County Public Schools, fortifies what Slaughter-Defoe, Carlson, and Howard posited. Black males often feel unheard and underestimated. To that point, the likelihood of [black] boys being taught effectively can be/is stifled if their sentiments, situations, and strengths are denounced and derailed by a system that puts [black] boys and their teachers in opposite corners. This polarizing of [white] teachers and [black] students can also happen when curricular content allows and/or places ethnic content inside a lesson but fails to provide time to have adequate and responsive discourse about the perceptions and understandings that the [black] boys have about the topic.

Having ethnic content in a lesson does not fully equate to culturally responsive teaching. Ladson-Billings (1994) asserts that culturally responsive teaching draws on the social, intellectual, and behavioral strengths of each child, which then evokes a level of inclusion that draws the [black] boys into the classroom; hence allowing the whole self to be engaged and seen as a contributive and included learner. In short, if [white] teachers are to reach [black] boys, allowances must be made to have what Deiro (1994) coined as "effective openness."

I maintain that effective openness cannot be timid and steeped in rhetoric that perpetuates hegemony, mediocrity, and [white] privilege. Effective openness must place [black] students at the nucleus of the classroom and acknowledge the one-sidedness of curriculum, cultural ignoring of certain groups, colorblindness, and systemic racism. In turn, effective openness yields affective expression that I believe will eventually allow both teacher and student to have mutual and genuine respect for each other, which is the prelude for building a relationship. This openness must be reciprocal. [Black] males cannot be muted for being different, distrusting, angry, gifted, and/or black. Instead [black] males must have [white] teachers who are open to difference, change, and challenge.

Understanding that critical race theory is the belief that race impacts the inputs and outcomes of all systems, I wholly subscribe to the belief that racism is the most powerful component contributing to the station of [black] students. By defaulting to or blaming poverty and other factors as the main reason for some [black] students not performing well in school, all the while minimizing racism, the U.S. education system is dismissing the tensions evoked in a classroom that seldom provides space for [black] boys to interact with or to react to what is being taught.

The United States is unhealed when it comes to race relations. In spite of attempts by some to mend the vestiges of slavery, Jim Crowism, fact dodging, and longstanding systemic racism, U.S. schools are still rife with supported segregation, relegation, and marginalization. The color line (Du Bois & Edwards, 2008) is the still elephantine in education. If [black] boys are still vulnerable to antiquated ways of teaching and profound (sometimes unknown) prejudices that are firmly embedded in the fiber of the school system, massive improvements will continue to be close to nonexistent.

Racial injustices, segregation [inside our school systems], and disenfranchisement will continue to wedge [white] teachers from [black] students. Even though [white] teachers may not purposefully uphold racist practices by dodging race and not investigating the impact of race, [white] teachers galvanize racism and demobilize racial equity. West (1993) evangelizes race dodging best when he states, "To confront the role of race and empire is to grapple with what we would like to avoid, but we avoid that confrontation at the risk of our democratic maturation" (p. 41). Can a white teacher teach a black boy? Only if the teacher recognizes her whiteness and his blackness and what that entails.

We hope that reading even one section of this book will leave readers with a new lens for seeing themselves and the Black boys they teach. That process of developing a new lens is powerful and can be emotionally exhausting. As you go through this process, you may want to refer back to this next chapter by Ali Michael. This chapter describes a framework of identity development that White people tend to go through as they learn more about racism. Each time you have strong feelings—whether they be enthusiasm, affirmation, gratitude, sadness, anger, guilt, or shame—consider that you are entering a new stage of identity development and that it is all part of a very normal process. We place this chapter here, in the first section of the book, because we want to give you tools for your journey.

CHAPTER 6

White Racial Identity Development

Ali Michael

I remember sitting in an African American literature course, hearing the words "White supremacy" and "White savior complex" and feeling the color drain from my face. "Are they talking about me?" I wondered. I didn't really know what these words meant, and I had never really thought about the fact that I was White. I grew up thinking I should be colorblind, that I shouldn't talk about race, that racism was a thing of the past. Personally, I had thought of myself as "normal" or as a woman, but not really as "White." I knew a little about racism, and I thought of it as something that affected Black people—not something that impacted me.

Later in college, I studied abroad in South Africa, I lived with a Black South African family, and, as I learned about the gruesome details of apartheid, I became highly critical of White people—especially White South Africans. The critique permeated my own sense of self and I started to become uncomfortable with my own Whiteness. I started dressing more ethnically African, I shaved my head, I started to learn Xhosa. I was doing my best to somehow shed my own Whiteness and be something else, something less harmful to the world.

A few years later, living in New York City, my hair had started growing back in, and I stopped trying to be someone I wasn't. But I still felt tremendous guilt for all the ways that my family and I had benefited from laws and policies that gave us access to jobs, education, medical care, and political agency—at the expense of people of color. I felt like this guilt was somehow my penance for the wrongs of the past—and that my guilt could heal the world. Clearly, I hadn't thought this through to its logical conclusion. Essentially, I thought the goal of racial justice was to create a world full of White people who feel bad about being White. It never occurred to me how pointless that would be.

Then one day, I read a book by a Black psychologist named Janet Helms, PhD, called, *A Race Is a Nice Thing to Have: A Guide to Being a White Person or Understanding the White Person in Your Life.* As I read this book, I began to recognize these different moments in my identity development as phases—phases that many White people go through as they learn about racism. And the most liberating part of this notion of phases was that I still had not gone through all of them. Helms suggested the radical notion that guilt is not actually the ultimate goal for White people who strive for racial justice. In fact, the end goal of racial justice is the kind of "beloved community" proposed by the Rev. Dr. Martin Luther King, Jr. (1957), and further conceptualized by scholar bell hooks (1995), who wrote:

> Like all *beloved communities* we affirm our differences. It is this generous spirit of affirmation that gives us the courage to challenge one another, to work through misunderstandings, especially those that have to do with race and racism. In a *beloved community* solidarity and trust are grounded in profound commitment to a shared vision. Those of us who are always anti-racist long for a world in which everyone can form a *beloved community* where borders can be crossed and cultural hybridity celebrated. Anyone can begin to make such a community by truly seeking to live in an anti-racist world (hooks, p. 272).

This was an epiphany for me. If love was really the goal, if beloved community through an end to unjust and oppressive structures was really the goal, how was my guilt going to help us get there? My guilt didn't make me more loving or more effective. It rendered me silent, unsure how to act, tentative in relationships across racial difference, sensitive to critical feedback, fearful of making a mistake, and paranoid that everyone might think I'm racist. Not to mention the fact that it made me relatively unpleasant to be around and uniformly unsupportive of other White people who had questions, doubts, or insecurities about race.

White racial identity development theory changed the whole game for me. I stopped trying to feel guilty and make others feel guilty. I started to look at how I could be proactive. Over time, I was able to return again and again to this framework to see where I was in my process and how I needed to grow in order to truly be an instrument for racial justice, and not just a guilty White person *or* a know-it-all White person *or* an activist White person who thinks my way of doing this is the best way, better even than the people of color who I'm supposedly allying myself with (all phases I know well, because I've been through them). The phases have been a guide for me in setting my developmental trajectory and seeing if I'm meeting it. They have also helped me cope, when I'm discouraged or sad—or even guilty or ashamed of my thoughts or actions—to remind myself that I'm simply in a phase and to push myself to keep moving through it, rather than get stuck there.

I currently work with classroom teachers almost every day. In my experience, White teachers fall into certain patterns with Black boys—and with Black colleagues—that are connected to their racial identity development. In the following paragraphs, I will describe the six original phases first outlined by Helms, as well as the ways that these phases typically manifest in the classrooms of White teachers. While Helms's phases were originally written in the context of relationships with people of color in general, I will use Black boys and their families as the reference point here because that is the group we are addressing in this book.

The phases most commonly cited[1] are as follows:

Contact: This is the first time a person has *contact* with the notion of racism, after years—sometimes a lifetime—of believing the world is fair and that racism doesn't really impact people's lives. In this phase, one's definition of racism is limited to individual acts of meanness, one believes that all people have equal opportunities regardless of race, and one has only superficial relationships with people of color, if any.

In schools, I often meet White teachers in the *Contact* phase who believe that it's better not to see color, who see racial difference as a bad thing, rather than a part of who they and their students are. They might whisper the word *Black* or pre-empt a description of a Black person with qualifiers (i.e., He's this really amazing, well-spoken, total teddy bear of a Black man), as if they are afraid that the descriptor *Black* on its own is an insult. Teachers in contact phase might quickly shut down conversations about race, whether those conversations are among students who want to talk about current events or among colleagues who are trying to diversify the faculty. These conversations make them uncomfortable, and they are generally unable to make the important differentiation between conversations about race that perpetuate racism, on the one hand, and those that confront or otherwise seek to dismantle racism on the other.

Disintegration: Disintegration is a phase in which part of the foundation of what a person knows literally begins to disintegrate because the reality of racism is so

---

[1] First by Helms, and then more popularly by Beverly Daniel Tatums in *Why Are all the Black Kids Sitting Together in the Cafeteria?*

different from the foundation of what they were taught (i.e., if a person was taught that the world is fair and that everyone had equal opportunity, the realization of historical racial discriminatory practices that may have benefitted their family for being White could be disorienting and could appear to discount the hard work that person's family contributed to their own success). After having contact with the reality of racism, people begin to question the foundation of their beliefs about the world and feel torn between different realities, different racial ideologies. Friends and colleagues might have a much greater awareness of racism than they do, whereas family and friends they are intimately connected to might not understand any of it. There's a lot of guilt and sadness in this phase as people become more and more aware of racism and racial privilege but still feel confused and conflicted about it.

When I meet teachers who have a lot of questions, who seem particularly emotionally torn up by discussions of racism, or who play the devil's advocate a lot, I often figure that they might be in the disintegration phase and that they probably need (1) to keep learning more and (2) to get support in answering questions posed to them by family and friends. Their need to play the devil's advocate is often coming from an inability to bridge their two worlds and a desire to find the language to explain things to others at home.

Reintegration: This phase is regressive. It comes about because it can be so hard when their foundation is rocked or disintegrates that people simply start to try to *reintegrate* their understandings of the world as it was before they started to see the stark realities of racism. In this phase, people try to avoid the feelings of guilt and shame by turning them outward and transforming them into hostility and anger. People in this phase blame people of color for racialized problems, suggesting that it's individual inferiority that causes disproportionate poverty in Black communities, not centuries of laws and policies that prevented Black people from having access to education, employment, and the housing market. People in this phase believe that to be White is to be wrong when it comes to conversations about race, and they often fear people of color while ridiculing White people who try to be racially conscious.

I recognize this phase in White teachers when they hesitate to call a Black parent, because they are scared of conflict. They may struggle to see parents of color—and colleagues of color—as equal partners in the education of students of color. They may not greet Black families or colleagues because the interaction raises anxiety in them as they start to realize that they too are raced, that they are being seen as a White person, and that they have this history of racism between themselves and people of color that they may not have previously acknowledged. A person in this phase might refuse to participate in professional development about racial or cultural competency, out of a belief that by virtue of being White, everything they say will necessarily be wrong. They will resist attempts to diversify faculty or increase outreach efforts to families of color.

People in this phase (and my own self in this phase) can get in the way of anti-racism efforts in schools (each of us can get in our own way in this phase). Often, people need support to get through this phase. They need to know that they can keep trying and that they have support to keep trying—that nobody is trying to trap them into looking racist, that their own personal struggles with oppression that are connected to their class background, sexuality, or gender, matter too. It can be hard for others to give support to people in this phase because the actions of people in the reintegration phase can be so alienating.

Pseudo-independence: In this phase, people start to understand racism but still have an internalized sense of superiority that comes from an internalization of a system of racism that suggests White people—and White ways of doing things—are better than people of color. Although they see racism, they may also believe that if Black people worked harder, or if Black people were more like White people (talked more like White people, dressed more like White people, ran the PTO meetings more like White people), maybe racism wouldn't affect them so much. They may not realize that having to be more like White people in and of itself is a demand for assimilation that is based on a value system that prizes White cultural styles over any other racial or ethnic cultural styles. In this phase, people still tend to *think* about racism much more than they *feel* about it.

People in this phase might see themselves as allies, but others may not see them this way. They want to help Black students and families, but they see themselves as saviors rather than supporters. They still judge Black teachers, Black administrators, and Black families harshly, assuming that they themselves know more about how to help a Black boy grow into a Black man than the Black people in that boy's life. Their presumed competence is often based on their knowledge and prioritization of Whiteness and White ways of being—not knowledge about the assets and struggles of Black people. Teachers who focus on their Black students exclusively, trying to befriend and support them, without also trying to change oppressive structures or other White people, might be in this phase.

Immersion: The immersion phase is about immersing oneself in understanding the reality of what it means to be White in a society in which resources and opportunities have historically been—and still often are—distributed unequally along racial lines. It's about working to understand how to be an antiracist White person who takes responsibility for racism and uses racial privilege to work against racism. This phase might involve feelings of guilt and anger, which may be directed toward other White people. It also may involve efforts to join communities of color and disown one's Whiteness. It involves reading and engaging with ideas about race and Whiteness to try to determine what kind of White person one wants to be.

Teachers engaged in extracurricular reading groups might be in this phase. At this point in their development, White people tend to be so outraged about racism that they are sometimes ineffective at communicating with other White people in a way that would help them understand the source of their outrage. They may assert that because they work in a predominantly Black space, or live in a predominantly Black space, that they somehow have less of a connection to Whiteness or are "less White" than other White people.

Autonomy: I have dubbed this "the beloved community" phase. In this phase, White people develop a new, positive antiracist identity in which they are conscious of their racial privilege and use it to take action. White people are then able to work in multiracial coalitions as healthy contributing members, not taking over or unconsciously using privilege to shape the agenda. They seek and accept feedback from people of color, while also thinking for themselves. They value racial diversity beyond the optics, understanding how language, parenting styles, and cultural styles get racialized, and then marginalized, within a society that repeatedly asserts the superiority of White ways of doing things. In this phase, White people are able to move beyond guilt because they understand the ways that racism is both systemic and historically rooted.

In this phase, White teachers will work to change oppressive structures, finding ways to hire more Black teachers, finding ways to connect Black boys and families with resources and opportunity. Rather than trying to change Black boys, they might change systems of evaluation so that Black cultural styles are not denigrated or downgraded. In this phase, White teachers fight all forms of oppression—not just racism—but homophobia, transphobia, sexism, and Islamaphobia, too. Teachers in this phase understand how to use their Whiteness strategically—in ways that are not always visible to outsiders. It is likely that Howard Stevenson's drama teacher was in one of these positive phases of identity development when she made the choice to produce *A Raisin in the Sun,* as Howard shared in his vignette earlier in this section. White people in this phase are able to "lean in" to other White people, supporting people in the early phases of identity development to move through those phases. They understand that they themselves are White, and they feel no shame about it—they may even be open to friendly teasing about it. But they know how to use their Whiteness to work against systems that hurt Black boys without having to be recognized as a hero or savior.

These phases do not usually occur for individuals in the same linear way that the theory broadly describes. Like the phases of grief, there's no right way to go through the phases, and everyone goes through them in their own order and on a different timeline. People often continue to cycle through the phases each time they have contact with a form of racism they didn't previously know or understand, just as people go through the phases of grief each time they experience a loss. It would be ridiculous to say, "I don't need to grieve again because I already went through the stages of grief four years ago." Similarly, people go through these phases again and again as they learn more about racism. But in my experience, I have been able to go through the phases more quickly with new experience. Rather than spending three years feeling guilty for something, I might spend a weekend, or even just a few minutes, before snapping out of it and moving toward understanding and action. Having knowledge of these phases does not necessarily make progression through the phases any easier, but it does take some of the panic out of the process. Rather than wondering, "Why do I feel this way?" I am able to say, "I feel defeated because I'm in the reintegration phase in which White people feel like they can never be right. I'll move through this. I just have to keep learning, keep asking questions, keep listening, get support, and keep connecting."

■ ■ Engaging the Mind ★ Taking Action ★ Inspiring Excellence
Identities at Play

1. Think back to a conflict or an uncomfortable moment that you had recently with a Black boy in your class, a Black colleague, or a Black parent.

2. Consider what phase of identity development you were in before that moment of conflict or awkwardness.

3. Consider what phase of identity development you were in after that moment.

4. Consider what phase the student, parent, or colleague might have been in at that time (see Chapter 18 from Bentley-Edwards et al.).

5. Write an action plan for how you might approach this person again next time you see them, knowing more about the phase of identity development you might have been in during your interaction, and knowing what phase of identity development they might have been in at that time.

For many White people, the "r"-word can be terrifying. Many teachers have experienced it, and many of those who haven't fear it. For many, the word is the end of a conversation. And often the blame for the shutdown of the conversation gets placed on the accuser, the one who wields the "r"-word. But, having read what we've read at this point in the book about the common patterns White women exhibit (from Julie Landsman) and the unconscious bias that is so ever-present in most of our unconscious thoughts (Diane Finnerty), it seems very possible that, despite their best intentions, many teachers still act in ways that evoke the "r"-word in the minds of Black students and parents. And Dr. Elizabeth Denevi asks, in this compelling piece, what if that's the beginning of the conversation—rather than the end? The key to this inquiry is really about the teacher—not the bearer of the word. It's an inflammatory word, yes. But sometimes it's the best a parent or a student can do, given the feelings they're feeling. And as teachers, we have the choice to let it open us up to something we didn't see before or to close us down.

What If Being Called *Racist* Is the Beginning, Not the End, of the Conversation?

Elizabeth Denevi

It's the mid-1990s, and I'm a young White teacher with a few years under my belt. I take a long-term substitute position because a teacher quit, and the school needs someone right away. So, the high school class has been meeting for a few weeks, and they've just read a short story by William Faulkner. On my first day, I jump right in. I open the class by asking what the students' reactions were to the short stories so I can get a sense of where they are in their analysis of the form.

There are three Black boys in the class. One raises his hand and says, "I'm tired of reading books with the n-word in them. For my entire life in school, I've had to read this word over and over. It's not right, and I'm not going to discuss it anymore." He and the other two Black students get up and leave.

What would you do?

I doubled-down. I thought, "Ah, these boys don't understand why it's important that we look at 'authentic' texts in English class. We cannot scrub the text of the original language. We must consider the historical context and teach the work of literature as an artifact of its time, and certainly, Faulkner's time in the South." Blah, blah, blah-blah-blah. I brought in articles the next day for the students to read so that I could prove to them why it was important to talk about the n-word in English class.

I can sense your groan and/or gasp for breath. I feel it now as I write. I still get goosebumps when I tell the story, evoking the racial stress that still lives in my body (thank you, Dr. Howard Stevenson (2013), for teaching me how to cope with racial stress).

And what did those well-educated, young Black boys do? They got up and left the class again. Good for them. They were demonstrating a healthy resistance to racism that I could neither see nor understand.

And what did I do? I kept right on going. And they came back. And we muddled through. I never discussed it with them. What I would give for a time machine so I could go back and try to see it again more clearly. Twenty years later, the details are fuzzy. But I have never forgotten those young men and what I learned from them.

The sociocultural aspect of this classroom was invisible to me; I had no understanding of the cumulative effect of hearing these slurs in the classroom over and over. For me, it was an intellectual exercise. For these young men, it was an assault on their very being.

While I now know that the greatest predictor of academic success is the teacher's expectation, I had not established any kind of relationship with these young men; thus, my explicit/implicit bias and privilege were in play. I still shudder at the power I had, but which I had no sense of. How terrifying, right? And how ordinary. I bet a lot of you could tell a similar story. And that's what makes it all so systemic and illusory. It was just the water I was swimming in at the time.

Here's my second example:

A few years later, I'm sitting in a parent-teacher conference. A Black mom sits across the table from me as we discuss her Black son. I have now been through my master's program and have been asked to join a diversity committee. I would consider myself a "good" White person, now "thinking" about racism (it's still an intellectual exercise for me). So, I'm particularly troubled by this young Black boy who "is not living up to his potential." I feel that he can do more, but he's not. I express my oh-so condescending concern as, "Look at all I'm doing. Why won't your son meet me half way?" a sentiment I have felt and heard in schools more times than I can count.

And this mom looked at me and said in a calm voice, "I think you're being racist toward my son."

And what did I do? I doubled-down again. I proceeded to explain to this mom all the ways that I certainly was *not* racist, how much I had worked with her son, given him extra time. I had not written him off as so many other teachers had done, telling me that I shouldn't waste my time with him. Couldn't she see how "good" I was? I defended myself, and my Whiteness, just as I had been taught to do by centuries of White superiority and White silence on this topic.

Are you cringing again? Years later, I shudder when I recall this conversation. And then I pose to you the central question of this article: What if being called *racist* was the beginning, not the end, of the conversation? What if, instead of a defensive rant about my intentions, I had taken this mom at her word? What if I considered that she might know her son's experience better than I did? What if I had owned the outcome of my behavior and considered with her how my work with her son was perpetuating racial stereotypes and prejudice? Do you think that might have impacted her son's experience in my class? In the school?

So here's what I wish I had known *before* I started teaching and what I try to communicate to all teachers.

I want other White women to know (1) that they are White, (2) that it matters because as Parker Palmer (1998) notes, "We teach who we are," (3) that their students see race either implicitly or explicitly, and (4) their failure to locate themselves as White and to talk about what that standpoint/position means is doing more harm than good. This is especially true for their White students.

When I first learned that I was white,[1] and I mean really White—not just the abstract concept that I was White—I was angry. Really, really mad.

And I was obnoxious about it. My husband often calls me the "white tornado," but a bulldozer metaphor works as well. I was going to solve the problem of racism once and for all: White privilege at its best. The hardest piece for me was getting over being colorblind. I had been carefully taught not to see race or comment on it. It was a huge shift for me to even use the term "students of color" because for me to see and notice race meant that I was racist. For me to have identified as *really* White would have been tantamount to saying I was a KKK member. I had no examples of White people who had worked for social justice. I had no idea that for as long as there was slavery in the United States, there were White people working to end it. But nobody taught me about those people.

---

[1] This happened while I was reading four authors: Beverly Daniel Tatum, Janet Helms (1992), Ruth Frankenberg (1993), and Peggy McIntosh (1998). Thank you to Randolph Carter, an inspiring Black male educator and father of two Black boys, who first asked me the question that serves as the title for this article.

I have been profoundly impacted by the research of John Dovidio and his work to illuminate aversive racism. He clearly explains why being colorblind is so pernicious:

> When Whites attempt to be colorblind, they tend to be self-focused and more oriented toward monitoring their own performance than toward learning about the particular needs and concerns of the person of color with whom they are interacting. In interracial interactions, this will impair the ability of people (particularly less explicitly prejudiced individuals) to engage in intimacy-building behaviors (Dovidio, Gaertner, Ufkes, Saguy, & Pearson, 2016, p. 27).

Those intimacy-building behaviors are what lead to strong, connected relationships in schools and to academic success. When White women teachers are worried about what they might say or that they might be called racist, they're not paying attention to our students. Thus, they are not grounding their teaching in who they are, what they know, and what they bring to the table. And when they're not doing that, they're not being excellent teachers.

Along the way, these have been additional critical points of learning:

- Difference as just difference, not deficit:

  The noticing of race is not racism. To understand that my students of color have a different experience is just that—different. Their experience is not a representation of deficit culture (Gonzalez, Moll, & Amanti, 2005, p. 71–88).

- Diversity vs. multiculturalism:

  While diversity is quantitative, meaning it speaks to differences that can be measured and counted, multiculturalism speaks to the quality of life that diversity experiences in a school. These two terms are related and connected, but they are not synonyms. White teachers need not only to think about representation but also to consider classroom climate and culture.

- Equality vs. equity:

  Equality means giving all students the same thing. Equity mandates that we give each student what he or she needs to be successful at school. Equity pedagogy signals that the playing field is not equal, thus including elements of power and privilege in our analysis of what students need (my gratitude to Paul Gorski (2013) for holding our feet to the fire on this topic).

- Safety vs. comfort:

  White folks will often say they are unsafe during conversations around race when what they are generally referring to is a feeling of discomfort. We must be willing to wade into this topic with our White colleagues as this "complaint" usually goes unchallenged in White circles. See Robin DiAngelo's research for the best analysis I have seen of "white fragility" around topics of race (2011, p. 54–70).

- Intent vs. impact:

  While I cannot crawl inside your head and know your intentions, I can feel, hear, and see the outcome of your behavior. If we spent even half as much time owning and dealing with the outcomes of our behaviors as we do defending our intentions, we might create classrooms that are more equitable.

I am deeply indebted to a whole host of White educators who have dedicated their careers to illuminating Whiteness and the inequities created by racism. We have inherited a carefully crafted structure by which White people avoid, ignore, challenge, and collude in any way possible to avoid being seen as racist—better known as the "Scarlet R." This kind of "white talk," as Alice McIntyre (1997) describes it, keeps White teachers from really learning why their awareness of White identity is so critical to being an excellent teacher.

I'm also grateful to the educators of color whom I've had the privilege to teach alongside of, learn from, and speak with.

At first I struggled with the title of this book. I just wanted it to be "The Guide for White Women Who Teach." Yet, if they had not proposed the title, I might not have remembered those Black boys I mis-taught. If White women can learn how whiteness impacts their teaching, it will certainly benefit Black boys. *But most important*, it will allow White women to be excellent teachers, educators who are wise to the fact that racial identity has, and will probably always, impact teaching and learning in profound ways.

■ ■ Engaging the Mind ★ Taking Action ★ Inspiring Excellence
Naming Whiteness

To better get at what it *really* means to be White, take this challenge. For one week, try to include people's racial identity each time you use their name. For example, "I had lunch with Amy, my white friend, and we . . ." Watch how people react. I couldn't make it through seven days. By Day 4, White people (not people of color) were so challenging, I gave up. What would it mean to make it seven days? Thirty days? A year?

*

One of our goals in this book is to give you as many personal stories as we can, so that you have a deep and complex picture of who White women teachers are and who Black boy students are. Their experiences are so completely broad and diverse, and yet our collective experiences as members of those racialized and gendered groups impact us in so many common and predictable ways. The following vignette is by Eli Searce, a White woman married to another White woman, who is the mother by adoption of two Black children. Eli would have sworn that this unconscious bias thing we're talking about here did not impact her. She didn't see it in herself until she adopted her son, and she caught herself seeing—out of the metaphorical corner of her eye—how she actually looked at the behavior of Black boys differently from the behavior of White boys.

Vignette: New Understandings

Eli Scearce

I am a White woman married to a White woman and together we are raising two African American children. After teaching in my private school for about six years, we fostered, then adopted, our daughter, a seven-year-old girl. Our son came to live with us, also through adoption, when he was two and half, about two years later.

I started teaching woodworking in a classroom after several years teaching multi-age levels in afterschool programs and summer camps. I thought of myself as bias-free especially with regard to race, especially Black folks. You know the story, "I have good friends who are Black." And racial equality was a value I was raised on. During the adoption process, the social workers helped us see that the only children racially different from us whom we could support culturally were African American. We felt certain we had plenty of folks in our community who could help us with that piece of raising our children. We also live in a predominantly Black area of the city. We felt we were prime for raising Black children. I didn't consciously think about race and teaching at all. I was sure I was unbiased when it came to race, believing racism was a conscious thing that didn't apply to me. After all, I adopted Black children, right?

At about the time we were adopting my children, I started to recognize something while I was writing reports. It was disturbing. I was describing the behavior of a student in my class. The way I was phrasing it was less egregious than a student I had written about just a little while earlier, even though I was describing the same behavior. The first time I realized it, I justified it and continued. However, it didn't happen just once. It happened almost every time I wrote reports. When I started looking at the differences in the children, I realized they were racially different. I was being much harsher on my Black boys than my White boys. What a rude awakening! I then started to look at the behaviors and recognized I was definitely biased toward the White boys. I would justify their behavior as "not that big a deal." With the African American children, I would make the problem out to be much more serious in my mind. I realized I had been doing this without consciousness even after welcoming my son into our home. Ouch. I was uncovering a bias that I had been sure I didn't have.

This was the first of many new understandings I faced. Another was how triggered I was when black boys were acting "hood." One year we had four fifth-grade boys of color who were trying on a kind of "street" behavior, mostly a visible body language of coolness. Many of the teaching team were also clearly triggered by this behavior. It felt like a challenge to authority conveying that school didn't matter to them. Ours is a highly rigorous school, and this behavior felt challenging to what we stood for, high academics. Being a non-academic teacher, I was surprised by how this behavior still triggered me. It was clear that unconscious bias was at play for me.

Another realization was that I called out Black children more often when there was a disruption in class. All of these understandings shifted my attitudes and behaviors in class, but it was hard to admit it happened at all.

As my son has grown, I started to identify more with some of the Black boys, seeing my son in them. He is a very impulsive but good-hearted child. The impulsive Black boys I was teaching started to seem much different to me. In fact, one time I went to the classroom teacher about the misdeeds of a student who had lashed out in class at another student. I was trying to talk about the impulsiveness and to point out that he wasn't malicious in his actions. The teacher jumped on my words and refused to hear me out. I felt she couldn't see him as I was seeing him. To her, his impulsiveness was an intentional sign of disrespect. For me, it was so clearly a developmentally appropriate (albeit frustrating) behavior in a good-natured, well-meaning child.

My son has had his share of bias when it came to his schooling. But as many parents of Black boys know, it's hard to pinpoint what is coming from bias and what is coming from other factors. I don't want my son to look for reasons he is getting called out on his behavior, but he needs to know, too, that he will often be the one nailed first, in spite of how guilty he actually is.

In my behavior reports, I have adopted a descriptive style with no judgment or allowances. I frame it in terms of what kids do, not who they are. I had no idea I was biased racially, and it took having a black son to help me recognize it. Recognizing it was the first step; understanding and owning it was the next step. I have since done a great deal of education and reading and working with others around this and other unconscious biases. Now that I am aware of my biases, I have become a better teacher.

The following chapter by teacher-educator and scholar of Whiteness Robin DiAngelo demonstrates how so many of the patterns of behavior that White women exhibit are a direct result of a much larger system. This chapter helps coalesce our understanding of how White women teachers—a massive and infinitely diverse group of people—could have so many of the same common issues with Black boys—another massive and infinitely diverse group of people. We see how one's placement in this system can shape one's attitudes, assumptions, and patterns of behavior, without them asking for it, or even realizing it.

CHAPTER 8

What Does It Mean to Be a White Teacher?

Robin DiAngelo

I am a teacher-educator. On the first day of the semester, I pass out paper with the following questions and ask my students to write their anonymous reflections:

> Discuss what it means to be part of your particular racial group(s). How racially diverse was your neighborhood(s) growing up? What messages have you received about race from your family, friends, schools, and neighborhoods about race? In other words, how has your race(s) shaped your life?

The following anonymous student response is representative of most I receive, both in content and length. Keep in mind that these students are in their junior and senior years of college and will be going on to be our nation's teachers:

> My neighborhood in itself was not that diverse, however, much of my hometown is. I have always been taught to treat everyone no matter what their race is equally. Overall, I do not think race has shaped me much at all because it really doesn't matter to me. When I look at someone, I do not look at the color of their skin but rather the person that they are.

I taught in an education program that is 97% white, and it was rare for me to have any students of color in my classes. Thus, this typical insistence that race doesn't matter comes from white students sitting in an all-white classroom, who grew up in primarily white neighborhoods and attended primarily white schools, and are currently being taught by a virtually all-white faculty (including me). The majority of white teachers have not lived near or attended school with people of color; have had few if any teachers, friends, family members, or authority figures of color; and do not interact with people of color in any direct or equal way in their personal lives or in their teacher preparation programs. Yet while most teacher education students live their lives in racial segregation, it is common for them to believe that racism is in the past, that segregation "just happens," that everyone is the same and therefore they don't see color, and that being white has no particular meaning.

While the following do not apply to every white person, they are well-documented white patterns that make it difficult for white people to understand racism as a system:

Segregation: Most white people live, grow, play, learn, love, work, and die primarily in racial segregation. Yet our society does not teach us to see this as a loss. Pause for a moment and consider the magnitude of this message: People lose nothing of value by not having cross-racial relationships. In fact, the whiter schools and neighborhoods are and the further away from Black people, the more likely they are to be seen as "good." The implicit message is that there is no inherent value in the presence or perspectives of people of color. At the same time, society gives us constant negative messages about Black people, and males in particular. Many white teachers, not having grown up having authentic cross-racial relationships, come to fear Black males, sometimes consciously but most often unconsciously. Left unexamined, this fear manifests in their interactions.

Segregation not only demonstrates that race does indeed matter, but also makes it difficult to see the racial disparity between whites and Blacks that is measurable in every area of life. If white teachers insist that race is meaningless, they are left to explain racial disparity in ways that blame the victim, such as "they just don't value education."

Individualism: White people are taught to see themselves as individuals, rather than as part of a racial group. It follows, then, that they see themselves as racially objective and thus feel they can represent the universal human experience; their view is not tainted by race. People of color, on the other hand, who are not seen as individuals but as members of a racialized group, are not seen as objective on race and thus can only represent a subjective and racialized viewpoint. Seeing themselves as unracialized individuals, White people take umbrage when generalizations are made about them as a group. This enables them to ignore systemic racial patterns. This is reflected in popular White teacher narratives such as, "I don't see color, I only see children." While teachers don't want to reduce students to race, they must never ignore the powerful role race plays in our society and in teacher perceptions of their students.

Racial arrogance: I was once asked to provide one-on-one mentoring for a White teacher who had made inappropriate racial comments to a black student. When the boy's mother complained, the teacher became defensive, and the conflict escalated. The incident ended up in the newspaper, and potential legal action was discussed. I will call this teacher Ms. Smith. During one of our sessions, Ms. Smith told me about a colleague who recently had two black male students at her desk. She prefaced something she said to one of them with, "*Boy, . . .*" The student was clearly taken aback and asked, "Did you just call me boy?" The other student said it was OK; the teacher called all her students "boy."

In relaying this story to me, Ms. Smith expressed the anger that she and her colleague felt about having to be "so careful" and not being able to "say anything anymore." They perceived my intervention with Ms. Smith as a form of punishment and felt that because of this incident, Black boys were now "oversensitive" and complaining about racism where it did not exist. This is a familiar teacher narrative, and in this instance, it was rationalized based on the following: (1) The teacher called all her students "boy" and so the comment had nothing to do with race, and (2) One of the students didn't have an issue with the comment, so the student who did was overreacting. The White teachers' response illustrates several problematic dynamics:

- The teachers never considered that in not understanding the student's reaction, *they* might be lacking in knowledge.

- The teachers did not demonstrate curiosity about the student's perspective or why he might have taken offense. Nor did the teachers demonstrate concern about the student's feelings.

- The teachers do not know their racial history.

- The teachers were not able to separate intentions from impact.

- In spite of the fact that Ms. Smith was so lacking in cross-racial skills and understanding that she was involved in a racial violation with potential legal repercussions, she remained confident that she was right and the student was wrong.

- Her colleague, aware that Ms. Smith was in serious trouble regarding a cross-racial incident, still maintained solidarity with her by validating their shared perspective and invalidating the student's.

- The teachers used the student who excused the comment as proof that the other student was wrong; he was the "correct" student because he denied any racial implications.

- The teachers used this interaction as an opportunity to increase racial divides rather than as an opportunity to bridge them.

Racial belonging: White people enjoy a deeply internalized, largely unconscious sense of racial belonging in U.S. society. In virtually any situation or image deemed valuable in dominant society, Whites belong. In dominant society, interruption of racial belonging is rare and thus destabilizing and frightening to White people and usually avoided. Conversely, *not belonging* is conveyed to Black males through their lack of representation in the curriculum, textbooks, and role models, as well as the well-documented lower expectations that White teachers hold for them.

Constant messages that White people are more valuable: Living in a White dominant context, White people receive constant messages that they are better and more important than people of color. For example: White people are central in history textbooks, historical representations and perspectives, media, and advertising; our teachers, role-models, heroes, and heroines are usually White; everyday discourse on "good" neighborhoods and schools and who is in them favors Whiteness; popular TV shows are often centered around friendship circles that are all White; religious iconography depicts god, Adam and Eve, and other key figures as white. While you may explicitly reject the notion that one group is inherently better than another, you cannot avoid internalizing the message of White superiority, as it is ubiquitous in mainstream culture. Of course, Black boys are getting the opposite message; they are inferior and undeserving. These messages powerfully shape the interactions between White teachers and Black boys. If teachers can't see these messages, or deny receiving them, they can't resist their influence on interactions.

Many people are taught that they have to "walk a mile in someone else's shoes" in order to understand the other's perspective. But walking in someone else's shoes is not truly possible. Although we can't fully walk in others' shoes, we can learn to draw connections, contrasts, and parallels between their experiences and our own. To do this, we must first begin with an understanding of our *own* worldview; considering those of others requires that we are able to consider our own.

■ ■ Engaging the Mind ★ Taking Action ★ Inspiring Excellence
Racial Socialization Reflection

To begin the lifelong work of examining and challenging what is below the surface of your conscious racial awareness, work through these reflection questions. If they don't match your specific background, adjust them accordingly.

(Continued)

At what point in your life were you aware that Black people existed? Most Black people recall a sense of "always having been" aware, while most White people recall being aware by at least age 5. Once you identify the earliest age at which you were aware of the existence of Black people, reflect on the following:

NEIGHBORHOODS

- Did your parents tell you race didn't matter and everyone was equal? Why did they need to tell you this?

- If everyone was equal, why didn't you live together?

- Where did Black people live? If they did not live in your neighborhood, why didn't they? What kind of neighborhood did they live in?

- Were their neighborhoods considered "good" or "bad"? What made a neighborhood good or bad? What images did you associate with these other neighborhoods? What about sounds? What kind of activities did you think went on there? Where did your ideas come from? Were you encouraged to visit these neighborhoods, or were you discouraged from visiting these neighborhoods?

SCHOOLS

- Did you go to a "good" school? What makes a school good or bad?

- Who went to good schools? Who went to bad schools?

- If the schools in your area were racially segregated (as most schools in the United States are), why didn't you attend school together? If this is because you lived in different neighborhoods, why did you live in different neighborhoods?

- Were "their" schools considered equal to, better than, or worse than yours? If you went to school together, did you all sit together in the cafeteria? If not, why not?

- Were the honors or advanced placement classes and the lower-track classes proportionately racially integrated? If not, why not?

TEACHERS

- When was the first time you had a White teacher? How often did this occur?

- When was the first time you had a Black teacher? How often did this occur?

- Why is it important to uncover our racial socialization and the messages we receive from schools?

- If your school was perceived as racially diverse, which races were more represented, and how did that impact the sense of value associated with the school? For example, if White and Asian heritage students were the primary racial groups in your school, your school was likely to be seen as better than a school with more representation from Black and Latinx[1] students. What were you learning about race from these dynamics?

---

[1] Latinx is used to avoid the gender-specific terms Latino/Latina.

As you reflect upon these questions, don't stop at your first response; go one step further and think critically about your answers. Ask yourself how they reveal the deeply internalized framework through which you make racial meaning. In other words, we are taught to rationalize many of these patterns. Given this, we need to continually challenge our rationalizations in order to identify how they function. Do they lend themselves to accepting the racial status quo or to challenging it? The way we think about the world drives our actions upon it. For example, if my explanation for why my neighborhood was predominately White is because "people just naturally prefer to live with people who are most like themselves," what further reflection on the impact of segregation on my identity is required of me? How does this explanation deny the decades of policies and practices that maintain racial segregation? Am I more or less likely to work to interrupt racial segregation in my own life and in my classroom? Am I more or less likely to build the cross-racial relationships that can lead to deeper self-knowledge and anti-racist action?

In conclusion, what does it mean to say that all people are equal but live in segregated groups? Our *lived* separation is a more powerful message because the separation is manifested in action, while inclusion is not. While these questions are challenging, this is the level at which we need to engage in self-awareness if we are going to challenge the unconscious reproduction of racism in the classroom.

PART 2

UNDERSTANDING THE CONSTRAINTS AND CHALLENGING THE NARRATIVES ABOUT WHO BLACK BOYS ARE AND WHO WHITE WOMEN CAN BE

If you have ever asked yourself, "How does *race matter* in the classroom?" the chapters in Part 2 are for you. In Chapter 9, Dr. Jawanza Kunjufu lays out a history of African-descended people that rarely gets told. He reminds us that if White people, White images, and White history are the only things taught in our classrooms, schools and teachers are not colorblind; they see only White. *Race matters* in the classroom because the story that gets told about Black people and about their ancestors impacts how Black students feel about themselves. This profound and poetic chapter is followed by a chapter on African American Vernacular English by Dr. April Baker-Bell. Baker-Bell challenges the idea of code-switching as an idea of privilege and asserts that linguistic racism is common in classrooms. She argues for valuing Black language in schools and shares with teachers an activity to expose the possible propagation of linguistic racism in their classroom. *Race matters* because even the language used in schools is raced and, as Dr. Baker-Bell points out, Black English is denigrated in schools because of its association with Blackness. In Chapter 11, Dr. Becki Cohn-Vargas, who has worked as a classroom teacher, principal, superintendent, and now the director of Not In Our School, writes about creating identity-safe classrooms. This is a strategy-based approach for addressing stereotype threat. *Race matters* because when students belong to a stereotyped group, the cognitive demand of managing that stereotype can be so great that they underperform. This has massive consequences for Black boys, who are stereotyped to be bad at math and science, as well as school in general.

In Krystal de'León's vignette, she shares a story of her young son being told by a classmate that his skin is the color of poop. *Race matters* because children—even our youngest students—pick up negative messages about brown skin color, and then they use them—intentionally or naively—to hurt one another. In Chapter 12, Dr. Darla Scott introduces the term verve, a concept originally developed by psychologist Wade Boykin, to help explain why some students prefer multiple simultaneous sensory inputs, and others can't handle it. In other words, why do some students work better with noise and chaos, while others seek silence? *Race matters* in schools because these preferences for verve sometimes line up around racial cultural background, and the assumption that everyone works better in a quiet setting is a subjective approach, not an objective reality. Chapter 13, by Dr. Chezare Warren and Justin Coles, examines commonsense practices in schools, which make no sense at all when looked at through a racialized lens. *Race matters* in the classroom because the lens teachers and students use to gauge what is "common" sense is shaped by their different racial perspectives. Finally, our last two chapters, by Toni Williams and Dr. Sharoni Little, look at the narratives that are told about Black boys and offer practical strategic ways of rewriting those narratives. The intervening vignette by Olugbala Williams describes historical archetypes of Black men and White women, which inform much of the narrative that continues to play out at the local, institutional, and systemic levels. *Race matters* in the classroom because we are all hemmed in by historical and present narratives that render us less human, less powerful, and less capable of connection.

We believe educators must start by respecting the history connected to Black boys. It is impossible to bring our Black boy students to a place of success, pride, and self - actualization if we don't know where that place is. The history of Black ancestors is one that blazed a trail of excellence, and educators need to know this greatness to encourage and inspire Black boys to the greatness of their forefathers and foremothers. The classroom must be an environment of respect and belief in the possibility of success.

Understanding and respecting language, culture, hopes, and fears is essential. Chapter 9 by Dr. Jawanza Kunjufu may raise more questions than answers but by the end of the chapter, readers should have a strong list of questions they need to explore. It is one of those pieces that helps to crystallize the entire landscape of what Black boys—and the White women who teach them—are up against in education and in the United States.

CHAPTER 9

Respecting Black Boys and Their History

Jawanza Kunjufu

Why do some Black boys associate being smart with acting White? Have you ever heard White boys associate being smart with acting Black? Why are most Black boys more confident in sports than science? Why are they more assured in music than math? Why are they more comfortable with rap than reading? I have observed Black boys arrogantly challenge White boys to a game of basketball but fail to compete against them in a science fair or spelling bee. Why is that?

Why do so many Black boys fight each other? Why are so many angry? Why do some carry a chip on their shoulder? Why are so many obsessed with demanding respect? How can we reduce the Black male rates of suspension, special education placement, retention, and dropout? How do we explain this situation? What can White female teachers do to enhance the educational experience of Black boys?

What can White female teachers do to empower their Black male students? What can schools do to empower Black boys? How important is history and culture to African American boys? How important is history and culture in the Asian, Jewish, and Nigerian communities? How do some groups use their history and culture to improve their educational achievement? In what months do most schools teach Black history? February. In what months do most schools teach White history?

Every month. Could that explain why some Black boys associate being smart with acting White, and White boys associate being smart with acting White? How do we explain that 86 percent of professional basketball players are Black, but only 2 percent of engineers and doctors?

Did Columbus really discover America? To best answer that question, we'll need to first understand the definition of *discover*. Was Columbus the first person in America? Was he the first White person in America?

Did Abraham Lincoln really free the Africans? Notice, I call them Africans, not slaves. The American South had seceded from the Union, and Lincoln had no control over them. The people he could have freed in the North, he did not. Lincoln saved the Union. The North wanted to change the economy from agriculture to industrialization. Northern businessmen wanted Africans to leave cotton fields for factories. Will White female educators teach Black boys the truth about Columbus and Lincoln?

Was Hippocrates the father of medicine? Have you ever read his oath? He acknowledged that he studied from the earlier Egyptian doctor, Imhotep. The oath uses his Greek name, Aesculapius. Will White female educators teach Black boys the truth about Hippocrates and Imhotep?

We would recommend that every teacher use the Black history textbook, *Lessons From History, Reading, and Writing for Urban Survival* and the curriculum, *SETCLAE (Self-Esteem Thru Culture Leads to Academic Excellence)* and African American Images' Best Books for Boys and Children's Library.

I evaluate a social studies curriculum by what they teach about Egypt and slavery. Some schools have taken Egypt out of Africa and placed it in the Middle East. Some maps have placed the United States in the center of the world and made it larger than Africa. In SETCLAE, they use the most accurate map, which is the Peters Map. How many continents are there on this map? What is the definition of a *continent*? *Webster* defines it as a large body of land surrounded by water on all four sides. Does that apply to Europe? Is North America really in the center of the world? Is the United States larger than Africa?

What year was the first pyramid in Egypt built? 2780 BCE. What year was the supposed father of medicine, Hippocrates, born? 460 BCE. What year was Pythagoras, the father of mathematics, born? 570 BCE. How did Africans build pyramids without the scholarship of Hippocrates and Pythagoras? We need White female educators to teach Black boys that their ancestors built the pyramids and the first civilization. We need White female teachers to keep Egypt in Africa and convince Black boys they are just as talented in science, math, and reading. We need White female teachers to overcome racism, White supremacy, and White privilege. We need White female teachers to have a different view of Hippocrates, Pythagoras, Columbus, and Lincoln.

The second area I evaluate in a social studies curriculum is slavery. What does your textbook say about slavery? How many pages? Does it include the number of lynchings and revolts? Does it show pictures of Whites having a lynching after church? Does it give the number of Africans who died in the slave trade? I am always amazed that most people know 6 million Jews died in another country, Germany, but they do not know how many Africans died in the United States. The range is between 5 and 30 million.

We need White female educators to teach Black boys about reparations. They need to teach Black boys that Jews, Asians, and Native Americans received reparations for the injustices they encountered.

Some textbooks have tried to whitewash slavery to the extent that the people were not slaves, but servants, happy well-fed workers or indentured servants. Some publishers have compared them to immigrants. Most books do not mention the hundreds of slave revolts. We need White female educators to teach Black boys that their ancestors resisted slavery in Africa, while in the dungeon, on the slave ship, and on the plantation.

The slave revolts were so numerous that they were affecting the existence of the institution. We need White female educators to teach Black boys that there were more than 300 slave revolts. Black boys need to know about Nat Turner, Denmark Vesey, Harriet Tubman, and many more of their ancestors. They need to know that Frederick Douglass was beaten because he loved reading and valued education.

In 1712, owners hired a consultant named Willie Lynch because there were so many slave revolts. He explained to the White owners that on a typical plantation, there were more Africans than Whites. Lynch explained to them, you must divide and conquer. You must convince Africans to hate themselves. You must make them look for differences. You cannot allow them to become united. You must teach Nigerians to hate Ghanaians. You must teach the Yoruba to hate the Ashanti. You must teach light-skinned Africans to hate dark-skinned Africans. You must teach those who work in the house to hate those who work in the field. Lynch projected that this self-hatred, if evoked successfully, would last over three centuries. (Some question whether Willie Lynch really existed. To me, what is more important is the lack of unity and self-hatred that exists within the African American community and its impact.)

We need White female educators to teach Black boys the Willie Lynch Syndrome. We need White female educators to teach some Black boys they are suffering from post-traumatic slavery disorder. We need White female teachers to recognize

White privilege, prejudice, and racism. We need White female educators to show Black boys fighting each other, using the "N" and "B" words, to stop associating being smart with being White, and to reject the assumption that they are deficient in science, math, and reading: all of these are illustrations of post-traumatic slavery disorder.

There is an historical law that is based on the premise that you can't exceed your origin. Most schools choose to start Black history in 1619 on a plantation rather than in 2780 BC on a pyramid. I want you to be honest. What date do you consider in tracing the history of Black boys? This question is especially urgent for White women teachers: Where will they start Black history—on a pyramid or a plantation?

We need White female educators to teach Black boys the significance of all the dates in the exercise that follows this chapter. White female educators cannot teach what they do not know. They cannot teach what they do not believe. White female educators cannot teach if they don't see color and are in denial. During slavery, less than 10 percent of Americans were slave owners. How could slavery have persisted? Because the larger majority were in denial. This reminds me of the teacher's lounge. Someone makes a derogatory comment about a Black boy. Are you a White teacher who thinks that because you did not make the comment, you are innocent? Why was the teacher so comfortable making the comment to you?

White women teachers must not be silent in the teacher's lounge. They must not remain quiet in the face of curriculum errors and oversights? They must not see colorblindness as an acceptable goal. The first step is to admit that race and culture exist. The second step is to understand these historical factors, and the third step is to appreciate the culture of Black boys. Teachers who attempt colorblindness are in the zero stage of denial. Notice, I said *attempt*. I believe teachers who say, "I don't see color" may often see it better than everyone else.

I am reminded of a workshop I conducted for teachers, when someone blurted out, "I don't see color; I see all children as children." I asked her if I could visit her classroom after my presentation. I have been an educational consultant for over forty years. You can tell me anything in a sterile conference room, but classroom bulletin boards, posters, and library collections don't lie. About 60 percent of this teacher's students were Black, 30 percent were Hispanic, and 10 percent were White. Her classroom decor and library collection was 95 percent White. She saw one color. White. She was deceived into thinking she was colorblind.

We need White female teachers who have the desire and will take the time to correctly pronounce Black boys' names. There is no better sound to students than the correct pronunciation of their names. I have heard many White teachers tell their Black students they cannot pronounce their name and ask for a nickname. These same teachers have no problems with pronouncing their peers' German, Russian, Polish, Italian, Greek, and other European multisyllabic names. Why is it easier to pronounce a European name and not a Black, Hispanic, or Asian name? Are we now talking about the elephant in the room? Prejudice and racism. What is the difference between the two?

We need White female educators who will see Black boys as handsome and extremely intelligent. We need White female educators who will not consider Black boys hyperactive but will help them channel their high energy level. We need White female educators who appreciate the slang and swagger of Black boys. We need White female teachers who are not afraid of Black boys. We need White female educators who will not rob Black boys of their childhood and innocence. Research shows some White female teachers view innocent Black boys in primary grades as young adults and middle and high school Black males as adult criminals.

To understand and appreciate the history of Black boys, I encourage you to read *The Destruction of Black Civilization* (Williams, 1987), *Nile Valley Contributions* (Browder, 2007), *Stolen Legacy* (James, 1992), *They Came before Columbus*, *Before the Mayflower* (Yardley, 1931), *Eyes on the Prize* (Carson, 1987) and many more in this genre. To understand Black boys and their learning styles, I encourage you to read *Changing School Culture for Black Males* (Kunjufu, 2013), *Understanding Black Male Learning Styles* (Kunjufu, 2011), *Keeping Black Boys out of Special Education* (Kunjufu, 2005), *Countering the Conspiracy to Destroy Black Boys* (Kunjufu, 1983), *Reducing the Black Male Dropout Rate* (Kunjufu, 2010), and *Raising Black Boys* (Kunjufu, 2010). This is especially important for White women teachers.

White women teachers should also listen to Black boys. I want these teachers to respect their students, to try to understand and nurture their sometimes large, insecure egos.

Last, for Black boys, relationships are more significant than content or pedagogy. Too many teachers believe they teach subjects, not Black boys. Too many educators give left-brain lessons to right-brain learners. We need White female educators who will meet the needs of Black boys who may be visual, oral, tactile, or kinesthetic learners.

We need White female teachers to understand their subject matter and make it relevant to Black boys. We need White female teachers who will teach the way their students learn. We need White female educators to give right-brain lesson plans to right-brain learners. We need White female teachers to internalize the African mantra, "If the student has not learned, the teacher has not taught." We need White female teachers to internalize that Black boys are relational learners. Black boys want to have a genuine relationship with their teachers. My closing question to White women teachers is: Do you want to have a genuine relationship with Black boys?

Listed below is a chart. Please answer what happened in Black history for each of these dates.

5 million BCE	
30,000 BCE	
2780 BCE	
2000 BCE	
1400 BCE	
1391 BCE	
1279 BCE	
1619	

1712	
1863	
1865	
1896	
1920	
1926	
1954	
1963	
1976	
1995	
2008	

NOTE: Answer key is available at the end of Part 2, on pp. 150-151.

We asked Dr. Baker-Bell to write the following chapter because teachers inevitably have questions about African American Vernacular English, or what Baker-Bell calls Black English. Language is connected to race, and teachers want to know, do I correct Black English, do I teach Standard English, do I ignore it all together? This is one of the enduring questions of teaching across racial and power differences. We encourage readers to listen to this chapter in which Dr. Baker-Bell challenges us to see the ways that Black English is denigrated precisely because it is a language spoken by Black people. While there are no easy answers about what to do in the classroom, we will begin to arrive at answers only when we understand Black English in the larger context of the American narrative about Black people, just like everything else. Baker-Bell also provides suggestions for the classroom.

CHAPTER 10

"I Can Switch My Language, But I Can't Switch My Skin"

What Teachers Must Understand About Linguistic Racism

April Baker-Bell

Danny: *I get that people from different cultures and backgrounds communicate differently with each other, but I also understand that my students will enter a land where they will be judged based on their language. Whether this is fair or not, as their teacher, isn't it my job to prepare my Black students to communicate in "standard English" so that they don't get discriminated against?*

Baker-Bell: *They are also living in a land where they are discriminated against based on the color of their skin, so how do you prepare them to avoid being discriminated against for being Black?*

This exchange took place in an English education course that I teach each semester that challenges students' dominant notions of language and engages them in critical conversations about the language practices of linguistically marginalized youth of color. During one of our earlier class discussions, Danny,[1] a White, monolingual in-service teacher, was wrestling with how to honor his Black students' language practices while preparing them for what he perceived to be their *linguistic reality*. Danny, like many well-intentioned teachers, assumed that if Black students communicate in *White Mainstream English*,[2] then they will somehow avoid discrimination. Unfortunately, many teachers are unaware of the role that race plays in shaping their ideologies about language (Alim, Rickford, & Ball, 2016).

In my response to Danny's question, I could hear the voices of so many Black students from my previous research and teaching experiences who reminded me that communicating in White Mainstream English does not always prevent *linguistic racism*.[3] I could hear the voice of Janel, a ninth-grade student from Detroit, telling me about her experiences being racialized regardless of whether she communicated in White Mainstream English or *Black* or *African American Language* (BL or AAL). My response also reflected the frustration that 15-year-old Lorenzo displayed during an interview as he tried to untangle his linguistic identity from his racial identity. I could hear Calvin, a student from one of my earlier studies, argue, "If African American Language was used by the dominant population and Dominant American English [see footnote 2] was used by the minority population, then African American Language would be deemed the superior language and Dominant American English would be viewed as inferior" (Baker-Bell, 2013, p. 365).

My question to Danny, along with the student voices that underpin it, illustrate how nearly impossible it is to separate a speaker's language from their racial positioning in society (Flores & Rosa, 2015). In this chapter, I provide a brief overview of how linguistic racism gets operationalized in our pedagogical practices, and I offer recommendations and a reflective activity that help teachers work against perpetuating linguistic racism in their classrooms.

---

[1] All names included in this chapter, outside of the author's, are pseudonyms.

[2] I use the terms *White Mainstream English* and *Black Language* in this piece to foreground the racial dimensions of language. White Mainstream English is commonly referred to as standard English or Dominant American English (DAE). Other aliases for Black Language include African American Language (AAL), African American English (AAE), African American Vernacular English (AAVE), and Ebonics.

[3] I use the term *linguistic racism* here to describe the role that racism plays in language.

Stating the Linguistic Facts: The Linguistic Dimensions Behind Race

Although Black Language is viewed as a symbol of linguistic and intellectual inferiority and is devalued in many classrooms, like "every naturally used language, it is systematic with regular rules and restrictions at the lexical, phonological and grammatical level" (Rickford, 2002, p. 1). Black Language is at least one of the languages spoken by most Black or African Americans (Paris, 2016). It is not merely "a set of deviations from the 'standard'" (Alim & Smitherman, 2012) or an informal language[4] that can be classified as solely slang or street talk. Like the slang in every language, Black slang represents the new and short-lived vocabulary of Black language (That party was *lit*) whereas a language refers to words (*ashy*), distinctive patterns of pronunciation (*aks* for ask), and grammar (see Table 10.1) that are more systematic, deeply rooted, and stable over time (Green, 2004; Rickford, 1997). Black Language is also unique for its rich rhetorical style. Features such as signifyin', semantic inversion, and call & response are a few examples of the Black cultural modes of discourse (see Table 10.2) that have survived for generations in the Black community (Williams, 2013).

TABLE 10.1

GRAMMATICAL FEATURES
Habitual Be: to indicate an action occurs habitually.   He <u>be</u> in the house studying.
Regularized Agreement: She told me <u>they was</u> going to be at the library after school.
Bin (Been): stressed *been* indicates an action happened in the remote past.   We <u>been</u> finished with our homework.

Although White Mainstream English is the standard used in many classrooms to measure Black students (Alim & Smitherman, 2012), linguists maintain that the idea of a standardized language is hypothetical and socially constructed (Lippi-Green, 2012). White Mainstream English is most widely accepted as being proper and correct (Lippi-Green, 2012), but if you ask anyone to define or describe it, many would define it using arbitrary ideas that reflect language superiority (Haddix, 2015). The belief that there exists a homogenous, standard, one-size-fits-all language is a myth that is used to justify discrimination on the basis of "language markers that signal alliance to certain social groups, primarily those having to do with race, ethnicity, [gender] and economic factors" (Lippi-Green, 2015, p. 15).

---

[4] There are formal and informal registers—a formal and informal way of using the language.

TABLE 10.2

BLACK CULTURAL MODES OF DISCOURSE
Signifyin': a mode of discourse that has a double meaning and can be used to provide playful commentary or a serious social critique (Smitherman, 2006). Example Daughter: I need $50 for the homecoming dance, Momma. Mother: You must think *money grow on trees*. (money is limited)
Semantic inversion: when a word takes on a reverse or opposite meaning. Example Sandra: I have not seen you in a long time. Where you been hiding? Barbara: I've been working and going to school. I'll be graduating in the spring. Sandra: Well, go on' with your *bad* self! (*bad means good*).
Call & response: "a mode of communication in which the audience constantly participates by responding to the speaker, and in most cases, the audience members act as co-producers of the text or discourse" (Williams, 2013, p. 414). Example Pastor: Weeping may endure for a night, but joy comes early in the morning. *Can I get a witness?* Congregation: Amen! Hallelujah!

Sociolinguists have long argued that so-called "standard English" reflects and legitimizes White, male, upper middle-class, mainstream ways of speaking English (Alim & Smitherman, 2012; Lippi-Green, 2012). As argued by Smitherman (2006), the only reason White Mainstream English is the "form of English that gets to be considered 'standard' [is] because it derives from the style of speaking and the language habits of the dominant race, class, and gender in U.S. society" (p. 6). The concept of *Whiteness* is important in understanding the silent and invisible ways in which White Mainstream English serves as the unstated norm in our classrooms (Pimentel, 2011). Alim and Smitherman (2012) assert:

> Whites can exercise power through overt (obvious) and covert (hidden) racist practices. The fact that it is the language and communicative norms of those in power, in any society, that tend to be labeled as "standard" "official," "normal," "appropriate," "respectful," and so on, often goes unrecognized, particularly by the members of the dominating group. In our case, White Mainstream English and White ways of speaking become the invisible—or better, inaudible—norms of what educators and uncritical scholars like to call academic English, the language of school, the language of power, or communicating in academic settings. (p. 171)

In this way, White Mainstream English-speaking students get erroneously positioned as academically prepared to achieve because their cultural ways of being (language, literacies, histories, values, knowledges) are privileged in classrooms. From this assumption, Black Language-speaking students and other linguistically marginalized students of color get falsely positioned as linguistically inadequate because their language practices are viewed as deficient. Some Black students have noted that when they use White Mainstream English in classrooms, they are often met with symbolic linguistic violence (Johnson, Jackson, Stovall, & Baszile, 2017; Martinez, 2017) and linguistic microaggressions—bias and negative messages such as "you are really articulate," "you speak very well," "you speak intelligently"—that imply that they should sound a certain way based on their race (Charity Hudley & Mallinson, 2014). These same messages are rarely directed at White students who communicate in White Mainstream English. This illustrates how Black students are not only racialized because of the color of their skin, but they are also racialized because of their language.

How Linguistic Racism Gets Perpetuated in our Pedagogical Practices

Linguistic racism gets normalized in classrooms every day through disciplinary discourses, curricular choices, and pedagogical practices. Here I use a commonly known approach in academic discourse, *code-switching pedagogies*, to illustrate how linguistic racism subtly gets propagated through our pedagogical practices.

In their book, *Code-Switching Lessons: Grammar Strategies for Linguistically Diverse Writers*, Wheeler and Swords (2010) model for teachers how to "lay down the red pen and use successful strategies—contrastive analysis and code-switching—for teaching Standard English grammar in linguistically diverse classrooms" (p. vii). In the box that follows, I include instructions and a few of the code-switching charts that Wheeler and Swords recommend teachers use to help their Black students code-switch. More specifically, the activities displayed below are from a lesson in their book entitled "Diversity in Life and Language." This lesson focuses on getting students to identify informal and formal places (Table 10.3) and informal and formal clothing (Table 10.4) as a pathway to understanding formal and informal English or how to use language by the formality of the situation (Table 10.5).

Instructions from Wheeler and Swords (2006) to teachers on creating code-switching charts:

In this unit, we begin to work with the T-chart, the graphic organizer that will underlie all our future work with students on code-switching. Just as we will in every lesson, we place the name of the category we're exploring at the top of the chart. Then we title the left-hand column Informal and the right-hand column Formal. This way, we will be able to lead the class in discovery of Informal clothing or places or language and Formal clothing or places or language. In this unit we build three charts with the students, contrasting formal and informal clothing, places, and language (Wheeler & Swords, 2010, p. 3).

TABLE 10.3   Informal and Formal Places

PLACES	
INFORMAL	FORMAL
your house	wedding
farm	church
outside	museum
mall	interview

TABLE 10.4   Informal and Formal Clothing

CLOTHING	
INFORMAL	FORMAL
jeans	suit
T-shirt	tuxedo
sneakers	nice dress
basketball uniform	military uniform

TABLE 10.5   Code-Switching: Informal and Formal Language Patterns (Wheeler & Swords, 2006).

HABITUAL *BE*	
INFORMAL	FORMAL
Y'all be playing.	You are <u>usually</u> playing.
	You are <u>always</u> playing.
	You are <u>typically</u> playing.

SOURCE: Wheeler, R. S., & Swords, R. (2006). Code-switching: Teaching standard English in urban classrooms. Urbana, IL: NCTE.

CRITICAL ANALYSIS OF THE
WHEELER AND SWORDS APPROACH

On the surface, the code-switching charts appear to be extremely helpful in getting students to think about how to use language based on the formality of a situation. However, as Young (2009) points out, "the code-switching approach implies a racist, segregationist response to the language habits of African Americans" (as cited in Baker-Bell, 2013, p. 357). First, classifying Black Language as informal and White Mainstream English as formal further legitimize a hierarchy that produces Blackness and Black Language as inferior and Whiteness and White Mainstream English as superior. Furthermore, by teaching Black children to restrict Black Language to informal contexts, teachers "ignore the many ways of producing formal speech in African American English in addition to informal uses of Standard English" (Young, Barrett, Young-Rivera, & Lovejoy, 2014, p. 45). Moreover, the code-switching charts imply that Black Language should not be used in formal places like *churches* and *weddings*, which can be problematic and confusing for Black children given that Black churches and weddings are two significant forces that nurture and preserve Black cultural traditions.

Finally, as I review the code-switching charts, I am reminded of a comment that Janel made during an interview: "it's not just about language or how you talk." Janel is suggesting that code-switching pedagogies ignore the relationship between language and one's racial identity. That is, code-switching is a response to the technical differences between Black Language and White Mainstream English but ignores the racial and cultural tensions that underlie such pedagogies (Baker-Bell, 2013).

"SHOW ME THE RECEIPTS!": BLACK STUDENTS AND UNCRITICAL LANGUAGE PEDAGOGIES

The Black youth that I have come to know through my teaching and research experiences indicate that they are fed up with cover-up and uncritical language pedagogies that do not consider their language intellectually valuable. Black youth want receipts![5] Many are well-aware that White Mainstream English is the expected language in school because it represents White linguistic norms, not because it is a universal, proper way of using language. They have concerns about why Black students are required to code-switch and learn White Mainstream English for aca-

---

[5] A phrase used in the Black Language community when someone is in disbelief about something (in this case, uncritical language pedagogies) and hard evidence (or receipts) is required to prove it to be true.

demic success when White students are not required to learn anything about Black Language or code-switch to be academically successful. They want to know how communicating in White Mainstream English is going to prevent them from being discriminated against when Black people are being killed in the streets across America left and right just for being Black (e.g. Trayvon Martin, Rekia Boyd, Jordan Davis, Tamir Rice, Renisha McBride, Jordan Edwards). They question why their teachers tell them that Black Language will not lead to success when it has been instrumental in protest and justice movements (Kynard, 2013), which have led to change in the structure and character of American society. Black youth are fed up with claims that Black Language will not get them jobs when they watch their linguistic and cultural creations get appropriated and used in promotional ads, at sporting events, and in cinema! Their concerns suggest that teachers cannot continue to cover up language politics with respectability language pedagogies.

To move toward transformation, teachers must first recognize that they are complicit in the reproduction of linguistic and racial inequality in schools and society. Too often, teachers look for cookie-cutter pedagogical approaches and easy-fix solutions to address what they perceive as a problem with their Black students' language practices; as a result, they fail to see how their own pedagogical practices uphold White supremacy and anti-Black racism.

■ ■ ■ Engaging the Mind ⋆ Taking Action ⋆ Inspiring Excellence
Beginning the Conversation With Students

In Table 10.6, I list eight questions that get teachers to thinking about the ways in which linguistic racism covertly and overtly gets propagated through their curricular choices and pedagogical practices. Teachers must interrogate their own practices as a first step toward working "against, racial, cultural, linguistic, and socioeconomic inequalities" (CEE Executive Committee, 2009).

TABLE 10.6 Activity: Do you propagate linguistic racism in your classroom?

1. Do you teach your students that White Mainstream English is the "standard," "official," "normal," "appropriate," "respectful" way of communicating?
2. Do you teach your students that Black Language is "slang," "informal," "inappropriate," or an "uneducated" way of communicating?

3.	Do you teach your students that Black Language should be restricted to informal situations and White Mainstream English should be used in every other situation?
4.	Is White Mainstream English the gold standard used in your class by which all students are measured?
5.	Do you teach students about the historical, cultural, political, racial, and linguistic dimensions of Black Language?
6.	Do you teach students that Black Language is systematic with regular rules and restrictions at the lexical, phonological, and grammatical level?
7.	Do you teach your students that the idea of a "standard language" is hypothetical and socially constructed?
8.	Do you teach your students about the intersections between language and race when teaching about language?

If you answered "YES" to questions 1 to 4 or "NO" to questions 4 to 8, then you probably recognize how your own curricular choices and pedagogical practices play a critical role in upholding and reproducing linguistic racism. To begin creating more linguistically inclusive and humane classrooms for Black youth, I recommend that teachers provide their students with a critical linguistic awareness of the historical, cultural, racial, and political underpinnings of Black Language." I provide an inquiry-based activity below (see Figures 10.1 and 10.2) that helps teachers begin this conversation by inviting students to participate in a dialogue about Black Language. The first character on the activity sheet questions: "What is African American Language (AAL)? Is it incorrect, improper, or broken-English? Is it slang?" This character represents the uniformed perspective of AAL typically held by the general public, including some Black people. The second character in the conversation was designed to counter or interrogate dominant assumptions about languages by providing a historical, political, or cultural perspective of Black Language. Finally, the worksheet includes a blank section that invites students to contribute their ideas, thoughts, and perspectives to the conversation. This activity is one of many steps that teachers can incorporate in their quest to create more linguistically humane classrooms where students and teachers learn to use language and literacy in critical and empowering ways.

FIGURE 10.1 Activity: A Conversation About African American Language

What is African American Language (AAL)? Is it incorrect, improper, or broken-English? Is it slang?

AAL can be defined as a legitimate Black-originated, rule-based language that is spoken by most (but not all) African Americans. It is not slang, broken-English, or street talk. AAL is intimately connected with a history of oppression, resistance, and rich linguistic and literary achievement among African Americans.

Your thoughts, questions, concerns:

1.

2.

3.

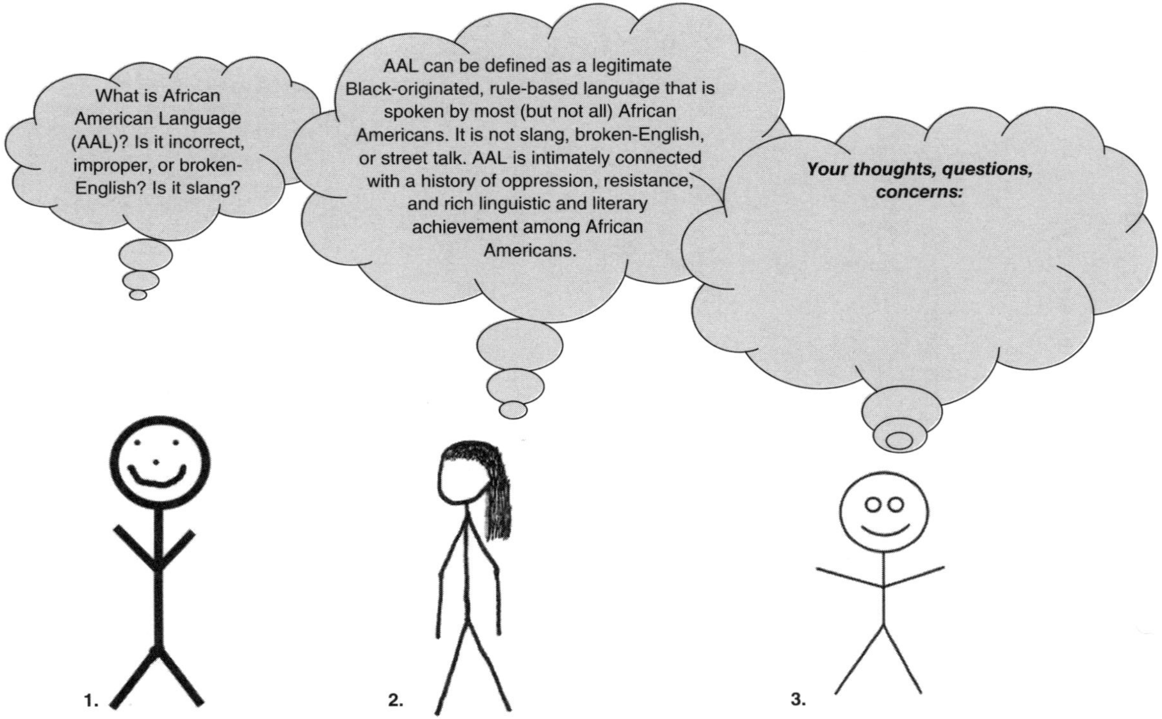

FIGURE 10.2

As the preceding chapter and the following vignette demonstrate, part of the work of teachers is to pay attention to the myriad ways that Blackness is denigrated and to correct it for their Black students, even as they are also correcting it in the larger society.

Vignette: The Color of Poop

Krystal de'León

My phone rings. It's my son's school. I answer the phone assuming that he missed the bus home. Right away I ask, "Do I need to come pick up Prince?" Mrs. F tells me, "No, he's on the bus. I've called to inform you of an incident." She tells me that while standing in line, another child said to my son, "Hey, your skin is brown like poop!" In shock, I remain quiet and listen as the teacher goes on to tell me she believes the student was only making an observation. She tells me at this age (four years old) bodily functions are interesting and "cool." I am speechless. The conversation ends.

I'm gathering my thoughts.

I am angry that this teacher doesn't seem to think it was a big deal that the only Black child in her class was told that his skin looks brown like poop. I am angry that she tried to validate the actions of this White child but did not once acknowledge my son and the possibility that his feelings were hurt. What about him?

I feel guilty. We are one of the only Black families at the school and in the community. I should have seen this coming.

When I asked my son what happened after the incident, he tells me his classmate was told, "If you say that again you're going to the principal." And he was given a time out. My son, Prince, was told to get a book and go to the reading rug. That was it. Nothing more was done or said in the moment. No one said to Prince, "Your skin isn't brown like poop." No one said, "That's not true." And no one bothered to ask my son to identify his own skin color. In that moment, nobody did anything to empower my son and protect his identity. Instead they told him to "go get a book . . ."

I decided to follow-up with Mrs. F. I validated her in saying, "I understand being young and making observations." But I said, "I think what happened was more than a simple observation. It was an observation that came along with a negative attachment. At a young age, we hear 'gross, stinky, poopy diaper' and move quickly to get away from it. I don't see anything cool about poop." I suggested having a conversation on how to describe skin color in ways beyond using brown, black, or white. The child could have chosen caramel or chocolate; he could even have compared my son's skin-color to being brown like a tree trunk. He chose poop. If you ask my son what color his skin is, he would tell you it's brown like the color of sand.

Situations like this can provide an opportunity to talk about these types of differences at a level that is age appropriate. I explained that while our school and community is limited in ethnic diversity, the wider world is very diverse. Right now, while our young children are growing and forming opinions that may last a lifetime is when we should help prepare them for all that they may encounter.

Mrs. F. just didn't get it. She said she still thought it was a harmless observation. She told me that if I would like to come in to the classroom and share what makes my family unique she would love to have me. She told me a story about her daughter, who performed a rap about Martin Luther King, Jr. She also offered that if I had additional questions and concerns, I could contact the early learning coordinator for the district, the school principal, or even the school psychologist.

I chose the latter, and a week later I was meeting with a White teacher, White principal, and White early learning coordinator. Going into this meeting, I asked myself, "How—as a Black woman—am I going to have this conversation with three White women? How am I going to convey how important it is not just to my son, but to all children, to be able to handle differences appropriately?"

The chapters in this section make it clear that the denigration of Blackness is one of the forces at play in teachers' relationships with Black boys, and it is a force they will have to contend with if they are going to reach Black children. Another such force is that of stereotype threat, which tends to impact members of stereotyped groups, like Black boys. The concept of stereotype threat comes from psychologist Claude Steele, who popularized the concept in his best-selling book, Whistling Vivaldi. *The concept helps concretize a complex threat to Black student achievement, which is practically unimaginable to most people, including Black men themselves. Steele literally spent a lifetime investigating this topic because he believed so fervently that something was underlying Black male underachievement besides the intellectual inferiority or lack of effort or passion for school that are so often assumed. In the spirit of universal design, he investigated this concept first with a focus on Black boys and subsequently discovered it has enormous salience for any person in a stigmatized group, including White women. White women navigating the stereotype threat that all White people are racist may be so cognitively distracted by trying not to fulfil the stereotype that they cannot fully learn what they need to know about race. The concept of stereotype threat has incredible value and consequence. But how, exactly, does a K–12 classroom teacher navigate stereotype threat in the classroom? Becki Cohn-Vargas, along with the late Dorothy Steele, wife of Dr. Claude Steele, developed the concept of identity safety as an antidote to stereotype threat in the classroom. They have written a book addressing this concept; Cohn-Vargas gives us a taste of its practicality and possibility here. Rather than having one activity at the end of the chapter, Cohn-Vargas has distributed activities throughout the chapter.*

CHAPTER 11

Identity Safety as an Antidote to Stereotype Threat

Becki Cohn-Vargas

When I was principal of an urban elementary school in Oakland, California, the father of Dewan, a fifth-grade Black boy, came to the school to complain. His son's teacher was not giving him homework. It was noon, so Dewan, his father, and I went to talk to Mrs. Thomas, a White teacher. Her classroom was full of students playing math games. She told Dewan's father that she indeed gave homework. She apologized for not informing him that Dewan was not completing his work. Dewan looked sheepish, and his father seemed embarrassed at being played. He turned angrily to Dewan. "Look at these students, one day you'll end up working for them. I just don't want you to end up being a statistic."

Just what kind of statistic? A school dropout? A gang member? Or perhaps one of many incarcerated men shown on TV? The fact that Mrs. Thomas had not communicated with Dewan's father about the missing homework was also concerning.

Over the years, I heard other students say, "My parents don't want me to be a statistic." It resonated when I learned about stereotype threat, the fear of confirming a negative stereotype (C. M. Steele, 2010; C. M. Steele & Aronson, 1995). When people feel their social group is negatively stereotyped, worrying that they might exemplify it diminishes performance—even if they do not believe the stereotype is true. This is a social psychological phenomenon called *stereotype threat.* Groups include gender, race, religion, age, and other negatively stereotyped social classifications. The insidious stereotype that Blacks are less intelligent than Whites has been found to lower academic performance of Black students.

STEREOTYPE THREAT RESEARCH

In one study, Black and White students (with comparable academic levels) were given part of the GRE (Graduate Records Examination) verbal exam. In the first group, students were told the test was "diagnostic of their abilities" (triggering the stereotype about Black intelligence). The second group was told the test was a problem-solving exercise, therefore not triggering stereotypes. Black students in the second group performed at higher levels than those in the first group. Black performance in the second group also matched White students, who performed equally well in both groups (C. M. Steele, 1995). This research established that stereotype threat impacted academic performance for Black students.

Over 300 stereotype threat studies have been done involving stereotypes of people of all backgrounds (e.g., women in mathematics, senior citizens with memory). Consistently, stereotype threat was evidenced when pervasive negative stereotypes were triggered (Stroessner & Good, 2009).

While stereotype threat is not the only cause of academic failure, it certainly merits serious consideration as educators work to improve equity and access for Black boys.

STEREOTYPES START EARLY

At a preschool in Los Angeles, Sean, a Black toddler, was regularly bumping into a White girl. The teachers discovered it was because he liked her and sought her attention. Her parents called saying "we're extremely upset." In response, the director told them, "Don't worry, we'll ensure your child's safety." In this way, a Black toddler's behavior was pathologized. Little Sean may not have realized it, but the first seeds of stereotype threat had been sown.

Imagine, Sean starting school as someone to be feared and then compounding it with unequal treatment throughout his schooling. Add in messages that put the fear of being a statistic into his mind. Stereotype threat runs deep. The question is how to counter it.

IDENTITY SAFETY: AN ANTIDOTE TO STEREOTYPE THREAT

Stereotype threat researcher Claude Steele, together with Dorothy Steele, began to investigate ways to counteract stereotype threat in schools. They considered that many teachers with good intentions strove to be "colorblind" by ignoring differences. They worried that efforts to "treat everyone the same" might diminish belonging for marginalized students. They posited that a colorblind classroom, where differences are ignored, allows stereotypes to flourish underground. Educators often do not realize when they react differently to the behavior of Black children (Markus, C. M. Steele, & D. M. Steele, 2000).

The researchers felt efforts should begin early, even before students could grasp the concept of stereotyping. They hypothesized that students need to be inoculated with messages that validate them not in spite of but because of their social identities. They defined *identity safe* classrooms as places where "teachers strive to ensure that students feel that their social identity is an *asset* rather than a barrier to success in the classroom and that they are welcomed, supported, and valued whatever their background" (D.M. Steele & Cohn-Vargas, 2013).

Solutions to improving academic outcomes for Black boys require a concerted effort to dismantle institutional racism in all forms. Because this book focuses on teachers, this chapter highlights identity safe classroom practices as an antidote to stereotype threat.

IDENTITY SAFETY RESEARCH

The Steeles and colleagues examined the theory of identity safety with a research study, the Stanford Integrated Schools Program (SISP), conducted in eighty-four urban elementary classrooms. SISP's goal was to identify environments where stereotype threats were lifted. A team of two observers visited the classrooms three times during a year. They sought evidence of practices that create identity safety in students. They also interviewed teachers, surveyed students, and collected achievement test data. When the data were analyzed, the study revealed a constellation of practices, when taken together, that create environments where students from all backgrounds feel a sense of identity safety, like school more, and improve achievement (D. M. Steele & Cohn-Vargas, 2013).

Identity safe practices are broken into four domains: *Child-Centered Teaching, Cultivating Diversity as a Resource, Classroom Relationships,* and *Caring Environments.* The domains include fourteen specific factors. Educators will find the factors familiar. However, identity safety emerges from the factors taken together and implemented through an equity lens. Factors will be described, together with ways educators might check themselves to assure they are not reproducing societal stereotypes or promoting lowered expectations for Black boys.

CHILD-CENTERED TEACHING

The factors in this domain:

Listening for student voices to ensure that each student can contribute to and shape classroom life;

Teaching for understanding so students will learn new knowledge and incorporate it into what they know;

Focus on cooperation rather than competition, so each student learns from and helps others; and

Classroom autonomy to promote responsibility and belonging in each student.

It may be tempting to tell Black boys that if they don't work hard in school, they won't get into college and have a better life. Rather than giving warning lectures, however, listen to the students. Child-centered teaching helps Black boys find their voice. In a varied learning environment, students can explain what they learned and why they are learning it. Data are carefully analyzed, and progress is monitored to assure understanding.

Students can write about what matters to them, choose areas of interest to research, learn to analyze and express ideas, and develop public-speaking skills. Activities that build autonomy strengthen students' confidence in their abilities. Cooperation is central with students grouped in dyads, triads, small and large groups, and cross-age partners. They learn to communicate and collaborate with peers.

Autonomy and Motivation. Students become autonomous by being taught in a way that is meaningful to them. Students can recognize that we all learn differently. Lessons can be designed to appeal to varied learning styles. They can learn to discuss and debate. They can choose to demonstrate knowledge through writing essays or narratives, videos, PowerPoint presentations, skits, and artwork. Interactive environments, with many physical activities, motivate Black boys (National Education Association, 2011).

Academic Identity. Developing varied expertise helps students form an academic identity. It begins with developing a sense of self-efficacy. Zaretta Hammond (2015, p. 109) describes four components of an academic mindset: I belong in this academic community, I can succeed at this, my ability and competence grow with effort, and this work has value for me.

How are the lessons scaffolded so all students understand the content and engage?

How are the student groups formed so that students get to know one another and learn to work together?

How do students find their voice and create their academic identities?

Are student choices authentic and motivating?

CULTIVATING DIVERSITY AS A RESOURCE

The factors in this domain:

Using diversity as a resource for teaching to include all students' curiosity and knowledge in the classroom;

High expectations and academic rigor to support all students in higher level learning; and

Challenging curriculum to motivate each student by providing meaningful, purposeful learning.

In identity safe classrooms, cultivating diversity is an approach drawing from what kids know and bring with them to school. Challenging curricular content in a rigorous curriculum combines with higher-level thinking that can be taught at every academic level. Teachers can show students that they believe in them and will support meeting high expectations (D. M. Steele & Cohn-Vargas, 2013).

Cultivating diversity as a resource through repertoires of practice. It may be daunting to bring in a student's cultural background without falling into reductionism and stereotyping different groups. Gutiérrez and Rogoff (2003) explain repertoires of practice. It refers to how people engage in cultural practices "because . . . variations reside not as traits of individuals or collections of individuals, but as proclivities of people with . . . histories of engagement with specific cultural activities" (p. 1). They propose educators focus on "individuals' and groups' experience in activities—not their traits." They recommend bringing students' lives into the classroom.

African American students, African students, Puerto Rican Black students, and Caribbean students all have different cultures and practices. By sharing from their families, students feel their lives matter and are valued. It also helps them discover their own identities and better understand their peers. Teachers cannot possibly learn about every culture, but by sharing from lived experiences, students are the ones who teach the others.

Critical multiculturalism. Starting in fourth grade, students can analyze messages from television and textbooks. They can be taught a process known as critical multiculturalism (Ladson-Billings, 1999). Through this lens, students critically examine the world in the context of historical inequities. They begin to notice biases and what is missing from textbooks. A critical eye is an important life skill. Students gain confidence in themselves to counteract times when they are inevitably faced with negative stereotypes, implicit bias, and microaggressions.

Equalizing student status and drawing on student expertise. In identity safe classrooms, educators work to equalize status. Status, an underlying part of all interactions, can be raised by allowing each student to authentically share his or her expertise. Identifying expertise involves valuing skills that contribute to others. Students can explore areas of expertise that benefit others (e.g., mentoring, creativity, translation). Status is equalized when they share their unique expertise.

Healing crushed hearts. Mitchell was the only Black student in the gifted program. His sixth-grade teacher ridiculed him and moved him from the gifted table in front to the back with disruptive kids. When he asked why, she said it was because he was tall and blocked the view. He recalls "At sixth-grade graduation, I said to Mrs. Frithy 'well, I made it.' She replied 'yes, just barely.' I was an A student! I remember all her words to this day." Mitchell went on to become a lawyer but experiences like these often lead to giving up.

Dewan's teacher in the opening anecdote may not have contacted his parents, assuming that his parents didn't care if he completed homework. In an identity safe classroom, teachers express belief in students and work to make up for past failures to do this. They give encouragement to students and parents.

What are the messages coming from the textbooks and literature?

What tools for a critical multicultural analysis have you taught?

Are you helping students bring their full social identities into the classroom through authentic activities that do not single out any student?

Have you taken steps to undo the damage of low expectations that a student may have brought with him to your classroom?

What are your assumptions about your students' parents?

CLASSROOM RELATIONSHIPS

The factors in this domain:

Teacher warmth and availability to support learning by building a trusting, encouraging relationship with each student; and

Positive student relationships built through interpersonal understanding and caring among students.

Belonging thrives with positive relationships between teacher and student and among students. Teachers monitor academic and social interactions. Teachers intervene when someone is teased, bullied, or excluded. Students learn conflict resolution techniques and ways to be accountable for their behavior through restorative practices.

Trust. Students need to trust that their teachers "have their backs." For White women teaching Black boys, this sometimes requires working harder to overcome past negative experiences. Trust is built by support and feedback (Cohen, C. M. Steele, & Ross, 1999). Approaching errors as learning opportunities liberates students from the sense of failure. One middle school teacher made analyzing errors on math quizzes fun. Whenever she asked students to analyze their mistakes, hands shot up. One kindergarten teacher simply told her students "mistakes are our friends" (D. M. Steele & Cohn-Vargas, 2013).

"Wise feedback" builds trust. Claude Steele (1999, para. 33) described wise feedback. "Some people think you should just give the feedback unalloyed, don't soften it. That doesn't work. Black students are in this ambiguous situation where they can't trust that . . . It's intriguing how race in that way creates a bubble that can isolate a person from feedback." Steele posed an alternate process. Say to the student: "Look, we're using high standards in evaluating this work. I have looked at your work, and think you can meet those standards.' That combination of high . . . standards plus affirmation of that person's potential to meet those standards deeply inspires the students." Once feedback is clearly communicated, Black students will be open to hear specific steps for improvement (Cohen & C. M. Steele, 2002).

Empathy. Teaching students to be upstanders who speak up and stand up for themselves and others helps them develop self-confidence. They learn to empathize and avoid victimizing their peers.

■ ■ Engaging the Mind ★ Taking Action ★ Inspiring Excellence
Check Yourself

Are students participating equally? Who is called on most often?

What is your reaction when students make mistakes?

Are you monitoring social status and group dynamics so that none are stigmatized or excluded?

CARING CLASSROOM

The factors in this domain:

Teacher skill to establish an orderly, purposeful classroom that facilitates student learning;

Emotional and physical comfort so each student feels safe and attached to school and one another; and

Attention to prosocial development to teach students how to live together, solve problems, and show respect and caring for others.

Teacher skill refers to how teachers foster a caring and identity safe environment where students are engaged rather than controlled. Procedures and behavioral expectations are clear. Activities draw on student strengths, cultures, and learning styles. Discipline practices are not punitive, but like academic mistakes, misbehavior offers a chance to learn.

Emotional and physical comfort help students feel safe and at ease. The room set-up, noise level, and transitions are not frenetic. A friendly environment does not preclude one that is rigorous and challenging. When students feel safe, they will take risks.

Students are taught, practice, and can articulate social and emotional learning skills. Respect, empathy, attentive listening, and kindness are infused all day long.

Practicing prosocial skills. Some students easily learn prosocial behaviors, while others keep "messing up" and need practice. When Black boys are constantly corrected or seen as pariahs, it leads to dis-identification with school. Behaviors that begin as impulse control issues can evolve into talking back to the teacher, bullying, and fighting. These behaviors should not go unchecked; rather, when a student repeatedly misbehaves or breaks rules, consider the cause while ensuring he is not publicly humiliated (D.M. Steele & Cohn-Vargas, 2013). Consider:

Did the student know he was breaking the rule?

If so, teach the expectations or procedures that were lacking.

Does he lack impulse control?

If so, help him become aware of and learn to monitor behavior. Practice techniques such as ways to control his reactions. It takes lots of practice!

Is there a social skill he needs to learn that will help him avoid the problem in the future?

Teach the skill, being sure to explain its importance. Model it and practice.

Is he experiencing frustration from repeated academic failures?

Consider how you can turn failures around by scaffolding success to ease the frustration.

Is he seeking attention?

Help him find positive ways to get attention.

Give him chances to repair harm through restorative justice. Ultimately, show care and build rapport with him. He needs to be a valued member of the class. The environment can be constructed to help him transform. It won't be instantaneous, but with support, students can shift behavior.

Positive presuppositions: What comes out of our mouths? Every word teachers utter gives an underlying message to students. The message can say "we believe in your capacity" or it can convey doubt. A popular poster says, "Time passes, will you?" That casts a subtle doubt, permeating the room. We can become aware of cues embedded in words. Making a positive assumption—saying "when you do your homework" rather than "if you do your homework"—expresses confidence that the student will do the homework. Using specific language to highlight strengths— "You showed me that you understood the concept of . . . because you . . ." tells the student exactly what he did right. By carefully considering each word we say, we have power to strengthen confidence.

■ ■ Engaging the Mind ★ Taking Action ★ Inspiring Excellence
Check Yourself

Are you treating Black boys fairly? Are you reacting differently to the same behaviors when a Black boy is involved?

Are you giving a positive message and throwing in a "but" that undermines what you are saying, invalidating the student? (e.g., "you did a good job, but . . .")

How can you keep a kid from being seen as a pariah while he repeatedly is misbehaving?

CONCLUSION

Creating an identity safe classroom is like making a tapestry. Every aspect of classroom life must be designed thoughtfully to create acceptance and belonging. Students' prosocial development is considered in all curricular and social interactions. Weaving together strategies for creating autonomy and belonging must accompany adding to a growing sense of student competence through valuing their unique identities. By carefully checking to uncover unconscious biases, teachers are more likely to treat students fairly and avoid contributing to stereotype threat. No student should be saddled with worry about failure or becoming a "statistic." This is not easy work, but it is highly rewarding. Inevitably, teachers make mistakes, but as with students, those mistakes are learning opportunities. This concerted effort has tremendous potential to provide equity and access for Black boys.

The following chapter introduces the concept of verve, which describes a person's capacity—and preference—for more or less sensory input. Some people like to listen to music in the car while having a conversation. Other people turn the music down or off during a conversation. Neither approach is right or wrong—but both may indicate a person's capacity for verve. As a reader, consider how many simultaneous sensory inputs you usually experienced in your house growing up. Did you grow up in a home in which people spoke softly one at a time, or a house in which people spoke over each other and/or escalated the volume to be heard? Did you grow up in a house with one, two, or three other people, or did you grow up in a house with four, five, six, or more people besides yourself? Was it considered a distraction to have the TV or radio playing while eating dinner, or was it a norm? Again, there are no right or wrong answers to these questions, but your response may give you some clues as to what role verve plays in your life. The answers to these questions also might be related to your ethnic background, your neighborhood, or the professions and interests of your parents. If your parents were musicians, you might have had more sensory input in your environment than if your parents were librarians. If you were a twin—or one of many children—you may have had more sensory input than if you were an only child, or one of two. As Dr. Darla Scott demonstrates in the next chapter, your capacity and preference for verve is related to what helps you focus: a silent classroom or simultaneous sensory inputs like music, talking, or noise. In the same way that New Yorkers can't sleep when they travel to quiet, rural areas, many non-New Yorkers struggle to sleep through the night in New York when the subway rumbles past underground and sirens go by on the street. There is no right or wrong. The key is to understand how we've all been shaped by our upbringing. As teachers, we can't assume that all students will thrive in a quiet setting, just because that's what may work for us.

CHAPTER 12

The Science Behind Psychological Verve and What It Means for Black Students

Darla Scott

for the energetic Black boys who come to school excited to learn . . .

Jesse arrived at school and could hardly contain his elation. It was the first day of first grade, and he felt like a big boy now! As he ran to his new class, the hall monitor reminded him to walk. Once in class, he danced to his seat and tried to make friends with his new classmates. While practicing a new skill, he drummed a beat on his desk and seemed to pay more attention when a new activity was introduced. Throughout the day, Jesse received different messages about himself, how he should behave, and what was expected of him. Will there be opportunities for Jesse to succeed in class and in school?

Psychological verve is a preference for and receptiveness to relatively high levels of physical stimulation (Boykin, 1979, 1982). There are three dimensions of physical stimulation, namely, variability, intensity, and density. Variability relates to the alternation between different activities. Intensity refers to the liveliness or loudness of the stimulation or activity. Density involves the number of stimuli or activities that occur concurrently in one's environment (Boykin, 1986). The Triple Quandary, which serves as the theoretical foundation for verve, conceptualizes the behavioral and personality implications for African Americans as they negotiate the majority, minority, and Afro-cultural realms of experience. Each of these realms of social negotiation results in different pressures and requires distinct repertoires of behavior (Boykin, 1983). Boykin (1986, 1994) identified nine interrelated dimensions of Afro-cultural ethos; those with relevance to academic settings include movement, verve, affect, communalism, expressive individualism, orality, and social time perspective. There are data to suggest that these ideologies are cultivated in the home and transmitted to school and community settings through the preferences and practices of African-American students (Tyler, Boykin, Miller, & Hurley, 2006). Schools, much like our homes, are cultural spaces. Many of our public schools espouse White, middle-class norms that can conflict with the cultural norm of Black households (Ellison, Boykin, Towns, & Stokes, 2000).

Thus, we have lively home environments with simultaneous high-energy activities cultivating a preference for higher levels of stimulation and related behavioral displays among children like Jesse. These behaviors are far too often interpreted as off-task, disruptive, or even maladaptive. This perception has far-reaching implications for Black students, especially boys. Gregory and Thompson (2010) found statistically significant differences indicating that individual African American students tended to be perceived differently by different teachers. Whether teachers perceived behavior as defiance or cooperation was connected to the number of discipline referrals (Gregory & Thompson, 2010). For these students, their teachers' perception is their reality.

Understanding psychological verve can help teachers to better understand their students. Verve is a tool that can be used to connect instructional strategies in meaningful ways with students, especially Black boys. It must be said that all Black children will not demonstrate or prefer this type of learning environment, as no community is a monolith. But, verve is a concept grounded in developmental psychology and cultural theories that help us understand the lived experiences of Black children. Guided by empirical tools that measure vervistic behavioral tendencies, teachers can identify the proclivity toward psychological verve in their students and weave it into the ways of thinking and knowing employed in their classroom.

EMPIRICAL SUPPORT

Over the years, researchers have investigated psychological verve to determine its utility in application to learning environments. The findings from these investigations have consistently shown that Black student performance improves in the more varied task presentations (Bailey, 1998; Boykin, 1979, 1982; Boykin & Bailey,

2000; Bullard, 1987; Hart, 1987; Tuck & Boykin, 1989; Walton, 1994, 1998), particularly when the students report highly stimulating home environments (Allen, 1987; Tuck & Boykin, 1989). In these studies, varied task presentation involved the alternation between activity types versus a blocked format with all similar tasks completed together. Bailey (2001), through manipulating the variability dimension of verve in academically relevant exercises (such as spelling), found that students working on varied tasks outperformed students working on blocked-format tasks. Scott (2006) revealed that variability significantly improved performance for fourth-grade participants with grade-appropriate tasks involving fractions, estimation, spelling, and context clues. In this study, students completed the four task types in a randomly generated sequence (high varied) or completed all the practices for each skill before moving to the next skill (low varied/blocked). Furthermore, researchers have found that psychological verve is empirically linked to motivation, engagement, and performance gains for African American elementary students (Griffin, 2004; Scott, 2006).

More recently, researchers have demonstrated the importance of variability in skill practice through the interleaved practice construct with middle school and college students (Rohrer, Dedrick, & Stershic, 2015; Sana, Yan, & Kim, 2016). This line of research provides evidence that varied (or interleaved) practice helps improve students' strategy selection and mathematics learning due to the distributed practice. The impact of the intensity dimension of verve can be seen in the literature around creating active classrooms, which has resulted in enhanced learning and achievement in physically active academic lessons (Erwin, Abel, Beighle, & Beets, 2011; Martin & Murtagh, 2015).

VERVE IN ACTION

Jesse, a Black boy, is in the fifth grade now, and he has demonstrated verve in his behaviors and preferences. Tessa, his fifth-grade teacher, wants to implement strategies in her classroom to support Jesse's culture and learning style, which will foster his academic success. But, before making any modifications, Tessa knows that she must understand Jesse's learning styles and preferences for verve by measuring it.

Three tools have been used to measure vervistic tendencies and learning preferences: Home Stimulation Perception Questionnaire, Pathway Preference Measure, and Questionnaire of Stimuli Preference. Each of these tools examines self-reported preferences for high levels of stimulation.

The Home Stimulation Perception Questionnaire (HSPQ) is a fourteen-item measure designed to assess the level/degree of perceived physical stimulation in the home environment (Boykin & Allen, 1988). A sample item from this tool is: "How often do people in your house read, study, or do homework with the TV on, with music playing, or with people talking?"

The Pathway Preference Measure (PPM) is an indirect measure of preference for variability, which resembles a maze map with various locations, such as home, school, and playground. Using this maze, the degree to which the student deviates from the most direct path from school to home provides an index of their preference for and receptiveness to variability (Bailey, 1998; Boykin & Bailey, 2000).

The Questionnaire of Stimuli Preference-Modified (QSP-M) is a thirteen-item scale that measures students' preference for vervistic pedagogical practices and activities across classroom, recreational, and social contexts at school (Bailey, 1998). A sample item from this tool is: "I have the best times playing when I'm playing, talking, laughing loudly, and making a lot of noise. How much do you like playing this way?"

Practitioner Development: Utilizing Psychological Verve in the Classroom

Tessa has been teaching for three years, and she knows her fifth-grade students well. She has embedded age-appropriate choice and variability into her classroom. During the fourth week of class, Tessa's students arrived at 8:20 am and selected one of three Opener activities. Today's Openers were a Library Book Do (when students react through text or art to a book they have read before), Reflective Writing Prompt using the prompt spinner, and New News (an opportunity to find interesting news to share, along with how it is relevant to them). Throughout the day, Tessa's teaching style brings variability and connected lively movement into her classroom. How will her students respond to these learning experiences? Will her Black boys, like Jesse, feel connected to the class? How will Tessa validate the voice of her diverse group of students? Will Tessa notice any signs of disengagement in contrast with behavioral displays that indicate a verve preference?

The authentic application of psychological verve in the classroom requires an understanding of the integrity in the lived experiences of African American students and a willingness to create culturally relevant learning opportunities. Beyond openness to the validity of the home practices that cultivate psychological verve, teachers should be willing to de-privatize their classrooms for the sake of working within teams of practitioners to develop multiple entry points, diverse learning exercises, and varied performance assessments. Researchers examined the implementation of a coaching model to support culturally responsive classroom management strategies and found that teachers responded positively to this ongoing professional development support (Pas, Larson, Reinke, Herman, & Bradshaw, 2016). These types of strategies have the potential to address equity issues in education, such as discipline disproportionality rates. Critical self-examination is vital so teachers can challenge presuppositions about how orderly and effective classrooms should look and sound. The ability to distinguish the signs of engagement will help reflective practitioners to know that their students are "getting it" in a lesson, regardless of the "noise" level in the classroom.

INSTRUCTIONAL DEVELOPMENT: CONCRETE WAYS TO MAKE BETTER USE OF PSYCHOLOGICAL VERVE

In most of the previous work on psychological verve, the variability dimension has occurred in the presentation of learning materials and has been imposed by the researcher. Furthermore, these varied learning practice opportunities have been contrasted with blocked-presentation formats, as in the interleaved practice literature (Rohrer et al., 2015; Sana et al., 2016). The implication of this work is that variability can be beneficial in the learning materials and skill practice segments of class. For the classroom, variability can be introduced in the presentation of learning material formats, practice opportunities, and skill reinforcement across several academic domains. For each learning exercise, the classroom should include opportunities for variety, age-appropriate choice, and student voice in how learning takes place. Varying learning blocks is a great way to introduce variability into instruction. For example, rather than a 45-minute block on mathematics followed by a 45-minute block on language arts, teachers could alternate 15-minute blocks between mathematics and language arts. Another method would be to introduce variability by having cross-disciplinary practice, alternating between math and science practice or between social studies and language arts practice.

Density has been demonstrated by adding multiple stimuli to a given learning environment. Thus, the implication for the classroom would be layering stimuli in learning lessons, such as using background music while practicing a skill in class. One teacher reported using instrumental music at a low volume with her ninth-grade students and found that they were calmer and more focused. Making meaningful use of multiple educational aids within a given lesson would also be an excellent manipulation of density. Music can be used as a signal and background motivator during various lesson segments, for example, playing a song during warm-ups or closing exercises. Also, it can have a performance enhancement effect during the independent or collaborative practice phase of the lesson.

Intensity is related to the loudness or vibrancy of the stimulation in classrooms. The challenge with integrating intensity in classrooms is the perception of how a good and orderly classroom looks and sounds. Are children talking and laughing? Is it loud or quiet? The answers to these questions involve "when": When should it be loud? Quiet? When should there be laughter? Talking? Teachers are encouraged to use intensity by making age-appropriate use of movement, high-energy activities, and music. While the focus of this work is getting children more physically active, the active classroom learning activities are a great example of ways to bring intensity to your classroom (see Martin & Murtagh, 2015, for sample lessons). Furthermore, teachers should focus on selecting lively learning materials (the main characters ran and jumped rather than sat and rested). We are optimistic that this conversation will continue, and gap-closing solutions will emerge as educators work to see and develop talents in all children (Boykin & Noguera, 2011).

■ ■ Engaging the Mind ★ Taking Action ★ Inspiring Excellence
Incorporating Verve

Small Group Exercise: In a group of eight to ten educators, each participant receives an index card. Ask participants to write a clear, brief description of two activities or assignments that they gave last week on their index card. Once everyone has finished writing, have people pass the index cards to the person on their right (continue passing four times). Participants then write three different ways that students could demonstrate the same (or similar) competency on the index card that they have received. Allow ten minutes to jot down ideas. Each participant shares with the group by explaining what activities they received and then their ideas. NOTE: Consider multiple entry points, multiple formats, and multiple demonstrations of expertise for this exercise. Finally, discuss the challenges with implementing the ideas generated in the same lesson/class session (i.e., choice or activity alternation) and possible solutions.

Reflection Exercise 1: Ask teachers to think about their students' behavioral displays and write as many examples as they can recall of their vervistic expressions (preferences for variability, intensity, or density). How can they connect these behavioral displays with learning activities? How do they typically respond to these behaviors? What resources do they need to improve how they use psychological verve in your classroom?

Reflection Exercise 2: Have teachers consider how to gather information on students' preferences at the beginning of the semester. What type of information would they want? What are creative ways of getting students to assist with gathering and sharing the data? How can teachers use the information that is gathered about the students' interests, preferences, and proclivities? Ask teachers to be specific about how they will use each piece of data so that they can hone tools and maximize time and efforts. Possible types of information to gather: favorite game(s), favorite sports or musical artist(s), preferred learning exercises, favorite social media platform(s), and things that enhance motivation (what makes them work hard).

One of the gifts of this project is that White women teachers get to go on figurative tours of schools guided by Black men teachers who can be straightforward and honest with them. We can't always do this among colleagues, but in this book, we are able to hear voices that are uncensored and open to share. In this chapter, two seasoned Black male educators describe a typical moment in an elementary school classroom and share with the reader how this relatively normal scene does harm to Black boys. The authors challenge readers to question some of the "commonsense" ideas they might have about where Black boys belong in the classroom, particularly when they are acting up. In light of the previous chapter by Dr. Darla Scott, readers might simultaneously challenge themselves to consider whether "acting up" could signify a child's propensity for verve that needs to be accommodated differently by the teacher. Reading this chapter gives readers a chance to build new common sense for the classroom.

CHAPTER 13

The Visit

Justin Coles and Chezare A. Warren

Justin, a black man from the western suburbs of Philadelphia, and his colleague, a black woman from Brooklyn named Janine, boarded a charter bus one brisk morning in late March with a group of preservice teachers. Upon arrival in Chicago, Justin and Janine reviewed the itinerary, which consisted of a variety of school visits. The first stop was an elementary school in the Hyde Park neighborhood, a racially diverse, solidly middle-class community on Chicago's south side. Toward the end of the visit, the group was elated to visit the third-grade classroom of a teacher who had graduated from their university's teacher education program. Ms. Williams (pseudonym) was eager for Justin's group of undergraduates to visit her classroom, considering she had been in their shoes just a few years earlier.

Upon entering the classroom, Justin thanked the young teacher for her willingness to host the group of eager preservice teachers. Just then, Janine tapped Justin on the shoulder. As Justin turned in Janine's direction, he immediately noticed that most of the black boys in the room were seated at their own separate desks on the margins of the classroom. The other students in the class looked to be working cooperatively on a math project, but these boys were lined up against a wall, working alone. Justin, a little befuddled, made eye contact with Janine, who was equally perplexed by the seating arrangement. They were growing impatient. The visual isolation of these boys was startling to Justin, the only black man in a room full of white women who hoped to be standing in this teacher's place one day.

From the looks on the young men's faces, Justin imagined the implicit and explicit messages they were receiving about their worthiness to be included in the class. This was happening in a context where historically, black people have never been viewed as fully human in the public imagination. Black people were involuntarily transported to the Americas as the property of white settlers, colonists whose only intention was to exploit black people's labor to drive agronomic productivity. In that moment, Justin contemplated the implications of antiblackness (Dumas, 2016) four hundred years after slavery for the ways it might explain how this classroom might be a site of black suffering and how segregation from their peers was a form of symbolic violence (Bourdieu, 2001).

"Are you OK?" asked Janine. "Yeah." responded Justin. He composed himself enough to inquire about the practice, hoping that the teacher would offer him a logical reason for her decision to isolate these black boys from the rest of the class. Eager to answer his question, Ms. Williams explained that these boys were referred to as "islanders". She went on to cite the effectiveness of this classroom management strategy to neutralize "bad" classroom behavior. Justin's mind was racing. "They just could not behave themselves." she lamented. "They were consistently unfocused while grouped with other students." The result was to sequester them to their own "island." Just then, Janine exclaimed, "Alright everyone the bus is here!" The group scuttled out of the room just as quickly as they had entered it.

THE DISCUSSION

Readers may be thinking that something as small as a seating assignment decision intended to keep students "focused" could never be harmful. The danger is in the commonsense thinking of this practice. Ms. Williams rationalized the need for black boys to be isolated from the group because they "could not behave." In other words, they failed to talk or sit or comport themselves in a way that was palatable or acceptable to the teacher. The result of their violation was being isolated: relegating their physical bodies to the periphery of the teaching and learning epicenter. Similar classroom scenarios are viewed as completely normal or appropriate in a society with an incredibly long history of racial subjugation for its non-white residents.

Disciplinary practices similar to the "islanders" take on new meaning when its utility is examined from the perspective of antiblackness. Antiblackness is the rendering of black flesh as disposable, broken, or in need of fixing, and it positions black people as not fully human in the public imagination. In a *Washington Post* article, Tunette Powell (2014) wrote about the ways black boys are criminalized in schools. "My son has been suspended 5 times. He's 3," she said, explaining that her preschool black boy had been suspended for throwing a chair that did not hit anyone.

While the behaviors of her child may have been wrong, she said, the consequences were inequitably distributed, developmentally inappropriate, and unnecessarily harsh. While at a birthday party for her son's classmate, Tunette recounted to other (white) mothers her son's suspension record. The other mothers were shocked. They could not comprehend why her son had been suspended when their own children had engaged in similar or worse behaviors without having been suspended at all. For example, one mother noted that her son intentionally threw an object at a child, who was rushed to the hospital as a result. She simply received a phone call from the school. No suspension was given to her son.

Examples like this one beg the question of why black boys are treated much more harshly or much more negatively than their non-black counterparts. This question sits at the core of our concern over the repercussions of antiblackness as a broader social construction and over the antiblack imaginations that guide or frame white teachers' classroom interactions with black male students. There are numerous examples of the ways that black men and boys get perceived as animalistic, deviant, and anti-intellectual in American society (Entman & Rojecki, 2001; Waytz, Hoffman, & Trawalter, 2015). Schools are institutions of socialization: young people learn how to interact socially with one another and other individuals in the world based on the interactions they are having in school. Students' assignment of worth and value for themselves and others who are culturally different is largely influenced by their experiences in school. Putting black boys on an "island" correlates to a larger societal tendency to *other* them, to position them as inherently deviant, which does nothing to avoid reifying an antiblack sentiment in the psyche of young people and adults who socialize with them. In this chapter, we admonish white women teachers to critically examine the implications of commonsense practices like this that only establish and maintain a silently assaultive school environment for young black men and boys.

The second author, Chezare, once interviewed a group of black boys at the request of school administrators to gather insight about why they were being disciplined and suspended at such high rates. He learned that these boys were not acting "bad" because of one isolated incident or interaction with a teacher or because they were "boys being boys." Their behavior was directly associated with perceptions about how others were viewing them in school. They consistently felt under duress. Simply walking down the hallway felt assaultive/disorienting/alienating/off-putting/disconcerting for these middle-school boys. They told stories about how they were treated in kindergarten, first grade, and all the way throughout the elementary and middle grades. Their stories suggest they, too, had been islanders, marginalized and perpetually held in contempt by school actors for "bad" behavior. Such disciplinary practices only added to their mistrust of the educational institution and the authority figures who are paid to inspire and nurture their intellectual development.

Because schools are a social institution—a microcosm of social interactions in society—it makes sense that black boys are punished when their behavior is not fully assimilated to standards of whiteness.[1] This is because black people, like the many young black men who have unlawfully lost their lives in confrontations with police, are punished when they don't concede to demands by authority. Another example is a study (Neal, McCray, Webb-Johnson, & Bridgest, 2003) that examined the movement/walking styles of African American males in comparison with European American males and how teachers evaluated students' academic capacities based on those movements. The teachers participating in the study perceived the males who walked in African American movement styles as "lower in achievement, higher in aggression, and more likely to need special education services than students with standard movement styles" (Neal et al., p. 49). Other research documents disproportionality in exclusionary discipline for black boys (Henry & Warren, 2017; Howard, 2008; Noguera, 2003). Practices like the islanders are antiblack. They reiterate the message to black youth that they deserve to be pushed out to the margins when their behaviors do not conform to the dominant social and cultural norms in the academic space, which tend to be norms most favorable to white cultural preferences (Howard, 2014).

This is especially true when such practices are enacted by white female teachers. Historically, white women are not the architects of white supremacy, but they are indeed propagators of white supremacist logic(s). This is logic that defends and validates the steady surveillance, control, and punishment of black bodies. It is doubtful that being sent to the island does anything to intrinsically motivate these young men to act "good." It is a physical display of the teacher's power to manage and manipulate black bodies, such that black youth are made fearful of authority and thus compelled to submit to the teacher's desires. Our argument here is that such a practice strips young people of their dignity. All human beings, especially those whose cultural heritage reflects centuries of racial subordination, should be treated with much care and concern. This means making extra effort to develop culturally responsive disciplinary practices that remind students of the high expectations a teacher has for them, while also affirming they are indeed capable of meeting those high expectations. Antiblack disciplinary practices like the islanders do little to communicate a young person's worth—to them or their classmates. Nor does this act effectively reconcile a young person's offense such that they are motivated not to repeat whatever they did to "warrant" such an action in the first place.

---

[1] By standards of whiteness, we mean the ways of talking, behaving, thinking, and being that are viewed as most preferred and acceptable by white people or white cultural norms.

Ms. Williams could have asked herself a litany of questions before reimagining these boys as islanders. Being an islander strips them of their identities as full citizens of the classroom, deserving of every single right and privilege of every student member of the classroom community. This is the essence of antiblackness. Here are some of the questions teachers might ask themselves to determine how their classroom might be assaultive to young black men and boys:

- What are the long-term consequences for black boys, as different and completely separate from other groups of youth, who spend an entire year in isolation (on their own island)? Do I have practices like these that separate my black boy students from the rest of the class?

- How does this practice enable these boys to cultivate positive attitudes toward schooling?

- What do I know about their interests and their motivations to behave in the ways they have chosen to behave in my classroom?

- What am I doing to celebrate the contributions my black boy students make to the classroom environment? How am I regularly affirming them?

- [After looking at school-wide data trends] What do I know about how black (male) students are generally viewed in my school? What am I doing in my classroom to oppose disproportionality in discipline?

These questions are intended to initiate the process of empathy's application (Warren, 2014; Warren & Lessner, 2014) and care for black male youth (Jackson, Sealey-Ruiz, & Watson, 2014; Watson, Sealey-Ruiz, & Jackson, 2014), such that teachers are aware of myriad perspectives needed to disrupt the maintenance of (symbolically) violent classroom spaces. Questions like these, and other professional discourses of race in a school are needed to (re)humanize teacher interactions with young black men and boys.

This book often refers to the "narratives" of Black boys that exist in media, schools, our heads, and often, even in the minds and hearts of Black boys. We sometimes refer to this as the "Black boy box," the narrow space of stereotype and expectation that traps Black boys into being more of a stereotype and less of themselves. The following two chapters offer strategies for rewriting the narrative that gets told about Black boys— rewriting it for the collective, but also with the individual. The intervening vignette gives more historical context to both the Black boy box, and the White woman box and why those raced and gendered identities have been so polarized. Readers of The Guide want to make a difference in the lives of Black boys. This section is designed to continue that process and offers both reflective and specific ideas for possible growth.

The following chapter by Toni Williamson could be forty pages long. In preparation for writing this chapter, she told us story after story of Black boys with whom she rewrote the narrative of how people thought about him and how he thought about himself. She is a seasoned educator, who specializes in helping Black boys see in themselves what they—and many others—do not.

CHAPTER 14

Rewriting the Narrative

Toni Graves Williamson

I remember getting my class list at the start of my first year teaching: twenty-four names of students who would walk into my fifth-grade classroom in a week. I carefully wrote their names on sentence strips for their desks and cubbies. Heather, Anthony, Dwight, Aniya, Keith, Steven, Mia, Ann, Deidra . . . . So far, just names, but pretty soon the seats would fill. As I contemplated whether to put the desks in small groups or have everyone facing the board, the fourth-grade teacher, Mrs. Green, came into my room and pointed to a desk. "I had her last year. Good kid, never does her homework, but always behaves." I started creating my bulletin board about the scientific process, only half listening.

"Oh, you have Bradley! Lucky you! He wasn't in my class; more experienced teachers get the gifted kids." I tried to wrap my brain around that uncomfortable fact.

Stopping in front of Dwight's name, she gasped, "Oh, my goodness! You have Dwight!" And then she said what all Southerners say when they want to make themselves feel better about the next thing that comes from their mouth: "Bless your heart." I looked up from my very bad drawing of a telescope and braced myself for whatever my heart needed a blessing for. She moved closer and said in a stage whisper, "Dwight was in my class last year. I would have held him back, but he has already been held back. He was one of my lowest-performing students. His skills aren't even on a third-grade level. And I could have dealt with that, but his attitude is terrible. Nothing helps! I met with his mother several times, but she has a lot on her hands with his other siblings. I really struggled with his refusal to do any of his work."

She worked her way around the room and gave me suggestions about who shouldn't sit together and who should sit near the front of the room. She even suggested that I should sit Dwight on the side of the room closest to my desk, not in a group. "If anything, you shouldn't put him next to Antonio. They are like oil and water."

I didn't hear much after that. I didn't know how to feel. At first, I had been so excited about my new students, but she had changed that mood. In that moment, though, I made up my mind to help rewrite the story that this kid—who had only been on the Earth a little over a decade—already had about who he was and who he wasn't. So I thanked her but didn't give her my soapbox speech about how I was going to prove her wrong.

When Dwight entered my classroom, I did treat him differently. I sat him in the group that was in the front next to me—not because I was worried that he was going to get in trouble but because I was going to love **on** him as much as I could. I made sure that I asked him to help me pass out pencils. I called on him to create groups when it was time to line up to go outside. I let him join the group that helped me design our classroom reading nook. I was determined not to avoid having his story influence my expectations of working with Dwight. As a matter of fact, I *wanted* it to influence me. But instead of influencing me to treat him differently in a negative way, I was going to do everything in my power to help him rewrite his story.

My first year of teaching was not an easy one. I had to figure out how to hold my bladder all day, how to have an effective parent/teacher conference, how to eat lunch in thirteen minutes, and how to use a grade book. I won't pretend that my time with Dwight was perfect. We struggled sometimes. He gave me attitude, he didn't always have his work done, and he fought with Antonio. What I did do that was most important was I worked to build a solid relationship with him so that when he got into trouble he knew that I loved him. I held him to the highest standards and didn't accept work that I didn't think was done to the best of his ability. Dr. James Comer's book, *Leave No Child Behind* says, "No significant learning occurs without a significant relationship." So even the day Dwight got so mad at me that he ripped all the papers off the wall on his way to the bathroom, he returned to the room ready to make amends. Over the course of the year, I also realized that his cognitive abilities did not line up with his performance. When we talked about what happened in a book or when I sat with him to do his math, he spoke confidently about what he had read and explained the problems to me almost poetically.

At the end of the year, Dwight's mother and I discussed his going to a different school for middle school. I had heard about a community school that was tuition-free and specifically designed to help boys of color who weren't performing to state standards. I had met some of the high school students from the school at a conference and had been impressed. I thought this would be the perfect place for Dwight. The school year ended; Dwight wore a purple suit to fifth-grade graduation. His mom told me that he had been accepted into the school. And then I didn't hear from them again.

When I sat down to write this chapter, I decided I would do a Google search for Dwight to see if I could find where life took him, now almost twenty years later. In minutes, I found him. He was in prison. I was disappointed but remembered the words of social justice activist Bryan Stevenson (2014):

> . . . (E)ach of us is more than the worst thing we've ever done . . . if someone tells a lie, that person is not *just* a liar. If you take something that doesn't belong to you, you are not *just* a thief. Even if you kill someone, you are not *just* a killer . . . When you experience mercy, you learn things that are hard to learn otherwise. You see things you can't otherwise see; you hear things you can't otherwise hear. You begin to recognize the humanity that resides in each of us. (p. 290)

Dwight's crime was armed robbery, and he was serving a six-year sentence. But I knew Dwight. I could see him putting away the pencil cases at the end of the day. I could feel him hug me on the last day of school. I could see his big smile when he realized that he passed his end-of-grade tests. So I had to write him.

In the letter, I told him about where my life had taken me as an educator. I told him that I was writing this chapter. I told him that despite the things he did wrong, I felt no judgment. I signed the letter, "Ms. Williamson," a name that I hadn't used since that first year of teaching, since students in my new school call me by my first name. But I knew that to Dwight, I was Ms. Williamson and he was the kid in the purple suit.

A few weeks later, I received a letter back. In perfect penmanship, he thanked me for reaching out to him. He told me how much of a difference I had made in his life. He explained to me that he had caught up with his right grade while at the community school. "Somehow school just started to click for me." He talked about the importance of the foundation that he had built in my class and at that school. He told me of the mistakes that had landed him in prison and his vision of a new life once he got out. Through my tears, I saw that he had included two more pieces of paper. One was a poem that he had written about having a new start and the other were his scores on his GED. In small writing beneath the scores he wrote, "I didn't do as well on the math because I ran out of time, but my reading scores were the highest in my group!"

The next day, I showed a good friend the letter. She said, "That must really make your day."

I told her, "No, that just made my career." For all of those black boys who had entered my life after Dwight—for all those times I had refused to accept the narrative that was given to me about them—I knew that the work I put into holding them to high standards and building solid relationships had been worth it. Perhaps their stories weren't quite like Dwight's but there was the possibility that I had helped them reshape their image so that others could see beyond stereotypes. I have had black boys in my classes since that year and have had people speak the same way that Mrs. Green spoke about Dwight. I've heard things like, "He gets in his own way." "He needs to be on a short leash." "Good luck with him." "His parents are not in partnership with our school." "Typical story of an athlete at this school." And I wish all of those who made these statements could meet my nephew, who is a big football player but has a sweet spirit and even at eighteen loves when I play with his ears. Or I wish they could know my other nephew, who when he lived with me would ask for help with his homework even if he didn't need it because he wanted the attention. And I wish that they could all meet Dwight, who made sure all the pencil cases were put away and who wore his purple suit to graduation.

When Mrs. Green entered my classroom all those years ago, she didn't just want to tell me about my new students, she wanted me to engage with her. She wanted to lure me into a conversation much like the conversations that I have heard all too often. People love gossip, and Mrs. Green would have loved to continue our year together hearing all about how Dwight and the other kids were doing in my class. After two decades of experience in the classroom, I have learned that we discuss quite a bit around the copier and on the sidelines of the playground. Sometimes the conversation is about the latest episode of *Survivor*, but more often it is about the students we teach. I started paying attention to how often the information that we shared about the black boys we teach was negative. So what if instead of spreading negative gossip, I started being intentional about sharing *positive* gossip? Instead of saying, Sam got in trouble again for wearing his pants too low, I'd say "Sam stayed after school and helped me to organize all of the handouts for my workshop." Instead of saying, "Sudan was late again!" I would say, "Sudan led an activity in the Black Student Union yesterday that had all the kids talking!" I am intentional about using positive words to paint a picture that rewrites the narrative that other teachers have of the black boys that we teach.

Each year, I choose three to four students to help me lead diversity facilitator training. I always make sure that at least one black boy is on that team. On purpose, I choose the black boys that are the "unlikely story" of someone who would be taking a risk to lead large numbers of students both in and out of school.

Recently, I reunited with a former student who is now in college. He remembered that I had put him in the lead role for his affinity group. I never asked him; I told him that he would be good at it. He said to me that although he was nervous, he did it because I told him that he could. I didn't sit down and have a long conversation with him—I just told him a fact. You can do this, so he did. Now he continues to lead the LGBTQ affinity group in college.

Rewriting the narrative for black boys starts with teachers telling themselves a different story about themselves and then giving them the support that they need to live up to those stories. Spreading these stories among other educators is not enough, though. It is important to tell the boys these stories, too. Teachers must tell black boys they are valued and smart and thoughtful and loving. When teachers tell these stories to themselves, their peers, and their boys, then eventually everyone will believe what was always true.

■ ■ Engaging the Mind ★ Taking Action ★ Inspiring Excellence
Spread Some Gossip

Spread some gossip! Look at a list of your students. For every black boy, think of a positive story that you can share about each of them. Tell three of your colleagues, the student's parents, and the student himself.

These do not have to be long and complicated stories. They can be snapshots. Here are some examples:

He turned in his homework three nights in a row.

He held the door open for the entire class when it was cold out at recess.

He remembered to take his hat off without being asked.

He asked if he could help me when I was carrying something from my car.

He contributed thoughtfully while doing group work.

He sat near me in the assembly instead of near his friends.

With two or three of your colleagues, read and discuss Robert Ferguson's article, "Helping Students of Color Meet High Standards, from Mica Pollock's book, *Everyday Anti-racism (2008)*.

The following vignette by Olugbala Williams helps us contextualize this conversation about Black boy narratives and White women narratives. These narratives are not new; they are as old as the notion of race itself.

Vignette: Slavery's Archetypes Affect White Women Teachers

Olugbala Williams

Power and politics in the United States are defined by institutions' influence and control over people's lives (including prisons, banks, and schools). These social constructs have historical and metaphorical antecedents rooted in the slave plantation, and they continue to condition American minds. White women overwhelmingly manage America's classrooms, raising the question of how they teach African American boys.

American slavery's archetypes and symbols, vile and reprehensible, have left a faint but recognizable imprint upon these teachers' mindsets. Due to segregation, racism, and poor teaching, African American students perform poorly in our schools.

American slavery, one of the most horrific crimes in human history, was sustained and made possible by lies (some would say myths), the central lie being that Africans are not humans, thus deserving of enslavement and its cruel debasement. From these myths come four major tropes that speak directly to a hierarchical society whose repugnant remnants lay strewn about our modern landscape.

According to Eldridge Cleaver (1968), if the United States is viewed allegorically as a human body, the white man is the brain, and the black man is the body. Four archetypes complete this metaphor, which come straight from the slave plantation.

The first is the Omnipotent Administrator, personified by the white man, the director who makes the rules and fosters the all-powerful status quo. He knows what is best for society and all its denizens and citizens. The white man is the brain that determines life circumstances for everyone, regardless of dissent or agreement. To assert and prove this role, the Omnipotent Administrator sets up a false competition system where life is rigged in his favor.

The second is the Hyper-masculine Menial Worker, personified by the black man and brutally strong, wild, and physical. The Menial Worker must be harnessed or subdued like any other wild animal. The black man is treated like a wild animal who is capable only of physical strength and adeptness and is devoid of cognitive ability. He lacks intelligence and is a buffoon who needs the direction of the Omnipotent Administrator, without which the Menial Worker would be lost, or more acutely, left uncivilized. Cleaver posits that the only thinking the black man does is enough to carry out the will of the white man.

The third archetype is the Beauty Queen, personified by the white woman, who is the Omnipotent Administrator's lesser counterpart. She is pristine, porcelain, and virtuous. The white woman is the acme of white beauty and because of racism, the standard of beauty imposed upon the world. She is a medal or prize that symbolically affirms the dominance of white supremacy.

The last archetype posited by Cleaver is the self-reliant Amazon, personified by the black woman: sexual, strong physically and spiritually, overtly motherly (for example, Aunt Jemima) and, because she has African features, ugly. The black woman is hard and perpetually angry. She also affirms the low status of black men since she is his woman. These lies affect our lives today, playing out in mass media, showing up on the movie screen, and directing what and how we teach our children.

The United States, the system writ large, seems to want African American boys to be, at best, low-level workers and, at worst, slaves (as in the prison labor system). One can look at the disproportionate number of African American men in prisons for verification. The white woman, in her attempt to move beyond being merely a symbol, has aped the white man and accepted the trope of African American boys as wild, unruly, and in need of strict control. For verification of this, see the disproportionate number of African American boys suspended and expelled in our public schools or branded as a "superpredator." To be fair, many white female teachers are not explicitly racist, but their pedagogy may remain informed by a script that says, in many different ways, that African American boys are a lost cause. The result is implicitly racist behavior.

Racism is a two-way street, affecting all participants: the oppressed and the oppressors. White women teachers belong to the oppressors class, not only because of white privilege, but also because their education reinforces behavior that treats black boys as disruptive, menial, or criminals. Many people may be well-intentioned, but sadly, mentalities inform actions. Too many white teachers see their students as failures and simply tolerate them because they have low expectations of a future criminal. And those white teachers who are invested and want to act morally forget to strengthen African American children by respecting their ancestry and culture and learning about their heroes and heroines. Last, these teachers could begin to dismantle institutional racism in schools by telling the truth about history and revealing how many historical "heroes" are actually monsters, not worthy of adulation.

Moreover, investing in these actions would help not only African American children, but all children, and it would help these teachers regain a large part of their humanity by recognizing the humanity in (someone deemed a predator or a body) all others.

As these archetypes demonstrate, Whiteness and Blackness have always been defined in opposition to each other. One does not exist without the other—historically they have been mutually defining: what is not Black is White; what is not White is Black. They are two ends of the racial spectrum. Historically, Whiteness, White people, and White spaces have been framed in association with goodness, safety, and intelligence. Blackness, in contrast, has been historically framed in association with badness, danger, and ignorance. White women have been constructed as virginal, innocent, fragile, and in need of protection against Black men. Black men have been constructed as aggressive, hypermasculine, hypersexual, violent, unintelligent, and particularly threatening to White women. White women's safety has historically been the justification for the control and oppression of Black men. To build a relationship between White women and Black boys requires an awareness and a refusal of this ubiquitous framing. This is the underlying thread of the narratives that Toni Williamson was battling with her Black boy students, and Dr. Sharoni Little confronts the same thread of the systemic narrative in the following chapter.

CHAPTER 15

"Don't Lean—*Jump* In"

The Fierce Urgency to Confront, Dismantle, and (Re)write the Historical Narrative of Black Boys in Educational Institutions

Sharoni Little

In many schools throughout the country, Black boys are "learning" under a perpetual state of surveillance or hypervisibility.[1] Fueled by a pathological narrative maintaining their inferiority and deficiency, many Black boys languish in schools that undermine their intellectual brilliance and curiosity, ignore and devalue their

---

[1] I argue this reality can be understood using Foucault's notion of the panopticon as a practical metaphor for explaining how social control and power are maintained. In his work on social disciplinary practices, Foucault demonstrated the hegemonic strategy of control through *perpetual surveillance* (Little, 2005). The panopticon is a prison tower where the imprisoned are constantly seen but cannot see if and when they are being guarded. Foucault (1979) contended that: "The major effect of the Panopticon: [Is] to induce in the inmate a state of conscious and permanent visibility that assures the automatic functioning of power. So to arrange things that the surveillance is permanent in its effect, even if it is discontinuous in its action; that the perfection of power should tend to render its actual exercise unnecessary" (p. 206).

cultural contributions, and instill doubt and anxiety. Studies show that such learning environments impact Black boys' self-esteem, self-efficacy, and overall learning outcomes and contribute to their disproportionate suspension, expulsion, and drop-out rates (Steele & Aronson, 1995, 1998).

As teachers, administrators, and educational institutions seek to address these disparities and create an affirming and inclusive learning environment, there must be, as Dr. Martin Luther King, Jr. (1967) declared, a "fierce urgency" to confront, dismantle, and rewrite the educational narrative that has historically plagued Black boys. This chapter examines the institutional mission, policies, practices, and organizational culture of schools and provides various institutional strategies to ensure the educational and personal success of Black boys.

Leon's Lessons?

Leon,[2] a bright, creative, and confident high school senior, has had an educational journey filled with academic curiosity, personal growth, and a passion for business and entrepreneurship. Throughout high school, Leon has participated in several leadership, mentoring, professional, and civic engagement programs. Leon serves as president of his school's entrepreneur club, is a member of the school band, and was elected to the state honor band. In sports, Leon has also been a member of the basketball team and is the first and only Black varsity golfer in his school's nearly seventy-year history.

Pursuing his passion for cars and entrepreneurship, Leon attended a Business Leadership Institute for young men of color, where he learned business fundamentals and devised a business plan that earned him a first-place award and the opportunity to serve as a peer mentor. Committed to enhancing his automotive design, drawing, and technical skills, Leon, the youngest student in his classes, successfully completed courses at a prestigious, world-renowned design college.

In addition to his traditional and entrepreneurial studies, Leon serves as a leader in his community. He is a member of a national youth program that teaches civic engagement and community advocacy, and he has worked as a summer writing mentor and instructor for writing and digital story-telling camps for fourth-to-sixth graders. Leon has also competed and won regionally in the NAACP, ACT-SO program in entrepreneurship and drawing, and he completed 345 hours of community service, earning him a Presidential Service Award.

Fueled by his passion for cars and his professional goal of becoming an automotive designer and manufacturer, Leon's tenacity, leadership, and fortitude has afforded

---

[2] "Leon" is a pseudonym to protect the student's privacy.

him many wonderful opportunities. To gain global knowledge and experience, Leon took on a new and exciting challenge to study abroad during his junior year of high school. While many of Leon's teachers affirmed his gregarious, good-natured, and self-assured manner, he also experienced unwarranted scrutiny and critique by a couple of teachers, who appeared uncomfortable and threatened by his presence and steadfast confidence.

> Leon is smart and has a sharp eye. His sensitivity for fine materials and harmonious color choice come out in his comments in class and even in the accessories he wears. Ironically, his gift for visual thinking may play a part in his awkward relationship with certain aspects of ancient theory. [It] requires analytical thought, background reading and rethinking first impressions.

This written commentary, an excerpt from Leon's first-quarter performance assessment by his teacher, exemplifies marginalizing, intellectual stereotypes, and deficit teacher expectations that often construct many Black boys in schools as unintelligent and nonanalytical. In her seminal book, *Other People's Children: Cultural Conflict in the Classroom*, noted scholar Lisa Delpit (1995) examines how the presumed deficits and pathologies of historically marginalized, racialized, and underrepresented students are intentionally and falsely promoted to explain social and educational disparities. Because of deficit thinking, these demeaning narratives assert students' supposed lack of motivation and discipline, as well as their cultural and family depravity and their limited intelligence. Deficit lenses prevent a more truthful, humane, and familial view, causing some students to be viewed as "other people's children," denying them the empathy, compassion, and care people would have for their own children or those whom they value.

From the onset of the academic year, Leon's teacher concluded that he, the only Black male, and only Black student in the class, lacked the critical thinking and overall intellectual acumen to understand the subject matter but was gifted "creatively," especially in his clothing and accessories decisions. Driven by her belief that Leon's "deficiencies" warranted additional academic support, his teacher's insistence eventually had an adverse academic and emotional impact. While some of Leon's academic habits and outcomes were the result of his need to improve his study skills, the teacher failed to understand how her low expectations and lack of support might influence his overall learning experience and outcomes. As with many Black boys who face such attacks on their intellect, integrity, or character, the teacher's actions would ultimately push Leon to demonstrate his intellectual fortitude and resilience, while exposing insidious entrenched racial and gender stereotypes, microaggressions, implicit bias, and perpetual surveillance on her part.

Determined that regularly meeting with Leon was the best way to address his apparent learning challenges, his teacher began scheduling conferences during his break time without conferring with him. After Leon could not make one of the meetings she had scheduled due to his own prior arrangements, his teacher became incensed and would later enlist the support of administrators to reify her assumptions and behavior.

In an email sent to administrators (and later shared with his parents), Leon's teacher wrote:

> As you know, he left school a moment after I invited him to join me for our most recent meeting (Nov. 3) and kept me waiting the entire period. He has not discussed this inappropriate behavior with me yet. While this episode is a minor issue, I'm more concerned about his struggle to take responsibility for his learning and to accept the help he needs to improve his academic performance.

Elevating this now very contentious situation, some administrators reinforced the teacher's behavior, ignored and diminished Leon's agency, and became an ardent defender of their white female colleague. Ignoring Leon's student status and the inherent power imbalance, he was "adultified" and blamed for his "avoidance" and "lack of accountability," as illustrated in an email he received from an administrator:

> We were particularly concerned with your failure during second period this morning to meet your teacher after she sought you out for your scheduled extra-help session. You told her that you would get your materials and be right back. Then, you left the school and never returned to the classroom. You had an explanation for your absence, but you did not share it with her because you rightly understood that she was upset with you. This example served as a great representation of the avoidance behavior you have exhibited in many of your classes. Leon, we want you to more specifically take ownership for your academics and respond by taking advantage of extra-help opportunities offered by your teachers, particularly when you do not understand the material at hand.

Shaped by an antagonistic racist and sexist lens fortifying their implicit bias, the teacher and supporting administrators perceived Leon as a disinterested, irresponsible, and educationally challenged student. Concerned about the emotional and academic impact this situation was having on Leon, his parents spoke with the teacher regarding their concerns and agreed that *Leon* would initiate requests for support, if needed. Clearly angered by this decision, Leon's teacher, who vehemently professed that her actions were merely in his "best interest," continued to convey coy messages littered with deficit sentiments, couched in a patronizing, "I'm just trying to help him" tone:

During the second half of the term, I no longer pursued the weekly meetings I had solicited in the first two months of school in agreement with his mother; Leon is able to take full responsibility for his work and communication. It is worrisome that he has difficulties retaining knowledge. For the second half of this term, I remain available to meet with Leon and encourage him to reconsider his study skills, habits, and time management so he can activate his potential.

His final oral presentation earned a 68%, much higher than his written work, but falling short of gathering visual evidence in support of a logical and overarching argument. I imagine Leon has had little to no practice thinking or writing like this before, especially in regard to visual material. Despite his lackluster performance, I am confident that his natural eye and sensitivity will be his allies in the second term. I am available to meet with him by appointment, as always.

Ignoring how her demeaning and often contradictory communication and behavior might impact Leon's self-efficacy, academic motivation, and performance, his teacher failed him on multiple levels. Despite this onslaught of personal and academic slights, Leon reached out to his teacher regarding a drastically lower participation grade he received although he felt he continued to remain engaged during class. In a personal and contradictory email to Leon, his teacher insinuated that he might have an inability to "concentrate":

> I'd be happy to talk with you about all your work and help you get on track. Your participation grade is low because your participation is sometimes rowdy and distracted. Today, for example, it looked like you were dozing off in class. I wonder if you find it hard to concentrate. What has your experience been?

Lacking training or credentials in school or educational psychology, his teacher proceeded to diagnose Leon and to ask him to substantiate her claim. In addition, her use of "sometimes rowdy" to describe his participation was not only contradictory to her "dozing" reference, but rhetorically constructed him using a menacing and threatening lens, often used to reify entrenched violent tropes about Black males. This teacher's behavior and unyielding negative focus on Leon actually led to what she later called a grading "mistake" that resulted in Leon receiving a failing quarter grade. This left him devastated and demoralized until it was corrected due to what she stated was an "unintentional technical mistake."

Despite this year-long assault on his humanity, intellectual curiosity, and emotional stability, Leon continued to thrive and receive a passing grade. Sadly, the teacher and administrators were surprised, asking him during a meeting the last week of class, "Why did you continue to work hard when it would have been easier to just give up?" Ironically, if these "educators" had recognized, honored, and leveraged Leon's tenacity and intellectual brilliance from the onset, his experience would have been more personally and academically rewarding.

INSTITUTIONAL LESSONS

Leon's academic experience and his teacher's egregious behavior are unfortunately not anomalous for many Black boys in schools. While the continuum of experiences ranges from various microaggressions to expulsion, Black boys continue to confront racist and sexist stereotypes and oppression in a place that should be safe and affirming—schools. As demonstrated in Leon's story, educators and institutions must confront, dismantle, and rewrite the dominant narrative about Black boys.

From preschool to college, a prevailing national narrative contends that Black boys and young men are difficult to teach, deviant, undisciplined, unintelligent, and problematic. Consistent with deficit-based narratives, Black boys are often associated with negative traits such as lazy, disengaged, nonattentive, lacking focus and motivation, disruptive, confrontational, and threatening. Conversely, Black boys are not often considered thoughtful, analytical, creative, determined, smart, collaborative, respectful, and hard-working.

■ ■ Engaging the Mind ★ Taking Action ★ Inspiring Excellence
Gauging and Changing Your Institutional Narrative

To gauge a school's current institutional narrative about Black boys, educators and administrators should engage in an analytical and reflective exercise to assess the prevailing culture and climate and to reveal implicit/explicit bias and marginalizing teacher expectations and perspectives. In small cross-functional institutional teams, conversations might discuss the following questions:

• What is the primary institutional narrative about Black boys? What stories are shared and perpetuated about and involving Black boys in this institution?

(Continued)

(Continued)

- Who promotes and reifies the educational narrative about Black boys?

- What is the most common lens by which Black boys are viewed at the institution—asset or deficit? Do teachers and others talk about their brilliance or focus on their brawn?

- Institutionally, is the school's ethos the same for Black boys as it is for all other students? If not, why?

- Are Black boys regularly regarded as intellectual exemplars? Are Black boys asked about their academic interests?

- How do teachers and others affirm Black boys' experiences, culture, history, and community in curricular and pedagogical strategies?

These queries allow institutions to honestly and transparently reflect on their perceptions, pedagogy, and behaviors related to Black boys.

To confront and dismantle historically marginalizing, deficit narratives, schools must courageously conduct an in-depth strategic analysis of their institutional practices, communication, and outcomes to determine their inclusivity and overall academic effectiveness related to the educational and personal success of Black boys. Questions can include:

- Are Black boys embodied in the institutional vision, mission, and ethos?

- Are Black boys at the forefront and center of academic objectives, curricula, and pedagogy?

- Are Black boys academically and personally succeeding at your institution? If so, is it because of or despite your institutional practices, beliefs, values, and culture?

- Do Black boys see positive reflections of themselves in the faculty, curricula, and administrators?

- How does the institution *operationalize* equity and inclusion efforts, specifically related to Black boys?

This analysis should inform and guide an honest, transparent, and sustainable institutional strategic plan involving stakeholders across and throughout all levels of the institution to ensure collective buy-in and accountability. Additional strategies include:

1. Confront and dismantle the historical narrative about Black boys and advance an asset narrative that values and leverages their diverse personal, cultural, and intellectual attributes.

2. Evaluate and change institutional systems, practices, and policies that reify the dominant narrative surrounding Black boys.

3. Adopt a racial equity strategy to determine the impact of a deficit narrative on the educational experiences, outcomes, and success of Black boys, while

ensuring transparency, honesty, and accountability.

4. Champion and include the authentic and diverse voices of Black boys to construct a realistic and inclusive narrative that positions them as valued members of the community.

5. Acknowledge the emotional and educational trauma experienced by Black boys when they are subjected to an institution and teachers who engage with them through a deficit lens.

While these efforts are complex and require sustained focus, schools must develop a fierce urgency to confront, dismantle, and rewrite an affirming and authentic narrative of Black boys. Educators and institutions must ensure the personal, social, and academic success of Black boys because their dignity as well as emotional, physical, and intellectual well-being is literally at stake.

The narrative about Black boys is deep and pervasive, and rooted in many people. Psychologists suggest dealing with stereotypes and false narratives like weeds. To grow a successful garden, you must recognize the weeds, pull them out, and then replace them with healthy flowers, fruits, and vegetables. We hope that the preceding chapters have helped you, as readers, to begin to recognize this narrative in your own thoughts and explanations and that the remaining chapters will help you find the seeds of counternarratives, accurate images, and positive visions of Black boys that will grow and flourish in your mind and heart over the next many years.

ANSWER KEY for "What Happened in Black History in the Year . . . " (Chapter 9, p. 96)

5 million B.C.E.—Known as Australopithecines, this is around the time when the first hominids walked, in East and Southern Africa.

30,000 B.C.E.—The first sculpture of a human figure can be traced to this date in Africa. It appears to be the work of Africans of Monomotapa.

2780 B.C.E.—The Egyptian Pyramids date back to this year.

2000 B.C.E.—King Sankhkare Metuhotep III became Pharoah of Egypt.

1400 B.C.E.—Thebes, the capital of Egypt, became the largest city in the world at that time.

1391 B.C.E.—The first university in the world was built in Egypt, the Temple of Wasat

1279 B.C.E.—This was the time of one of Africa's greatest kings—King Ramesses the 2nd

1619—This is the year that most schools begin teaching Black history, when the first enslaved Africans arrived in the North American Colonies. Records show that approximately 20 Africans were purchased for the English settlement of Jamestown from a Dutch ship.

1712—Following a series of revolts by enslaved Africans, Southern plantation owners hired Willie Lynch as a consultant. Lynch suggested the slave owners must divide and conquer the enslaved Africans, who at that point outnumbered Whites on plantations. He suggested that they must convince Africans to hate themselves and to divide against one another, and that if they were successful, such hatred would last for generations.

1863—Abraham Lincoln issued the Emancipation Proclamation, which freed all enslaved people in the Confederate States.

1865—The Thirteenth Amendment, which eliminated slavery, was ratified in this year.

1896—Plessy vs. Ferguson. This historic Supreme Court case, decided on May 18, 1896, was the first major test of the 14th Amendment, which granted African Americans full and equal citizenship under the law. It was in this case that the Court established the legality of "separate but equal," which persisted until 1954 when it was reversed in the case of Brown v. Board of Education.

1920—The 1920's and 30's became known as the Harlem Renaissance a time when Black culture and identity flourished through literature, art, music, and intellectual achievements. On August 26, 1920, the 19th Amendment to the Constitution is ratified giving all women the right to vote. Nonetheless, African American women, like African American men, are denied the franchise in most Southern states.

1926—The famous historian Carter G. Woodson in collaboration with the Association for the Study of Negro Life started the first "Negro History Week" in 1926. This week would go on to become Black History Month which has been celebrated every year since 1976.

1954—In 1954, Plessy v. Ferguson is overruled in the landmark case of *Brown v. Board of Education of Topeka, Kans.* where the Supreme Court unanimously rules that segregation in public schools is unconstitutional.

1963—In 1963, one of the largest civil rights demonstrations occurred during the march on Washington, D.C., where Martin Luther King, Jr. gives his "I Have a Dream" speech. In the same year Martin Luther King, Jr. writes his "Letter from Birmingham Jail," arguing that individuals have a moral duty to disobey unjust laws.

1976—Black History Month grew out of "Negro History Week." Carter G. Woodson and other well-known African Americans started "Negro History Week" in 1926. The month of February was chosen because it is the birthday month of Frederick Douglass and Abraham Lincoln.

1995—In October 1995, hundreds of thousands of black men came to Washington, D.C. for the Million Man March, which was one of the largest demonstrations in the capital's history. The march intended to spark motivation and inspiration among black men to take on a personal responsibility for improving their circumstances. It was also the hope of some organizers that the march would help challenge some of the negative stereotypes that black men face every day in America.

2008—On November 4, with a clear mandate to govern, Barack Obama became America's first Black President. President Obama went on to serve two consecutive terms in office.

RESPECTING

Under the theme of *respecting,* this book aims to show White women teachers the incredible strength and resilience of Black boys, their culture, families, history, hopes, and dreams. Part 1 of *The Guide* asked White women teachers to take a good hard look at themselves, their own histories, cultures, implicit biases, and the stereotypes they may bring to a classroom. This work must be done first. After that, Part 2 asked readers to understand Black boys, in their broad diversity and multiplicity. But once minds are open to understanding self and student, learning to respect Black boys—and the particular constraints that U.S. society puts on them—is essential. The work of cross-racial relationships may be about love, but it is not only about love. It is also about building skills. As Dr. Howard Stevenson has said in public talks, nobody is born knowing how to navigate cross-racial relationships, just like nobody is born knowing the best strategies for teaching math. Being able to build strong relationships with Black boys is a core competency of the work of any teacher, and the chapters in Part 3 were chosen to disrupt and counteract negative stereotypes and narratives that act as barriers to authentic connection.

PART 3

RESPECTING THE BROAD DIVERSITY OF BLACK BOYS' EXPERIENCES AND IDENTITIES

Understanding Black boys' experiences in schools requires that we see their collective identity as Black boys, as well as their many different individual identities. Part 3 was designed to help readers get familiar with who Black boys are, in all their complex intersectionality.

Part 3 starts with a vignette from Jack Hill who, growing up in Baltimore with a single mom, has a story that may fit some of the stereotypical narratives of Black boys. Yet reading his narrative, you can picture him, sitting on the steps of a Baltimore rowhouse, listening to Prince and dreaming his way out of the narrative that society had constructed for him into a story that is more complex and more personal. We hope the stories and chapters in this section will help challenge the common narratives that paint all Black boys with the same brush and, especially, will persuade teachers to create school experiences that have their individual and collective stories in mind. In Chapter 16, the first chapter in this section, Rev. Dr. Jamie Washington describes those limiting narratives and offers ways for teachers to put their arms around the Black boy within and love him through and beyond the narratives so he can become his full self outside of those constraints. Chapter 17 comes from fourth- and fifth-grade teacher David Stills, who writes about the two phrases that scared him the most when he was growing up: Black excellence and White privilege. In Chapter 18, psychologists Drs. Paul Robbins, Leann Smith, and Keisha Bentley-Edwards write about Black racial identity development, which can help teachers orient themselves around what their Black boy students might be going through as they grow up in and try to make sense of a world that judges them harshly because of their Blackness and their boyness. Adrian Chandler's vignette, written from his perspective as a sophomore in high school, demonstrates just how this plays out in the life of a child. Dr. Joseph Derrick Nelson, scholar of Black masculinity in education, writes about strategies for reaching the Black boy learner, in Chapter 19.

In the vignette that follows, Sean Norman shares his experience growing up as a deaf Black boy, who did not know of one successful deaf Black grown man until he went to college. Vignettes like these are crying out to us to find ways to put mirrors in front of our students, to find experiences to which they can connect. In Chapter 20, Dr. Rich Milner, professor of education, writes about why it is not enough to look at a student's economic background without also acknowledging their race. In Chapter 21, Dr. Eddie Moore Jr. addresses the N-word, that ubiquitous word that no middle- or high school teacher can get away with ignoring. But in typical Eddie fashion, he doesn't let readers get away with thinking about the word only as it's written, said, or used as a slur; he insists that we begin to see how the N-word lives in us. This chapter is followed by a vignette from Marguerite W. Penick-Parks, a professor of education, who writes about an early teaching experience in which she was unprepared for a discussion of the N-word. In Chapter 22, college student Zeam Porter, writes about growing up trans and Black, describing the particular struggles that Black trans students face. This is followed by a vignette by Phillipe Cunningham on how teachers can support trans students of color.

Part 3 starts with a vignette from Jack Hill, Dean of Multicultural Education at an elementary school in Denver, Colorado, who writes about growing up in Baltimore City, where the narrative about who he was—and who he was supposed to become—was already written for him. It wasn't a narrative he identified with, or even wanted, but it was almost impossible to escape. What Jack needed was a different model of a Black man, and he found that model in what some people might consider an unlikely place: the artist formerly known as Prince.

Vignette: Prince Taught Me the Redefinition of Black Masculinity

Jack Hill

As a young man, I always enjoyed the pleasures of music. At the time, I never realized how much it was a refuge from Baltimore's unforgiving streets. I was raised by a single mother who often reminded me that I was fortunate to have survived the visceral, and systematic attack on Black-youth culture, the crack-cocaine epidemic, and the intolerant streets that decimated Baltimore City in the 80's.

Being a young Black male in urban America was tough, but growing up fatherless was even worse. And because I had very little guidance, the gender messages I received from my neighborhood and local public school were inextricably linked to systems of power and patriarchy, survival and violence.

I inherited an old-school version of masculinity that taught me vulnerability and emotion were signs of weakness. I was told never to drop the heavy armor of toughness—to live by the street code, to be more than willing to demonstrate my manhood, should threats of violence find me. At twelve years old, I found it unbearable and, at times, exhausting to navigate the school system's institutionalized norms and discursive structures, which framed how I saw myself and the world around me. Little did I know that this would all change one day.

I remember being propped on the steps of an inner-city East Baltimore neighborhood, listening to my cousin's vintage portable Lasonic boom box, cranking Prince's tenth studio album, *Lovesexy.* His spiritual, soul-searching, cathartic sound served as a refuge for so many of us in a world where violence, uncertainty, and hopelessness were reality, and not some social or political construct.

His lyrics pushed me deeper into the corners of my own mind, forcing me to critically confront and think hard about my own identity and the voices of my environment that dictated who the world around me said I was. His lyrics helped me to rewrite my own history and to decipher the negative and positives images that mirrored the many voices and faces in my neighborhood, local church, and barbershop. The first track on *Lovesexy* was the song, *Eye No.*

The formidable lyrics embodied a consummate struggle between good and evil, self-empowerment, and self-degradation. I was fascinated by the songs' dreamlike atmosphere, and I entered a world where I wasn't categorically defined by, or hostage to, my own Blackness or the social context in which I lived.

Prince had awakened me to his world, his voice, his style, his masterful, seductive, symphonic sound; his added Jheri curl and gyrating hips offered me, and I'd gladly accepted and affirmed—even if only for a moment—the freedom to break through the negative and complex American filters that dictate the image of Black masculinity. Through his bold, assertive, demagogic stance toward discovering his own identity and voice—I discovered my own. And while his shocking death in 2016 illustrated the makings of a Shakespearean tragedy, the end of his life is certainly not the climax of it. It's amazing to me that Prince maintained his authentic self amid an ever-changing culture that unfairly demands young Black men to lose their authentic selves—I hope we never lose sight of Prince's refusal to be anything other than himself and the way in which he used it to transform our community, our lives, our America.

We start with this vignette by Jack Hill because he makes it so painfully clear that the narrative that gets written by and about Black boys is a destructive narrative that not even they themselves may want to buy into. The next chapter was written by the Rev. Dr. Jamie Washington, an internationally recognized diversity expert, minister, and facilitator, who knows a thing or two about the power of love. We start this section with Dr. Washington's chapter because he demonstrates how loving Black boys requires knowing them as individuals. And knowing them as individuals requires seeing how quickly and easily their individuality gets blotted out by the broad brush of stereotyping and misrepresentation. Seeing Black boys clearly enough to love them cannot be done with a colorblind lens. Seeing Black boys clearly requires us to see the lenses that have been put before our eyes by a society that is very much color conscious, and then to peek around, behind, and beyond those lenses to locate the individual.

CHAPTER 16

Strategies for Showing Love to Black Boys

Jamie Washington

In the eighth grade, I had a music teacher who saw that I enjoyed music and performing, and she challenged me to do something for the spring concert. She said, "Here is what you're going to do," and then provided opportunities for me to practice and gave me feedback on what I was doing. She encouraged me; she said, "Nope that's not sufficient, that's not good; here's what you need to do, practice some more."

In my 20s, I worked with a White woman who is still my mentor. When I first met her, she'd say, "Jamie you know you're brilliant?" And I had this moment where I looked at her like she'd lost her mind, like, "What are you talking about?" She'd say, "You are brilliant, the way that you can talk about this, and figure it out, and put it together. You're just brilliant." When she said to me, "You are brilliant," she introduced a counternarrative of self. And that counternarrative has informed the rest of my life.

Loving Black boys means inviting them to know that we see the narrative that gets told about them, that we don't buy it, and that we don't want them to buy it either. Black boys are navigating the narrative of "All you're good for is . . ." "Maybe you won't be alive by . . ." "You just have to survive . . ." Even the Black boy who is coming from an incredibly supportive and loving family, where he gets pure love, encouragement, and support, is still operating within a world that believes the negative narrative. That story says Black boys are scary, they're violent, they're apathetic, aggressive, not smart, not capable, not beautiful, not loving, not capable of being loved. Kids growing up in middle-class or upper-class Black families are going to have some different tools or experiences for confronting the negative narrative because they are often living with or experiencing role models that demonstrate some of the counternarratives. Black boys from lower-middle, working-class, and low-income families not only hear the negative narrative, they are living in the story. They leave you after fifty minutes or after four or five hours, and they go back to a different reality from the one you try to tell them about.

Loving Black boys requires creating a counternarrative to the one that gets told about them. Creating the counternarrative requires that we first see the current narrative, the story that gets told about Black boys, then recognize it and know that it's false. To counter it requires seeing Black boys as a collective. Not a monolith. Not a homogenous group. A collective. Every Black boy is unique. However, everyone belongs to a collective. Some belong to the collective of old people or immigrants or White women. All Black boys are part of the Black male collective. And the narrative that gets told about Black boys and men is a story that gets told about each one of us, no matter how different, how special, how precious, or how rare each of us is.

If teachers want to love Black boys, they need to know that they should meet the boys wherever they are—sometimes deeply embedded in the "Black boy" narrative—and love them through it and beyond it. Teachers must be able to show up with a counternarrative and to love them with this current context, where Black men and young people are killed every day—and some of that is at the hands of their own people because of internalized oppression. This means that sometimes—often—it's going to be challenging for Black boys to be able to receive that love.

But that is not the biggest problem. Teachers must first acknowledge that the negative narrative lives in them. Even as a Black man, I have had to recognize this dynamic as well. Teachers have to ask themselves, "What is it we are carrying? What are the ideas, what are the images, what are the issues, what are our frameworks around who Black boys and Black men are? How do those ideas shape how I engage with them?" If teachers don't know to look for that, if they don't know that they carry the narrative, then it affects how they show up in their relationships with Black boys. It becomes self-fulfilling. It's hard for the individual teacher to see, but it's very real. It's called implicit bias, and this silent killer has an enormous impact on Black students. When I was a student, it wasn't what my teachers *did* that hurt me; it was that they often did nothing. The indifference was ten times more hurtful. When teachers would turn back a paper with a bad grade on it, with energy that said, "That was what I expected of you," it was devastating because it confirmed the larger narrative about me. I needed them to show me the energy that said, "What can I do to support you more? How can I help you more? Have you considered doing this?" I felt isolated and blamed for my failure, rather than supported to navigate the meaning and the context of my failure. Some days, kids come to school having spent the previous night navigating where they were going to eat, or *if* they were going to eat. Naturally, the biology homework is not their top priority the next day. But when psychologist Abraham Maslow's hierarchy of needs leads to homework neglect, teachers treat the failure as inevitable, and it just feeds the narrative the kid already buys about himself.

But teachers don't know it's a narrative. They think it's the truth. And it's hard to undo because nothing has forced them to counter it in themselves. If teachers don't have relationships with Black people, what evidence do they have that contradicts the narrative? The social world supports the narrative. It's hard to wrap your mind around that when you're a teacher who is supposed to love all your students, treat them all the same, and want to see them all succeed—especially if you're trying to be colorblind. But remember, Black boys are a part of a collective from which they can't break loose. It doesn't serve teachers to pretend that there is no narrative. That just pushes Black boys to think, "You don't see my reality, you don't understand my experiences, you are just here doing some fake stuff to try and make your life easier." It's not just White people and other people of color that have a story about Black people: Black people have a narrative about themselves as well. And Black men and boys must navigate what that means. So too do the people who love us.

Once teachers have done the work to explore and examine what they believe about Black boys, they will land on this understanding: Black boys are like other boys. They are born with desires and hearts of brilliance, potential, just as all children are. Then teachers can ask, "What do I need to do that helps me to show love to them in a context where many of the messages that they may be getting say that they are not loveable, or not deserving of love?"

If Black boys don't receive love in the first way you try, then you must try another way. You must be willing to not give up. Teachers must fight through a narrative that is very strong, and depending on where their boys are and what kind of home circle situation they are in, teachers might be having to burrow through some intense stuff, which can feel like extra work. It can feel like you're giving more time, more energy, more attention to this and you've got twenty-eight to thirty other kids in your classroom that need your attention. It is a lot of work.

The message to convey is: I see you. I know that you are of value. I want you to be able to find your power, your skills, and your gifts, and I want to do that not only individually but collectively with yourself and other Black boys. I want you not only to be able to receive love from me, but also to give love to each other. Part of loving Black boys is helping them to love themselves and other Black boys.

My music teacher—she encouraged me and helped my potential emerge. But what she did not do—what I had to navigate on my own—was help me see that there is a narrative about me as a Black boy that I didn't write and I don't have to believe. That's what my mentor did for me when she told me I was brilliant. She gave me a counternarrative of self. That is what love looks like from teachers.

■ ■ Engaging the Mind ★ Taking Action ★ Inspiring Excellence
How Do I Invite Him In?

This exercise is addressed to teachers. Read the paragraph below and think of some of the Black boys in your classroom and how you have, and have not, coded their behavior. And then look at the final three questions and make a list of answers. Keep a running total of answers for a week and then spend a week implementing a different approach in your classroom. Then reflect on changes you see in your students.

It's not uncommon for many young children to be silent and withdraw sometimes, or to joke around. But we don't treat the same behaviors the same way—we code the black boys' behavior differently. If we have a young white child who is disengaged and not being involved, we don't code it as, "Well that's just how they are." We usually look at what's causing it. We don't have that collective narrative around White boys that we have around Black boys. We need to start to wonder, what that's about for him? He's always joking, or he's always got to be the life of the party, or he shows with aggression, or he's disengaged. How do I invite him in? How do I pull him in? How do I not give up?

As teachers engage in Dr. Washington's activity, it's useful to look at your Black boys, consider the stories you tell to explain the behavior that you see, and consider this: When Black boys are depressed, their behavior is often misinterpreted by others as aggression (Cassidy & Stevenson, 2005). This is generally true for boys and men, who have been socialized to express sadness or fear as anger and hostility. But even beyond that, the silence, the downcast eyes, the inward emotion of depression, gets read by many in our society as aggressive behavior in Black boys. Knowing that the stereotype of aggressive, angry Black males is just a stereotype, if a Black boy is described as "aggressive" or "angry," it's important to stop and reconsider whether he might be depressed, or merely quiet. Whenever a person codes a child in a way that resonates with stereotypes, it should be a catalyst to double-check other possibilities. It doesn't mean that the child is not angry. Given the brutality that Black people experience in the U.S., it is hard to imagine being a Black boy in America and not being angry. But the person you encounter may not be angry. Or he may be angry and something else. But look again. Is that accurate? Is that all that is there? Is that what's going on for him, or is that what's going on for you? Remind yourself that boys—Black boys—deserve to have access to the full range of human emotion, which includes joy, sadness, anger, fear, disgust, and much more. The following chapter illustrates these ideas in the life of one young Black boy—now a fourth- and fifth-grade teacher.

CHAPTER 17

White Privilege and Black Excellence

Two Terms That I've Been "Afraid" of for Much of My Life

David Stills

Growing up in the neighborhood I did, White privilege was a term people didn't use or even think about much. Although I always understood that my skin was darker than most of my classmates, I never gave this any substantial consideration until I was seven. I was in second grade. My class had just come in from playing outside, and all of us were sweaty and out of breath. A child asked me: "Why does your hair look like that when you sweat?" To this day, I have no idea what the child meant. Was he asking about why my hair stayed frizzy? Was he referring to the way perspiration beaded at the end of my newly formed sideburns and fell across my cheek?

Looking back, I realize that it doesn't matter what he meant. After he asked the question, I went to the bathroom, and stared in the mirror for so long that my teacher sent someone to see if I was OK. I lied and said my stomach was acting up. In truth, I was looking at my Black face in a way I never had before. I remember feeling disappointment and shame. Why didn't my hair flop this way and that? Why couldn't I run my hand through it and change its shape in the same way as my classmates? And that nose! And those lips—Dammit! What was this new feeling?

In that moment, I became extremely aware of my physical appearance. Naturally, when I observed my unmistakable Blackness in the mirror, I detested it. In noticing the physical differences, I had to accept that I was not White, and I would never enjoy that kind of privilege.

The comparisons, and the questions continued as I grew older, and I became so used to the disgusted feeling, I began to think it was normal.

Although I grew up in a house with two Black parents and two Black siblings, I slowly became aware of a real difference every time I left my home. The question began to form: If I feel this much disgust when I look at my own face in the mirror, how much hate must they feel when they look at me?

I didn't understand then, that I'd come up hard against my own implicit bias and that my disappointment was a natural reaction to the constant message I'd been getting: "Whites are excellent. Blacks are mediocre, at best (or: "Whites are excellent; Blacks are subpar"). Naturally, when I observed my unmistakable Blackness in that mirror at the age of seven, I detested it.

Like every other American individual, I was raised in the land of White privilege, without any real sense of Black achievement or excellence.

The privilege was everywhere, and touched everything. My heroes in comic books and movies were White. My role models on television were White. In the 1980s and '90s, nearly everyone in the media who was beautiful, intelligent, and successful was white.

Both of my parents had grown up in what they called "rough" inner-city neighborhoods, and they had sworn to raise a family in "safe" rural America. I grew up in a predominantly White neighborhood, and so my teachers and pastors and coaches, my friends and classmates, were White. As a result of being raised in a racially homogenized society of White heroes and role models, there was never a question of White Excellence. There was never a question of White anything.

My parents did keep "the culture" in our household. My mother and father often spoke openly about being Black. I grew up with soul food on Sundays and family dance parties listening to Diana Ross, the Jackson Five, Smokey Robinson, Stevie Wonder—Motown and more. Gospel music was a staple in our house.

My mother and father regularly spoke to me about the differences between their upbringing and mine; my mother grew up in Harlem in the late 1940s, and my father grew up in both Wilkes-Barre, Pennsylvania, and South Philadelphia in the 1940s. Both referred to their neighborhoods as "rough" and explained that you had to know everyone in order to make it. People became addicted to drugs, got into trouble and went to jail, or died in their neighborhoods. Kids who couldn't afford books or pencils and had to share twenty-year-old textbooks with their classmates lost hope and stopped going to school in their neighborhoods. Police rarely came to their neighborhoods, and when they did, they weren't looking to help the people in their neighborhoods. Entire populations were depressed and stagnant in their neighborhoods. Being "blessed" meant graduating from high school, in their neighborhood; being better-off meant leaving their neighborhoods.

My parents explained that although it was hard to grow up in a town that was mostly White, I would receive opportunities there that they could only have dreamt of as children. And they talked to me about some of the unfair things I noticed as I became more aware. They prepared me for what I would face as I became older and bigger and my voice became deeper. And they were right. I cannot tell you how many times my younger brother and I have been pulled over and placed in the back of police cars while a cop "called in a license." I remember one evening when I was home from college over winter break. I was driving home from a friend's house, and as I pulled into the driveway, I saw the flashing lights of a police car. I stopped my car at the beginning of our driveway, got out of slowly, and half raised my hands (indicating they were empty) as I walked toward the car. When I got closer, I saw my brother in the back seat. My pace sped up slightly, and the young police officer who was calling in my brother's license plate told me to leave. I explained to the officer that this was my house and that the man in the backseat was my brother. The officer didn't believe me and told me to get in the back as well. I told him to look at my brother and to look at me. The officer scratched his head (my brother and I look very much alike), and at that moment, my mother came out of the house.

She said: "David, it's alright. I just called the police office. He's new, he doesn't know you two." A few minutes later, the sheriff, who was familiar with our family, came and explained to the new cop that we were all who we claimed to be, that we owned the cars we were driving, that we did in fact grow up in that house as we claimed and were a family. This kind of thing has happened to me so many times, I've lost count. And yes, I've had a police officer pull his gun on me. It happened a few years before college. He was in plainclothes and drunk, and I was using a public restroom. When he entered the restroom and asked me if I was selling drugs, I became offended and told him to go to hell. It was then that he pulled his gun. I still didn't know he was a cop, but I did think I was going to die. One of my White friends decided to be an ally right then and there. He refused to leave the bathroom, despite the fact that the cop started waving his badge and saying that he would arrest both of us. I was fifteen years old then. Nothing was the same after that. I couldn't go back to being relaxed about my status. Everything was suddenly much more serious.

I guess I'd been afraid of the concept of White privilege because if it existed, it meant that the cards were stacked against me. I didn't want to see that.

Growing up, I never put much effort into my academics. My father was constantly pressuring me to do well in school, and I think I pushed against that. It never felt right. Why did I *have* to do perfectly in every subject? I can still remember a report card I brought home in third grade. Four As and three Bs. I was reprimanded and punished. My father said: "I don't want you to be good. I want you to be the best!"

I stopped trying then. It was too much pressure, and it didn't make any sense at the time, so I stopped trying.

By the time high school came, I didn't know any other way to perform in school. My parents had just split up, and I was lost. I was looking for meaning in many different areas, and academics was the farthest thing from my heart and mind. I was afraid to push myself. What if I really was stupid?

I remember being invited to the Urban League of Rochester Black Scholars Award ceremony in Rochester, New York. My parents were proud. I was so embarrassed. How was I being awarded for my mediocre effort and achievement? It felt like they were just handing out "Good job for being able to read and write!" awards to any Black kids who met the minimum standard. Looking back, I realize that this program was extremely well-intentioned and provided an immense boost to the African American population in the greater Rochester area. We were underrepresented in everything. Being recognized as a scholar was powerful. Many of the children came to the ceremony in their "Sunday best." They were motivated to make it back next year. They liked their teachers and their pastors and their younger siblings speaking about their academic achievements. But I didn't feel like I deserved an award for my ability just to show up.

I didn't realize that my feeling came from the fact that I needed a boost in my own confidence. I spent most of my free time hanging out with White 4.0 students whose parents were doctors and lawyers, college professors, business owners, and other professionals. School seemed to be second nature for these families.

I didn't feel like I would ever measure up, and I wondered what the difference was.

Years later, my mother would reveal to me that I was the first person in my mother's family to receive a college degree. My brother and my sister are the second and the third. She didn't tell me this information when I was in high school because she didn't want to put that kind of pressure on me.

And I didn't realize the kind of pressure my father was experiencing, the pressure that caused him to push me so hard. He wanted me to push myself because he understood the uphill battle I would eventually be facing. It wasn't fair, but it's OK. I get it now. And it isn't fair.

Receiving a college degree wasn't enough for me. Even though I did my best in college, somehow it didn't make the cut. I needed more. I needed to be better.

I remember feeling really small after the officer pulled his gun on me. For a few moments, I was convinced that my life had come to an end, and I couldn't shake that feeling for a long time. It stayed with me. I knew I needed to find a way to become my best, in the face of every negative and unfair circumstance I'd faced.

I'm still finding my way, but I know now that my decision to seek excellence was an act of survival. A way to rise above my shock and my anger. A way to not believe what even my own mind was telling me: "You just aren't as good as them. You deserve this. You'll always be less-than."

So I looked to Black, wealthy, intelligent heroes beating the system: Puff Daddy, Jay Z, Oprah, Michael Jordan. I still idolize these kinds of people because of the unequivocal excellence they represent. Nobody can say, "Well, has Oprah really made it?" These people give me something to shoot for. As I explored further, it occurred to me that Black excellence is something I'm seeking *and* building. I need to be encouraged by the examples around me, and I need to be an example.

Now I see excellence in the family that is working toward something together. I see it in the daughter who knows she is special and refuses to give in to peer pressure. And I see it in the son who stays relaxed when he is being baited, giving a calm, intelligent response to the person holding power. It's in the parents, working to earn advanced degrees while maintaining careers and doing a magnificent job of raising their children. It's in the father who remembers to eat right and breathe and who talks to his children about injustice but also radiates enthusiasm and power. And in the mother who is powerful because she understands what it means to be empowered. And in the parents who live their lives as an example that their children will learn from.

Looking back, I realize that my parents invested all their hopes and dreams in us. Many of our teachers and coaches believed in us, and this message was more powerful and important than any of the other negative messages we received.

Black excellence isn't just recognizable in billionaires. To truly be understood, it must first be recognized in yourself. Excellence is learned, and the lesson is, "I am worth it!" Live, fight, believe, learn, love yourself, and keep believing! Embrace the culture. Do not give up on the dreams of those who came before you, and remember to take pride in your victories. Find peace in your unwavering commitment and strength in the knowledge that you are lifting yourself and others higher.

Remember: You are worth it. You are excellent.

Now that you've read "White Privilege and Black Excellence", please take a few minutes to complete the following exercise.

2-Minute Reflection:
"Self-Consciousness"

- When do you feel like you "belong"?

- What does is look like when you are questioning whether or not you have been fully included, or whether or not you should be part of a (discussion, get-together, project at your workplace etc.)?

- Throughout your day, how often are you aware of your physical appearance?

- What triggers this awareness?

7-Minute Activity:
"Sit With Yourself":

- Find a quiet place to sit. Close your eyes, resting your hands on your lap. Inhale and exhale ten times, making sure to focus on the sound and feel of the air entering and leaving your nose.

- If you can, take note of where you feel tension in your body.

- Open your eyes. Ask yourself: "What in my life causes me to experience stress?"

- Consider your Socio Economic status growing up. Were you aware of it?

- If you were, why were you? If you weren't, why weren't you?

- Close your eyes once more. Relax your shoulders, arms, and hands.

- Inhale and exhale ten more times, paying attention to the inward and outward movement of your breath.

- What makes you feel ashamed (how often do you feel shame)?

- What makes you proud?

5-Minute Activity:
"Alternative Life":

- Visualize your immediate family. Next, think about your aunts, uncles, grandparents, and cousins. Now, bring to mind your friends, and your "family-friends" growing up.

- What kinds of people are you close with now?

- What do they look like? What level of education have they completed? What books do they read? Where do they shop? Are they "worldly"?

- What do their families look like? Do their families possess any material wealth?

- Now, use your imagination to change the circumstances you've visualized.

- For example: If your family has long history of undergraduate, or postgraduate degrees, imagine your family with no college degrees.

- What else would be different?

The following chapter is the corollary to Chapter 6 on White racial identity development, which describes the phases of identity development that White people go through as they learn about racism. This chapter, by Dr. Paul A. Robbins, Dr. Leann V. Smith, and Dr. Keisha L. Bentley-Edwards, describes the stages that Black boys go through as they learn about racism and begin to grasp the reality of what it means to be a Black boy—and later a Black man—in the context of a racist society. It describes common psychological phases that one might go through after experiences like those David Stills relayed in the previous chapter. Having a gun pulled on you by an undercover police officer, for example, is an experience of racial trauma that necessarily requires periods of processing and healing. But in the context of colorblind schools and classrooms, students rarely have the opportunity to process such moments of trauma in school. This chapter is meant to give you more resources to understand what might be going on for your Black boy students when they express sadness, anger, frustration, or disgust in response to their own experiences of racism (either personal or vicarious). If a child says, "I hate White people," you might react to them differently if you have a sense of where that statement is coming from in terms of their identity development. You might react still differently if you are able to gauge for yourself where you are in your own identity development (see Chapter 6 for White racial identity development) and how that impacts the way you hear and understand the student's statement. We hope that you come back to this chapter again and again as you read this book, especially those of you who work with Black boys.

CHAPTER 18

Black Boys and Their Racial Identity

Learning How They Fit Into Society and in Your Classroom

Paul A. Robbins, Leann V. Smith, and Keisha L. Bentley-Edwards

Have you ever tried to pinpoint the exact moment when you first realized that you had been assigned to a race in American society? Did you consider what your position as a White person or a Black person in the United States meant to yourself and to others? Go ahead and take a minute to flash back into your personal history. My personal Black realization moment could have come while discussing being Black in America in the context of the Rodney King beating, the subsequent riots (social uprising), and the O. J. Simpson trial with my parents. Instead, it came on the eve of a middle-school dance; friends of mine who were in an interracial relationship were looking for dates. After I suggested that they go together, one of my White friends pulled me aside and said, "Her dad won't let them. She's White, and he's Black. Some people don't go for that." He said it like it was universally understood; yet, as a Black person, I spent hours trying to make sense of my new reality.

You can imagine how simultaneously enlightening and traumatizing these moments can be for a child who believes people are judged based on character and not skin color. Scholars have examined the process through which that shift occurs and have coined the moment an *encounter*. In a broader sense, an encounter is just one of five theoretical stages of racial identity development. According to Cross (1991,1995), in the stage prior to having an encounter (*pre-encounter*), a person interprets their interactions through a colorblind lens, not considering (or at times, actively ignoring) their status as a member of a racial group and the implications that has on other aspects of their life. Suddenly, their status of being racially different from others is recognized through the form of an encounter or event that causes a shift in worldview. After that stage, Black individuals begin to fully immerse themselves into their culture and explore everything related to their Blackness, a phase aptly called the *immersion* period. During this time of exploration, a Black boy may choose to actively reject mainstream (White) ideologies and people who he feels imposed subordinate thinking on him. Eventually the individual comes to a place of *internalization*, in which his culture is still celebrated and a primary component of his identity, but without the rage. He begins to explore areas of difference and understand others of different racial groups.

To parallel the story provided at the beginning of the chapter, the child remained in the pre-encounter stage until he was enlightened that his friends in an interracial relationship would be negatively appraised by their parents. Presumably, after this encounter, he went on to ask more questions and research more about Blackness. Reading this chapter's narratives, which are inspired by real events, keep in mind this idea of Blackness and its shifting salience over the course of an individual's lifespan is based on their personal experiences. Think about how some Black boys may have already had their own racial encounters. The absence or presence of these encounters will undoubtedly shape the way they see themselves and others, as well as how they interact with their teacher and the rest of their world.

The vignettes that follow demonstrate that other factors may affect the ways in which Black boys' identities will manifest in classroom behaviors. One of the main factors will be the salience of race (i.e., Blackness) and racial identity stage. Racial salience can be defined as the extent to which race is an important component of a person's self-concept (Sellers, Smith, Shelton, Rowley, & Chavous, 1998). The relationship between racial salience and racial identity is such that as people explore more about their racial identity, their racial salience presumably increases and vice versa. In the following scenarios, Black students from various academic tracks and different levels of racial saliences are presented with potential encounters that either change or represent a shift in their worldview. It is our hope that through reflecting on the concrete examples provided, teachers can use the information to help navigate the complexity of Black students' racial identity development.

Demetrius

Demetrius is the only Black student in his advanced placement history class. During a lesson on slavery, a classmate comments, "I heard that some slaves lived a decent life." Ms. Peterson disagrees but wants to seem neutral so she deflects, "Interesting thought . . . Demetrius, do you mind giving us the Black perspective on this?" Demetrius interjects, "My previous history teacher explained that some of the masters took good care of their slaves. Plus, with the economic benefits, I probably would have done the same." Stunned, Ms. Peterson retorts, "If I were Black, I would have problems with slavery rationalizations."

Two months later, Demetrius enters class in a somber mood because the previous night, he saw a news story about an unarmed Black boy who was killed by a citizen who felt threatened. Ms. Peterson refuses to discuss the killing because it is not in her lesson plan. She warns Demetrius that if he continues to derail the lesson with this distraction, she will have him removed from class. Demetrius accuses her of being afraid to let a Black student speak or being secretly racist. Demetrius remarks, "This probably wouldn't happen if we had a Black teacher." Ms. Peterson responds, "I love all of my students the same, regardless of race" and calls the office to have him removed.

Ms. Peterson was correct in seeking a more critical evaluation of slavery, but several things could have been done differently. Presenting one Black student's opinion as representative of "the Black perspective" puts unnecessary pressure on the very children who are supposed to be learning from their teacher. Thus, it is not Demetrius's responsibility to teach his classmates a culturally informed curriculum. Demetrius's opinions represent *his own* views, and having a Black child's endorsement does not make a point any more or less valid. In addition, once she realized his opinion did not value Blackness, she indirectly questioned his identity. It is important to remember that some Black boys have not had an encounter, and trying to force one will typically be futile. For Black boys who are high achieving and also do not identify strongly with their Blackness, their beliefs and behaviors will likely model those of their teachers and peers, emphasizing colorblindness. For them, the goal is not to stand out or be singled out as being different or having a different perspective because of race. Teachers who imply otherwise might receive some pushback.

Later, Ms. Peterson did what many teachers do when confronted with behavior perceived as aggressive, disrespectful, or disruptive; she removed the threat. Sometimes a student's words or actions will feel threatening, especially if teachers are concerned about their ability to manage the classroom. It can also feel extremely threatening for a White teacher to have her identity as an unbiased

White person challenged. Ms. Peterson did not like the idea of adapting her discussion, but the accusation of racism seemed to elevate her threat level exponentially. Teachers must understand that newly "awakened" Black students are still learning the impact of their words. They aren't necessarily attacking their teachers, so much as they are fighting against the status quo. Teachers should not treat a Black student in the same way they might treat an adult who calls them a racist on the streets. In this case, the actual threat was minor and likely could have been resolved without removing Demetrius from class. Rather than being defensive, she could have resolved this issue by adapting the lesson for a five-minute class discussion. It likely took longer than that to argue with Demetrius and then have him removed.

Many high-achieving Black students who see Blackness as an important part of their identity are unafraid to speak freely and challenge authority. For many students like Demetrius, speaking in class is a way to ensure they are not overlooked and to fight the Black boy academic disengagement stereotype.

Jordan and Tyrod

It is the first week of school for Jordan and Tyrod, who attend a racially diverse school. Jordan notices that most of his classes contain only Black students. His math teacher, Ms. Maxwell, questions Jordan about his lack of effort. She reminds him that he will need this information in college. "What's the point? People from these classes don't go to college," Jordan responds. "Haven't you seen the school report card? You must think you're teaching the White kids down the hall or at the school across town." Tyrod chimes in, "It has nothing to do with race. You could have registered for those classes, too. We're in here because we need extra help." "You would agree with her," Jordan quips, before putting his head down for the rest of class to avoid another office visit.

Many teachers would see Jordan as a lazy or disengaged student. He might also be labeled combative or low performing for rejecting his class work. His lack of effort may say very little about who he is as a student, however, and a lot about his perceptions of academic inequality in his school and city. He seems to be aware of statistics that say that Black students experience disparate educational outcomes compared to White peers at his school and in his district. Maybe he sees a system that has failed the generations before him, and seeing mostly segregated classes reminds him that his outcome might not be different. It would probably be best to speak privately with Jordan. Attempt to better understand why he feels this way and how you can use your power as a teacher to help him feel like his work will be rewarded.

Tyrod was technically correct when he said that students in his class could have registered for advanced classes, but Jordan may know that at many schools, legitimate barriers prevent switching tracks easily. Tyrod attempted to remove race from the discussion and presented an alternative explanation. In doing so, he might be indicating that he has not had a moment in which he thinks race has impacted his schooling. This might not mean that he doesn't understand racial inequality or believes he is not Black, as Jordan indirectly implies. Tyrod may have seen Black academic stereotypes confirmed in his academic track, which may generate cognitive dissonance about being Black. Instead of seeing lower academic achievement as a symptom of systemic issues, he might have attributed academic racial disparities to Black students' behaviors or attitudes. That sounds good in theory, but teachers have probably had students who do almost everything right, but still can't seem to get ahead in school. Blaming it on individual behaviors removes the teacher's responsibility to make sure that the system works for all children. Witnessing misbehavior makes it harder for people to look at the bigger picture.

OTHER CONSIDERATIONS

High-achieving Black students may see themselves as Black people who are fighting the system by doing well in school or as people who are providing evidence that the system can be conquered with a little bit of hard work. As high-achievers become exposed to the influence of race in society and in their social lives, their behavior is likely to reflect this knowledge. Boys who see the value in being Black might start behaving in ways that help them preserve a Black image among their peers. Those who see Blackness as a deficit will likely gravitate toward behaviors that they believe will set them apart from other Blacks. These behavior changes are normal and can be exacerbated by peer approval or disapproval. Teachers should avoid pathologizing either set of behaviors, while exploring the motivation behind them. Since some of these actions will be based on stereotypes, teachers should reject the notion that a student talks or acts White or Black. They should also stay away from the idea that high-achievers are somehow better or an exception to the rule of Black underachievement. This perspective perpetuates the belief that Black students are destined to fail unless they are one of the few with specific characteristics.

Finally, it is important for us to discuss Black boys who display atypical behaviors or have hobbies that are not traditionally associated with Black boys. These boys might have trouble fitting in with their peers, or they might be well liked. Either way, remember that teachers have no responsibility to guide them toward Blacker norms. These boys are important because they highlight the fact that the Black community is not monolithic and that Blackness can have many forms. Teachers should intervene only if the student's peers or other teachers are implying that these boys are not Black, as many of them are very racially aware and are regularly impacted by their race; remind students and colleagues of the myriad ways to be Black.

CONCLUSION

It is our hope that this chapter will be used as a beneficial resource that can be referenced as a reminder of the complex and ever-changing process of racial identity development for children, and Black male children in particular. Of course, not every possible scenario or Black male response to an evolving identity has been covered here. Given the diversity within the Black racial group, as well as the plethora of other unrelated but equally important characteristics, it is unrealistic to capture every potential student that will enter a classroom. However, teachers who continuously examine their own racial identity may find themselves better equipped to relate to their students and to challenge their own beliefs about Whiteness and other racial groups. They will also be more cognizant to avoid some of the teacher pitfalls mentioned throughout this chapter.

■ ■ Engaging the Mind ⋆ Taking Action ⋆ Inspiring Excellence
Black Racial Identity Development

This exercise is provided for teachers and others who work in a school setting. Now that you have read about possible ways that racial identity development can influence your classroom interactions with students, we invite you to reflect upon your interactions with two Black boys (whom you have personally taught) at differing stages of racial identity development. As you think of a past interaction with each of these students during a racial discussion or conflict, consider the following:

- What made you choose these two students over others?

- How much did each student seem to understand race and racism?

- What are some of the ways in which their racial identity development stage may have impacted their interactions with others in the classroom?

- How did you (and others in the classroom) initially react to each students' ideas about race?

- Did you seek advice regarding the students' behaviors? Who did you go to for this advice and was it constructive?

- In hindsight, was there anything that you would have done differently in response to these students' identity development? If yes, what resources will you gather and utilize to aid future students like these in navigating their racial identity development?

The following vignette by Adrian Chandler, a 15-year-old sophomore in high school, describes one of his "Encounter" moments, as defined by the racial identity development framework just described in Chapter 18. Notice how, in the course of one day, Adrian's entire worldview shifts, and he realizes that the world is not as fair—at least not for boys who are Black—as he previously thought it was.

Vignette: *I Had a Right*

Adrian Chandler

Growing up, kids learn what adults teach them directly and indirectly. A lot of the rules around race are taught in schools indirectly. I am currently a high school sophomore, and I identify as a male and my race as Black. When I was in middle school, over 90 percent of the students in the school were White, and all the teachers and administrators were White. I was one of the very few students of color at my middle school. To me, it seemed like when a situation arose, the first person the teachers blamed was me.

One day I remember vividly. I was in gym class learning floor hockey. There was a White boy on the team we were playing against whom I considered my friend. I was going full out to win like I always do in sports. Running after the puck, my friend and I collided. I popped back up ready to keep playing. He got up, took one step closer, and socked me in the face, right in my jaw. I stepped back, giving him a nudge to separate us and to give me time to recover. I had never gotten punched before, so it surprised me, especially coming from a friend. The two co-teachers ran over to us. I told them what happened, and they took the other boy to the principal's office. The rest of us continued the game.

After class, I was called to the principal's office. The principal and the school liaison police officer were there with the kid who had punched me. The principal explained that she was giving me a three-day in-school suspension and the other kid was getting a detention. This was all done in a span of about five minutes, without any recount from me and without any parent contact. I didn't realize what was happening at the time. I expected people to be rational and fair. I expected the adults in the situation to figure out what really happened and to be fair about discipline. I was attacked, and I defended myself. I thought that the adults would agree that I have a right to do that. They did not believe that I had a right to defend myself.

The stress every day after this incident, knowing that whatever I did, I would still be blamed for any kind of incident, was exhausting. I couldn't be myself. I couldn't focus on learning. I had to be on guard all the time. I had to be on the lookout for any kind of situation that might lead to some kind of problem. The hardest part about it was that the adults in the school believed that I didn't have the right to defend myself. After that experience, my mother decided to home-school me.

This was tough on my mom and me, transitioning into home-school. Not seeing other kids at school every day bothered me a lot at first. I thought I was getting an even worse deal by being singled out and separated from my friends. I felt like I was being punished for something that the school was failing at. Instead of the teachers and principal at the school stepping up to take care of their problem, they dumped it all on me. That was not fair—not at all. I felt like my life was being put on pause, and it felt scary. The fear didn't last very long, but the feeling that the school unfairly dumped its problems on me has never left me. That feeling makes it hard to trust teachers in general. My mom is a teacher, so she helps with that.

I had to be very independent and diligent about my learning when my mom home-schooled me. She and I would have to create my lesson plans and figure out different ways to teach me the materials my mom did not know. Home-schooling was an interesting experience, and it allowed me to practice and fine-tune my independence skills. Having experienced this whole situation with the school, and having to transition and adapt, has allowed me to expand my mindset and realize that not even the most basic things like school can be healthy and safe. It also allowed me to respect home-schooled students whom I have met since then. We don't live in that city anymore, and the school I go to now is a place where I feel safe and I can learn in a supportive environment.

As we put together this volume, we paid special attention to how it would serve teachers. We hoped that, by virtue of reading the book and practicing the suggestions within it, teachers would transform their consciousness and subsequently their classrooms. To do that, we recognized that we needed to acknowledge not only the racialized aspect of Black boys' experiences in schools but also their gendered experiences. Traditional schooling expectations, including sitting still, staying quiet, and following directions, are generally more attainable for girls than for boys. Gender is not a binary, of course, and every child is on a spectrum of gender. For some girls, those traditional expectations prohibit their success, and for many boys, they are well within their habits of body and mind. But for the most part, it is boys who are disadvantaged by traditional expectations of schooling, and Black boys even more so. White boys who are overactive and restless in class may be identified as unchallenged and placed in a higher-level course, or at the very least given the benefit of the doubt that "boys will be boys." Overactive and restless Black boys face a much more extreme response, given how quickly and easily they might be diagnosed with ADHD, designated as in need of special education, or worse, seen as aggressive and violent. Given these disparate outcomes for Black boys, it becomes even more critical that teachers know and implement strategies for engaging boy learners. For some children, it can mean the difference between success and failure, which sometimes means life and death. The following chapter was written by Dr. Joseph Derrick Nelson, a sociologist of education, who studies Black boys, masculinity, and schooling. He provides multiple ideas and strategies for accommodating Black boy learners. In the spirit of universal design, we believe if teachers implement these strategies that have been demonstrated to support the learning of boys, all students will benefit.

CHAPTER 19

Teaching Black Boys During Childhood

A Counternarrative and Considerations

Joseph Derrick Nelson

LAFAYETTE: A YOUNG SCIENTIST

Lafayette would like to be a bench scientist or play for the National Football League when he grows up. His 98-average in science, and a stellar recommendation from his science teacher, recently earned him a scholarship to attend a summer camp for young scientists in New York City, where he lives with his mother and little brother in Harlem. Lafayette is an African American fifth-grader at a single-sex school for low-income Black and Latino boys in Manhattan. He was thankful and honored that his favorite teacher, a White woman named Mrs. Carson (pseudonym), thought of him for this coveted learning opportunity, and he was also excited to participate in the camp with two of his closest friends at school, both of whom had also earned scholarships. Lafayette said:

> I have a good relationship with my science teacher; she's my favorite teacher. She teaches us everything she knows about science . . . And I'm glad that Aaron and Nathan (pseudonyms) get to go too. It's going to be fun to do a

lot of science experiments with friends from school—who love science just as much as I do.

A football career was the back-up plan for Lafayette, if science becomes too difficult for him—a genuine fear that Lafayette had expressed. His interest in the sport began early in his education. In school, Lafayette regularly encountered reactions to what he considered his husky physique for a fifth-grader, as well as his dark brown complexion and earnest facial expressions. This appearance, he said, kept his school peers from disturbing him while he was trying to focus on his schoolwork in class. Teachers and administrators, who then inadvertently influenced his peers, were the individuals who often suggested he pursue an athletic career path. Lafayette was adamant, however, "I want to be a scientist first; then I'll try football." He had fun playing for a neighborhood football league over the weekends, but he loved doing "science stuff" after school with Mrs. Carson, Aaron, and Nathan.

Lafayette did not always love science. In third grade, when he attended a co-ed elementary school closer to his home, he recalled being frequently "yelled at" by his teacher—a White woman named Miss Briggs (pseudonym). She would ask, for example, right after she announced a class science project, "Why are you moving around in your seat?" In response to "messing with" science materials during a lesson, she would ask, "Is that what you should be doing right now?" After he blurted out the answer to a question that Miss Briggs posed to the class, she would ask, "Why are you talking so loudly?" Lafayette often felt he was being closely watched, and any misconduct or genuine mistake would be met with a stiff consequence, such as not being able to participate in the science project. This happened to Lafayette, who felt little or no effort by his teacher to empathize with or understand his behavior in class.

He attributed this treatment to "not being liked" by Miss Briggs, and he related her reaction to his being physically larger than his classmates, compounded by his darker skin complexion and his stern comportment. "I stand out," he said. Miss Briggs would particularly act in such a manner toward Lafayette when there was a rare science lesson—a "special treat" for the class. Lafayette was not only excited by the novel occasion, but he also found the subject matter fascinating. He said, "I couldn't control myself . . . I would get so excited, that I bounced around with anticipation—I couldn't stop moving around in my seat."

In contrast, Mrs. Carson was perplexed yet intrigued by Lafayette's excited behaviors during science lessons and sought to understand their motivation. Through asking Lafayette, she learned of his pure joy and excitement in relation to science, which compelled her to harness this energy to drive his learning; for instance, Mrs. Carson would assign him tasks, such as lab helper, and partner him with

Aaron and Nathan for class experiments. From Lafayette's perspective, his actions were a deep expression of interest, and more important, not a malicious effort to disrupt the learning of his peers, although he did admit to playful mischief from time to time. His teacher's gestures strengthened Lafayette's relationships at school, especially with Mrs. Carson herself, as well as Aaron and Nathan, and furthered his intrinsic joy and love for science.

TEACHING BLACK BOYS DURING CHILDHOOD

Negative race and gender stereotypes of Black males in the United States are strongly correlated with racism and poverty in urban neighborhoods. This chapter operates from this premise to offer a preliminary set of pedagogical considerations for White women who teach Black boys during childhood. Lafayette's profile, derived from a three-year ethnography of a single-sex school for boys of color in New York City, provides a counternarrative that challenges these pervasive stereotypes, which are largely perpetuated by the popular media and have historically deprived Black boys of the curiosity, discovery, and naïveté of childhood. In U.S. society, Black boys are essentially *adultified* (Ferguson, 2000), deemed inherently suspect and malicious soon-to-be criminals. At school, Black boys become a physical threat and a "problem" to be monitored and controlled, rather than a student to be taught and developed socioemotionally. School professionals tend to presume that Black boys are disinterested students or less academically inclined; prone to sinister, disruptive, and willful acts of misconduct; preoccupied with horseplay or sports; and view close relationships with teachers and school peers as less important or frivolous.

The recommendations that follow are informed by theories of child development (Mooney, 2013; Wood, 2010) as well as evidence-based frameworks related to effectively teaching boys broadly (Reichert & Hawley, 2010) and teaching Black boys more specifically in light of race and gender stereotypes. Other frameworks demonstrate how *relational teaching with Black boys* (Nelson, 2016) is central to their learning: School relationships are deemed valuable and essential to school success, especially during childhood, when social stresses tied to racism and poverty in their neighborhoods and at home may at times prevent secure relational attachments with parents that are vital for healthy child development. Together, these interrelated frameworks strive to contribute to a *(re)imagining of Black boyhood* (Dumas & Nelson, 2016) in U.S. schools and society.

In *Reaching Boys, Teaching Boys*, Reichert and Hawley (2010) advance eight approaches to effectively teach adolescent boys specifically. Gleaned from more than 1,000 teachers, lesson plans that successfully engaged boys toward learning involved: (1) creating products, (2) gaming, (3) motor activity, (4) role play/performance,

(5) open inquiry, (6) teamwork, (7) personal realization, and (8) novelty, drama, and surprise. When fifth-grade Black boys from the school ethnography are considered, particularly as boys contend with stereotypes, urban poverty, and childhood, four of these approaches held more significance for Black boys and constitute what White woman can do in their classrooms to support their learning and development: (1) open inquiry with novelty, drama, and surprise embedded; (2) role play/performance; (3) teamwork; and (4) personal realization.

For Lafayette, his love of science emerged from his excited curiosity (e.g., bouncing around in his seat during science); anticipation and discovery were embedded in the science inquiry process (i.e., open inquiry and surprise). He assumed the role of a young scientist (i.e., role play and lab helper) or future professional scientist with pride (e.g., scientist first, football player second), but his science-football contention reflects a sociocultural stronghold that sports typically have on Black boys' professional worldviews, especially during childhood. It also reveals the critical need for targeted learning opportunities (e.g., summer camp for young scientists) that affirm life aspirations that are opposed to stereotypes of Black boys in U.S. schools. Lafayette thoroughly enjoyed collaborating with Aaron and Nathan on science experiments (i.e., teamwork), which reinforced his ability to embrace the joy of discovery and inquiry with school peers who shared his adoration for the subject matter. Collectively, these facets of his childhood education helped him arrive at a professional aspiration (i.e., bench scientist) and overcome his fear that science may be too difficult for him (i.e., personal realization). Spending a lot of time with Mrs. Carson after school in the science lab, along with his two closest friends, served to enrich his science learning and revealed his genuine desire to be in relationship with others at school. Miss Briggs, in contrast, had enabled negative stereotypes of Black boys (e.g., willfully mischievous) to obscure her view of Lafayette's inquisitive school behavior in relation to learning scientific knowledge (e.g., yelling at Lafayette); and professional development is arguably needed to shift her view of Black boys and grant them a robust childhood in her classroom.

Contributing to a (re)imagining of Black boyhood in the classroom requires teachers to develop pedagogical interventions that create learning environments in which Black boys can experience robust childhoods. Informing these interventions must be empirical research that asks Black boys, "who they are, what they think, and what they desire in their lives" (Dumas & Nelson, 2016, p. 27). This inquiry focus or lens for classroom teaching counteracts negative stereotypes that are "destructive, operate unconsciously, and skew teachers' perceptions of who boys are, and distort teachers' efforts to meet boys' distinct learning needs" (Nelson, 2016, p. 1; Reichert & Hawley, 2014). With effective pedagogy, relational teaching, and Black boyhood in mind, this chapter encourages White women to creatively act on the considerations below while teaching Black boys during early and middle childhood.

- Black boys want to be cared for and seen outside of negative race and gender stereotypes associated with Black males in the United States. For boys to feel "seen," teachers must mitigate assumptions and biases that impair their ability to recognize the potential of Black boys in school and life and tailor their relationship-building approaches and classroom practice accordingly.

- Black boys long for their perspectives and opinions, talents and gifts, and interests and passions to be valued by their teachers and authentically used to facilitate and enrich their learning in the classroom; and boys furthermore desire to see themselves in their learning environments, evidenced by the topics explored, literature read, and instructional approaches taken.

- Black boys want learning-based relationships at school, whereby teachers: (a) go above and beyond school policy or procedure to meet their distinct learning needs; (b) personally advocate on boys' behalf to marshal school resources to ensure their academic success; (c) find where boys' interests and hobbies converge with their own; and (d) accommodate opposition from them at times when they, despite genuine effort, fall short of doing their best to excel in school (Nelson, 2016; Reichert & Nelson, in press).

- Last, Black boys ask that the instructional strategies and relationship-building approaches of their teachers reflect that they are indeed children, with the needs and desires associated with this foundational stage of human development, where "Black boys can giggle, play, cry, pout, and be just as silly and frivolous as other children without these activities being perceived as an impediment to their educational attainment, or a threat to the well-being of others" (Dumas & Nelson, 2016, p. 39).

To support the school success of counternarratives like Lafayette's, White women teaching Black boys in early-childhood centers and elementary schools must routinely ask themselves: In what ways do I engage these considerations with the Black boys that I teach? Where and how do I fall short? And how can I do better in the future?

These considerations are important but insufficient if they do not lead to classroom practice that builds on effectively teaching Black boys. Identity Maps (e.g., https://www.visualthesaurus.com/cm/lessons/mapping-your-identity-a-back-to-school-ice-breaker/), for example, have become an increasingly popular approach in elementary schools to get to know Black boys outside of negative stereotypes and help teachers see Black boys as students with distinct perspectives, talents, and interests. Teachers and Black boys themselves are often surprised by how much they learn and how these dynamic maps enable both constituencies to see limitless potential and aspects of Black boys' identities that they had never seen before—revelations much needed to (re)imagine Black boyhood going forward.

■ ■ Engaging the Mind ★ Taking Action ★ Inspiring Excellence
Who They Are, What They Think, and What They Desire in Their Lives

In the spirit of basing classroom interventions on empirical research that asks Black boys "who they are, what they think, and what they desire in their lives," teachers are invited to print an Identity Map (https://www .visualthesaurus.com/cm/lessons/ mapping-your-identity-a-back-to-school- ice-breaker/) and have a Black boy student complete it in school this week. Use that Identity Map to influence a lesson next week. Remember the principle of Universal Design which states that a design based on the deep and specific needs or interests of one individual can be even more effective for an entire group than a lesson based on broad and superficial understandings of the group at large. After completing this task, assess its value, and then proceed to do Identity Maps with all Black boys. Teachers might choose to do Identity Maps with every student at the beginning of the next school year.

One valuable frame for considering the books, curricula, and images that teachers put in front of students is that of "windows and mirrors" (Style, 1996). The idea is that every student needs mirrors of his or her own identity and experience, mirrors that reflect people of similar racial and gender backgrounds. Students also need windows that give them insight into the lives and experiences of people who differ from them. Black boys tend to have plenty of windows onto the experiences of other people, but mirrors are rare. According to the Cooperative Children's Book Center's Survey of 3600 books, only 3 percent of the children's books in 2012 had an African American protagonist of any gender. That's ninety-nine books. Of those, only some of them depict Black boys. And of those, how many might depict a Black deaf boy?

The following vignette was written by Sean Norman, a student at Gallaudet University, who writes about the double stigma of being Black and deaf. His story drives home Nelson's point in the previous chapter: Teachers need to design lessons based on the individual students in their classroom. One of the most salient pieces of advice that Sean gives is this: Show Black deaf students that they can grow up to be healthy and productive Black deaf adults. Give them role models. Teach them about Black deaf people throughout history. This advice does not seem novel or new—essentially, he is asking teachers to give students mirrors to see themselves and their own stories in the world around them. Doing so will also give Sean's classmates windows that they too sorely need. It seems simple, and yet, hearing it again, from one student who spent years wondering if there was a place for him in the world because he had no evidence of it, is a powerful reminder of the importance of mirrors.

Vignette: Being Black and Deaf Is a Double Stigma

Sean Norman

I was always very skilled with history, very interested in history. In my deaf classes, I felt like the material wasn't interesting. It was very slow. I wanted to be put into a mainstream class because I felt the content would be more suited to my needs. My reading was never perfect, but I could do the work. I wanted to be put in the higher-level classes, and my parents wanted it, too. The deaf class moved at a slower pace; it wasn't as interesting. But my White teachers wanted to keep me in the deaf class. It was too much of a fight to get put into a class that was more suited to my needs—I felt oppressed in a sense. I got my degree after high school, and I wish that if I would've known, I could have put up more of a fight because I could have graduated and gone to college sooner.

Something I really want White teachers to know is to listen to the Black male voice. What I mean by that—not as much the content and the curriculum—but not to ignore when the kids want to use their voice. Being Black and deaf, it's a double stigma, and it's a lot for parents to bear. And the communication problem, too. A lot of deaf Black youth don't make it to college because they're perceived as unable to communicate because they're stuck under this double ceiling. A lot of people think that Black deaf youth have problems, but really they're just frustrated because they don't know how to get support. It's not that they're dumb, but they're being oppressed—they're not given the option to succeed.

Here's my advice for teachers of Black deaf students:

1. Pay attention. Believe what they're saying. Many people take one look and think Black deaf students can't do the work, they can't be successful. Parents do it, too.

2. Mainstream teachers—regardless of who the teacher is—it's important for that teacher to learn some sort of sign language to have a connection and to understand the background of the student.

3. Find out:

   What's the student's home life like?

   Do their parents sign?

   Do they have communication at home?

   Are they on their own at home?

   Are they emotionally stable?

   Do they have supports at home or not?

4. Find a Black deaf role model for the youth, someone who is successful, someone who could come to the school, so youth can see they can grow up to be a successful deaf Black person (male or a female). I'm Black, and it wasn't until college that I found a deaf Black role model like me who could sign and who was successful. Find someone who can come into the school and present to give them support and help them feel like they don't have to give up. As a deaf Black man, especially with my female teachers, it was very hard to find a mentor, someone to identify with. Especially with Black deaf students as well, it's good to have a mentor so they can understand their experience, they're not alone. My parents never communicated with me well either, so it really influenced my youth.

5. As a Black man and a Black person, it wasn't until high school and college that I learned about racism. It started in elementary school, but I didn't know anything about it. In my life, my experiences with racism, I wasn't aware of labeling it racism, but I was aware of people looking at me differently, and I didn't realize it was because of the color of my skin. It's something you have to learn to recognize over time. That should be happening from the beginning of K–12 to show some project about starting with slavery in the South, or showing the 1950s, or introducing Malcolm X—give those role models so they can start to learn about the Black experience in America today. For Black and deaf boys, many are unaware—like myself. It would be important for them to know what's happening in the world too, so they're aware and not sheltered. They need to know the truth. I didn't know about any of that until college. We don't get taught that information.

6. Teach them about prominent Black deaf people. It's funny because I went to Gallaudet University, and I was really surprised because the first Black man to

graduate from there was Andrew Foster. He went to Gallaudet University and I didn't learn more about him until I went to Gallaudet. He established many residential deaf schools in America, he was well-known in deaf community, and I never learned about him in my life growing up. Here's a role model for a deaf Black man, and I didn't learn about him until I was well out of my youth.

7. Listen to them. Really believe in the students and what they're saying. Help them be comfortable at school whether they're comfortable at home or not. They can learn that at school. Even if their home situation isn't comfortable, they can see there's support out there. They need that support. When my mother and I did not have a good relationship, school was important to me. The teachers were very important role models to me. Teachers almost become like a motherly role in the school—they take that role on. The students cherish that support.

8. Understand the complex relationship that students have with interpreters. I use an interpreter. Interpreters tend to be White women. That's a hard relationship to be involved in as a deaf student. They're so important. When the students are looking at the interpreter as a teacher, they're there to help me, they know the information, they have access to the communication, and that's my only inlet to the communication with others in the classroom, this White woman, and we need to work together. It's a partnership, and we're trying to develop that relationship. But sometimes I feel like I'm left out of the classroom. I want to make sure I'm participating, I want to feel involved in the classroom with the teachers, too. The interpreters have to understand that connection and voice appropriately for me from my point of view—not as a White female—but as a representative of me. They need to understand where I'm coming from, which is difficult because they're not Black. They're typically White women, and it's hard to get a connection that is accurate.

9. If there are any Black deaf people at home, or in the area, advocates or role models, invite them into the classroom, to meet the students, because that would be fantastic—they need to see adults as resources and there are many in the area that are successful. Find places and organizations where they can go and meet these people—there are quite a lot of pockets of these people all over the states—that would be a great resource for teachers to incorporate in the classroom as well. There are Black deaf advocate groups in Illinois and the District of Columbia. It would be great to have that connection to an organization. Ask if they have events, if they provide interpreters, and if the teacher can attend with the students.

Sometimes, when we talk about race, people will protest, "But isn't this really about class? Why are you making this about race, when there wouldn't even be a problem if we all had access to money and resources?" And while this statement is not entirely false—race is inextricable from class in the United States, it's not possible to talk only about class without talking about race—because, again, race is inextricable from class. That doesn't mean that race is predictive of socioeconomic status—there are more poor White people in the United States than poor Black people, even though the proportion of the Black population that is poor is higher than the proportion of the White population. There are also many wealthy and middle-class Black families in the United States who often get stereotyped as being poor or having minimal access to power and resources because of their skin color. Discussions of class are always also discussions about race. In the following chapter, Professor of Education Dr. Rich Milner demonstrates how discussions about poverty cannot be separated from discussions of race.

CHAPTER 20

"How Dare You Make This About Race?!"

Centering Race, Gender, and Poverty

H. Richard Milner

Derrick and his best friend, Alvin, had been good students. Current ninth-graders in a public high school, they have been friends since Little League baseball. As two Black males (I use *Black* and *African American* interchangeably throughout this essay), they are conscientious about prejudgments and stereotypes that people may have of them. Not only have these Black males been good students, they are charismatic. People (adolescents and adults alike) are drawn to their personalities. They love to make their friends and teachers laugh. Derrick's mother is a teacher, having taught in the school district where Derrick and Alvin attend for almost two decades. His father is a mechanic, and Derrick and his brother and sister have a good relationship with both parents.

Alvin's mother was a nurse practitioner at a convalescent home. Recently, the facility closed, and she was out of a job. She has been working part-time at a local hospital, working about ten hours a week, but has not been able to secure full-time employment. Alvin's father has been out of work for several years now due to a back injury he incurred on the job. Until recently, his family was moderately comfortable with his mother's nursing income. While Alvin's father receives disability benefits, he is not earning nearly as much as he earned when he was working, and the medical bills and medicine he takes for his back financially stretch the family in serious ways. Alvin has two younger brothers, and while he wants to get a job to help the family, most employers won't hire him until he turns sixteen—still almost a year away.

Lately, Alvin's teachers have noticed serious shifts in his academic performance as well as his attitude. He appears depressed and frustrated, and the change in his academic performance is quickly (and obviously) linked by his teachers to his social situation outside of school. Residents of Atlanta, Georgia, Alvin and his family are now living below the poverty line, with five total people in a household earning less than $28,410 a year (see Table 20.1 below).

TABLE 20.1   2015 Poverty Guidelines From the U.S. Department of Health and Human Services

PERSONS IN FAMILY	48 CONTIGUOUS STATES AND D.C.	ALASKA	HAWAII
1	$11,770	$14,720	$13,550
2	15,930	19,920	18,330
3	20,090	25,120	23,110
4	24,250	30,320	27,890
5	28,410	35,520	32,670
6	32,570	40,720	37,450
7	36,730	45,920	42,230
8	40,890	51,120	47,010
For each additional person, add	4,160	5,200	4,780

SOURCE: Federal Register, 80 FR 3236, pp. 3236-3237

His teachers in math, science, social studies, English language arts, physical education, and band (all of whom identify as White) are keen to focus their attention on his financial situation. But what his White teachers seem not to understand is that their attention needs to be placed as well on his race and his gender. The fact that Alvin is Black and a Black male is not trivial by any means in the grand frame of centering his socioeconomic status. His teachers believe that these social constructions are irrelevant and certainly inconsequential to the ways in which they respond to the shifts in Alvin's behavior. They believe that the focus should be on his family's financial situation—period.

White Teachers' Response

Excited, the White teachers in the school welcomed me as the professional development facilitator who was invited by the building principal to help them develop lessons and related experiences that responded to students living below the poverty line. Interestingly, some of the teachers assumed that there were some magic lessons that students living in poverty should experience. However, when I suggested that the teachers needed to consider race, gender, and poverty in their plans to be responsive to Alvin and similar students, the teachers were appalled. The issue for the teachers was about poverty, not about race! One teacher spoke on behalf of her colleagues to me as the professional development facilitator: "How dare you make this about race?! The problem with kids like Alvin is their lack of resources not their race!"

Alvin's situation is not unique in his school and community. To the contrary, other students were grappling with the same or very similar issues, with parents losing their jobs. But the teachers wanted to focus on this situation with Alvin and not think seriously about broader structures and systems that needed to be in place to support other students as well as Alvin. And the teachers, with good intentions, wanted to focus mostly on addressing Alvin's new situation living below the poverty line without attention to other matters. But it *does matter* that Alvin is Black and male in addition to now living below the poverty line.

Why Being Black Matters

Race is socially constructed. For as long as he can remember, Alvin has heard news reports, read articles in the newspaper and online, and overheard his teachers talk about a *state of emergency* for Black students and Black people. He understood that his being Black was an issue that others consistently tried to "fix" or change. Teachers should understand that racial messages Alvin received, such as those in the news media, consistently pointed out that Black male students were underachieving in comparison to their White counterparts. To be clear, while it is important to address and respond to all students living below the poverty line, White students' experiences were likely analogous but not identical to the issues Alvin and other Black students faced (Ladson-Billings, 2000). White students might understand financial challenges, for instance, but they do not understand the breadth and depth of what it means to live as a Black person in a racist society. Thus, attempting to support Alvin academically without deeply interrogating what it means to be Black in school and society would lead to an incomplete set of supports. Both poverty and his race must be considered in a project aimed at supporting Alvin and students like him (Milner, 2015).

For instance, in schools, Black students are overrepresented in special education classes, and the research shows that many of these students are teacher-referred for defiant behavior. Black students are also underidentified as gifted, while their White counterparts are consistently being recommended for the most rigorous learning opportunities in school. Another example of the ways in which race influences student experiences concerns the fact that Black students are disproportionally referred to the office for disciplinary infractions. Research shows that teachers tend to refer Black students to the office for subjective infractions ("you are too loud" or "you are disrespectful") whereas White students are referred to the office for objective ones ("you are late for class" or "I saw you push that chair over.") (Skiba, Michael, Nardo & Peterson, 2002). Consequently, these Black students are suspended (in-school and outside of school) as well as expelled at alarmingly higher rates than White students. In this sense, it is essential that teachers understand that student experiences inside of school are shaped not only by their socioeconomic status but also based on their race.

WHY BEING BLACK AND MALE MATTERS

What if, in addition to his family's financial situation, Alvin is grappling with broader societal realities relating to his being Black and male? Indeed, some believe Black males are supposed to be masculine and emotionless, and it can be tough for them to show vulnerability. Although Alvin is struggling, he finds it difficult to show his vulnerability because he has to present himself in a particular kind of way among his peers. Thus, poverty, his race, and his gender (maleness) must be considered in a project aimed at supporting Alvin and students like him (Milner, 2015).

The timing of his mother's job loss is essential in the grand emphasis of teachers responding to Alvin and his family. In other words, we need to consider what else is happening in society when Alvin's mother loses her job. For instance, although unjustifiable and counterproductive, the shooting of five Dallas police officers by a Black man, Micah Xavier Johnson (age 25) of Mesquite, Texas, serves as a reminder to Black males about what criminal stereotype they embody with their presence. Although Alvin and Derrick (or their fellow family members or friends, for that matter) were not the actual shooters of the police officers, the image of a Black male committing the crimes can cause social and psychological strain. In what ways do those in society see Alvin when they imagine Micah?

Black males must also deal with the consistent shootings of and harm to unarmed Black male bodies by police including but not limited to the following:

Amadou Diallo, 23, shot dead while unarmed, February 4, 1999

Sean Bell, 23, shot dead while unarmed, November 25, 2006

Oscar Grant, 23, shot dead while unarmed, January 1, 2009

Trayvon Martin, 17, shot dead while unarmed, February 26, 2012

Jonathon Ferrell, 24, shot dead while unarmed, September 14, 2013

Michael Brown, 19, shot dead while unarmed, August 9, 2014

These incidents send a message to Black males about their worth and their place in society and school. Attempting to understand Alvin's situation in poverty without understanding the time and place of his poverty status is insufficient (Milner, 2015). Put simply, Alvin is now living below the poverty line during a time when Black males are consistently being shot by police officers and vilified for crimes that they did not personally commit on police officers. As a middle-class student, Alvin did not have the same level of strain and stress on him about the financial challenges his family faced. His parents also were not as stressed about finances and could spend more time talking with Alvin about the shootings. This is not to say that his parents were not engaging Alvin with the shootings, but the additional financial pressures could make focusing on the shootings less of a priority for them. Moreover, when Alvin's parents were making more money, they could provide additional services to support him, such as setting up appointments to meet with a counselor or psychologist if they believed those resources were needed for their son as he was grappling with these unfortunate situations.

In addition to negotiating societal realities as mentioned above, Black male students are also simply having to live in and through peer and youth culture in the twenty-first century.

UNDERSTANDING RACE, POVERTY, AND GENDER INTERSECTIONALITY

As I have conducted professional development with teachers across the United States, I am often met with resistance and downright disregard of the role and salience of race (and gender) in the work teachers do. During a recent professional development session, one elementary school teacher made her frustrations with me clear. In her words, "Our principal invited you here to talk to us about specific strategies to teach our poor children. I was devouring what you had to say—you were right on target—until you got to this race stuff. *Race has nothing to do with how to teach my kids living in poverty.* What does it matter? Really!" Frustrated, the teacher disengaged for the remainder of the professional development session, despite my efforts to draw her back into the professional development opportunity.

Offended, the teacher did not find the focus on race or the intersected nature of race, class, and gender relevant to understanding the needs of her students. What was particularly striking as I reflect on the teacher's words and her unwillingness to address race was the privilege and power she exhibited in that moment to ignore what she found uncomfortable. A liberal but dangerous position that many teachers adopt is that issues of inequity are connected mostly to social class or poverty and that race does not matter any longer. They, in fact, believe we are postracial. Of course, poverty is important for teachers to consider in their practices, but poverty is only part of what is essential for teachers to consider in the complexity of meeting the needs of students who are experiencing the world like Alvin.

CONCLUSIONS AND RECOMMENDATIONS

In conclusion, teachers should be concerned about Alvin, but they should also be concerned about building practices that support other students as well. Building structures and systems to support all students does not mean that they treat all students the same (equally) but that they support and cultivate support and learning opportunities equitably, depending on the needs of each student. This means that what is appropriate to support one student living below the poverty line might be qualitatively different from what is necessary to support another. Centering issues of social class, race, and gender are critical dimensions of what is essential to build equitable practices. Focusing solely on Alvin and not broader challenges other students may be facing is problematic. My point is not that Alvin is not important. My point is that teachers sometimes try to become saviors—heroes and "she-roes"—to individual students without working to transform an entire system, structure, or situation for a broad range of students. For teachers in the classroom, this means that they develop instructional practices that are in fact responsive to a wider range of students. For instance, being responsive to a diverse range of students means that teachers should do the following:

(1) Immerse themselves in students' life worlds: Attempt to understand what it means to live in the world of their students through music, sport, film, and pop culture. This knowledge and understanding can enhance learning opportunities in the classroom.

(2) Reject deficit worldviews and ideologies: Concentrate on the assets that students bring into the classroom and build on those assets in the learning contexts. Understand their own assets as teachers and use those as a foundation to bridge learning opportunities in the classrooms.

(3) <u>Understand equity in practice</u>: Understand the difference between *equality* and *equity*, and work to meet the needs of individual students while realizing that their curriculum and instructional practices may not be the exact same between and among all students.

(4) <u>Build and sustain relationships</u>: Understand that students need to get to know teachers, and teachers need to get to know their students. Maintaining some professional distance, teachers see their work as a family affair and view their students as their own.

(5) <u>Provide student entry into their life world</u>: Allow students to learn about themselves and make connections to show the commonalities that exist between students and teachers. Share their stories with their students and allow students to share theirs with them.

(6) <u>Deal with the (for)ever presence of race and culture</u>: See themselves and their students as racialized and cultural beings.

■ ■ **Engaging the Mind** ★ **Taking Action** ★ **Inspiring Excellence**
Race and Class Reflection

Because race is so difficult for many teachers to understand and reflect about, this activity is designed for teachers to reflect on their own race and racial background (also, see, Johnson, 2002).

Identify and write about your memories and thoughts about how you came to see yourself as a racial being with a particular class background. On a small scale, pose questions to your parents, teachers, and/or siblings about events, episodes, and moments that shape how you see yourself as an individual with a race and class. Mostly, you should rely on your own memories, thoughts, and reflections about how you came to understand, represent, and develop your racial and class awareness. Locate artifacts that help shape your story about your race and class,

such as photos with family, friends, and classmates and other memorabilia. You might consider organizing your response around phases (early years, middle years, high school, college, adulthood).

Then consider how your race and class memories may influence your work as an educator.

Some guiding questions include:

(a) When did I start seeing myself as a person with a race and a class?

(b) What experiences and moments (in particular) have helped shape my racial and class awareness?

(c) How might my experiences as a racial being with a particular class background affect me as an educator?

Remember that chapter on White racial identity development? You may want to return to it as you read the following chapter. Dr. Eddie Moore Jr. is famous for his N!gga(er) word certification workshop, in which he helps participants confront a word that many of us have been taught to put out of our conscious minds. He takes readers through the workshop in the text here. We encourage you to pause as you read this chapter and participate in all the activities that Eddie puts forth as you read. His chapter is followed by a vignette by Marguerite W. Penick-Parks, a professor of education, who recounts her struggle with the N-word in her classroom as a young, inexperienced White teacher. Both Eddie's chapter and Marguerite's vignette close with practical suggestions for how to deal with the N-word as a White teacher.

CHAPTER 21

The N!gga(er) in Me . . .

Eddie Moore Jr.

It is very hard to recall every N!gga(er) moment while growing up in a poor area/ public housing in Florida. My real questions are related to the ongoing psychological impact of hearing the N!gga(er) word throughout my most impressionable years. The word was at the community center, on the basketball court, at house parties, at school, and other gatherings with family, friends, mentors, and Moore. In my mind, you instantly became cool, popular, and accepted by using, embracing, and becoming the word. Over time, you start feeling powerful because of the N!gga(er) in you. Eventually, N!gga(er) becomes almost impossible to shake from your identity development. You're actually embracing the persona and stereotypical characteristics of N!gga(er). The way you talk and walk. The people you respect and disrespect. The institutions you support and oppose. By embracing N!gga(er), I'm cool, I'm tough, I'm hard, I'm accepted, and I'm respected. Over time, N!gga(er) became synonymous with being a real Black man. This is and was part of my identity development growing up. Every day seemed to be a constant struggle with coolness, anger, acceptance, respect, pain, and fear. In fact, today, the struggle continues. Yeah that's right, I'm still dealing with the N!gga(er) in Me. It's still a part of my identity development, my identity struggle, and my psychological state of mind. Ya feel me? Ya hear me? Unfortunately, I don't think I'm alone. In fact, I'm saying N!gga(er) has become much more than a word mentioned too many times in a movie or rap song; N!gga(er) has been ingrained inside all of us. In fact, I'm arguing that the N!gga(er) word has been impacting folks since birth (possibly). Imagine that, educators, community leaders, policymakers and the like: Could it be true, do you have the N!gga(er) word inside of you? How would you know? How would you be impacted every day? What would be (are) the real life consequences and realities of the N!gga(er) word?

This chapter is designed to examine and understand the psychological, emotional, and educational impact of the N!gga(er) word on everyday people. More specifically, how the N!gga(er) word shapes and impacts the everyday realities and educational experiences of young Black boys taught by White women. In addition, this chapter is about the need for Moore courageous conversations and critical analysis related to how the N!gga(er) word has influenced and continues to influence generations of young people across all race, gender, social class, and Moore. Last, we will examine how the N!gga(er) word is often misunderstood, misconstrued, and filled with stereo-typical images that become the foundation for fear, oppression, and White supremacy.

The best way I've found to explore and understand all the complexities related to this word is to walk you through my N!gga(er) word presentation. I've been sharing this presentation with diverse groups across the nation for over fifteen years. It's part of a larger professional development presentation for educators, parents, and students called the "N!gga(er) Certification Program." This step-by-step process is designed so participants (readers) will consider a much different approach specifi-cally focused on understanding the psychological impact of N!gga(er). I also want participants (readers) to be inspired to take action. Most important, as part of our commitment to closing all the achievement, discipline, dropout, and other gaps related to Black Boys, we must examine, explore, and better understand N!gga(er) and the lifelong impact and influences it has on them and their White Women Teachers. Ok, Ok, here we go . . .

Step One: I turn off the lights. I tell the group, "Close your eyes, take a deep breath, stay quiet and please clear your mind." Then, I open/shut the door.

Step Two: Now I say, "With the room dark (ish), quiet (ish) and your eyes closed, the question is . . . a N!gga(er) just walked in the door, what's the picture in your head?" Go ahead, you try it. Close your eyes, quiet, clear your mind, and then I say, "a N!gga(er) just walked through the door." In one word, tell me, what's the picture or visual that comes into your mind? You can only use one word to describe the picture. What's the one word to describe the picture in your head.

Participants are encouraged to say the first word that comes to their mind as quickly as possible. There's no time for overthinking it or political correctness. I want the truth, the whole truth and nothing but the truth! If (when) folks are honest and real, then we can begin to uncover some hidden biases, blind spots, misperceptions, and stereotypes. Over the years, the words that have shown up consistently include but aren't limited to big, Black, male, young, athlete, gangster, thug, drugs, tattoos, thief, violent, Air Force 1s (shoes). Try it! What words did you come up with?

Step Three. It's time for a courageous conversation about where this picture comes from. It is very important to steer yourself away from who said it or where they heard it and to get to the visual/picture of N!gga(er) that is in your head. This is especially true if you are thinking, "I've never said that word." This is very important because even those (White women) teachers who will never utter the word and believe they don't have negative behavior associated with the word need to understand they still have images in their mind. More important, the word and images could have an impact on how they think about, treat, or teach Black boys. The pictures in the head don't lie. Even if participants don't believe it or never said it or listened to it, in presentation after presentation, their image of N!gga(er) is still there. It's often buried deep in the subconscious, but it's still there, ready to emerge inside of the various educational settings like classrooms, interventions, discipline, moments of needed empathy, academic expectations, parent/teacher conferences, dress code, vernacular, self-awareness, testing—the list goes on. As soon as the Young Black Male arrives, that student is judged, characterized, supervised, understood, or misunderstood through the lens of "N!gga(er)"

In my thirty years as an educator and twenty-five years as a father to two Black boys, and my fifty years as a Black man, it appears Black boys are often assumed to be more aggressive and violent. In situations involving physical altercations, it seems the Black boys receive harsher penalties or they are disciplined more quickly as the instigator rather than the victim. The tone for the Black boys is often one of suspicion. There is often a feeling of fear and danger coming from the students and teachers.

Sometimes it's even more subtle than that. One Saturday morning, I led the N!gga(er) word in Philly, and I went to a center city food court to buy some food at the lunch break. As I waited for my order in my three-piece suit, which I wear for presentations, a White woman approached and asked me where to find the plastic silverware. In that moment, I had to ask myself, "Was she seeing Eddie, or was she seeing the N!gga(er) word?" She saw my skin color and not my suit, not my shoes, not my body language. She saw my skin color and assumed inferiority, servitude.

Step Four. After a challenging look into the behavioral and psychological impact of N!gga(er), the next step is to explore the history of the word. Placing the word into a historical context creates an opportunity to discuss how the word has evolved, or not evolved, from the earliest time of being a word that controlled and demeaned a group of people, primarily African Americans, and more specifically, Black males. There are many questions we explore related to the history of the word. What's the history across different racial groups? How is the impact different for Black males, White women, and others? What does N!gga(er) really mean?

This idea of looking at the history of the word includes an individual assessment of where their image attached to N!gga(er) started. There is another very important (bonus) question I like to raise in each session which comes from a Lady Gaga song. The question is, "Were you 'born this way?'" My challenge is this: Is it possible that you were born with this image in your head, or is the N!gga(er) word (picture) learned behavior? I believe I learned my most (self) hate during my most innocent state. Many people believe the picture/psychological behavior tied to this word comes from society, television, rap music, or family members. But few people talk about the Gaga question: Were you "born this way?" I think we need to spend Moore time considering this question because the earlier the image enters the psyche, the harder it is to erase. Researchers suggest that the high rate of miscarriages among Black women in the United States is attributable to racial stress because miscarriages occur even when controlling for other factors like health care access and class. The United States is a country where there are racially disparate levels of prenatal care, in which White babies tend to get better and more comprehensive care than Black babies before they are even conceived. Baby Einstein sells music to play for babies in the womb because we know that even prenatal exposure to music impacts fetuses. What other types of exposure did you get in the womb? How was your birth mother cared for? When you were born, what was the racial background of the doctor? The nurses? What kind of facility were you born in? Even the care we get as babies begins to shape us, our experiences of the world, and our image of the N!gga(er) word. What did you see with your wide eyes at ages one, two, and three? Who did you live near? Who took care of you? Were there neighborhoods that your family avoided? What about your Black boy students? What were each of them hearing in the womb and seeing in infancy?

The process to unlearn N!gga(er) is different and much more difficult to unlearn if it is part of you from birth as opposed to something you heard for the first time at summer camp. I believe N!gga(er) socialization is what one sees every day all day, and it is Convincing, Undermining, and Powerful (CUP). It comes in a CUP that's filled every day. And whether we want to admit it or not, whether we have been taught we don't have it, even if we are disgusted by the word, we still have the word/image in our heads. Even if people don't make a joke or comment, we still think it. The image is around us, and it is kept alive by social media, by systemic racism, by the educational system, and by our very inability to admit it is there.

There is another important piece essential to the process of learning to own the word and the image. This piece involves not only understanding the visual but also how the visual may be different across groups. In addition, we need to recognize not only how the word impacts us individually, but more important, how it shapes how we do our job and how we make critical decisions. One place we consistently see the results of this image systematically appearing in people's minds is in the educational system. Teachers have to ask, "How does this image we carry around manifest in education: in our classrooms, in our curriculum, assessment, discipline, tracking, and so much Moore?" Examples of the image appearing in the system include a lack of representation of African Americans (especially African American males) in advanced placement courses; the overrepresentation of African American males in special education; the inability, or unwillingness, to recognize the whitewashing of the curriculum; and the discomfort with readings and discussions that allow for the much-needed courageous conversations. Many people who are making these decisions have that picture at the forefront of their minds even though they may never say the word. There is also the consistent impact on policy because of the visual: who is hired, how much they are paid, who is sent to the office, and who gets in trouble for teaching a book that looks like me (Moore).

The book *Nigger: The Strange Career of a Troublesome Word* by Randall Kennedy is a must-read for any teacher, parent, or administrator who is going to support, challenge, or stop the use of the word in their schools. Teachers who do not understand the relationship between Huck and Jim, especially in historical context, will talk about the characters as "friends" or equals. But is it really possible for Huck to pretend not to see the color of Jim's skin? That is a conversation teachers must have, but without the historical understanding of the embedded image in their head, the fallback is simply to say, "It is a bad word that we don't use today." But it *is* used; it is in social media, it is in rap music, it is used to describe the former president of the United States. The image is there when you look at police shootings, jury perceptions, and whether a Black boy belongs in talented and gifted classes. Literature such as *To Kill a Mockingbird* or *March* or *Huckleberry Finn* is exactly where these issues should be discussed to explore the image in students' minds. But to do that, teachers need to be educated on N!igga/er and have an understanding of the true image, not necessarily the one politically correct one they think they are supposed to have.

■ ■ Engaging the Mind ★ Taking Action ★ Inspiring Excellence
Addressing N!gga(er) in the Classroom, School and System

The big question is how is N!gga(er) being introduced to people. Where do they hear it, where do they see it, and when it appears in a text, what do they do with it? What are the skills educators need to know to address the word in their schools?

1. Educators need to understand the impact N!gga(er) has on them and how they can grow and understand the impact and influences of the word on their students. Teachers must talk with their students about personal challenges and struggles they

had/have with the word over their lifetime. It allows for trust and an opportunity for honest dialogue with their students, parents, and others.

2. Educators should have a zero tolerance policy in their schools and classrooms. It doesn't matter what students say in their house or in social media or listen to in their music. In the classroom and in the school, there must be zero tolerance. If that means you don't read *To Kill a Mockingbird* aloud, then you don't read it aloud. Zero tolerance!

3. Educators need to acknowledge how to apply zero tolerance to real-life situations, decisions, friendships, and so on. They must be strong and consistent when applying their policy because N!gga(er) is not going away. It is everywhere we turn, from the news headlines, students having "African" or gangster themed parties, to rap music, jokes, or coded language like "you're so ghetto," and even in social media with people addressing the first Black president as N!gga(er) The educator must play a key role, always.

4. Last, let's not overlook White students. Educators must know how to respond to White students who think it is cool to use the word. What does it mean when they do? Is it different? Those students should not get a free pass, and denial of that fact puts educators back at the beginning: what is the image you have of N!gga(er) in your head?

5. If you are not prepared for the myriad ways students will respond to this word, don't bring it into your classroom through literature or any other means. Nobody can be perfect in every situation, but you need to feel comfortable and competent for any kind of scenario or know where you can get help if you need it.

Vignette: Die N-word Die

Marguerite W. Penick-Parks

This is not about working with black boys, but it is about being a white woman teaching in a predominately black urban high school. And it is certainly about lack of either personal or professional preparation to be a culturally responsive and competent teacher of students who did not grow up in Iowa.

It was my second year of teaching. I was a 22-year-old, five-foot two-inch white woman teaching in a predominately African American urban school, and I thought I was prepared for anything. I was a student teacher in a special program to teach in urban schools and had done fine my first year. Now, I was not only the English and drama teacher but also the debate and forensics coach.

My first year had been eye-opening in terms of literature. Even though I was a speech/theater major and an English minor, the only African American author I knew when I started was Langston Hughes. Thus, for oral interpretation, I did not have a lot to offer my students beyond Shakespeare, Emily Dickinson, Mark Twain, Robert Frost, Edgar Allen Poe, and a whole host of authors whose works certainly did not fall in the realm of being culturally relevant. It was fortunate for me my first year that my students introduced me to Gwendolyn Brooks, Leroi Jones, Ntozake Shange, Countee Cullen, and numerous authors whose words my students loved to bring to life. And so, being the "cool" teacher I wanted to be, by the second year, I was trying to let them choose their own works for oral interpretation.

I did have a rule about language, which I had learned my first year. Students could say damn and hell because they are in the Bible, and if they used other words for the reason the author had chosen it, I allowed it. If they used any profanity for the purpose of getting a laugh out of the class, they would lose points. Students were fairly good about following the rule because they really wanted to do their own selection, and this allowed them dramatic freedom.

But then came the day of H. Rap Brown. I had a young woman in my class who struggled. She was behind academically, she was constantly in trouble with teachers because she often "spoke back," and she missed a lot of school. However, she loved drama, and she was good at it, so forensics was one of the things that kept her coming to school. I expected her to perform an African American author because I had helped her look for some, and I knew she would choose something with a lot of emotion. What I did not expect was a selection from H. Rap Brown's book, *Die Nigger Die: A Political Autobiography.* And yes, that word was repeated over and over in her selection.

How did I handle the uncomfortable, constant, and emotional use of the N word? All I can remember is just sitting there. I really don't remember anything else except sitting there thinking, what do I do? Do I stop her? What are the other students thinking? She was so proud of herself, of her selection, of how well she did it, of how much it meant to her. And I just sat there gaping.

How did I address it? I didn't. I had absolutely no idea what to do. So I just gave her a grade and kept my mouth shut. What teacher education institute from Iowa was going to prepare me for this? I know what I would do now. Now I have the tools and the knowledge to address the history, the impact, the media. I have read Michelle Alexander, Joy De Gruy, and Randall Kennedy, and I have attended Dr. Eddie Moore's N!gga/er workshop three times. Now I would have a discussion. I would ask her why she chose that selection, how it spoke to her. Why she felt the need to use that specific word. I would have a discussion on the history of the word, maybe have students read part of the Kennedy book. I would talk about how the word is used in music and why white people should never say it. I would let the class discuss how they felt having her use the word and why they think H. Rap Brown titled the book as he did and wrote what he did. Now I am a little more ready. But I wasn't then. I was a twenty-two-year-old five-foot-two white woman who thought she knew it all, who sat there with her mouth wide open, gasping, like a beached white belly up flounder. I remember that much. Ick.

We are so lucky to have the following chapter by Zeam Porter with contributions from Ty Gale. Lucky because we were put in touch with this bold young man, who writes with so much clarity about his experience of being Black and trans, and lucky because, somehow, Zeam made it through high school. According to Zeam, he spent more time in high school imagining his funeral than his graduation. As we read Zeam's words, we wonder how many brilliant minds we have never heard from because depression or suicide—caused by the incredible ignorance that our society has about the experience of transgender people—rendered them unable to access and share their gifts. The vignette by Phillipe Cunningham, which follows Zeam's chapter, focuses on how educators can create classrooms in which Black trans students can grow and thrive.

CHAPTER 22

Blackness/Transness

Two Targets on My Back

Zeam Porter with Ty Gale

Black: an adjective describing a person descended from the African diaspora.

Trans/transgender: an adjective describing a person whose gender identity does not directly correspond to the marker they were assigned at birth.

Cis/cisgender: an adjective describing a person whose gender identity corresponds to the marker they were assigned at birth.

Falling in love with economics was like Sisyphus finding the joy in pushing a boulder up a hill: slow, painful, lonely, but thoroughly captivating. One might find it difficult to understand why I looked forward to that class every day, especially with Ms. Youmans (a White woman born and raised in Minnesota) as my teacher. Every day I walked into a classroom where I held the weight of being both the lone Black student and the lone trans student. Every night my parents would walk by my room, seeing tears streaming down my face and hearing me ramble on and on about where all the moral economies had gone, and worry for me.

But I still practically ran to class, and not just because of my inherent obsession with theories and facts and figures. Economics fit right into that, certainly, but much more important, it was the only class where my identity as a Black transgender man was truly appreciated. There was no grudging acceptance in that class.

My identity and all the insights and hardships that come with it were explicitly encouraged to show up with me.

Ms. Youmans met the basic expectations for anyone interacting with a transgender person: she got my pronouns right, used my preferred name rather than my birth name, and corrected herself when she slipped up. But she didn't just lead by example, she used her position as a teacher to encourage class dialogue on gender, gender identity, race, misogyny, and how oppression and identity contributed to every economic system we studied. She regularly sent me home with extra reading materials on discrimination lawsuits from trans employees against various states. When learning about capitalism, she did not shy away from the hard conversation around Black people, my people, being seen as capital. She had our class read sections from *The New Jim Crow* to remind us that Black exploitation and other systems of oppression are rooted in profiting from vulnerable demographics, and their legacies still live on in our economic system to this day.

In short, Ms. Youmans wholeheartedly invested in my education. She saw how the curriculum in front of her was never meant to teach minority students like myself and decided to flip those lessons on their heads. She would bluntly state where resources and material did not recognize my existence in the classroom and tried her best to fill in the gaps. This does not mean she was an impossibly perfect teacher who fixed every part of our broken education system without a single misstep. What it means is that she did the necessary work to make her classroom into one that recognized my humanity and kept me engaged. She held space for me to be angry, for me to fumble, for me to be too tired to give 100 percent. I saw her trying her hardest to acknowledge the complex intersections of my identity and the identities of the rest of the class, and I never felt like it was some liberal guilt-driven attempt to let her pat herself on the back. She learned where school was failing and sincerely did her best to make up for it. With me, she succeeded. The fact that her success is remarkable points to fundamental negligence in the American education system, something I'm very familiar with.

Your Black trans students are operating in a world that only acknowledges them to highlight their death or define them as perverse. Your Black trans male students, in particular, are dealing with emotion too heavy to bear. They are then told that a real man—a real Black man—does not express those feelings, he uses them to grow strong and hard. Your Black trans male students are dealing with a cocktail of transphobia, racism, and toxic masculinity and are expected to somehow thrive in spite of that or end up dead or in jail.

I am Black, I am transgender, I am 19 years old, and narratives of death have surrounded me for my entire life. Every time I look at my high school diploma, I become overwhelmed. What should be a symbol of pride only dredges up lingering feelings of urgency and exhaustion. My graduation came from necessity, not a desire for success. I cannot celebrate the academic achievement of graduating when the institution that handed me my diploma hurt me in ways I'm still trying to understand. The Black poet Lucille Clifton (1993) once wrote what became the only purely positive sentiment I can see in my transition from high school to college.

> *. . . come celebrate*
>
> *with me that every day*
>
> *something has tried to kill me*
>
> *and has failed.*

Could you celebrate any more deeply than a sigh of survival when your school never acknowledged that Black trans women are murdered almost every week like clockwork? Could you exalt your education when you were the one forced to constantly educate your peers, teachers, and school administrators about trans identity? Could you salute your school when you became the center of a statewide debate about whether or not you should be allowed to play sports with the boys? Could you muster the strength to do schoolwork, to even show up to class, when your existence is practically invisible? Could you concentrate in class when you haven't used the bathroom for six hours for fear of getting kicked out, beaten up, or suspended? Could you raise your hand when you know your teacher will get your name and pronouns wrong, cementing the lifelong lesson that no one will ever recognize or validate you? Could you feel safe in an environment tailor-made to resemble a prison?

These questions aren't rhetorical. I urge you to deeply ponder your students' reality and your role in either hurting or helping their quest to survive it.

PRONOUNS AS ACTS OF VALIDATION OR VIOLENCE

Pronouns: how we refer to others in the third person: he/him/his, she/her/hers, they/them/theirs, and other pronouns outside of the binary of male or female.

Misgendering: the act of using the incorrect pronouns to refer to a transgender individual.

Gaslighting: a form of psychological abuse in which a victim is manipulated into doubting his or her own memory, perception, and sanity.

Microaggressions: intentional and unintentional acts of everyday, subtle hostility to members of marginalized groups.

Dissociation: the unconscious act of separating oneself from one's moment-to-moment experiences. A common symptom among victims of trauma.

As a Black trans student, how people refer to me reflects how important they believe my identities to be. Pronouns are either a statement that a teacher sees me and acknowledges who I really am or a reinforcement of the idea that how a teacher perceives my gender is everything and the truth of my existence doesn't matter. Even if a teacher apologizes for misgendering me, it doesn't heal the wound created by years of transphobia. Apologizing without putting in the effort to change the behavior gaslights trans people.

There is an unavoidable (and necessary) power dynamic between teachers and students. Trans students' sanity and self-worth is put on the chopping block every time a teacher doesn't respect their chosen name and pronouns solely for the convenience of refusing to appropriately engage with them. It is similar to having someone consistently get your name wrong and telling you that your name is too hard to pronounce and they have no interest in trying. The power imbalance is such that the student often cannot demand respect from the teacher without suffering consequences in the classroom. Having to deal with incorrect names and pronouns alongside a host of other transphobic microaggressions makes concentration difficult, and dissociation is a common survival technique. Whether intentional or unintentional, transphobic microaggressions from teachers and other authority figures actively interfere with trans students' academic success.

UNDERSTANDING THE BLACK TRANS SCHOOL EXPERIENCE

> **Cisheteronormativity:** the ingrained social assumption that straight cisgender identity is the norm and that anyone who deviates from it by holding Queer/ trans identity is lesser.

Every single day, Black trans students deal with an environment that is almost overwhelmingly hostile to them. Racism, transphobia, and all other oppressive systems are intertwined and interdependent. Living at the intersection of multiple minority identities only magnifies the experience of oppression. There is often no safe haven.

Education is a system through which oppression is taught and reinforced. Through the unconscious externalization of their ingrained racism and transphobia, teachers often act as barriers to the education of Black trans students. I discussed how this manifests through direct interactions with students, but it's also prevalent in curricula across all areas of study. According to many classes that discuss history, trans people don't exist, and Black people are uncivilized savages who only become relevant in death. Curricula must move to acknowledge the contributions of Black people and trans people to math, science, art, and overall culture. Erasing those legacies teaches Black trans students that their imagination and their drive are irrelevant, that their impact on society is negligible unless they become martyrs.

Teachers must work to actively and intentionally combat cisheteronormativity. That starts with understanding the fundamentals of trans identity, getting names and pronouns right, and setting a tone of respect in the classroom. Students follow the examples set by teachers, and too often those examples erase and delegitimize transness.

Educators must realize that holding multiple marginalized identities means facing systemic oppression from every direction. To put it bluntly: *Your students are combating death daily.*

UNDERSTANDING THE BIGGER PICTURE

The True Colors Fund found that LGBTQ-identified youth make up 7 percent of the general population and 40 percent of the youth homeless population, with a disproportionate amount of those specifically identifying as trans or gender nonconforming. In a survey by The National Gay and Lesbian Task Force and the National Center for Transgender Equality, 41 percent of trans respondents reported attempting suicide compared to less than 2 percent of the general population. Too many transgender students wake up each day wondering how they will survive. Where will I live? What will I eat? Where can I bathe? How do I keep from self-harm? How am I supposed to concentrate in school when I have to worry about staying alive? Many trans youth are also forced to engage in the underground economy, selling narcotics or participating in sex work as a means of survival. The shame attached to such activities only helps to push trans students out of school and into unsafe situations.

The best teachers acknowledge trans students and the specific challenges life has for them: academic disparities, increased rates of murder and suicide, employment and housing discrimination, health care discrimination, increased rates of mental health issues, and dozens of other complications.

■ ■ Engaging the Mind ★ Taking Action ★ Inspiring Excellence
Concrete Steps Teachers Can Take to Help
Black Trans Students

- Creating a school committee or work group focused on addressing racism, homophobia, and transphobia in the school environment is a good way not only to increase the impact of an individual's efforts, but also to create a supportive environment that can help to alleviate the stress and pressure that often comes with confronting racism and combating its effects.

- Protect trans youth access to bathrooms and locker rooms.

  o A study done by GLSEN (2015) found that 56 percent of trans students were denied access to facilities that align with their gender identity.

  o This directly affects a student's success in the classroom and can lead to physical harm, including urinary tract infections from students withholding relief for eight hours a day.

- Take a deep look at curriculum and notice how Black and trans folks, much less Black trans folks, are not represented.

- Speak up on queerphobic, transphobic, and/or racist violence, including police brutality and incidents like the Pulse Orlando shooting, without triggering or tokenizing your students.

- Allow personal narratives to be included in class work, recognizing that your students have insight you don't that deserves to be incorporated into your class.

- Take time out of class to identify other students' problematic/violent attacks and commentary.

- Provide access to suicide hotlines.

- Lead by example.

  o If you do not get your students' pronouns right and recognize their humanity, why should they show up and work hard?

- Be aware that Queer/trans people of color are significantly more likely to experience homelessness.

- Talk with sexual education providers about how to employ harm reduction practices and not perpetuate misinformation.

  o A 2008 study from the National Center for Transgender Equality (NCTE) and the National Gay and Lesbian Task Force found that "Black transgender and gender non-conforming people are affected by HIV in devastating numbers. Over one-fifth of Black respondents reported being HIV positive (20.23 percent) and an additional 10 percent reported that they did not know their status. This compares to rates of 2.64 percent for transgender respondents of all races, 2.4 percent for the general Black population, and 0.60 percent for the general U.S. population."

- Understand that having hard conversations and educating oneself is mandatory, and not doing so perpetuates violence.

Vignette: What Educators Can Do to Support Trans Students

Phillipe Cunningham

In the education field, there has been an increased awareness of the need for culturally competent practices. Expanding cultural competency helps youth-serving professionals to have awareness of their own cultural identity, norms, and perspective on difference and to create learning environments that meet the cultural and social needs of youth of color. As we continue to see youth of color being left behind, there is an urgent need to begin intentionally incorporating cultural competency in learning opportunities, both in the classroom and outside of school time. This need rings particularly true for Black transmasculine youth as they are growing and maturing in a hostile social climate. They are forced to navigate the world combating prejudice and discrimination on multiple fronts due to the combination of their Black identity, their gender identity, and any number of other marginalized identities, such as a feminine gender expression, disability status, and so on.

In a study conducted on the transgender experience, almost half (49 percent) of Black respondents reported having attempted suicide, compared to 41 percent of all study respondents, and 1.6 percent of the general U.S. population (Harrison-Quintana, Lettman-Hicks, & Grant, 2009). Other research has shown that LGBTQ students are three times more likely to feel unsafe at school, which leads to poor academic performance and chronic absenteeism. LGBTQ youth are significantly more likely than their heterosexual and cisgender peers to have been bullied, threatened, or injured with a weapon; to experience dating violence; to carry a weapon; and to be in physical altercations or involved in gang-related activity at school. Disaggregated data show that Black LGBTQ youth are disproportionately negatively impacted in the school setting with these issues; they also face a higher likelihood of getting trapped in the school-to-prison pipeline by punitive discipline practices (Burdge, Licona, & Hyemingway, 2014).

To begin building culturally competent practices in the classroom requires, first, a clear understanding of one of the most significant barriers to youth from marginalized communities: Eurocentric values being prioritized over all other cultures. Eurocentrism is the interpretation of non-European societies' cultures and histories through a European perspective, as well as the dismissal and undervaluation of non-European societies as inferior (Mackerras, 2005). Eurocentrism is pervasive in every aspect of U.S. culture, media, arts, the business sector, government decision-making, the American identity, and so on. It is a massive roadblock for young people of color in their development process. Because they are undervalued, along with their experiences, young people of color lose the opportunities to learn valuable information about their heritage and culture's positive aspects and contributions to society during critical development years. The loss of this information is a form of oppression to youth of color.

Individual educators and other youth work professionals must take responsibility for dismantling this oppression within their classrooms and programs. One direction is to proactively identify and address cultural needs. Positive racial socialization—a proactive strategy to guide youth of color through the process of developing a positive racial identity—has been shown to inoculate Black boys and young men of color against risk factors for engaging in violent behaviors (Degruy, Kjellstrand, Briggs, & Brennan, 2012). Unraveling the Eurocentrism that is woven into the learning experience will reorient education to center on the strengths and contributions of *all* communities and identities, which in turn lifts *everyone* up, not just those from marginalized communities.

Developing a positive racial identity is crucial for Black trans boys and young men, but this alone does not fully address their more nuanced developmental needs. A lack of self-determination within the school environment has been shown to negatively impact LGBTQ youth, not only in their academic achievement, but also their physical and emotional health outcomes (Grossman et al., 2006). One strategy to address the disempowering effects of a lack of self-determination is to incorporate positive youth development into the learning experience and school environment. Positive youth development is a strengths-based approach in which young people are regarded as partners in their development and resources to be developed (Lerner, 2004).

Traditional education frameworks typically view youth as empty vessels who are to be filled with content knowledge; however, young people bring to the table a richness of stories and talents. Incorporating positive youth development in lesson planning and implementation will not only empower their personal agency but will also develop leadership skills as young people become active partners in their learning experiences rather than passive followers simply absorbing content.

Tying it all together, there are three areas where youth-work professionals can begin to leverage their lesson and program planning to address the needs of Black transmasculine youth to emotionally thrive and reach their full potential:

- Increasing representation of Black and trans people in content areas

- Building opportunities to increase agency and self-determination in the learning environment

- Empowering young people to cocreate their learning experience in a way that gives space for cultural and racial identity development

Some examples include providing a menu of diverse authors whom students can choose to read; incorporating historical research in science projects to explore scientific pioneers of color; and facilitating discussions about the experience of race and manifestation of racism within the context of the teacher's content area. Setting up an environment that promotes self-determination can be as simple as honoring and defending the answer to the question, "Who are you and who do you want to be?"

This may feel like a large task at first, but be empowered to work through being overwhelmed. Feeling overwhelmed, which often leads to shutting down, is one of the many ways that racism and transphobia protect themselves so they can remain unchecked. As educators and other youth-work professionals, it is our responsibility to work through these feelings of discomfort to fully show up for our most vulnerable students.

We turn now to early childhood, a time when Black children leave their home or sometimes their neighborhood day care or preschool, and go to a school with White teachers. For many, this is a new encounter. Many White teachers believe that children are colorblind, and race should not matter. And yet, as Dr. Chonika Coleman-King and Jabina Coleman write in this next piece, during this time, Black boys are suspended or expelled from school at the highest rates across kindergarten through twelfth grade. Unfamiliar with White schools and teachers, Black boys in kindergarten are maximally unconscious of society's demand that they code-switch to White cultural norms and behaviors. Black parents are still learning to navigate the educational system. White early childhood teachers, many of whom are trying to be colorblind, have rarely been trained to see this entry point into school as such a risky time for their Black boys. The boys' actions are often criminalized or demonized (e.g., running with scissors is seen as a threatening action) in ways that simply don't apply in the same way to White children (Okonofua and Eberhardt, 2015). We encourage teachers to recognize this as a vulnerable moment, when Black parents hand their precious babies over to White teachers. Will you hand them back whole at the end of the day, at the end of the year?

CHAPTER 23

White Teachers and the Power to Transform

Early Childhood Educators and the Potential for Lasting Harm

Chonika Coleman-King and Jabina Coleman

As a Black scholar who studies the intersections between education and race, the announcement that my sister was expecting a baby boy—a Black baby boy—brought both excitement and fear. I was excited because he was the first of his generation, and I couldn't wait to use my educational expertise to help give him a firm foundation, but I had also learned from my village of aunts and uncles how important my role as an aunt would be. I'd be his second mother, the person he could talk to when he felt he couldn't talk to his parents. I'd pick him up from school, buy him cool things, take him to museums and parks—I was thrilled by the idea that I could pour into his life in the same way my village poured into mine when I was a child.

However, I was also afraid. I knew that based on his genetics (both his parents are dark-skinned), he would most likely be a dark-skinned Black boy; in the United States, he would be perceived as a significant threat to people in positions of authority. Nonetheless, I was sure that because his mother and I had solid educational backgrounds from top public and Ivy League universities, we were well-equipped to advocate for him in ways that many Black boys are not afforded. His mother sought small, affordable, and educationally rich preschools for him. He was exposed to an array of books, music, and educational programming as well as fun and stimulating activities like arts and crafts, trips to the zoo; and most important, he too had a village. He was loved, and he knew it. He was always smiling and a fun-loving boy. We couldn't ask for much more.

When the time came for him to begin formal schooling, we did our research. We looked at the neighborhood public schools, public charters, private and elite independent private schools. Ultimately, our desire for him to have "the best" education landed him at an independent private school with tuition exceeding $16,000 per year. The student population was fairly diverse, and during the open house, school representatives mentioned how much they would nurture the individual gifts and characteristics of each child. We knew it would be a good fit. Randall loved people; he was an extrovert. He would make jokes, play tricks, laugh, and smile with everyone with whom he came in contact. We wanted him to be in a place that would nurture his vivacious spirit and intellectual curiosity. He had begun reading by age three and was beyond proficient in all the necessary foundational skills. We were excited about the prospects for his future.

Up until this point, Randall had little experience with White teachers and children, and not long after his enrollment into school, things changed. We were not in his classroom to know exactly what happened, but we did know that his spirit was broken. His mother received numerous calls home and complaints from the teacher. Randall, the darkest Black boy in the entire lower school, was a *problem*. In one meeting with his teacher, administrators, and the school counselor, who had observed him in class in preparation for the meeting, Randall was described using all the common catchphrases ascribed to little Black boys. He was deemed manipulative, inattentive, hyperactive, impulsive, and constantly in need of redirection—all buzzwords used to legitimize the systematic failure of Black boys in schools. For his mother and me, these issues were new; Randall's African American childcare providers had never complained, even though their programs required discipline and attentiveness to preschool-level academic instruction and developmentally appropriate play.

We knew the routine; we had read it in educational and social science texts. Still, to experience how "the best" education could take a smart, curious, and happy child and deem him deviant and in need of behavioral health services in a matter of months blew our minds and crushed our spirits. We tried to communicate that he needed more academic engagement, but school personnel ignored the thought that this Black boy wasn't being challenged enough or would be better suited to a different instructional style. According to them, the only plausible course of action was for the school psychologist to continue to observe and evaluate Randall for further recommendations.

According to research, Black children are punished more frequently and more harshly than their White counterparts for similar infractions (Townsend, 2000). In preschools, Black children often are suspended and expelled before they are given an opportunity to adapt to school norms and mainstream culture (Gilliam, 2005). These trends continue well into middle- and high school years, leading to staggering rates of school push-out, further strengthening the school-to-prison pipeline (Bentley-Edwards, Thomas, Stevenson, 2013; Monroe, 2005). In essence, what happens in the early elementary years can have a lasting effect on the educational outcomes and life trajectory of Black boys.

Although Randall began kindergarten as an enthusiastic child with a courageous spirit, that did not last long. With constant redirection and notes home to his parents, Randall began to dislike the idea of school. His peers blamed him regularly for classroom mishaps and labeled him a troublemaker. On several occasions, he mentioned that no one at school liked him, and he did not want to return to the school he initially loved. His parents were frustrated that their attempts to provide their child with the best possible education appeared to be doing more harm than good.

One day, upon entering the school, Randall's mother was met by an African American father who had been there to observe the school to determine whether it was a good fit for his child. The man said to Randall's parents, "Is that your son? I observed him in the classroom today and, boy, was he enthusiastic and eager to learn. He raised his hand for every question and gave very intelligent answers." This had been one of few positive reports Randall's parents heard that year, and it took someone who was an outsider to the school to acknowledge Randall's brilliance. At that point, Randall's parents truly understood the extent to which the color of their son's skin shaped the perceptions of his behavior and astuteness. Eagerness to learn was dubbed disruptive behavior, jokes told using clever plays on words were deemed troublesome, and his use of physical touch was demonized. His parents realized that providing him with the best education also came with exposure to prejudices, stereotypes, and labels that continue to shape his identity in educational settings years later.

We tell this story to help capture the harm that can be done to perfectly normal Black boys who love life and love learning. Just one teacher, with the support of institutionalized systems of racism, can transform a smile into a frown, an angel into a monster, a prospect into a problem. Once the damage is done, it is incredibly difficult to undo. To White teachers who are routinely entrusted with families' most precious gifts, this is what we want you to know:

- You have immense power, and it can be used to build up or tear down children. Think critically about the effects of your behavior on the child and not just whether you approve of the child's behavior or whether your expectations are being met. Value the needs and expectations of the child and family.

- Go with the flow, step out of your box, and learn from the exuberance or quietness of students who are different from the group. Follow their lead at times.

- Trust the knowledge of parents, guardians, and other family to help you in the instruction of their loved one. You (and other school personnel) are not the *only* experts, and your norm is not the *only* norm.

- Always give positive feedback to children and parents. If you cannot find the positive in a child, you are not engaging him or her in the right way.

- Know that many families of Black children are strict, clear, and direct in their instruction to children, as are many Black preschool teachers. This is often the result of needing to ensure that Black children are clear about expectations for them in a society that judges them harshly. If a Black child is acting out in your class, it may be that you are using language that is not clear and direct. A culturally competent teacher recognizes and accommodates areas of cultural mismatch between students and teachers. Observe Black teachers in your school, and ask for feedback from Black parents with regard to your communication style with children.

- Take notice when you have a child in your class who is different. Protect and advocate for that child. Help him or her to develop positive relationships with others. If you show care toward a child, his or her peers will follow suit.

- Always be cognizant of the kinds of words you use to describe the behaviors and attributes of children of color. If they sound like common buzzwords ascribed to particular groups, evaluate the role that race, class, and culture might play in your perspective.

- Reflect on how you treat children of color compared to White children with similar dispositions. Ask yourself, "To which children do I give the benefit of the doubt?"

- Remind yourself that all parents love their children, value education, and are doing the best they can to ensure their child's success.

- Remember that all children have a lot to learn, and that the people and cultures that they have been exposed to before coming to your classroom shape their expectations about what behavior, community, and school should look like. Take time to learn what those things have been for them.

This suggested activity is for our teacher-readers. If you find yourself having a difficult time with a Black boy (or girl) at school, do not seek punitive retribution. You will gain that child's trust and respect by drawing him closer. Eat lunch with that child or go to one of his extracurricular activities. Go out to dinner with his family. Do a home visit to experience the child in his space. Talk to parents about their goals and aspirations for their child. After spending time with a child outside of the classroom, you will never view that child or his family the same again. Your relationship with that child and his family will forever be changed with just a little intentionality, openness, and time.

The following two-part vignette is by Jillian Best Adler, an early-childhood practitioner who has witnessed racial dynamics with children for years. She recalls her own experience of caring for African American cousins and raising a mixed race son who appears White. From her vantage point, she has been able to bear witness, in ways that many White people never experience, to the marked difference in the way that Black children get treated in public relative to White children or children who appear White. Stories like these push us, as readers, to ask, "How much of this unconscious bias and judgement lives in me?"

Vignette: Brown Mothers, White Children

Jillian Best Adler

I acted as a regular caregiver for many of my cousins when they were young. My teen years were spent with brown-skinned, curly-haired children—African American and biracial—and I followed the example of our parents in holding them to certain standards in public. I tried to expose them to things that I valued, like spending hours at the playground, looking for creatures in the creek, dancing in the rain, and getting messy while making crafts, but when other people were around, I made sure that these children were clean, well-dressed, and well-behaved. I quieted their wild antics when we were under the watchful eye of black elders, and more important, white people. I wanted white people to value the children that I loved so much, so it felt vital that the children look like they deserved that value.

I grew to learn that this responsibility should not have been placed on their brown shoulders (or mine) because all children deserve to be valued and appreciated as divinely imperfect and playful. I committed myself never to force a black child to live up to the unspoken expectations of the watchful gaze of others. Although I am now a parent, I have never had to put my commitment into practice. My child appears white and benefits from White privilege. When he is in public, I experience the usual mild parental shame when he cries or fights, but I know that he is not being judged based on his race. I do not worry when his face is crusty, his clothes stained, or his behavior rowdy. People look at him and smile and comment on his golden curls. In those moments, I feel relief that they appreciate him and allow him to be a child, but I also feel ashamed that I, by proxy, am taking advantage of his White privilege when so many children can't.

This difference was palpable during a family get-together in Lexington, Kentucky, for my cousin's wedding. My black mother, my biracial sister and me, and two of our sons, fair-skinned and blond, waited in the lobby of the Hilton, while we waited for our rooms to be ready. We were just an hour away from the start of the ceremony in an upstairs ballroom, and our children were restless from a long car ride together. The boys, ages one and a half and four, ran in circles around us, giggling and squealing as we haggled with the shift manager. My uncle, large, bald, and black, walked up to us and, with some bass in his voice, told our children, "Settle down. This ain't no playground." I swivelled, redirecting the frustration that had been aimed at the hotel staff, and declared, "It is a playground for them because we don't have a room for them to run in, and they have to be ready to sit still during the wedding in forty-five minutes."

Once all was said and done, my uncle ushered them through foot races up and down the hallway on the ninth floor, and, later, we ended up leaving the wedding ceremony anyway because they were simply too young to sit quietly for so long. Yet, what strikes me is that my uncle and I were at odds because of our fundamental difference in belief about how children should behave in public. He's always had to protect his brown-skinned children from the disapproving gaze of others. They had to be better than other children, just to be granted the right to exist. In spite of their actual racial makeup, my son and nephew benefit from White privilege. Even when their behavior is downright naughty in public, they are judged only for their behavior (and maybe for their parents' abilities), rather than being seen as bad or dangerous, as African American children often are judged.

The following chapter comes from Benny Vásquez, one of the co-directors of Border Crossers in New York City, who writes with extraordinary candor about being Black and Queer in the classroom of White heterosexual—and Queer—teachers who don't know how to support him in the wholeness of himself. It is not enough, he says, to recognize his Blackness. Or his queerness. To truly support our Black Queer boys, he says, we need to support their Black queerness with role models and acknowledgment, and access to Black Queer adults whose existence can demonstrate to children who are wondering: Is there a pathway to adulthood for me? Is there a place in this world for me, as a Black and Queer person? Benny's activity and challenge to readers comes in the middle of his chapter, as an invitation to track your emotional response and then keep reading, even as it might evoke strong feelings. This chapter, like this book, asks White women teachers to reckon with their group-level identity in a way that can sometimes be hard for White people because White people tend to be accustomed to seeing themselves as individuals. As any of our Black boy students could probably tell us, each of us is an individual, and each of us is also represented and shaped by our group identities, whether we like it or not. Remember that if this piece—or any piece— pushes you outside of your comfort zone, that is not a sign that you should put it down. It is a sign that you are learning and growing. While the chapter offers thoughts useful to all readers, it is directly addressed to White women teachers.

CHAPTER 24

Learn About Us Before You Teach (About) Us

Queer Black Boys

Benny Vásquez

At the age of six, I had my first White teacher stand in front of me, put her hand on her hip, and yell, "If you play with those dolls again, I'm going to tell your mother," *making me realize what I could and could not do.*

At the age of eight, I was told by my White teacher, boys would quit calling me "Ben-Gay" if I stopped hanging out with Tanya, Theresa, Martha, and Kathy. She sat me down, put her hand on my shoulder and lovingly said, "For your own good, play more kickball with the boys and leave the girls alone, go be with the boys," *making me realize I was "different."*

At the age of ten, I was told by my White teacher that I need to sit up straight, stop speaking like those "Black boys" in the other class, *making me realize that I needed to talk, act, and speak the White way.*

At the age of twelve, I was told by my White teacher that I should spend my Sunday studying and learning how to read, rather than walking with "those people for that "AIDS thing," *making me realize that she was talking about people like me.*

At age of fifteen, I was told by my White teacher that Harvey Milk was the "best gay activist in history," *and I thought he was the only one.*

At the age of eighteen, I was told by my White teacher that Audre Lorde, Cherrie Moraga, and Gloria Anzaldua existed and was also told that being a woman **and** being a woman of color must be so *"beautifully painful." It was then that I asked myself, "Will my life always also be beautifully painful?"*

I could go on and on and on. White women were everywhere in my schooling and rarely did they provide a framework to support my development as a Queer Man of Color. I often wish I could hop on the car with Doc and Mc'fly and stop my White women teachers in their tracks, preventing them from perpetuating patriarchy, heterosexism, homophobia, and genderism. White women must realize that teaching children of color (whether it's Black, brown, Queer, or not) needs to be accompanied with accountability, consciousness, and the reality that your desire to "help" is not needed. Teachers: Learn before you act, teach yourself before you teach others, question how White supremacy has shaped you, and identify how white culture stands beside you in every classroom you enter. Most important, listen. Listen. Listen.

I have been a student, a teacher, a colleague, a fellow social justice organizer, and a dear friend of yours, White Woman. I have spent a lot of time with you and I ask that you continue to read this knowing that: Teaching Queer Black Boys is an art, not a science. I do not have all the answers, no blue pill to give you, nor do I represent all the Queer brown and black boys in the world. I am speaking to you from my heart, experiences, and the pain that many well-intentioned White women have caused, that many of you have caused my community.

■ ■ Engaging the Mind ★ Taking Action ★ Inspiring Excellence
Notice Your Feelings. Don't Panic.
Establish an Inquiry Stance.

Sometimes when I am honest with White women, I experience a sense of fragility, guilt, and anger. Rather than save a task for the end of this chapter, I invite you to monitor your own fragility, guilt, and anger as you read this chapter. Notice what is coming up for you as you read my words. Feel the feelings, but don't panic. Then, think about a question you want to explore moving forward as you grapple with your role as a White teacher. These six recommendations are ones I wished my White teachers would have followed, and I offer them as a gift to you.

1. SIMPLICITY HAS ITS FAULTS.

"Line up, boys and girls! Boys go here, girls go there! If you're a boy please listen . . ."
I remember hearing these short phrases and countless times questioning where

I was going to go. It wasn't because I questioned my gender but rather because whenever I heard those words, I panicked. You see, I was a spirited, "effeminate" kid who quickly became an outsider when forced to be with only the boys. When they played kickball and chose their teammates, I would cringe at the idea of being the last one picked. I often was. As they talked about what girl they wanted to kiss, all I could think about was what was wrong with me that I wanted to kiss them.

I ask that you challenge simplicity. Challenge and question how you assign groups, make teams, or even figure out seating assignments. Begin to think broadly about gender and its nuances. Think about the young Black boys who are questioning their gender and concepts of masculinity; they are right in front of you wondering if they are "broken" because they are not reflected in the words that are coming out of your mouth.

2. HARVEY MILK IS NOT MY HERO.

I can appreciate Harvey Milk as much as any other Queer man in this country, and I can strongly say that he is *not* my hero. If you are a White woman teacher and are going to celebrate LGBTQ History Month by teaching about Harvey Milk, marriage equality, and Ellen DeGeneres, then I ask that you stop. You are not doing any Black or Brown Queer students any favors, nor are you advancing any other student in your classroom. You are perpetuating a system of White supremacy that speciously links LGBTQ issues in schools as being solely a White issue. Break away from that paradigm and know that we are not just Queer, we are Brown, we are Black, and we are intersectional. Talk about Sylvia Rivera, Bayard Rustin, James Baldwin. Talk about Queer activists who are alive and continuously fighting for the survival of Queer communities of color. Go beyond White LGBTQ figures; know they don't represent the entire Queer community. Learn about us before you teach (about) us.

3. YOU ARE PRIVILEGED.

There I said it. I often wish I had said it to all my white teachers. Having them become aware of their everyday white privilege would have allowed me to be fully Queer and fully black in anti-racist classrooms. When White people know they're privileged, then they understand that my oppression is not just incidental to me, it's part of a system that affects us both. Think about your own relationship to racism and your privilege. Are you resisting it or accepting it? Regardless of your feelings, I ask that you reflect on the following questions. As a white woman teacher consider that your role as a teacher does not stop after the bell rings. Think about opportunities where you can become an active and intentional part of the cohort fighting against racism and Queer-phobia, and use your positionality for change.

- What are policies and practices that marginalize Queer boys of color? Examine your school through a racial justice and Queer-affirming lens. Think about discipline practices, academic success measurements, discipline practices, gender-binary policies (gender-neutral bathrooms, locker rooms), social events, and so on.

- How do we talk about relationships? Do you assume that everyone is heterosexual, gender-conforming, and white? When you talk about gender and sexuality, are you functioning through a lens that supports a gender-binary based in heteronormativity or through an anti-oppressive lens that affirms various experiences?

- What are your biases? As teachers, we bring our own biases and prejudices into the way we teach and what we choose to teach. Consider how Black Queer voices are underrepresented in your curriculum: How often do you ensure that the Queer black community is represented in what you teach? How have your internalized white superiority and (internalized) homophobia affected your pedagogy and the way you teach children who are both Black and Queer?

- Explore what it means to be White. Explore what it means to be a White Teacher. Explore what it means to be a White teacher who identifies as a woman. If you also identify as hetero, how does that affect how you relate, talk to, and form relationships with Queer Black boys? If you also identify as queer, how does *that* affect how you relate, talk to, and form relationships with Queer Black boys? What are you going to do to build classrooms that are fundamentally anti-racist and anti-queerphobic?

Write about these questions. Share them with other white educators. The more conscious you are of how *you* perpetuate white supremacy, the clearer the action steps will become.

You've made it this far, are you ready to keep on going?

4. We don't need saving.

I still admire and love one of my white teachers. She's the first white teacher who taught me that the voices of those who are Queer and black should be heard. She introduced me to the writings of Black Queer feminists and made me reflect on my own identity as a Queer young Black man. Being Queer herself, she had and wanted a special relationship with the few Queer students. I remember her taking on a motherly role in our lives, one that we didn't ask for but accepted. She cooked for us, used our slang and our language, told stories of working in the 'hood and teaching black boys about themselves, talked about how rough we had it and how she wanted to help us be "free." She often said to us, "I really understand and know your pain, believe me I want to be here for you." In retrospect, I realize that she had no idea of our pain and the experience we had as young Black Queer men living in the midst of AIDS, don't ask/don't tell, being labeled "super-predators," and witnessing the beating of Rodney King. Although her intentions were out of love, the impact we received as young Queer Black boys was that we mistakenly thought we needed her to survive.

White Woman teacher, please know, you are not our saviors, even if you identify as a member of the larger LGBTQ community. Rather than save, inspire. Spark inspiration by being authentic, clear of your positionality in this world, speak to your power and privilege in ways that show your humanity. Expand the narrative of how we talk about "gay issues" in schools; not all of us are White. I challenge you to start a sentence with "As a white (insert sexual orientation here) teacher . . ." while teaching and relate to your Queer Black boys without trying to *be them*, save them, or take on our identities.

Remember, you are not our mothers, and we do not need to be saved.

5. As Queer Black Boys, WE COME OUT EVERY DAY.

I've had the opportunity of working with several Black and Brown Queer students across the country in supporting their efforts in creating safer schools. During my time with these students, I met Johnny, who identified as a trans black boy and went to a predominantly white school in a major city in the South. Johnny was a fierce activist and eleventh grader who was consistently holding his school accountable for the racist and transphobic polices he had to endure. As a trans boy of color, Johnny had to endure a school culture that was not made for him to succeed. He often shared how every time he entered the school building, he felt that he was coming out as trans and as Black—every single day it was a new coming-out process. Not only did Johnny refuse to use the school bathroom due to safety concerns, but he was at a school (taught by majority white women) that disproportionately disciplined and suspended Black Boys like him. He would often express how many of his white teachers did not advocate for him to be comfortable, and nor did he feel that any part of his identity was accepted. Unfortunately, Johnny left his school after being physically attacked his junior year. He was attacked in a classroom where the white teacher did nothing.

Let it be clear, White teacher, you will not be a successful teacher for Queer Black boys unless you are challenging school policies that perpetuate institutional racism, institutional transphobia, and institutional homophobia simultaneously. You can't fight one issue at a time; all issues are connected. Be vigilant that the cycle of inequity is multilayered for Queer Black boys, and multiple approaches must be taken to address systemic oppressions. If you are going to teach us, then use your voice, privilege, and whiteness to dismantle the patterns that forced Johnny to drop out of high school. If you don't, you are making an active decision to support and maintain white supremacy in your schools.

6. YOU ARE NOT AN ALLY.

Do you consider yourself an ally? If so, I ask that you reconsider. Too many white women in our schools use this label as a badge of honor and proudly state, "I am a white ally! I am a straight ally!" without considering the implications. We don't need you to be an ally to Queer Black boys. We need you to speak up and get messy. Being an ally assumes that *we* are the ones responsible to tear down a system that continuously oppresses us and that you are here to support our "fight." You as a white woman and as a member of the largest population of teachers in the country take the lead, and we will hold you accountable as you do it. We, as Queer boys/men of color, will be allies to you as you take on a system that was made for your benefit while disadvantaging others.

WHAT CAN YOU DO?

Here are some ideas: organizing, sharing this book with other white women in education, starting racial affinity groups across lines of sexual orientation, working in partnership and in accountability to Queer Black men, and not giving up when it gets too hard or painful. White women, please realize that lives are being affected because of the fear of uncovering your whiteness. Ask yourself: What does it mean for me to be a white educator and teach Queer boys of color? Get uncomfortable.

Queer Black Boys don't have the time to wait for your comfort.

White Women, I want you to know that doing this work will not be easy, but you don't have a choice. As you continue, you will fail, and you will need to pick yourself up and try again. Do not give up. Lean on each other for support, guidance, and love. You can't afford to wait.

Time is of the essence and urgency is pivotal.

White Women, what are you going to do?

No discussion of Black males in school is complete without a discussion of Black male teachers and what we can do to increase their number. There may be no greater action educators could take on behalf of Black boy learners than making it possible for them to learn from Black men because so much happens for students when they see themselves reflected in a teacher. First, the possibilities for personal connections multiply, and we know that relationships with teachers are one of the primary predictors of investment and success in school. Second, teachers are the purveyors of knowledge and access in our society. To not see oneself among the force of people called teachers conveys a message that only White people can do that work, that Black people are not capable. And third, within their relationship with teachers, Black boys can see pathways for themselves they do not often see in our society. But there are so many reasons, as Dr. Chance Lewis and Amber Bryant point out in this following chapter, why Black men don't go into teaching or stay in teaching. Part of the work of creating schools that serve Black boys is to create faculties that Black men want to join.

CHAPTER 25

Black Male Students and Teachers in K–12 Classrooms

Strategies for Support to Increase Performance as Students and Professionals

Chance Lewis and Amber Bryant

This chapter seeks to advance the conversations on teaching Black male students and supporting Black male teachers by adding an informed perspective from a member of both groups. As a former Black male student and a current educator, my perspective on the topic is critical to shining light on the complexities that Black males face in educational and social institutions, in which they have often been misunderstood. This chapter is intended to provide a framework for which you can support Black male teachers in schools. It starts with a brief history and current status of Black male teachers in the United States and extends to a practical guide and reflective activity that can help others think more critically about their interactions with Black male teachers and students.

Brief History

The current racial and demographic makeup of the teacher workforce is no longer a surprise. Most educational research on the topic of diversifying the teacher workforce highlights the majority status of White women in the field. Much of this, as Anderson (1988) points out, is a result of the numerous obstacles Blacks faced entering into the public school system as both students and teachers during the late nineteenth century. Historically, the Black community in the United States has struggled to develop schools and curricula representative of themselves that reflects the uniqueness of their community. In the early nineteenth century, immediately after the American Civil War, the obstacles included persistent racial discrimination, limited financial resources, slow community economic development, and the insurmountable demands of Northern philanthropic funders (Anderson, 1988). Nevertheless, during this period, the teaching profession was viewed as a profession of honor, status, and respect within the African American community (Lewis, 2006).

In 2013, the National Center for Education reported that 82 percent of teachers in the United States were White and 7 percent were Black; only about 2 percent of teachers were Black males (Feistritzer, 2011; NCES, 2013). The status of Black boys in the U.S. school system is not drastically different as far as numerical representation in K–12 schools (see Figure 25.1). Academically, the high school graduation rate of African American students is the lowest compared to other major racial groups (Green, White, & Green, 2012). Research findings further suggest a relationship between the poor academic success of Black youth, particularly males, and their social isolation and academic achievement in the classroom; Black males are the least represented and are performing the worst academically.

We know that implicit discipline bias causes overrepresentation of Black boys in school suspensions and that teacher and student-deficit ideologies toward Black boys' academic success (Toldson, 2013) result in the disengagement and underperformance of Black boys. These negative perceptions of Black boys persist into larger society as they age. In regard to Black male teachers, Lynn (2006) explains that racist ideologies about Black men in society make it difficult for them to find themselves comfortable in a classroom. Lynn (2006) explains a commonly held sentiment within today's social norms: "Black men are not only considered incapable of providing children with a sense of emotional safety, but they also are considered to be threatening and intimidating to teachers and parents" (pp. 2499–2500). Black male teachers' presence in the classroom does much to lessen the negative stereotypes of Black men, and this promotion of social tolerance and acceptance is ultimately beneficial for all groups in society. Black males are less likely to enter the field of education due to low pay, demanding training and certification requirements, and more appealing career options (Lewis, 2006). In addition, Lewis (2006)

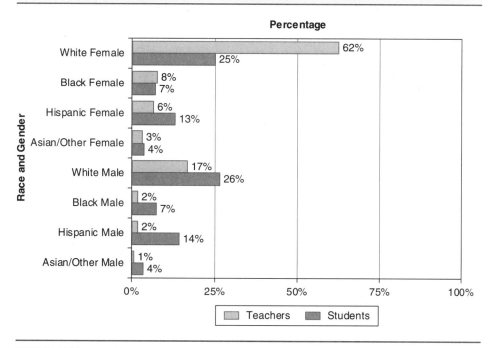

Percentage

White Female — Teachers 62%, Students 25%
Black Female — Teachers 8%, Students 7%
Hispanic Female — Teachers 6%, Students 13%
Asian/Other Female — Teachers 3%, Students 4%
White Male — Teachers 17%, Students 26%
Black Male — Teachers 2%, Students 7%
Hispanic Male — Teachers 2%, Students 14%
Asian/Other Male — Teachers 1%, Students 4%

Legend: Teachers, Students

SOURCE: Toldson, I. (2013). Race matter in the classroom. In C.W. Lewis & I.A. Toldson (Eds.), *Black Male Teachers: Diversifying the United States' Teacher Workforce* (pp. 15–21). Wagon Lane: Emerald Group Publishing.

explains that many Black male teachers describe social and cultural difficulties within the teaching profession, including racism and lack of encouragement and support, which serve as deterrents to staying in the field. Black male teachers are less likely to stay in the teaching profession than other racial demographics (Lewis, 2006, 2013). The rest of this chapter provides recommendations to help support current Black male teachers and Black boy students.

How to Support Black Male Colleagues

Black male educators need to feel direct support in the areas of classroom instruction and management. This is generally true of all K–12 educators; however, the uniqueness of Black male teachers requires a specific approach that recognizes and acknowledges the balance that must be struck between being a classroom teacher and a racial minority in a school. Often, Black male teachers are found to work in social isolation and take on extra and unintended responsibilities associated with being the only (or one of few) Black male teachers in the school. Black male educators tend to carry the burden of representing the entire race and gender of Black men and are often called upon to be spokespersons on diversity (Lewis, 2006).

Specific White teachers, both male and female, are not chronically called upon to speak for the whole of the race. Another unintended consequences of their status is that Black male teachers are often seen as disciplinarians or father figures to the Black students; discipline should be the responsibility of the school staff as a whole in regard to all children of all races (Lewis, 2006). Certainly, the presence of Black teachers is beneficial to Black students specifically; however, their presence is also beneficial to other races of students, as all children should receive an education from a diverse body of teachers with varying cultural backgrounds. Contrary to popular belief, it is not necessary to "befriend" Black male colleagues. Black male teachers want to feel respected and seen as equal colleagues more than anything; befriending can be a by-product of this process. This approach fosters ideologies of respect, inclusion, and empathy with both students and teaching staff, which are necessary to enable a successful global community.

Several tips that White teachers can employ to help support their fellow Black male colleagues are listed below. This list—excerpted from my prior work, *White Teachers/ Diverse Classrooms: A Guide to Building Inclusive Schools, Promoting High Expectations, and Eliminating Racism*—is not exhaustive but can serve as an informative beginning framework for those seeking deeper and more sustainable engagement.

1. **Show students and colleagues respect, and it will be reciprocated.** Black male teachers are just as qualified and educated as other teachers in the building. The "Golden Rule" of treating others as you would like applies here.

2. **Consider your first impression. Avoid judging based on stereotypes.** Work to intentionally reduce stereotyping, which has been indicated as an impediment to Black boys succeeding and engaging academically as well as Black males persisting in the field of education.

3. **Take the time to learn about your students' and colleagues' backgrounds and interests.** This will help you develop a connection with them that may create an environment conducive to teaching and learning. Cultural understanding and tolerance helps to reduce stereotypes and social threats of inclusion. For Black boys and Black male teachers, this means actively learning about diverse students and teachers, which will help to increase your understanding of and impact with such groups.

4. **Recognize cultural differences and develop a multicultural curriculum.** Attempt to decentralize your beliefs and paradigms associated with education and society, and try to be open to varying perspectives and other ways of knowing. Attempt to be explicit and inclusive in your curriculum choices and supplementary material. Highlight Black leaders and make their contributions to your content area known. Also, work to uncover

critical perspectives in history that may have been initially overlooked when planning lessons.

5. **Establish high expectations and standards for all students, and they will meet the challenge.** Set the bar high for your Black boy students and recognize in them what the Black male educators have—an ability to achieve as a child and to live up to their optimum potential such as they have as a minority teacher.

SOURCE: Garrison-Wade, D. & Lewis, C. (2006). Tips for school principals and teachers: Helping black student achieve. In J. Landsman & C.W. Lewis (Eds.), *White teachers/ diverse classrooms: A guide to building inclusive schools, promoting high expectations, and eliminating racism* (pp. 150–161). Sterling, VA: Stylus.

■ ■ Engaging the Mind ★ Taking Action ★ Inspiring Excellence
Supporting Your Black Male Colleagues

Part of turning theory into practice is understanding ideas and awareness of actions. This reflection activity is designed to help readers think critically and to honestly assess how you can adjust, adapt, or grow to develop a more supportive approach to Black male colleagues and Black boy students.

Directions: Rate the following statements according to the Likert scale provided.

SA - Agree Strongly	A - Agree	D - Disagree	SD - Strongly Disagree

1. _____I do not see color and this is a good thing.

2. _____I assume that my Black male colleagues are just as capable as I am.

3. _____I personally see Black male teachers as father figures to Black children.

4. _____I seek out my Black male colleagues when addressing discipline issues with Black boys.

5. _____I expect the same behavior and academic performance for my Black boys as I do from all my other students.

Think about what you considered when writing your responses. Did your approach reaffirm negative stereotypes? Was your approach from an inclusive mentality? In what ways do you need to adjust your thinking around the groups discussed? Being conscious of these factors will serve to have a positive effect on your teaching and relationships with Black boys and Black male educators while interacting with them in schools.

Black professionals are frequently undermined in education. Dr. Chris Emdin of Columbia University writes about the way that so many Black male teachers are given disciplinary positions, such as dean, because they are seen as capable of disciplining Black students—and particularly Black boys—in ways that White women can't (Emdin, 2016). When White women are unable, due to a lack of exposure and cultural competency, to discipline a Black boy student effectively, the burden gets unfairly placed on Black colleagues. Very few teachers went into education to be disciplinarians. And yet that becomes the entire job for some Black male educators. This inevitably drives them out of education early. The next vignette sheds light on a different issue: the overlooked Black professionals who serve Black students in a teaching and mentoring role but who are not recognized for this unpaid labor. Many of the Black support staff in schools take on the role of a loving and connecting adult to Black students whose White teachers cannot know, for lack of experience, what it is like to attend a predominantly White school as a Black child.

Vignette: The Administrative Assistant
Staff Member: Oh, and *Black*!

Deneen R. Young

I had one middle-school young man come to me yesterday. I didn't realize he even remembered me or remembered when I had told him, "You can stop me anytime if you just need a familiar, safe, and friendly face." Well, yesterday he needed that. He said hello as he passed, but then he turned around and came back to make conversation with me. I checked in with him and asked, "Are you good, or do you need that extra high five"? He smiled and nodded yes. I proceeded to let him know it's all going to be OK. "You are good!" I told him. I tell you, he smiled the biggest smile. I cracked a joke, and he walked away with a different step.

I am the assistant to the principal, assistant registrar, coordinator of end of the year events, and co-advisor for the Black Student Union. What most people don't know is that I'm usually the first person that African American students (and some students of color) come to when:

- They don't know how to be themselves or "flip the switch."

- They don't know how to manage their academics.

- They need an ear to share with someone who understands the difference between school life and home life—and they don't how to balance both.

- They can't figure out how to transition into an environment they know nothing about.

- They are unfamiliar with the do's and don'ts coming from a different culture or socioeconomic background.

- They don't have lunch money or haven't been able to order all their schoolbooks.

- They want to cry out of frustration or a sense of being alone or being "the only one"—and won't because of pride—but need the space to know it's okay to cry.

- They feel fearful that they cannot speak out when they are the only African Americans in a classroom and a teacher has shared something that hits home for them negatively and is insensitive.

- They have been mistaken for another African American student and don't know who to tell or that it is a microaggression.

- They've had a white student begin to touch their hair and wanted to speak up to say "stop" but were made to feel they can't because they will be viewed as aggressive.

- They are out of their comfort zone and need comfort (big or small).

- They need to be encouraged and lifted up because they don't think they are good enough or even smart enough.

- They feel how some teachers treat them differently from students who don't look like them.

- They don't know how to not be themselves because they're afraid they will be made to change.

- They need me to listen through their tears (and at times mine) and reassure them that they belong—they have everything already in them that will allow them to succeed and graduate.

It is my hope that my position—and the role of other Black staff members who do this same unpaid, unseen work—isn't just recognized when needed in a crisis. I want schools to realize that Black support staff, including cafeteria workers and custodians at many schools, are the glue that helps to keep Black children together. While I may not be an official part of the faculty, I am a teacher, an entire position, a department unto myself that is part of the heart that keeps the growth going.

I believe if we are all charged to meet each child where they are and support their growth academically, emotionally, and socially, it is each person's responsibility to do just that! Step out of your discomfort, know that you are not saving a child but supporting and teaching a child.

As a staff member, I am not always appreciated. My presence is needed not only in the high school but at every grade level. I purposely make connections with students and families of color across the school; sometimes I'm the only person at the school to whom they feel connected. And yet I'm often undervalued. But I'm usually the first person that my colleagues on the faculty and in the administration come to when someone uses the "n-word," when teachers have questions, when parents are unhappy.

Tears

Understands when called the wrong name

Understands when jokes are made about how you
talk or look

Understands that you learn differently but it doesn't mean
you're stupid but you may feel as though you are

Understands that the support you need is just an ear to
hear and understand

Knows how to support your needs entirely

Support

PART 4

RELATIONSHIPS WITH PARENTS, COLLEAGUES, AND COMMUNITY

Sometimes we just need to sit back and listen to the words of those who have spent their lives raising Black boys, fighting for the rights of their sons, and moving beyond to fight for the rights of all who have been marginalized, excluded, dehumanized, and isolated from opportunities to become who they want to be and know they can be. Two incredible women, Vernā Myers, Esq. and Dr. Shakti Butler, share their stories as mothers of Black boys, providing valuable lessons for teachers that they alone could write. Their chapters are followed by the voice of Orinthia Swindell who also shares her experience, of raising two Black sons. Listen to their voices, listen to their pain, and especially, listen to their advice as they speak words of wisdom for those who will determine the future of their children and millions of others.

CHAPTER 26

Helping Amazing Black Boys Become Amazing Black Men

An interview with *Vernā Myers*

In my mind, I'm saying, "Please conduct yourself in a way that someone is not going to kill you. Please conduct yourself in a way that no one is going to imprison you." This is the narrative in my brain from the sixth grade till today.

Let Me Tell How School Started for My Amazing Son

My son is now a twenty-nine-year-old, 6'5" tall, wonderful, kind, and social justice-oriented black man. He currently works at a nonprofit, helping young people who have family members in the criminal justice system. As a little kid, he was vocal, strong-willed, energetic, and all over the place. I found his energy difficult, because I grew up in a strict black family where kids were seen but not heard and were required to be compliant. No one was really interested in what children had to say; they just had to get and stay in line.

I think this idea of obedience is deeply engrained in our history because of its importance for survival through slavery, the Jim Crow and civil rights eras, and even today. As a parent, I quickly realized that if I used a heavy hand on him, I would destroy his spirit, so I spent a lot of time trying to learn strategies to keep his spirit alive while also giving him the parameters he needed to be successful.

That was fine until he went to school. When he entered kindergarten, I asked myself, "What are we going to do with this kid?" I remember walking down the hall to his kindergarten class. I could hear his loud voice, and I thought, "Oh, Lord, what was I thinking when I moved him to a school with only two black boys in his class?" He was really tall and really loud, and he was active, with unpredictable gross motor skills. That first day, as he walked down the hall, his hand hooked a little blonde girl's hair by mistake, and he dragged her with him halfway down the hall. This is how school started.

I WAS WORRIED ABOUT BIAS AND STEREOTYPE

Biases are the stories we make up about people before we know who they actually are. Everyone has biases, but the biases white teachers carry into the classroom about black boys have a detrimental effect. (I should mention black teachers have biases, too, but many also have more experience with black people generally and a level of investment in the success of black children that can outweigh those biases.) It is imperative for white teachers to ask themselves how they are going to get to know their young black male students when most of them have been told (directly and indirectly) all their lives to avoid and fear black boys and men. Research shows that implicit bias rears its head in the disciplining of young black men in the class-room when teachers are white women. The work of Okonofua and Eberhardt (2015) shows that black students exist in a system that, instead of keeping their spirits alive, doubles down and increases the discipline applied in classrooms. This increase in discipline breaks their spirit, which leads to opposition, which in turn leads to more discipline. This cycle continues until the child drops out, is pushed out, or worse, ends up in juvenile detention facilities (Okonofua & Eberhardt, 2015).

In their research, Okonofua and Eberhardt (2015) provided white teachers with the school records of black boys and white boys that described two instances of negative behavior. Then, the researchers looked at what the teachers proposed for discipline for the first and second infractions. Results indicated that on the first infraction, teachers disciplined white and black children identically and typically not harshly. For the second infraction, however, the teachers made presumptions about who that child was and what was possible for him. After the second incident, teachers perceived the black students differently.

This is the point where preconceived bias and stereotypes are confirmed. If the student was not black, teachers made excuses for what happened and were more lenient. The study shows that teachers discipline black students more harshly on second infractions, even when the infractions are identical, hence the title of the article: "Two Strikes: Race and the Disciplining of Young Students."

Studies such as this one that examine hidden biases demonstrate the need for white teachers to think about how they need to move toward young black men instead of away from them. If teachers can get past their implicit biases and move toward understanding students' individual needs, they may be amazed at what they find.

YOUNG BLACK MEN GROW UP TO BE AMAZING BLACK MEN WHO CHANGE OUR LIVES

In kindergarten when my son was one of two black boys, he had an outstanding teacher: an artistic white woman who showed me a lot of respect as a parent. She noticed my son was smart and articulate . . . not articulate for a black student, just articulate. But even though he was well-spoken, he couldn't draw to save his life, as his fine and gross motor skills were still undeveloped. He was loud. He stuck out because of these things and because he was black. He also couldn't sit in a circle and cross his legs because his legs were longer than everyone else's. His teacher said, "Oh, that's fine. He can just sit in a chair." I worried that he was going to feel like he was not part of the class, but she said, "No, I'll just explain to the kids that different people have different bodies; some people are more comfortable in chairs, and some people can sit easily on the floor, and if other children want to sit in a chair, they can, too." What she did was to normalize my son's different needs, instead of limiting him. She approached it head on, openly and simply stated: "That is what he needs." Not only did she move toward my son, she moved him toward her; he felt seen and she helped bring the whole class with him.

The other great thing this teacher did was to find a supportive way to address the fact that he had a lot of energy. Instead of talking about how he was a "bad boy," she worked with other teachers to find a solution. They decided that when he was behaving really well, they would give him a star, and he could translate these stars into time in the gym. Up until the fourth grade, he was given time to go to the gym, supervised, of course. So instead of demonizing the fact that he had the need to move around, the teachers found a way to normalize his needs and incentivize good behavior. The school adjusted to him instead of requiring him to do all the adjusting. This teacher saw that my son did not quite fit the norm. He was not bad, but he didn't follow mainstream white educational expectations, and she was willing to adapt and modify. She saw students as individuals and tried to modify accordingly. This is important for all students but especially for black boys because the societal presumptions start off against them.

Understand the Fears of Parents of Black Boys

Here is the thing that teachers need to know about the parents of black boys: we, the parents, are constantly wrestling with our future fear for our sons. In sixth grade, the school would call me, sometimes weekly, saying, "Tres had a problem today." And in my mind, I was saying, "Please conduct yourself in a way that someone is not going to kill you. Please conduct yourself in a way that no one is going to imprison you!" This was the narrative in my brain from sixth grade until today.

In middle school, all kinds of weird things started happening—to Tres and all his friends. I think it is developmental; many of them are acting crazy. And I get the call, "Your son has been in a fight with Mark Feldman." My son had been in a fight with one of his closest friends, who was white. When I got that call, my heart started beating really fast, and my brain was saying, "He's going to mess up his future. He can't afford to misbehave. Doesn't he understand that he's playing into the stereotype?" I thought then that somehow by crossing every "t" and dotting every "i" and being perfectly comported and having the correct diction at all times that somehow he could free himself from this cage of sorts. Despite all my efforts, in middle school, I had to deal with the fact that I had a young black son in a mostly white school who was acting out and seemingly confirming every stereotype about black boys as violent and troublemakers. I was doing all I could to make sure that people didn't have this presumption about him, and he was confirming it! I would explain to him every day that it was important for him to behave well, and yet I was being called by the school to come retrieve him due to his suspension. So I had all these ideas and emotions flooding in when I got that phone call. Mostly, I was angry!

But before I went to pick him up, I was wise enough to call a friend. I said, "Tres just got suspended; he's fighting again, and I'm so mad at him." She just started listening to me, and I went on and on, "He's going to keep getting in trouble; he's going to go to jail or he's going to get killed! I don't understand what's wrong with him and he's embarrassing, and he does bad things, and we do everything for him." She listened to me until I ran out of steam; there was silence, and then she said, "Sounds like you really love him." And something just cracked inside me. I cried and cried and cried. She added, "It sounds like you're afraid for him." And I said, "Yes, I'm really afraid for him." She reminded me that he was only in middle school, and my fears were based on a future worry, not what was happening now. Something about that conversation allowed me to get clearer about what I wanted to tell my son that day.

So I picked him up from school, and he walked out with that slouchy look, that said, "I am in trouble. I am useless as a person. I have done a terrible thing. My mother can't stand me." You know that body posture? He slinked into the back seat, and I asked, "Do you want to go to McDonalds?" And he remarked in a surprised way, "Umm . . . Yeah?" He knew that McDonald's was the place he got to go for a treat. So we went to McDonalds and he asked, "We aren't doing take out?" I said, "No. we are going in and you can get whatever you want." He ordered, and we sat down, and he began eating. Then I said, "I've been really trying to figure out how to tell you . . ." And he interjected, "How mad you are at me?" I said, "No, how much I love you." And tears just started falling from his eyes, and he began confessing, "I'm so sorry. It's all bad. Mark, he's my friend, and he said this and then I don't know what happened, I just started hitting him. And I don't know what to do with myself and I feel so scared." And he just sort of kept talking and talking, and I just listened. I hugged him and then I said, "We are going to figure it out. We are going to learn things so that when it gets scary for you, you know what you can do instead of fighting."

We left McDonald's, and driving home, we began passing the street where Mark lived. My son asked, "Mom can I stop at Mark's? I want to apologize." So, I took him to Mark's house and waited for him in the car. A few minutes later, Mark's Dad came out and said, "Well, they're on the trampoline right now, so I guess they're okay, right?"

As I reflect on the whole situation, I ask myself now, "How dare I burden an individual black child, who is in middle school, with the entire history of the marginalization of black males? But that's what we do, and I'm not the only one. We take that behavior and fast forward it to the future and we treat children like they are full grown adults. That's what some teachers are doing when they go to harsh discipline. They discipline young people as if they're old and they've been committed and sent to jail already. And as a mother who has done the same thing in my own brain, I understand how quickly one can escalate to that fear and act on that presumption.

Educators, like all human beings, are biased. Teachers who want to overcome their biases need to acknowledge the power of racism and the negative biases and stereotypes that have been embedded in our society and psyche—even when we are good, well-meaning people. Once they accept that we have all been impacted by racism and that they may have negative biases against certain groups like black men, there are things they can do to offset or counter that bias. For example, they can think about specific counterexamples to these biases and stereotypes. In other words, they need to understand that a child in their classroom could be the next Paul Laurence Dunbar, Nat Turner, W. E. B. DuBois, or Barack Obama. Teachers need to be aware that these black men used to be black boys sitting in a classroom. Sydney Poitier didn't just come from nowhere, and Colin Powell didn't just appear as a general. Not all of them were straight-A students who never got in trouble. They were all young boys, and along the way to adulthood, people made a difference in their lives and encouraged them. Teachers need to read and know and understand this history of black people because if they have that body of knowledge, they can visualize a future leader in the children before them, rather than a stereotype with limited expectations.

■ ■ Engaging the Mind ★ Taking Action ★ Inspiring Excellence
Four Suggestions for Teachers

1. Read, Read, Read. I suggest all teachers, and especially white teachers, read Beverly Tatum's classic book *Why Are All the Black Kids Sitting Together in the Cafeteria?* (1997). It is important and powerful. It will help tremendously to read studies on bias because they will be better able to find their own biases and get out of denial about them. The hardest thing for good people to believe is that they have biases and, more important, that the biases are impacting their behavior. It's the unconscious thought that is more predictive of a person's behavior than their explicit views. Therefore, all teachers should take the Harvard University's "Implicit Bias Test." https://implicit.harvard.edu/implicit/takeatest.html

Another highly recommended reading on bias is *Blink* (2005) by Malcolm Gladwell. Also, one of the major scholars in the field of the education of black boys is Dr. Jawanza Kunjufu. His works include *Black Students, Middle Class Teachers* (2002), *Keeping Black Boys Out of Special Education* (2005), *Changing School Culture for Black Males* (2013), and many more. It is critical that educators read at least some of these works because the texts explore multiple critical issues from discipline to bias as well as how awesome our black boys are.

2. Try to walk in the shoes of black parents. Know what may be happening for parents of black boys when you call them about discipline issues. Listen to their fears. Work with them as partners. Discipline the child in developmentally appropriate ways, and do not escalate the situation with your fears or presumptions about the future. Calm down, don't go overboard; track and compare discipline of black boys with non-black boys; ask yourself, "whose behavior am I watching?" "Am I looking at all the data over time about this child?" Am I being more lenient or more exacting with certain kids?"

(Continued)

(Continued)

3. Help boys figure out how they feel. Help them develop their emotional intelligence. When Tres was younger, he exuded a level of bravado that was ridiculous. We were like, "What are you doing? Why are you acting like this?" Meanwhile, he was also crying all the time. What we realized was that he didn't have a vocabulary for his emotions and feelings, so he was expressing extremes. And if you don't have a vocabulary for your feelings, you almost can't figure out what your feelings are. When Tres got mad, he would say, "I'm so mad, I'm so mad, I'm so mad." I had a "feeling wheel" chart that shows lots of emotions. I would take it out and say, "Let's see if you can find other feelings on this wheel because the "mad thing" isn't getting you anywhere." And he would respond, "Oh yeah, well I am embarrassed and ashamed." And I would explain looking at the chart, "Well, actually, that's fear and sadness." And he would say, "Oh, OK, I guess I'm afraid and sad then." Sexism and racism force black men into a certain way of being, a certain tiny range of acceptable emotions. Sexism does this to all men, and then racism intensifies the situation for black men. Black boys start getting this message very early about being tough, and as their teachers and their parents, we need to give them other ways of understanding and expressing themselves so they have a wider range of and permission for self-expression.

4. Teachers need to know the history of people of color. Because it is rarely part of either the K-12 curriculum or preservice training, teachers have to do their own work to understand the culture, history, and experience of black people and other people of color. It is also imperative they know more than a little about slavery, Jim Crow, and the civil rights movement. Teachers need to know the struggles and obstacles and disparities black people face as the impact of institutional racism. But they also need to know the triumphs and contributions of people of color because once they understand how smart black people are and once they understand how much black people, Latinx people, Asian people, and others have overcome and contributed, they will see the true legacy and history. Teachers need to look at the positive capabilities of a group of people to overcome their miseducation.

I invite you to sit down with a paper and pencil and answer the following questions:

How many accomplished black men can you name?

Can you explain why they are famous or what they have accomplished?

Can you tell your students why they should look up to them?

What books do you have to share with your students that will help them celebrate the accomplishments of black men and women?

Match the following facts about these very accomplished Black men with their names.

Paul Robeson   Frederick Douglass   Martin Luther King, Jr.

      Nat Turner   Malcolm X

Thurgood Marshall   Bayard Rustin   Booker T. Washington

      Marcus Garvey   Ronald E. McNair

WHAT DO YOU KNOW ABOUT ME?	WHO AM I?
1. • Seen as a prophet because of marks on his chest present at birth • Born into slavery in 1800 • Because of learning to read young and excellent oratory skills he became a respected preacher • Led a slave rebellion in 1831—recruiting other enslaved people, distributing weapons • Was hung November 5, 1831, for his role in the insurrection • This rebellion is seen by many as a major point in the search for freedom and basic human rights by African Americans	
2. • First prominent African American architect • Graduate of Penn School of Architecture • Senior Architect on Philadelphia's Museum of Art and Philadelphia Free Library • Born 1881 in Philadelphia, already home to generations of free Blacks because of Quakerism • Designed Duke University (37 years before he had a right to attend it because of Jim Crow laws) • Helped design Harvard's Widener Memorial Library	

(Continued)

(Continued)

WHO AM I?		WHAT DO YOU KNOW ABOUT ME?
3.	• Born in Jamaica 1887 • Speaker and leader in Black nationalism and pan Africanism • Helped found the Universal Negro Improvement and Association in 1914 • Strong relationship between the ideology of Garvey and others such as Rastafarians and the Nation of Islam • Known by many as the "Black Moses" • In 1918 he started the newspaper "The Negro World"	
4.	• Received a BA in 1948 from Morehouse College, also attended by both his father and grandfather, a BD from Crozer Theological Seminary in 1951, and a doctorate from Boston University in 1955 • Recruited in 1955 to be the spokesperson for the Montgomery Bus Boycott, which lasted 382 days • At the age of 35 was then the youngest person to win the Nobel Peace Prize • The only non-president to have a National Holiday and a memorial on the Washington Mall • Letters from Birmingham Jail continues to be one of the most read books in academia • Fought against segregation, for equality in working wages, for voting rights, discrimination in education and economic change	
5.	• Organizer of the 1963 March on Washington • Civil rights activist and strategist • Openly gay man—target of discrimination • Helped shape MLK's approach to non-violence—convinced Dr. King of the importance of non-violence • Learned his Quaker "values" from his grandparents • Performed with Paul Robeson • Helped organize the Southern Christian Leadership Conference (SCLC) • In 2013 President Obama posthumously awarded the Presidential Medal of Honor to Rustin who died in 1987	
6.	• Son of an enslaved mother and an unknown White man • Grew up in brutal slavery with grandparents at young age • Was sent to live in Baltimore at age 8, where he learned to read and write • Escaped to NYC then to Boston in 1838 when he was 20 • Published his first autobiography in 1845 and his second *My Bondage and My Freedom in 1855* • Served under five Presidents • Abolitionist who spoke and wrote against slavery his entire life	
7.	• Grandson of an enslaved African • Identified himself as a "hellraiser " in school for talking too much. One teacher punished him by learning parts of the Constitution • Attended Lincoln U. in Chester County with Langston Hughes and the future President of Ghana Kwame Nkrumah • Denied admission into the University of Maryland Law School because he was Black • Chief council for NAACP • US Solicitor General for Lyndon Johnson • First African American Supreme Court Justice 1967	

WHAT DO YOU KNOW ABOUT ME?	WHO AM I?
8. • Valedictorian of Carver High School in 1967 • Graduated Magna Cum Laude from North Carolina AT&T State University • Obtained a PhD at the age of 26 from the Massachusetts Institute of Technology in laser physics • Was a Presidential Scholar, a Ford Foundation Fellow, a NATO Fellow, and a National Fellowship Fund Fellow • Played the saxophone and was a sixth degree black belt in karate • Won the Congressional Medal of Honor after he died • Astronaut—logged 191 hours in space • Died in 1986 on the Challenger • Awarded the Congressional Space Medal of Honor posthumously • In 1986 Congress awarded funding to establish the Ronald E. McNair Post-Baccalaureate Achievement Program. This program encourages low income and first generation students to enroll in PhD programs.	
9. • Athlete, singer, activist, actor • Went to Rutgers, 15 varsity letters, graduated as valedictorian, endured racism and violence from teammates • His father was a runaway enslaved African who went to Lincoln University • Attended Columbia Law School • Performed Shakespeare, made 11 movies • Donated all the proceeds of one of his films to Jews escaping Nazis in Europe • Labor activist, peace activist, friends with Albert Einstein, WEB DuBois, Ernest Hemingway • Retired and died in Philadelphia	
10. • Born Malcolm Little; Muslim name, el-Hajj Malik el-Shabazz • Born in Nebraska, raised in Lansing, Michigan • Father, Rev. Earl Little, was a supporter of Marcus Garvey • Stopped his formal education when a teacher told him he should be a carpenter instead of an attorney • Was a minister for Temple No. 11 in Boston and Temple No. 7 in Harlem • Civil rights leader • Leader in the Nation of Islam	

Dr. Shakti Butler, filmmaker and educator, has a list of things that White teachers need to know about Black boys and what they learn in the families because so few White teachers are privy to that information via their private lives.

CHAPTER 27

Connecting With Black Students and Parents

Equal Vision

Shakti Butler

I grew up in a family where race was always part of the context and conversations that shaped our family life. And the same was true for all the friends and families within the immediate Harlem community that was a central part of our lives. Yes, we talked about race every day! At my new school, we never talked about race. My sense of self was clearly impacted as I interfaced with dominant white culture. I quickly came to understand that part of my role was to get used to—to fit into—this "new world" and a painful discomfort that I could not understand. My experience at home was one of acceptance, with rules and expectations informing how I was meant to find my place in the world; these directly contradicted what I was learning at school. In addition, I did not find myself represented in the learning or stories of civilization, knowledge, or power being taught in class. These lessons repeated themselves: who belongs, who does not; who is assumed to be intelligent and who is not; who has contributed to Western civilization and who has not, and on and on. As a parent of a black child I see these ideas still confronting our children, and as teachers, white women need to know and understand that my child's home does not and should not look like yours. Just as you expect my children to understand your world, please know that I need you to understand and accept theirs.

Black parents are watchful and somewhat apprehensive about how their children are being seen and how they are being assessed based on assumptions being made about them. Black parents know the family must teach kids about injustice, including having conversations about race that are not taking place at school or with their peers. Black parents point out the fallacy of the messages children receive from television. We talk about who is missing in terms of heroes, heroines; who is missing in the history lessons and leadership models presented to them. We identify the misinformation and absence of a lens that includes black folks and people of color in general. We point out the history of struggles for justice that inform the society in which we live. And, we instill in our children the importance of taking a stand for justice. We teach our children to name injustice, analyze it, and take action even if that means simply having a conversation, asking questions, or resisting unfair treatment for themselves and others. When black students confront teachers on issues of fairness, it is not because they are rude, it is because their parents taught them to stand up for themselves, because in this society they have to do so.

White teachers need to know this. Black students are resisters; their families taught them to resist because they have to learn how to survive. And parents who taught their children to resist are also going to resist patterns of injustice and possible misinterpretations of behavior because they are our children.

In the following lessons, I address white teachers directly as a black parent. As a white teacher of black children, no one may have ever told you these things. As a parent, I see these behaviors toward our black children all the time. I ask you to read these lessons and internalize them. Please think, really think, about how as a white teacher you can be there for my child, my beautiful black boy.

Lesson No. 1: Learn to have authentic conversations about race; Black and Brown children are already having these conversations at home.

Early on in the relationship with your students and children, you have to talk about race. This means acknowledging that children are impacted by race, that they grow up and form ideas about who they are based upon race. The tendency in dominant white culture is to not talk about race. The ability to have a meaningful conversation and to name what's actually happening is an important skillset, especially for educators, and it has to be developed. Like any new skill, it can be awkward and intimidating, at first. And the learning never comes to an end especially for white people; you will continue to develop this as a lifelong skill.

LESSON No. 2: You will need to work to earn respect, but that is okay.

A teacher has to earn respect, both from students and parents. One requirement is to communicate effectively by telling the truth, to feel comfortable talking with both the student and the parent. Rather than saying, "you did this bad thing," say "what happened that you behaved this way . . . what was going on with you?" It's about reaching into the child or young person and trying to understand what's happening. There is a delicate balance in communicating this way, which develops via trial and error with respect, love, and accountability. It often will take some time to build the trust that comes from truth-telling and compassionate inquiry with students and their parents.

LESSON No. 3: Look for the best.

White people, specifically white teachers, can become more comfortable with students and parents of color when they start seeing with what I refer to as *equal vision*. This means seeing the best in people and actively looking for that best, no matter how behavior might play out. With equal vision, people understand that underneath "bad" behavior, there's some damage, some hurt. It could be historical or could be temporary: it doesn't matter. Instead of getting triggered emotionally in the process of an interaction, we must look for places and spaces inside people where we can connect. It is an active and engaging process to look for the places to connect with children and their parents. Even if it's with someone we do not like, we may connect around something completely different than the issue at hand and vastly improve the relationship, but that means looking for the link.

I used to teach "special ed" junior high school boys in the South Bronx. I made it a point to get to know the parents of my kids by going to their homes. Of course, when teachers have thirty to forty kids, they can't do that, but they still need to be reaching out to parents and acknowledging them as the primary caretakers of their children. I would go to each kid's house, and my conversation with parents let them know at every opportunity—whether at the home or under other circumstances—the great qualities I saw in their children. Usually, when teachers are talking to parents, they focus on something that needs support or improvement: the student did something wrong. This is particularly so for children of color. Parents I visited were delighted by conversations that highlighted their children as amazing and helped them find the qualities in their children that were malleable, that were yearning to be recognized, and were wonderful. I could see how parents metabolized the praise as extensions of their own goodness and worth, even if they were experiencing hardship or battling serious problems of their own.

LESSON NO. 4: Know your community.

Joy DeGruy, well-known for her work on post-traumatic slave syndrome, stresses how teachers must make it their business to know parents, leaders, and members of the community where they teach so they can reach out to them when there is a problem.

Dr. DeGruy tells a story about a little girl who came to school, a first or second grader, and as soon as she arrived, she would sit down at her desk and pull her coat over her head. She would stay like that the entire day. No one could do anything to rouse her—you could peep in there and get down on her level, but there was a problem—obviously, there was a big problem. So, Dr. DeGruy had to go into the community to find out what was going on in her home. The mother was on welfare and on drugs, and the child didn't own any clean clothes. Dr. DeGruy and others at the school made some interventions with the mother and their community, attending to the girl's most immediate needs such as getting her some clothes and making sure she was fed. By the end of that school year, this little child was voted the most improved: as she started feeling and looking better, receiving positive attention and being under less stress at home, she came to school and would not be under her coat the whole day. She even caught up academically. Dr. DeGruy had been able to make real changes in this child's life because she connected with the little girl's mother and community.

At the awards assembly, everybody stood up and gave this child a standing ovation. She sat down and pulled her coat over her head. Dr. DeGruy's work was not done! What does it mean to be hiding from the world? People can hide from the world in many different ways: because they're being traumatized, because they're shy, or because they don't have any skills to allow themselves to shine. It is the job of the teacher to help every child to stop hiding and to shine.

LESSON NO. 5: Despite what the media or experience may say in terms of the ravages of space, place, and poverty, people of color love their children.

A Mexican gentleman, Jerry, who grew up in Compton, talks about how his grandma would wake up early every morning to "pray for her children." He explains that when he was a kid, it would frustrate him that she would wake him up with her prayers, but now as an adult, he understood that what she was doing was inoculating them to go out into a racist, unjust world where people didn't see small Mexican children as sacred, didn't see that they were beautiful, didn't see that they had something to offer, didn't see them as anything more than potential problems, criminals, or gang bangers. So, she would pray early in the morning, passing down the prayers that she had learned from her grandma and her grandma before her: a lineage of prayer.

When Jerry was small, he would say, "Oh grandma, why do you have to pray so early in the morning, can't you talk to God later in the day?" or "You prayed over us last night, why do you have to pray over us again?" But as he got older, he began to see the wisdom of being able to lean into his grandmother's ritual because she knew what they were facing in a hostile world. So how do teachers inoculate their students? How might teachers "pray them up"?

Teachers can help children connect to their parents, to one another, to history, to their own family's history. Draw family members into the storytelling of history that speaks to how people of color survived, how they became strong, how they developed great qualities, and how the values that are inherent in those family stories become a living, breathing part of children in the classroom. Teachers can help relate the child's family's experiences and identity to a part of the larger history that helps everyone understand who they really are and how we are all connected. Let the parents into the classroom, the school and the teacher's life. For that year you are one of the most important people in a child's life and you need to know and understand the whole life, because what happens outside the classroom doors comes into the classroom.

Lesson No. 6: What do white teachers need to know to talk to the parents of black boys?

I would urge all teachers to read an article called "Strategic Questioning for Social Justice," by Fran Peavey. The article will support teachers to be curious and ask questions about what parents' conceptions are such as: "What do I need to know about your child to help them shine?"

Some parents of color, especially African American parents, will tell you everything that's wrong about their kid. This response is often a legacy from slave-owning times when parents did not want to highlight the good qualities of their children in an attempt to try to protect them from further exploitation, from being sold and separated from them. The teacher's job here is to contradict the negative impulse, these racialized impulses to amplify what's wrong and instead to highlight what is positive and encouraging about their child's development.

The challenges of a white teacher of black and brown children can be their own fear and lack of knowledge about the lived experiences of people of color. What is it that you want to know about these young black boys, (and I'll add girls)? What is it that you are curious about? How do you see them? What are you afraid of? That self-inquiry is very important for teachers, but also for the parents of the children with whom teachers will interact. Teachers are well-equipped to observe, research, analyze, and see students and their parents as teachers as well.

Orinthia Swindell is a diversity educator and teacher who has worked with children of all ages from preschool to twelfth grade. She is the mother of two amazing, radical, thoughtful, successful Black men.

Vignette: Being a Black Mom of Black Boys

Orinthia Swindell

I am a proud mother of two young black men. My children were born seven years apart. I often think back to the time that I spent parenting my oldest son for those first seven years before the birth of my youngest son. It was the training ground that helped to inform who I'd become as a mother. During this time, I realized that I wanted to be the person my children felt they could ask questions of and receive honest answers. I also wanted to be the type of parent who could admit when she didn't know the answer, yet invite my children to work along with me to discover the answers together. I knew that I wanted to be the parent who helped to shape my children's worldview and instill in them the desire to make change and stand up against injustice. Both of my boys attended public school at some point; however, when my youngest son, Jacob, was entering middle school, we made the decision for him to attend an independent school. Jacob was somewhat familiar with this environment because I worked at the school that he'd be attending. He'd also attended the school for two years when he was in preschool before attending public school during the elementary school years. Over the years, Jacob and I engaged in conversations about the differences between the independent school and public school environments. A few of the things that he noticed immediately as stark differences was the level of cleanliness that existed between the two spaces, the visible presence of and access to resources, and the greater presence of white people in the independent school environment. When he changed schools, Jacob's day-to-day reality shifted from existing in a predominantly people-of-color space to a white-dominated space.

For some people of color, learning to navigate these two spaces requires a dramatic shift in one's being in order to exist between these two cultures. Jacob would often remark about how his peers took things for granted with regard to their expensive personal possessions, and he was keenly aware of the differences in how school administration—and particularly white women teachers—treated him and other children of color, in comparison to their white peers. I remember the time when Jacob was given a written assignment by his white female middle-school English teacher. She requested that students write about their observations of the advertising they saw around the city and the subtle messages that were conveyed. He followed the instructions for the assignment and wrote about the changing nature of neighborhoods in Brooklyn due to gentrification. He wrote about how the language used during the selection process for housing was geared toward obtaining white residents. Jacob presented research to support his point. He handed in his assignment feeling confident about his work only to have it returned to him with numerous corrections and comments urging him to rethink his ideas! When Jacob came home from school that day, he spoke with me about how he felt that he was being penalized for sharing his thoughts and experiences because they were different from his teacher's. He felt that she wanted him to shift his thinking to align with hers; otherwise, she somehow felt threatened by hearing a perspective that made her feel bad as a person. This resulted in Jacob changing his writing in order to receive credit for the assignment.

Another poignant incident that occurred during the middle-school years took place during advisory time, when they met with a teacher to be filled in on school news and to gather together before and after classes met. Jacob shared with me that when he was in his advisory, the students mostly gathered according to their friendship circles. Jacob sat with two black male friends, and there were clusters of peers spread throughout the classroom. He began to notice that every day during advisory time, his white female teacher would publicly reprimand him and his friends for being too noisy. Jacob also noticed that a group of white girls who gathered together closest to the teacher's desk talked and laughed loudly, yet the teacher never scolded them. As I listened to Jacob process what was happening each evening when he came home, I saw that he was deeply impacted by this difference in treatment that the young white girls were receiving. I will never forget the look on my son's face when he said to me, "Mom, I'm not cute anymore. When I first came back to the school, people would talk to me and treat me in a much nicer way then I'm being treated now that I'm getting older." I felt shattered by his comment, yet I asked him how I could be of help to him. Jacob's initial response to me was that he wanted to have a strike outside of the school building to protest the racism that this teacher as well as other white teachers displayed. I looked into my son's eyes and let him know that I understood how he was feeling; together we came up with a plan that didn't involve a strike, yet would get to the core of the matter with this particular teacher.

We decided that Jacob and I, along with the school pyschological consultant, would talk with this teacher about her actions and the impact they had on him. This was one of the proudest moments of my life! I witnessed my thirteen-year-old son speak from the heart to his teacher, supported by two people who love him and see all that he brings to the world. The teacher listened to my son, apologized, and did not ask the boys to quiet down anymore during advisory. I'm not sure what affect Jacob's words had on his teacher. My only concern in that moment was having her hear and see the effects that her bias had on my son. I'm not sure that in either of these incidences, the two white women teachers knew or fully understood the lessons that Jacob learned through his interactions with them or the things that he internalized about himself. On the one hand, he received the message that what he felt, thought, heard, or knew to be true based on his lived experiences and research was being questioned. In that moment, he was being told to rethink his position and to second-guess his frame of thought because the person with the power in the situation didn't agree or have the same experience. In the other situation, Jacob and his friends were being told that their way of being in the world wasn't acceptable, that they needed to be policed, scrutinized, and demonized for being thirteen-year-old black boys. Jacob realized in that moment that he and his friends were being seen as threats. These lessons were implicitly as well as explicitly taught and deeply internalized. The most profound aspect of all is that neither of these teachers was aware of how their actions required substantial rebuilding of Jacob's self-esteem. Jacob comes from a loving family that recognizes his brilliance, his creativity, his humor, his insight, his joy, his pain, and his passion to speak up and out against the injustice that he sees and experiences in the world. We embrace all that he brings! I'm sure Jacob experienced moments of cognitive dissonance as he tried to make sense of all that he was experiencing in school based on who teachers thought he was, compared to how his family members perceive him and reflect that vision back to him.

These experiences are just two of many! Unfortunately, the accumulation of experiences with whiteness and white women teachers over the middle-school and high school years led my son to dislike school at the time, and it greatly impacted the way he navigated that space. His level of participation in classroom discussions waned as well as his overall involvement in events at school. Imagine being part of a community every day where people treat you in a way that's at odds with who you know yourself to be. My hope in writing this vignette is that white female teachers will spend time doing their own work to reflect on how the various aspects of their identities frames their thoughts, actions, and ways of being in the world. Failing to examine this is damaging to young black males and their ways of being in the world.

In his work as an educator and now a director at Stepping Stones, Chris Avery has worked with youth for more than twenty years. This chapter is a summary of Avery's research, which is an asset-based investigation of effective practices that White women teachers use to engage and support Black boys. He interviewed African American students at his school to identify which White teachers made a difference in their lives and experience. He then interviewed the teachers they named to develop a set of principles and practices that White teachers can use when teaching Black boys.

CHAPTER 28

Activating Inclusiveness

Chris Avery

As an African American boy attending an independent all-boys school, I rarely saw reflections of myself in the classroom, and therefore, I failed to grasp my value to the school and, more profoundly, to embrace my own self-worth. Too often, I felt like a consumer rather than a contributor within the school setting. Because there were extremely few examples of African American heritage in the curriculum and even fewer examples in the faculty, most of my experience was isolating. However, along with faculty of color, a few White adults in my school life worked to move past tolerance of my presence in the school to including me in the overall school experience.

When speaking with African American boys attending the school where I taught for thirteen years, many of their reflections mirror my own. In addition to the feelings of alienation, they too felt that they had a few White teachers, overwhelmingly female, who valued them and worked to identify with them. I interviewed these white female educators and share below what they said helped them create a culture of inclusion for boys like me.

THE ROLE OF COMMUNICATION

Be polite. Don't assume. Don't threaten. Take all students seriously. Respect all students.

When working with African American boys, several White female educators described that they often had to overcome their own bias around race, particularly about behavior of African American boys. This mirrors Gary Howard's (2006) assertion that White educators must recognize their own biases to effectively educate their students. Several teachers described how they had to recognize social cues and differences that too often resulted in mishandling their interactions; for example, if they were talking with a student who looked away from them, standing tall and stiff, they often perceived him as angry. Many of the teachers recounted instances when they first began working with African American male students when they could not discern when a student was angry or frustrated. Unfortunately, most of them could reference an instance where their misassumptions damaged a relationship. Regarding language and interactions, one middle-school teacher advised:

> Be courteous and clear, and don't assume. Some White kids know how to look an adult in the eye, smile at the adult, and then do what they please, and they get away with a lot things because of that. It isn't easy to be an African American student in a White community. And it can be really, horribly isolating . . . It takes a long time for kids to trust a White woman (for good reason) and just because you smile at them, that doesn't necessarily make you a nice person in their eyes. Be reliable and consistent, and just keep on doing it, and don't expect trust right away. Or ever. Just be trustworthy yourself and don't worry about the kids trusting you.

The theme of trust consistently arose from the students and the faculty. Each group referenced that being reliable and using speech that emphasizes transparency and confidentiality builds trust. By making a consistent effort to greet them and sincerely ask them about their own lives, faculty found their relationships with African American boys improving. They recognized that for most of these students, it took longer for trust to grow, and their consistency became even more important. If teachers checked in on the students even when they had left their classroom, students would continue to come back or contact them years later. However, they also saw that these relationships were often more fragile than their relationships with students from other ethnic backgrounds. Be clear and direct (but courteous) about your expectations when giving directions; the teacher must not expect students of color to pick up on indirect hints or offhand comments. One teacher cautions: "If you are White, you belong to a culture of Whiteness in which White cues seem obvious to you and to some other White people, but don't assume everyone understands you."

White cues too often hold increased weight in the classroom and result in unbalanced management of behavior. When a White teacher works to create a culture of respect and equality, students of color are more willing to engage and take social risks. The teacher must model this by not shying away from difficult conversations about inequality. A lower school teacher put it like this:

> During conversations about race, I make sure I refer to White people with racial tags, just as I would for people of color. For example, I say, "The White settlers . . ." as well as "the people of the Cherokee Nation" If I use myself as an example during a conversation about cultural experience I say, "As a White person, this is my experience" My goal is to model open conversation about all cultural experiences, including experiences influenced by race.

In other words, a teacher's language can be inviting or isolating. By creating a culture of open dialogue and intentional language, educators limit damaging missteps in the classroom. While instances can and likely will still occur, creating this space for conversation and safety is essential to fostering inclusion.

THE ROLE OF RELATIONAL TEACHING

Relational teaching is at the core of education. There is something to be said about the teacher who goes the extra mile to get to know a student's likes, dislikes, and cultural background (Reichert & Hawley, 2014). It places an importance on the individual and shows the student that he matters. An educator's responsibility is to demonstrate an unconditional regard and belief in a student's capacity. Conversations increase when students recognize a White teacher's willingness to push against whatever barriers—sometimes institutional—stand in their way.

Many of the teachers asserted that African American boys are likely to be given harsher punishment for the same behavior than their White counterparts, which serves as a reminder for teachers to self-monitor when responding to misbehavior. For example, a lower-school teacher uses a behavior-monitoring system that provides points for good and bad behavior, with a greater emphasis on positive reinforcement. She finds that the system allows her to pay closer attention if a student has an disproportionate number of points, and ask why is that and what needs to be done.

She continues by saying that misassumptions break down trust and can permanently damage relationships, particularly with African American boys. Furthermore, when issues of racism occur, adults must respond appropriately and seriously and not in any way minimize the act (Stevenson 2014). Many students have become accustomed to seeing these instances mishandled and often have grown to expect it. Consequently, it becomes even more important that adults are prepared to handle these situations. To do so requires self-reflection and study (Stevenson 2014).

The Role of Curriculum

Students and teachers alike describe the importance of breaking the habit of only teaching the White male perspective of history. This perspective fails to provide a balanced view of the world and augments the perception that only White men can be successful. When teachers use a variety of windows into other cultures and peoples and provide mirrors that reflect the variety of backgrounds of the students in the classroom, students will become more engaged in the curriculum (Strand et al., 2011; Style, 1996).

A lower-school teacher stated that she finds it important to have books in the classroom that serve as mirrors for African American students. She gives each student choices throughout the year, understanding that not all African American boys will choose these books, while boys of other racial backgrounds may chose them:

> During our American history unit on Western expansion, I include readings and conversation about the experience of Native Americans and enslaved and free African Americans. We discuss how the mindset of "otherness" opens the door to inhumane treatment of others and how the dominant White culture took advantage of many subgroups. I am also sure to include positive examples of people of color from the time period.

These efforts do not go unnoticed: Several of the boys who were interviewed acknowledged and appreciated her intentional efforts to create affirming, inclusive curricular content.

The Role of Parents

Many faculty contend that creating trust with the *parents* of African American boys is even more challenging than creating relationships with their sons. Teachers have limited interactions with parents, which means that consistency and humility are even more essential components for building understanding. Many African American parents, including my mother during my time as a student, distrust the educational establishment (Webb-Johnson, 2002). Due to this distrust, conclusions may quickly be drawn as well-intentioned actions align with preconceived notions or worse, previous experiences of mistreatment. A teacher recounts how she had to recognize this and move past her own hurt and recognize the larger situation.

> Another example comes from my first year. . . . . I had a parent go to my division head the day after Back to School Night and complain that I was "racist." I had to push through the embarrassment and anger that I felt before I could honestly address this complaint. It was uncomfortable for me to meet with her throughout the year, as she continued to be unhappy with the school and the curriculum materials, but I did meet with her because I felt hearing her

was important. I used this difficult opportunity to take a look at the areas of the program that upset her. Some of her concerns were regarding things I had the ability to change right away, such as giving her son more access to the computer during the school day, as they did not have a computer at home. Other concerns, such as the history curriculum, I have addressed little by little each year since then. As a White person, I have to remain open to conversations about race relations even when they are difficult or personal.

To aid in these discussions about race, White teachers need to develop relationships with White peers that can provide honest feedback. It is important that they openly discuss issues of race in the classroom with other White allies as well as with teachers of color. Honest conversation is vital to solving the inequalities that continue to impact our African American boys.

CONCLUSION

While many White faculty or staff may feel like they have difficulty working with African American boys, they must be reminded that all students do not fit into the same categories. Different strategies will work with different boys from the same ethnic background, and educators need to be equipped with a variety of strategies to create a welcoming community. Educators must be acutely aware of the statistics regarding African American boys in American education. The reality is that the U.S. education system does not treat this group of children equal to their White or female classmates. As a part of the greater system, it is an educator's responsibility to ask: "How am I unwittingly perpetuating these inequalities, and how do I need to change my practices to equalize the experiences of Black male students, and all of my students of color?" Through this question, White educators can best understand their role in creating a supportive and balanced learning experience for Black male students that will allow them to feel fully included in their school environment.

■ ■ Engaging the Mind ★ Taking Action ★ Inspiring Excellence
Criteria for Trusting an Adult

When working with students within a classroom, ask all of the students to describe adults in the building whom they trust and who they feel support their identity. Have them describe what criteria they use and how it is reinforced. Have them talk in pairs about ways they can express the importance of an adult to them. It will be important to follow up with teachers named by the students and discuss what it means if any students could not name any adults.

Part of connecting Black boys to the classroom, to one another, and to their classmates, is leading activities that will support students to talk about those things that matter to them in a sanctioned and structured way. Doing so creates mutual vulnerability and an opportunity for students to share about their lives. In the following piece, Drs. Stefanie Rome and Ty-Ron Douglas share three activities that teachers could use in their classrooms—or that administrators could use with their faculties—to build a community in which people have spaces to share what matters to them. This chapter is followed by a vignette that includes another activity—more tools for teachers' growing toolbelts—by Dr. Carl Moore, professor of education, addressed directly to teachers.

CHAPTER 29

Belief, Pedagogy, and Practice

Strategies for Building Powerful Classroom Communities

Stefanie Rome and Ty-Ron Douglas

Psychologist, teacher, and scholar, Asa Hilliard III, devoted his life to educating and empowering Black children and teaching the truth about peoples of Africa and African descent. In 2008, Dr. Hilliard was interviewed on the subject of the academic achievement of Black children. When asked about the most important thing for White teachers to understand about Black students, Hilliard's response shifted the already compelling discourse toward the power of relationships, *"You have to start with 'the who'. Of course it is important to know your content and your curriculum, but you can't truly reach the children if you don't first start by getting to know who they are as people."* Notably, learning who Black boys are as people on an individual level cannot be disassociated from larger understandings and respect for *their people*—the Black families, Black communities, Black cultures, and Black history that undergird the beauty, power, and potential of the individual students who sit in classrooms. In addition, white teachers who want to believe in and build strong relationships with Black boys must first evaluate their epistemological frameworks—their ways of knowing and *seeing* the identities and promise of Black males—to ensure that they are operating from antideficit, asset-based ideologies and approaches.

We offer a small set of antideficit, asset-based practical tools designed to surface student strengths, elicit student cultures, and facilitate the building of genuine, mutually respectful relationships. Each activity has three-parts: *What* is it? *How* does it work? and *How long* might it take?[1]

BELIEVE TO ACHIEVE

In 2008, Dr. Reuven Feuerstein addressed attendees at the Teaching for Intelligence Conference, sponsored by the National Urban Alliance for Effective Education. The mixed group of teachers, leaders, and thinkers from across the country was completely engaged as Dr. Feuerstein spoke to the theme, "Believe to Achieve":

> Believe to achieve is not just belief. It is the origins of the belief. Belief is generated by a need . . . the need to ensure a quality of life for your fellow man. You can't see your fellow man stay in this very difficult condition and not come up with the belief that it can be changed. If you need to help your fellow man, your child, then you start to believe and if you believe you will achieve.[2]

Dr. Feuerstein, a cognitive psychologist and career educator who studied under Dr. Jean Piaget, devoted his life to the position that intelligence is modifiable; that the structure of the human brain can be changed and developed with strategic, culture-centered mediation. A refugee who fled from his homeland during the Nazi invasion, Dr. Feuerstein found himself teaching child refugees who had also fled seeking survival. The children were subjected to a series of IQ tests, which indicated that they were uneducable and intellectually deficient. This diagnosis prompted Dr. Feuerstein's lifelong quest to prove that intelligence is not fixed and can be enriched when learning experiences are individualized and challenging. The children had been deprived of rich cognitive and academic experiences, provided in a nurturing environment (Steinberg, 2011). The children did not know themselves and, as a result, had no idea what they were capable of. Feuerstein discovered, "Once cognitive skills are taught and cultural experiences are enriched, even the [most underperforming] individuals can extend their intellectual powers dramatically" (Kristinsdóttir, 2008).

---

[1] The activities are inserted at appropriate spots in the chapter. They were developed by Stefanie Rome and contributed to the work of the National Urban Alliance for Effective Education.
[2] To see this speech, follow this link: https://www.youtube.com/watch?v=uXopVpQwivY

ACTIVITY 1: CULTURAL CROSSOVER

(Inspired by UCLA's California Reading and Literature Project)

What Is It?

A tool for sharing personal frames of reference. Each student shares specific aspects of personal culture, and the large group has the opportunity to respond. Students discover and share their individual and collective uniqueness.

How Does It Work?

1. Students individually-silently, consider an aspect or characteristic of her or his culture.

2. The class forms a circle.

3. Each student shares one cultural aspect/characteristic, as they feel led, using this speaking frame:

   "In my culture, _____."

4. The "sharer", immediately after sharing, crosses the circle to stand in another spot.

5. Simultaneously, anyone who shares that aspect crosses the circle to stand in a new spot.*

6. Students share until everyone has contributed at least one aspect or until time allotted for the activity ends.

7. Debrief. Possible questions:

   a. What have we learned?

   b. How did it feel to share an aspect of your culture?

   c. How did it feel to have someone cross the circle when you shared?

   d. How might this information make us a stronger community?

How Long Does It Take?

Twenty minutes

*STUDENTS may find themselves crossing the circle alone. This is an excellent opportunity to honor students' personal and cultural uniqueness. In the debriefing period, provide these students the opportunity to share more deeply about their cultural characteristic. This kind of affirmation allows students to feel like valued members of their classroom communities.

PEDAGOGY OF CONFIDENCE

Inspired by Feuerstein's work, Dr. Yvette Jackson (2011) developed *The Pedagogy of Confidence*, a framework rooted in what Jackson describes as the belief that all students have an intellectual scope that is larger and more capacious than most educators dare to imagine (Jackson, 2013). She believes teachers have the agency to generate and ignite that capacity. Jackson proposes teachers devote a significant amount of time to eliciting and identifying student strengths, learning how to communicate about those strengths and using strengths to develop underutilized skills as they push students to the "frontier of their intelligence" (Jackson, 2013). *The Pedagogy of Confidence* rests upon seven High Operational Practices (Jackson, 2011):

- Identifying and activating student strengths
- Building relationships
- Eliciting high intellectual performance
- Providing enrichment
- Situating learning in the lives of students
- Integrating prerequisites for academic learning
- Amplifying student voice for self-directed learning and self-actualization

Jackson implores teachers to make strategic efforts to build relationships with students. Relationship building is a major prerequisite for meaningful student-teacher interaction. (Jackson, 2013). The University of Chicago reports that the quality of the relationships between staff and students defines the safety of a school (Steinberg, Allensworth, & Johnson, 2011). Jackson posits that quality relationships not only contribute to a physically safe school, they are vital to creating an intellectually safe school. Dr. James Comer (2005) found that the interaction between children and the authority figures that surround them builds their brains and allows them to strengthen the developmental pathways necessary for academic and life success. Comer posits that significant student learning requires the positive relationships and sense of belonging that a healthy school culture provides. Whether consciously or subconsciously, the relationships between teachers and students are what motivate students to grant teachers permission to lead them to places of self-direction, usher them into spaces of self-knowledge, and escort them into taking the responsible risks that lead to self-actualization.

■ ■ Engaging the Mind ★ Taking Action ★ Inspiring Excellence

ACTIVITY 2: I AM, I LIKE, I ALWAYS

What Is It?

A structure for speaking with confidence about a most familiar topic, *oneself*. It provides prerequisite practice for students

to compose and verbalize declarative statements about mastered content.

How Does It Work?

Explain to students that they are going to write and share information about a topic that they know better than anyone else, *themselves*.

Have students:

1. Complete this writing this frame:

   I am _____.
   I like _____.
   I always _____.

2. Complete each statement, including the stems, with any information they choose.

3. Share statements with the whole group, individually.

4. Continue the process until everyone has shared or until the time allotted for the activity runs out.

5. Debrief. Possible questions:

   a. What do we know now that we didn't know before?

   b. How did it feel to share characteristics about yourself with our group?

   c. If we did this again next month, do you believe your statements would be the same? Why? Why not?

How Long Does It Take?

Ten minutes

Dr. Jawanza Kunjufu (2011) specifies varying levels of effective teachers in his book, *Understanding Black Male Learning Styles*. Second from the top level is *Master Teachers*. According to Kunjufu, Master Teachers understand and successfully teach their content and know the importance of developing pedagogy that is compatible with their students' learning styles. Teachers at the top level, *Coaches*, are the most effective: Besides deeply understanding their content and the learning styles and individual cultures of their students, they esteem each culture with genuine respect. Through the consistent and carefully executed effort to elicit students' cultures, Coaches and their students are able to thrive in the classroom.

■ ■ Engaging the Mind ★ Taking Action ★ Inspiring Excellence

ACTIVITY 3: SUPER POWERS

What Is It?

A space to elicit internal, personal power. Students surface and share individual strengths and combine strengths with others to illustrate the power of the collective.

How Does It Work?

Have students:

(Continued)

(Continued)

- Choose *just one* of their many strengths for this activity.
- Work individually to write and complete the following strength statement: *My greatest strength is* _____.
- Work in groups of three or four.
- Share their strength statements individually with their small group.

Get creative! Each group must:

- Imagine they are a unit of super heroes
- Decide on a <u>supername</u> for each person
- Develop a <u>superstance</u> for each person
- Decide on a <u>supername</u> for the *entire unit* based on the individual powers in the group.

Show Time! Each group must introduce their superunit in thirty seconds, creatively including the following:

- Superunit name
- Individual supernames
- Individual superstances

Debrief. Possible questions:

- Which was easier, to decide on a supername for yourself or for your unit?
- How did your group come up with the name for your unit?
- What have we learned about our classroom community?

How Long Does It Take?

Twenty minutes

■ ■ Engaging the Mind ★ Taking Action ★ Inspiring Excellence

ACTIVITY 4: POWERFUL MESSAGES

What Is It?

An opportunity to affirm others. It is particularly powerful when students engage in this activity before a particularly rigorous or stressful task.

How Does It Work?

Have students:

1. Consider a soon-to-come stressful or rigorous classwide task.
2. Work individually to generate one written, powerful statement that contains a quality their classmates should be mindful of as they approach the stressful or rigorous task, using this frame: You are _____. (example: *You are unstoppable.*)

3. Add a tag sentence to their powerful statement that gives it an added boost. (example: *You can accomplish anything you set your mind to.*)

4. Personalize their statements by adding their signature at the bottom.

5. Circulate around the room carrying their written statements and without talking.

6. At the signal, stop. Find a partner. Share statements.

7. Circulate again, without talking.

8. At the signal, stop. Find a new partner. Share statements.

9. Repeat the process one more time.

10. Debrief. Possible questions:

    a. How did it feel being affirmed the first time? Second time? By the third time?

    b. How did it feel to affirm your classmates?

    c. Why do you believe we engaged in this activity today?

Extension: "Messages Internalized": After the third circulation, have students:

- Exchange statements with their partners.

- Return to their seats and take one minute of silent time to read and reflect on the message they received.

- Write a response to the author of the original message, careful to include every aspect of the statement *(example: Craig, I **am** unstoppable and I believe I can accomplish anything I set my mind to!)*

- Add how this quality will be evidenced in the upcoming task. (example: *"This will be evidenced when we take the exam this morning. I have worked hard and studied hard. All I need to do now is show that I know what I know!"*)

How Long Does It Take?

Twenty to thirty minutes

CONCLUSION

These tools may inspire teachers and school staff to seek and develop additional resources for building strong classroom relationships. The possibilities are endless. The time to implement is always, and the benefits are beyond measure.

Vignette: The Symbolic Teacher

Carl Moore

TEACHER AS A SYMBOL

When thinking about teaching black boys, it is important to remember that you are a symbol. What does this mean? Simply put, it means that you represent something to the students whom you are teaching. Depending upon the exposure and levels of awareness of the students, you could symbolize all sorts of things: You could symbolize the white teacher coming to "try" to teach, who is a part of the system that students fear or hate; you could symbolize a previous teacher that was a caring motherly figure or strict authoritative force; or you could symbolize the Michelle Pfeiffer character from the movie *Dangerous Minds*. In sum, being in front of the class and in front of a class of black boy students could mean so many things to different students.

You may ask yourself how to account for the many different perspectives and vantage points that may be present in the classroom. It may not be as difficult a task, once you realize that you are a symbol to the students. From this vantage point, you can design classroom experiences and activities that break the ice and account for the ways those students may see you. Crafting learning experiences accounting for varying perspectives may work not only for black boys but for all students, as all students view teachers in many different ways. However, because of the legacy of oppression in the United States, considering their perspectives is particularly important when teaching a group of historically disadvantaged and oppressed individuals such as black boys.

To account for and unpack the range of perspectives present among black boy students (and others), there are many activities that can be done. Generally speaking, activities that allow for students to anonymously discuss and voice their biases are ideal. One example of an impactful activity is *Hopes and Fears*. Rojzman's (1999) work argues that their fears limit individuals when they are learning from those who are different then themselves. He posits that understanding those fears can assist in creating harmony for reaching a common goal. The hopes and fears activity allows all students to anonymously write on a note card their hopes and fears about taking the class and having you as a teacher. The teacher collects these note cards and then shares with the class. They become a source of discussion for the class and also a means for the instructor to know what ideas and feelings are present in the room. Instead of note cards, students can write anonymously on sticky notes, which are then collected and posted around the room so that students can see the hopes and fears of their peers. Other ways to anonymously collect students' thoughts use technologies such as twitter, Poll Everywhere, and classroom clickers.

Anonymity of student voice in activities such as *Hopes and Fears* will assist in drawing out student perspectives, but it also can be used as a tool to help students learn. Sometimes the fear of having the "wrong" answer will limit participation of black boy students. In some cases, many stigmas are connected to being "smart" or "dumb." Anonymity may alleviate these concerns and increase participation for black boys and any other students who may not feel comfortable. This is particularly important for black boys because of stereotypes and internalized oppressions, which can limit the student's self-efficacy. Student learning theory informs us that a student's ability to learn without being judged will increase their self-efficacy and thus positively impact their motivation. In addition, being able to voice thoughts without judgment adds to the supportive nature of the classroom. When students feel they are able to learn and are supported in doing so, their motivation to learn increases (Ambrose et al. 2012).

Another strategy to helping ease the concerns of black boy students is displaying vulnerability. This can be done by participating in the activities mentioned previously or telling stories about yourself as a student and any struggles or triumphs you may have had. Being honest with the students regarding your own limited knowledge about working with them or your concerns is very helpful. It allows the students to see you as an individual who also has hopes and fears. The strategy can be quite effective when working with black boys because they will see you as a real person and may be able to open up as well. Depending on the age level of the students, discretion should be used with how much is shared of your fears as a teacher. But, it is important for the students to know that you have both excitement and concerns about working with them. The activity can be varied in any way when you are presenting it to the students.

We have multiple voices from parents in this section, most of them speaking directly to the White women teachers—and other professionals who work with children. Dr. Shemariah Arki, demonstrates the tension that parents feel when they want to get help and support for their children—in this case, therapy after a death in the family—but it requires trusting a White woman therapist, who does not seem to have spent much time considering her own biases. When she starts the session by asking about anger, Shemariah is ready to leave. White women teachers have to know that Black parents are sitting and watching and waiting, when they first meet White teachers, for an indication that they could or should trust this person with their precious child, whom the world already does not see clearly. And this is not because they're "reverse racist" or because they hate White people. It is because they grew up in a world where the narratives and stories shared in this book happened to them. Or they happened to friends, siblings, cousins, or parents. They are able to see the common behavioral patterns of White women, and they are waiting, hoping, for a White woman who will demonstrate a different kind of consciousness from the mainstream one to which they are accustomed.

CHAPTER 30

Ruminations From the Intersections of a #BlackMommyActivist[1]

Shemariah Arki

The therapist looked at my six-year-old son and said, "How have you been managing your anger? Are you still fighting?" I wanted to end it right there. I wanted to take my little Black boys out of her office, into our car, back across Green Road to our side of town. Yes, I set up the appointment. I reached out to the school counselor, a Black woman, to check on my sons during the school day. I knew my children needed an outlet to talk about the last year, their grandfather's death, and the Black family drama that ensued afterward, which we were all trying to live through.

"I've been better," my son told the therapist, after looking at me, then his brother. He looked down, nervous about being in the spotlight for such an interrogation. I spoke up on his behalf: "He's been much better." I recounted a story of sharing and how my sons used their words and a game of rock/paper/scissors to come to consensus. She smiled, said, "Great job guys!" and proceeded with her litany of questions.

Becky the therapist has a great way to build trust with the boys. The toys and games accessible to the children in her office help warm the space. She builds rapport with them by speaking directly to them, not me. They are excited to visit her; she centers

---

[1] The hashtag "BlackMommyActivist" comes from Karsonya Wise Whitehead (2016), who originally created and popularized the expression.

them and their needs in conversation, which has proven to be an effective tactic. It was me she needed to convince, though. She needed to convince me that she got it. By *it*, I mean, the sociopolitical context, or what Nieto and Bode (2012) identify as laws, regulations, policies, practices, traditions, and ideologies. The sociopolitical context in which Black boys are often interpreted according to the popular trope of the bastardized man-child and the hypersexed troublemaker. These harmful and systemic stereotypes are inadvertently manifested in the behavior of White women educators and other youth-serving professionals as failed personal attempts at equity. Becky is viewing and assessing my son through her own worldview, primarily Eurocentric, highly individualized, and grossly disconnected from our community.

As a Mom . . .

Considering the current state of the world today, mothers of Black boys are reluctant to release them to school, sports, or the streets, in an effort to keep them physically and emotionally safe. "Spirit murdering," what we ultimately are attempting to shield our boys from, is the piercing and existential experience young Black boys have on a daily basis. Defined as "the personal, psychological, and spiritual injuries to people of color through the fixed, yet fluid and moldable, structures of racism, privilege, and power, spirit-murdering denies inclusion, protection, safety, nurturance, and acceptance—all things a person needs to be human and to be educated" (Love, 2014, p. 302). Deemed powerless by the dominant patriarchy, Black mothers have been the primary bystanders, specifically with our boys. We are forced to watch, and sometimes even participate in, the emasculation and usurping of our heads of households, our fathers, our uncles, our brothers, and our sons, knowing the damage done cannot be easily undone. As a mom, I can conceptualize how individual acts of racism, in conjunction with the pervasive tropes of hypermasculinity in young Black males, unconsciously create the environment for spirit murdering.

Consider this conversation I had with Man-Man, a fourth-grade friend of my son.

Me: Man-Man, what you wanna be when you grow up?

Man-Man: A basketball player and/or a rapper, cus they be gettin' PAID Ms. Shemariah!!!

Man-Man's primary goal is to make a lot of money and to take care of his family. Somewhere, Man-Man has learned that being a man means physically taking care of your family. From a neo-indigenous cultural perspective, taking care of your family is centered on one's spiritual awakening and leadership, which includes the physical but centers masculinity through spiritual and metaphysical practices. If Man-Man's worldview includes only tropes, and the athlete/rapper is the only trope that makes millions, it then becomes the dominant message that he receives. In reality, Man-Man may know that there are other ways to do this, but he hasn't seen them, therefore, they don't exist in his reality.

As an Educator . . .

In addition to being a mother, I also work in the field of social justice education and ask those who are in our schools day in and day out to really think about the role they have with our children. Those who commit to the role of educator in today's urban public education system must commit to unpacking "the images of Black males in U.S. culture that make it possible for too many teachers to see some of their Black male students as threatening, arrogant, disdainful of authority, and uncontrollable except by force or removal" (Love, 2014, p. 293). As a former elementary educator, a current teacher-educator, and hip-hop feminist author, Bettina Love (2014) is committed to unpacking her own identity development; she uses the untimely death of Trayvon Martin as a backdrop. Love discusses how a member of the block watch killed Trayvon, a teenage Black male, and felt justified in taking Trayvon's life because of the messages the killer had been socialized to believe about Black boys.

What I know as both a mother and an educator is that many of the messages Trayvon's killer had been socialized to believe can be found in the White teachers interactions with our children. Trayvon's story often revolves around his choice to wear a hoodie, a strong and necessary nonverbal contributor to his swag-a hip-hop colloquialism that refers to a boisterous display of confidence through words and deeds with a foundational goal of likability and popularity (Love, 2014). For those who are unfamiliar with the hip-hop culture, swag can be misinterpreted, as it was in the case of Trayvon, as communicating arrogance, or simply opposition to the current power structure (Love, 2014).

While it is true hip-hop culture perpetuates negative tropes about young Black males, the social construction of the violent, threatening young Black male trope has deep roots in American history, White supremacy, and the culture of Whiteness. These tropes can become embedded in the psyche of preservice and inservice teachers, long before they walk into a classroom, and this mindset often leads to many of the negative interactions between White teachers and Black boys in the classroom. White female teachers must recognize how imperative it is for Black children that these tropes are interrupted.

As an educator, I know that previous research highlights how a Black feminist pedagogy, one that uses personal experiences and narratives as empirical evidence, can help educators and professionals engaging with youth to transform theory into practice (Arki, 2016; Collins, 1986). While implementing such pedagogy, professionals engaging with youth can use their intersectional identities and personal experience to disclose the longstanding history of bias in the education system. Introducing additional intersecting identities of Trayvon into this story helps educators conclude that his identity as a seventeen-year-old high school student involves more than his hoodie and hip-hop persona, in contrast to those identities placed on him by society. The ability for youth-serving professionals to see youth as people, as boys, as a child with multiple realities, is crucial to creating safe and inclusive learning environments for all youth.

BACK TO BECKY . . .

Becky seems clueless to this. Yes, I'm sure she's been to some type of professional development workshop targeting working with our population. What has she learned? How has she been tasked to implement these learnings into her daily practice? How is she evaluated? Who is there to mentor and guide her? It's not that she was bad. My boys liked her and worked well with her. But she had no sense of this larger societal context in which their individual trauma had taken place. She was not concerned, as I was, about inoculating them against spirit murdering. Seeing them with a colorblind lens meant she couldn't treat them—or their trauma—in their complex wholeness. Many White women, educator and youth-serving professionals alike, are like Becky. Guess what? Most White women have been, or still are, therapist Becky. Here are some concluding thoughts for her (and other white women tasked with working with our sons)

Young folks know more than we think they do. Consider the sociopolitical context in your work. Know what is going on in the world, specifically in the city and communities you serve. The dominant media outlets (CNN, MSNBC, FOX, etc.) are biased. Pay attention to new media—(youtube, podcasts, or any other user-uploaded content-supported platforms). Subscribe to a blog (www.upwithcommunity.org; www.crunkfeministcollective.com), or follow the weekly live conversations with #HipHopEd Movement on twitter (currently Tuesdays at 9pm EST). Get out in the community. Construct knowledge—listen to your students describe their community. It has a lot to do with how they see you and the rest of the world.

Don't make assumptions about families from what you read in the file; continue to build relationships with families, not just children. Today's families are becoming increasingly diverse. As you seek to build community with your students, introduce different types of families. For example, my fourth-grade son brought home an assignment from his teacher, the "Me Museum." He was empowered to choose the items that represented his family and culture to introduce himself to his peers. As a parent, this activity helped me to learn more about what my son values; valuable information as we seek to place him in environments where he can be respected, connected, and valued. Encourage students to tell their own stories. Use reflection prompts and examples of cultural happenings throughout the curriculum.

Believe none of what you see about Black boys, and half of everything you hear about Black boys. Our boys don't have an opportunity to tell their own stories. Listen to their voices. Hear their stories. The activity that follows can provide some practice. Little Red Riding Hood. Have you heard this story before? Whose perspective was it told from? How does the narrator's perspective change the story? How does it change how you feel about the story? What can you do differently?

■ ■ Engaging the Mind ★ Taking Action ★ Inspiring Excellence
The Maligned Wolf

As a mom and an educator, I recognize that perception equals reality. Therefore, I must acknowledge that same reality for everyone, including my children and students. The story of the Maligned Wolf is most often used with a variety of audiences to introduce the short- and long-term effects of cross-cultural communication. It's a story we are all familiar with, Little Red Riding Hood. This time, the story is told from the perspective of the wolf. As we learn the context from a new perspective, we are allowed to hold multiples realities. This becomes an acknowledgment of the dynamic nature of the world and the systems we operate in on a daily basis. The following discussion questions are designed to discuss the presence of multiple realities in us first. At a minimum, we must acknowledge our existence in the same world as those we serve. Such acknowledgment becomes foundational to our pedagogy as we educate and empower our young people to build a society better than the one they have been born into.

Download the free curriculum guide here: www.shemariaharki.com

The curriculum guide includes a printable version of the story as well as the discussion questions listed here. As a bonus, the printed guide also includes alternate activities, suggestions for future engagement on the topic, and an action planning worksheet!

DISCUSSION QUESTIONS:

- Have you heard this story before? If so, where?

- Whose perspective was it told from?

- How does the narrator's perspective change the story?

- Ask yourself this: How does it change how I feel about the story?

- What can I do differently?

- Create your action plan: What can I change now? What can I change soon? What can I change next?

We asked Dr. Chonika Coleman-King to write the following vignette because it is rare to have conversations in schools on the nuances of racialized differences in child rearing. Teachers tend to have a common sense about how to talk to children—and how to punish children—that is not universal. We have heard from teachers who are afraid to call home because they believe the parents enforce discipline using physical force, and they seek to protect the child from what they perceive to be abuse. We invited this vignette to help explore this issue further. We encourage teachers to consider that communication between home and school is one of the primary protective mechanisms in children's lives. Knowing there is no communication—or that they can manipulate the impressions that parents and teachers have of each other—makes students less safe in the world. We also encourage you, as you read this chapter, to consider the difference between physical punishment and abuse. Finally, we encourage you to consider the evidence that you have and to remember what you have learned throughout this book regarding the larger unquestioned social narratives about violent Black men and women. Consider that perhaps these narratives impact how you hear reports that your student is afraid of punishment. Remember that your communication with families is a critical part of your students' sense of safety, continuity, and consistency in the world. Reach out to families early and often to build a relationship, so you have a foundation for dealing together with the challenges that arise, as they do for all children.

Vignette: Discipline Practices of Caribbean Families

Chonika Coleman-King

As an urban teacher-educator, my students often ask me how to deal with students of color, namely Black boys who are routinely being reprimanded at school. Generally, my students describe the types of behaviors they encounter and the behavior management strategies of their classroom mentors. In most cases, preservice teachers acknowledge that many of the discipline strategies being used to address the behaviors of Black children are ineffective.

As frequently as these conversations arise, I find myself asking my students the question, "Did the teacher contact the parent?" The answer to my question is no, more times than not. I am always baffled by this response. How could a teacher who is having so much difficulty with a child at school not take steps to inform parents? Over the years, I have noticed an interesting trend. White teachers often determine which parents should know about a child's academic performance and behavior at school. These decisions are made for a variety of reasons. In some cases, teachers believe that most parents of color are not responsive to schools and do not value their child's education; some teachers fear interactions with parents of color; and others believe they are protecting students from parents' harsh discipline practices by withholding reports of problematic behavior.

I do not believe that teachers can effectively address routine classroom challenges if parents and caregivers are not informed and on board regarding ways to remedy behavioral issues. In my research on Black immigrant populations, I vividly remember the anger and frustration of a parent whose discipline of her child was scrutinized and criminalized. Hope, a Jamaican immigrant and certified public accountant with a military background, worked hard to instill a sense of academic and personal discipline in her son. Like Asian mothers, Jamaican mothers have been described as "tiger moms" who stop at nothing to ensure their children's high academic achievement (Chua, 2011).

Hope's son was in advanced classes in middle school, but making only mediocre grades because he was not completing homework assignments. However, he did well on standardized assessments and class tests with little effort. One day, Joshua was reprimanded for squirting lotion on a White girl in one of his classes. Joshua pleaded with administrators to not call his parents because he was afraid of the consequences. Because of Joshua's reported fear, school administrators called the Department of Child Services (DCS) on his parents, which resulted in a social worker being sent to their home.

Joshua did not have a history of being an unruly child, nor were there any signs that he was being abused. Hope argued, "if you look at the kid, and you listen to [his] stories, you would know . . . he's not abused, he's just defiant." Joshua knew his parents took teacher complaints seriously and would have taken away many of his privileges as a result of the teacher's complaint. Hope couldn't understand why school administrators simply did not call to ask, "Is something going on in the home?" Calling DCS seemed to be an absurd first step. An easy way to address any concerns would have been to call home *first*.

This situation undermined Hope's authority to engage in discipline practices that she and her husband knew to be effective. The more permissive parenting styles of some White families (sometimes described as progressive) don't always resonate with Black parents. Joshua's parents understood that police, employers, or teachers might not give their son, a Black boy, second chances. The unfortunate reality is that there are grave consequences for even the slightest missteps.

In Hope's estimation, it was only right for Joshua to be afraid of the consequences for misbehaving at school. He knew the high standards his parents had for him. Hope met with the administrators involved so that they would see the problem with their decision not to further investigate the matter or contact her with their concerns. After this meeting, Joshua was later called into the administrators' office and told that his mother loves him and only wants for him to be successful. However, the real question is, isn't that what all parents want for their children? Don't we assume that parents love their children and want what is best for them? Why, in this situation, was the first assumption that Joshua's parents were abusive? Why did Hope have to jump through hoops and risk the loss of her military security clearance due to a DCS complaint for school personnel to understand what they assume about most of the White families under their care?

In a world that is rarely kind to Black children, Black parents feel they must be aggressive in their support and discipline of their children. Teachers, most of whom are White, rarely have experiences with race and racism that will help them understand this intuitively. If you're White, you might not even realize how unkind the world is to Black children, day in and day out sanctioning their behavior and questioning the parenting skills of their caregivers. However, the teacher's role is not to undermine the work of Black parents, but to support them in the hard work of raising a Black child in a racist world. As Hope said, "I *love* [Joshua], that's why I fight for him and I'm always gonna fight for him, but at the same token he has to know when he's wrong." Teachers must not undermine parents by judging their discipline strategies, but join parents in their fight against a system in which the odds are always stacked against their children.

Ultimately, parents, grandparents, or guardians are responsible for a child's growth and development. And they might discipline their child in a way that you disagree with, or that child psychologists have shown to be suboptimal. But remember that many psychologists are not Black. And many psychologists are not raising Black sons in a racist society. That doesn't mean their word is irrelevant. But remember that the parents of your Black male students likely know something about raising Black boys that many White teachers and psychologists have possibly never even thought about.

The following chapter is by Professor of Education, Dr. Crystal Laura, author of Being Bad: My Baby Brother and the School to Prison Pipeline. *In her book, Laura shows how her brother, the son of a Black family in a middle-class suburban school district, seemed no more destined for prison than any of his White peers. But, as Laura traces the events that led him to prison, it is clear that the system within which we live, and the narratives that live in people's heads, created a pathway to prison that her brother could not escape. Dr. Laura writes this chapter as a letter to White women teachers, from the mother of two Black boys. It is clear from her letter that it's going to take all of us—all educators—to change the direction of this pipeline.*

CHAPTER 31

Find Freedom in the Classroom

A Love Letter to My Babies' Teachers

Crystal Laura

Hi there.

I don't think we've yet had the pleasure of meeting. This world is small, though, and I've recently been struck by wanderlust, which is to say that there is a real possibility our paths might cross and my babies—the ones I birthed—may one day be your students.

So let us assume they will, and that this isn't an academic book chapter at all, but rather a love letter penned especially for you.

***

October 2016.

Dear Comrade,

Welcome back to school! I'm Crystal Laura, Zachary and Logan's mom. I know that we'll soon have an opportunity to get better acquainted, but I thought to write and tell you more about me and what I care about to begin the school-family connection straightaway.

In addition to mothering my boys, I teach teachers and principals in the College of Education at Chicago State University. As part of my university work, I travel often to lecture and lead professional development trainings on critical issues in urban education. Recently, I left the boys for a couple of days to spend time with older youth—kids of fifteen and sixteen, who live in New York City, on Rikers Island.

The name precedes it. Rikers Island covers 413 acres of land in the middle of the East River between Queens and the Bronx, adjacent to the runways of LaGuardia Airport. Sitting on that land is a complex of jails: ten of them. It is one of the world's largest correctional institutions—it's a penal colony, really—and from what I hear, it's one of world's worst, too. It is notorious for abuse and neglect of people who are locked up there. You might remember the story that surfaced a couple of years ago of Kalief Browder, who spent three years on Rikers waiting for a trial that never happened—two of those three years in solitary confinement—and he was so deeply impacted by his experiences there that two full years after he left the Island, and after Jay Z and Rosie O'Donell and others donated materials and funds to get his life back in order, he hung himself.

There are over 11,000 other men, women, and children on Rikers—the youngest of them are mandated to attend school. That means that we also have colleagues on Rikers—general grade-level teachers, special education teachers, counselors, social workers, paraprofessionals, principals, and district staff—who work with incarcerated students behind the walls.

On the first day of the visit, I toured the school sites on Rikers—sat in on classes, met with young people, asked the adults some questions, really became a student of that place—and then on the second day, I gave a reflective talk to our colleagues about what I learned. What I told them was this: Without question, our current systems need complete overhauls; but, in the meantime, they can work wonders— what one counselor called acting as a "cool drink of water in hell"—and with proper training, a strong network of support, and whole lot of conviction, they can make great strides toward rethinking, reimagining, redesigning altogether how we approach harm, healing, and justice.

I see you like I saw them, as a cool drink of water in what is, quite frankly, for some young people hell. I see this letter as our first real opportunity to put our heads together about how to better understand and radically shift the hellish context within which many students find themselves.

So, I don't want to blow this opportunity. I don't want to waste it by going on and on about issues that you are likely already fully aware of. I want to touch on some things that you might not regularly engage in discussions about. As you begin this school year, I want to seize this little moment to help you frame your thinking about your intentions and purpose for teaching.

I Wonder . . .

I wonder if you know that as a teacher, you are either engaged in incarceration prevention or incarceration expansion. Incarceration prevention or incarceration expansion. It's just that real.

Because here and now, in the twenty-first century, we are seeing and experiencing an age of mass incarceration, a time when, as the professor Marc Lamont Hill (2016) argues, the prison is our go-to mechanism of isolation and containment, the central way that we adjudicate disputes, and the primary site where we deal with social trauma and social dilemmas.

Right now 1 in 31 American adults is under some form of correctional control—meaning incarcerated, on parole, or on probation. 1 in every 31. More than 2 million men and women are locked up in the United States—including my twenty-three-year-old brother—and besides the extraordinary number of incarcerated people, an even bigger problem is that we think that's normal. Today our nation cages more of its people than any other country in the world, more Black folks than were enslaved 165 years ago. This is the contemporary context, and I wonder if you know that.

But it's important for us, as educators, to stay alive to our expanding prison nation. Not just when somebody escapes and not only when we catch a marathon of those juicy, addictive documentaries—Snapped, Drugs, Inc., Lockdown, or—if you're old school—Cops. It's crucial for us to pay attention to prisons partly because in our profession, we ourselves are parties to barricading people in them. It's true. On every measure of academic attainment—earning a diploma, a GED, or some form of postsecondary education—those who are incarcerated lag behind us in the free world. They have lower literacy levels, fewer marketable skills, and a greater prevalence of disability. With regard to education and schooling, incarcerated people are often those who once needed the most from their teachers and somehow got the least.

I wonder if you know that and if you are keeping your eyes open wide to our current situation, which is largely defined by jails and prisons that are so full of brown and black bodies that most everyone who knows what I'm talking about and has good sense is practically begging schools to stop feeding them.

The School-to-Prison Pipeline

I want to say a bit about the school-to-prison pipeline because it strikes a special chord in me every time I meet someone—someone in the field of education, especially—who has never heard of the phrase. Now I suspect that this wouldn't apply to you. I imagine that uncomfortable, justice-oriented conversations are certainly happening in your classes and in your school. But ask a classroom teacher, a director, a principal, a parent, or school board member who is not well-versed in critical issues of urban education about the school-to-prison pipeline, and you can expect little more than a polite nod and smart use of context clues. I'm just saying. No offense, I've gotten that "I don't know what you're talking about, but something tells me I should" response more than a few times.

I often assume that the problem is one of semantics. Let's be honest, the term "school-to-prison pipeline" is not exactly part of everyday lingo, and even across activist circles, the mind-blowing idea that kids get funneled from systems of education to systems of juvenile and criminal justice has actually been captured by a number of other nifty metaphors. Off the top, I can think of three: one is the "schoolhouse-to-jailhouse track," another is the "cradle-to-prison pipeline," and a third is the "school-prison nexus." Write those down: schoolhouse-to-jailhouse track, cradle-to-prison pipeline, and school-prison nexus. In the interest of time, I will discuss only the first one, but all three of these school-to-prison pipeline derivatives, if you will, highlight the fact that our profession is hardly the great equalizer that it's hyped up to be. I want you to remember that these expressions are like close cousins not twins—and this distinction is important because if we are to dismantle the school-to-prison pipeline, which we will, then we've got to be clear about not only our language, but how we are directing our efforts and where to seek support.

SCHOOLHOUSE-TO-JAILHOUSE TRACK

For example, if you are deeply concerned about the ways in which school-based policies and practices help young people along to jails and prisons, then—in addition to reading my book, *Being Bad: My Baby Brother and the School-to-Prison Pipeline*—you have to take a look at reports published by the Advancement Project. The Advancement Project is a multiracial civil rights organization founded by a team of lawyers who have taken on a variety of social issues, including redistricting, voter protection, immigrant justice, and the on-the-ground realities of zero tolerance.

By now, zero tolerance in our schools and workplaces is as common as dirt, but some of us are too young to remember how things got this way. In the early 1990s, a spike of juvenile homicides led to public panic, fueled by a racially coded media frenzy around teenage "superpredators." This was followed by the passage of federal and state laws to mete out sentences. This sequence of events could have easily gone over our heads, but the staff at the Advancement Project, and others, started putting out reports that help us understand what it means when school adults have zero tolerance for children and youth in their buildings.

To understand what it means when school adults have zero tolerance for young people is to first acknowledge that as absolute as zero tolerance sounds, we aren't equally intolerant of all kids. Of course, I won't argue that we should be, but why is it that poor students, students of color, LGBTQ students, and students with disabilities so frequently get the short end of the stick?

I remember one spring semester I taught a teacher education course on urban ed policy, and the topic of "bad kids" emerged as a particular favorite among my students. Most everyone wanted to know how to run a tight ship, stay sane, and keep safe with so many "troublemakers" and "class clowns" in Chicago public schools. Whenever I pushed people to unpack the beliefs embedded within this kind of philosophy and everyday language, things always got ugly. Public schools were equated with city schools, city kids with cultural poverty and dysfunction. The stock stories commodified by the mainstream media—the news, Hollywood films, cable network television, and the music industry—about pathological and dangerous youth poured out in my classroom. And the grapevine, with its salacious tales from the field, was tagged as proof positive that some children will inevitably fall through the cracks.

As lively as these discussions were, no one ever seemed to want to talk about the connections between how we think and talk about children and how we treat them in social and academic contexts. A hush usually fell over the crowd when I suggested that demonizing ideology and discourse enables a whole web of relationships, conditions, and social processes—a social ecology of discipline—which works on and through the youth who rub against our understanding of "good" students. Granted, these were young, preservice teachers who had very little, if any, direct experience with children in urban schools. So, I'm guessing that part of their silence was rooted in ignorance. It's also true, however, that challenging and unlearning what we assume we know about people, places, and things is uncomfortable and that finagling around contradictions and tensions of implicit and explicit bias is easier than diving into and grappling with these ideas. But that's exactly what we educators ought to be doing, diving into the wreckage.

Because if we don't, then we will continue to build schools like "Rosa Parks Elementary," a fake name for a real place, where educational researcher Ann Ferguson (2001) found that Black male students of ten and eleven years old were routinely and openly described by school adults as "at risk" of failing, "unsalvageable," and "bound for jail." Help me out here: sticks and stones may break my bones, but what? Words will never hurt me. Bull*%!#. Yes, they will.

Because when our perceptions are so profoundly distorted that we can think and talk about our students in these ways, then we have no trouble acting accordingly. In a room of thirty students, with precious few resources to go around, and with the alphabet soup of standardized tests never far away—we have no space, no patience, zero tolerance for "misbehavior." The problem, of course, is that what counts as "misbehavior" depends.

Black boys, for example, are often refracted through cultural images of Black males as both dangerous and endangered, and their transgressions are sometimes framed as different from those of other children. Black boys are what Ann Ferguson (2001) calls, "doubly displaced"—meaning, that as Black children, they are not seen as childlike, but "adultified"; their misdeeds are "made to take on a sinister, intentional, fully conscious tone that is stripped of any element of childish naivete" (p. 83). As Black males, they are often denied the masculine dispensation that White male students get as being "naturally naughty"; instead, Black boys are discerned as willfully bad (p. 80).

So we put them out of class and out of school. We suspend them. We punish them excessively, usually for minor offenses, like talking about a Hello Kitty bubble gun, hugging a friend, and chewing a pop tart into the shape of a gun. In Chicago, where I live and work, zero tolerance policies in the district's schools were abolished in 2006 in favor of restorative justice approaches to harm and healing, but still the number of suspensions has nearly doubled since then. Black boys in my hometown are five times more likely to be suspended than any other group of students in the city's public school system. Black boys comprise 23 percent of the district's student population, but amount to 44 percent of those who are suspended and 61 percent of those who are expelled. Black boys are the only group of Chicago Public School students whose suspension rates are higher in elementary school than in high school.

Chicago has its issues. Chicago is the epicenter of neoliberal school reform, the third-largest school district in the country and one of the few without an elected school board. We've had over one hundred neighborhood school closures since 2001 and an eightfold increase in money going to charters. At the same time, 126 schools don't have libraries. You know what, don't get me started. School politics in Chicago is for another letter.

Let's be clear—wherever you work or live likely has its issues too. But the problem is much bigger than where we work because when we have zero tolerance for our kids, we not only suspend them, but we expel them. We not only suspend and expel them, but we arrest them—in schools, we have cops or school resource officers on deck (as we saw in South Carolina), and we've constructed booking stations in the school buildings to make school-based arrests easier, faster, and more efficient.

When we have zero tolerance for our kids, we lose all concept of kids being kids—wiggling, jumping, giggling, fidgeting somehow gets diagnosed and labeled and medicated. And when that doesn't work, we beat them. Yes, beat them—with canes, straps, paddles, and yardsticks. Corporal punishment is still allowed in twenty states.

When we have zero tolerance for kids and their "misbehavior," we even fine them. Back home, Noble charter school collects about $200,000 annually from student discipline fees, including $5 per infraction for things like missing a button on your shirt or being seen with a bag of chips; add that to the revenue from a summer behavior class at $140 per registrant and you've got yourself a promising fundraiser on the backs of the poor, Black students, and their families.

And if the kids for whom we have zero tolerance have not yet dropped out, we transfer them to other schools or counsel them toward programs like the Job Corps, what has been called the U.S. Department of Labor's boarding school for the "bottom of society" and what I would argue is an intermediary or pit stop in the schoolhouse-to-jailhouse track.

I could go on, but I think that you get the point, which is that these school policies and practices are systems of surveillance, exercises of power used to continuously and purposefully monitor poor youth and youth of color (Foucault, 1977/1979). I am a Black woman, a mother of two beautiful Black sons, so you'll understand why I am particularly attuned to the ways that schools wound Black boys. Black boys are unevenly punished and tracked into educational disability categories in their early years, practices that tend to reinforce the very problems they intend to correct. And although this is enough to make reasonable people want to holler, even more insidious is when those under surveillance internalize the experiences and labels assigned to them, when they believe the exclusion and isolation have been defensible, and when they learn to condition themselves. Then, Black boys who have been sorted, contained, and then pushed out of schools become Black men—men whose patterns of hardship are pronounced and deeply entrenched—men who constitute nearly 50 percent of the adult males in prison—men who have been well primed for neither college, career, nor full participation in our democracy, but instead for punitive institutionalization.

This is what the "schoolhouse-to-jailhouse track" tries to show us.

If you are moved by this—this brief description of how school policies and practices nudge youth to drop out—then I hope you'll consider grounding your approach to teaching in dismantling the schoolhouse-to-jailhouse track and in reframing your work in such a way that the school is not a place of punishment, that the school doesn't label more people ID and LD than it does PhD and JD, that the school is not the primary gateway to menial labor, the streets, and permanent detention. I think your job is to yearn for and create the kinds of schools that folks don't need to recover from. I want you to look at your position as disrupting the school-to-prison pipeline and as engaging in antiprison work.

I am happy to support you in this endeavor. Let's make time to talk soon.

All love, always.

Crystal

■ ■ Engaging the Mind ★ Taking Action ★ Inspiring Excellence
Love Letters

P.S. What do you think of responding to my love letter with one of your own? It'd be helpful for you to put in writing who you are, what you care and wonder about, and how you plan to collaborate with parents to find freedom in the classroom. Try addressing the letter to someone— maybe me, or a parent whose son you currently teach—to remind yourself that this is not an abstract activity or busy work, but rather a conscious effort to engage in thoughtful dialogue with a real-life comrade who wants as much for Black boys as you do. When you are ready, share your letter with whomever it concerns and watch the seed grow.

CONNECTING

In the process of interviewing both Black men and boys, as well as White women teachers, we heard people asking loudly for this book. White women want a resource that supports them to think and speak more honestly about themselves as racialized beings and about their Black boy students as a specific group with particular needs: *The Guide* does exactly that. Black boys need *The Guide* to be better understood, to be seen as individuals, as Black students, and as boys. When White women teachers read it, learn its strategies, and internalize its values, it will change the way school happens for Black boys. Parts I and II have led the way. Under the theme Understanding, the authors challenged teachers to consider how their identity impacts their teaching and to recognize potentially negative unintended impacts. Under the theme of Respecting, authors helped us get a sense of who Black boys are, in all of their diversity and collective identity and opened up pathways to see and respect them. In this third part, having done the hard work of the first two parts, we are ready to connect.

The Guide is premised on the idea that relationships between teachers and students are key to student success in schools. From prekindergarten all the way through college, having a personal connection with a teacher helps students feel invested in their school community. But beyond being an adult in their students' lives, teachers play an incredibly important role, not only as mentors, friends, and allies, but as gatekeepers. Teachers recommend students for honors placements or special education, identify students for testing that could lead to a giftedness placement or a psychological evaluation, for initiating suspension or expulsion, and for writing letters of recommendation for the next level: new schools, college, or jobs. To effectively support students as they pass through the gates (which is what great teachers do) rather than closing off student access, teachers need to be able to see students clearly, to connect with them authentically, and to understand the way the gates are rigged to make it harder for Black students to move through them. For White teachers to be allies to, or advocates for, their Black boy students, they must understand not only their students, but also the struggles their students incur simply by being Black and male in the United States.

PART 5

CONNECTING STUDENT SUCCESS AND FAILURE TO SCHOOL STRUCTURES AND CLASSROOM STRATEGIES

In the introduction to this book, we (the editors) brought forth the idea that if a teacher does not connect with a student, it is not the fault of the student. It is the adult's responsibility to find a way to create that connection. The following methods, strategies, readings, and models are key to successfully implementing lessons that connect to the often most marginalized students in the classroom, Black boys. Good teaching, like the ideas presented here, however, will enhance the education of all students, especially as they are introduced to ideas and content that will challenge and engage them. The strategies presented in this book are often simply examples of good teaching, but they are especially critical for the success of Black boys, those who have notoriously and systemically been marginalized from educational institutions.

When cultural styles do not match between teachers and students, students are expected to code-switch and to fit the styles of the teacher. They meet serious consequences if they do not. Teachers, however, are rarely sanctioned for not having the competency to adjust to different cultural styles of students and their parents. This is one of the fundamental assumptions we hope to reframe through-out this guide. Rather than blaming students when teachers do not or cannot connect, we need to search for explanations that start with teachers and schools. Adults must learn how to code-switch to connect with students. Code-switching is not a skill we can teach unless it is one that we already have. Furthermore, students will learn nothing from us—code-switching or otherwise—unless we have a relationship first.

But teachers cannot just implement the strategies without having done the groundwork of understanding and respecting outlined earlier in this book. Consider the recent controversy following the publication of *A Fine Dessert: Four Centuries, Four Families, One Delicious Treat* by Emily Jenkins, considered at first a book that incorporated national traditions. Because of its inclusion of an African American family the book fell into the multicultural realm and was praised as a book to make connections and discuss similarities. What quickly became clear to those who critically analyzed the book, however, was how it perpetuates privilege, stereotypes, and supports opportunities for microaggressions. Look at it closely for the images of "happy slaves." Educators who know how to "spot the stuff" (Tatum, p. 47) would have recognized the microaggression immediately and not incorporated the book into their curriculum. If White teachers have done their own work, they will learn to recognize the oppressive aspects of the curriculum before others have to point it out—and without simply just eliminating all references to people of color, which sometimes happens as teachers try to sidestep potentially controversial things.

Readers are therefore asked to work through the following chapters with pedagogy in mind. How does what is shared below impact the academic achievement of Black boys?

INTERRUPTING SCHOOL STRUCTURES

Many White teachers "go easy" on Black children. They feel bad because of a history of racism. They don't want to be perceived as racist. They want the satisfaction of an emotional connection. They want to respond to Black children the same way that they do to White children, without acknowledging the possible difference in cultural approaches to authority and respect. In this next chapter, Valerie Adams-Bass talks about the importance of firmness when starting relationships with Black boys—particularly boys in Grades 7–12. This advice may seem contradictory to the advice in other chapters, such as creating interactive classrooms that are premised on individual identities and preferences, showing love, challenging narratives of deviance, and so on. But it is not. Starting out firm, establishing authority, and setting high expectations, in our experience, only makes it more possible for teachers to have the control and structure necessary for a classroom to be flexible and responsive to individual student interests and needs. Think about the importance of having a tightly responsive steering wheel for making sharp turns in response to the specific conditions of the road. If you have a loose steering wheel, you may not be able to respond quickly to the road you are on and hazards it may contain. Adams-Bass's advice in this chapter should provide teachers a mechanism for tightening their steering wheel so that they can be more—not less—prepared to implement suggestions from throughout the rest of the book. That said, none of the suggestions in this book are absolutes. While broad cultural generalizations are helpful to know about different groups, no single orientation will necessarily serve the child sitting in front of you. To find out what works for that child, you need to know that child. We present this array of strategies so that teachers have an idea of the spectrum of possible responses. But we leave it to them to explore the gray area within the spectrum as they consider what works for their classroom and their students.

CHAPTER 32

Start Out Firm

Valerie Adams-Bass

I have spent seventeen years working with African American middle- and high school youth as an afterschool provider. For the most part, I have worked alongside or managed White American females to deliver youth development programming year-round during out-of-school time. More often than not, our approach to working with African American youth differs distinctly. I take a firm stance as I start my relationship with young people. I explicitly set a precedent of addressing me by "Ms. First name" or "Ms. Last name." Either is acceptable, but addressing me by my first name only is not. My colleagues have often started their relationships by allowing youth to address them by first name.

Against the backdrop of positive youth development (PYD) research, we work with the youth to collaboratively establish program rules and guiding principles for acceptable and expected behavior in the early stages of programming. PYD suggests providing opportunities for autonomy and ownership to teens as a best practice (Dotterweich, 2016) that has been proven to result in better social and academic outcomes for youth. Together, the youth, my colleagues, and I review the rules. Frequently, youth establish rules for handling behaviors identified as unacceptable, such as fighting, using illegal substances, or using profane language. If important rules are missing, I am usually the one who pushes the youth to think about adding another, such as one person speaks at a time—-the "one mic" rule— and to ask them to explain their definition of respect. Respect is almost *always* one of the first items youth add to the list. After we finish with revisions, my colleagues, the youth, and I sign and post the rules as a reminder of our mutual agreement.

Once programming begins, the rules come to life as do the preferences and early precedents we, the adults, set for addressing us. If a youth has had a bad day, we make room for them to attend the program: Everyone is welcome, but from my perspective, being disruptive to the group is not acceptable. When this has occurred, I direct the young person or the group to the rules for accountability. In contrast, my colleagues have waivered, allowing students to participate without accountability for the standards they have helped to set. Youth are adept at using the "call me by my first name" policy to persuade my White colleagues to bend or even to overlook the rules. A quick acquiescence is a set-up for a frustrated relationship and low standards for the youth. Ask yourself, why am I choosing to allow the students or youth to address me by my first name? What purpose does it serve? Will this genuinely help them? Being *friendly*, being addressed by your first name signals that you are a friend or peer, not a person to whom youth should show deference.

No matter the mood of the young people I serve, I remain firm. My decision to remain firm, requiring youth to address me as "Ms." and holding them accountable for their actions, has often resulted in students considering me "mean" or *unfriendly* early in the program. I choose to remain firm. I am not interested in either being the most liked adult or being considered mean. However, I prefer an early reputation of being "mean" to earning the reputation of being a *friendly* pushover. Starting firm requires that you become comfortable being uncomfortable as you establish and maintain boundaries that are acceptable and beneficial for the youth you serve.

Certainly, on more than one occasion, a youth has come to a program that I was facilitating unprepared to be "present" and to participate. Once, two African American male teens arrived late, under the influence of an illegal substance; my preference was to send them home without the tokens that are earned through active program participation. They were not participating; they had not earned the tokens. Instead of overlooking their condition, I spoke with them directly about my observations. My co-facilitator, a White woman, was uncomfortable with this decision and found it hard to send them home. We sent them home. They did not return to the program again in that condition, and they apologized for their behavior during our next meeting.

I have found that my White female colleagues, rather than express empathy—an understanding or acknowledgment of the experiences of youth they serve—respond out of pity, feeling sorry for the adverse experiences many Black youth encounter. They often relax program rules, blurring the lines of authority and being a responsive caring adult in exchange for likability. While relaxing expectations might make you feel good, or may feel like the right thing to do in that moment, more than likely it is not. Ask yourself, would you do the same for your child, niece, or nephew, or would you hold them accountable to a high standard? Why are you relaxing the rules? Are you establishing a pattern of behavior that can have long-term repercussions for youth? Remember, if you are working with youth-teens, developmentally, they are learning to test their boundaries and push limits (Dotterweich, 2016). Once they learn boundaries are superficial or unreal, they are keen to use this to their advantage. This applies to all youth, including urban African American youth.

For example, while facilitating a program, we learned from a participant's mother—I'll call her Ms. Roosevelt and I will refer to the teen as Diane—that Diane was not going to school because she wanted to be transferred to her friends' school, but she was attending our program regularly. Ms. Roosevelt asked for our support to advise Diane to attend school, to keep an open door for her, but not to allow her daughter to continue participating until she sorted through the truancy issue. We collectively decided Diane could not continue to participate in the program. Despite this agreement, she continued to be truant and to come to the program. My colleague chose to override the mother's request and my recommendation that we support Ms. Roosevelt by continuing to allow Diane to participate. When we discussed Diane's participation, my colleague explained that she felt bad for her and that she believed allowing her to actively participate would help persuade Diane to return to school. Had it been my decision exclusively, I would have remained firm. Diane would have been permitted to come by the office and to attend the community functions we hosted; our doors would have remained open to her, but I would not have rewarded her behavior. Diane received the stipend and tokens for full participation in the entire program. It didn't matter to my colleague that we agreed with Ms. Roosevelt that Diane would not be permitted to participate.

Relaxing the boundaries for Diane lowered the standards of expectation for her. What about the mother's request for support? What would you have done with Diane? Would you have allowed her to continue attending? Is your answer yes? If so, why?

Reinforcing unfavorable behavior sends a message that this behavior will have favorable results. At a minimum, reinforcing unfavorable behavior is risky for African American youth. Unlike other youth who are testing boundaries through similar behaviors, African American youth are judged more harshly when they have encounters with police or are disciplined in schools (Morris, 2016). Although they are youth, they are often not given the opportunity to make youthful mistakes (Bottiani, Bradshaw, & Mendelson, 2016). Lowering your standard of expectations because the youth you serve must manage racism daily, may live in challenged communities, or may have difficult home lives doesn't give them the opportunity to achieve at a high level. Start firm.

Black children and youth deserve equitable opportunities that include being held to high standards and high expectations. Start out firm. It sends a message that you have high expectations for them, that you plan to hold them accountable for their actions, and that you expect them to participate and to be engaged.

Be yourself. While it may be difficult to be firm, at a minimum, you should be yourself. Acknowledge your differences, be honest about what you don't know, while honoring what assets students bring into the classroom, and keep your expectations high. Don't make attempts to conform to what you assume students expect from you. Being yourself will likely earn you genuine respect from the students.

■ ■ Engaging the Mind ★ Taking Action ★ Inspiring Excellence
What Makes a Good Teacher?

Youth use all kinds of tactics to get control over the classroom. The kryptonite for White teachers seems to be "You're a racist." Fear of being called a racist or being perceived as racist often holds White teachers back from being firm. Try the following activity to help you parse racism from good teaching. Make a list of five characteristics of a racist and five characteristics of a good teacher and look for overlap. Notice the vast differences, and stand firm if students use the "r-word" to try to get you to loosen up.

The following chapter demonstrates the way that implicit bias on the part of teachers can set students on the wrong pathway for their lives. Dr. Ed Smith writes about the "undermatch," an underknown concept, in which high school students tend to apply to and attend colleges that are less selective than the ones for which they are qualified. He demonstrates how teachers can misdirect students—even if college counseling is not their role—with just a few unthoughtful words during their college search. This is one of the many insidious ways that both implicit bias and our inability to acknowledge what we don't know (i.e., giving college advice without knowing the admissions requirements of different colleges) can have devastating consequences for students.

CHAPTER 33

A Parable of Academic Misgivings

The Educator's Role in Addressing College Undermatch

Edward J. Smith

It was October of senior year, and Jonathan was filled with excitement as he prepared his college applications. As the only child of a single-parent household, his family, neighbors, and peers coalesced around his academic and athletic interests. The communal support had helped Jonathan evolve from an inquisitive child into a thriving scholar-athlete during his high school career. Immediately following graduation, Jonathan planned to enroll in college, seeking an intellectually vibrant campus, featuring an abundance of opportunities for deep learning, critical reflection, and self-examination. He was convinced that these opportunities were offered primarily at highly selective four-year universities.

Despite his excitement about the process, Jonathan was disinclined to apply to many such institutions. He was confident that his 3.65 cumulative grade point average (on a 4.0 scale) would position him for a multitude of college options. Yet still, Jonathan had a number of concerns that tempered his self-assurance, including his scores on the Scholastic Aptitude Test (SAT), his family's financial background, and his ongoing struggles in pre-calculus.

For example, Jonathan's highest score on the SAT landed him in the seventieth percentile of test-takers, which he thought was fine. However, after perusing a few websites, he realized the scores obtained by the incoming students at the colleges in which he was interested were much higher. Moreover, Jonathan experienced an intense case of sticker-shock[1] when he stumbled on the institutions' published tuition prices (each of which was well beyond $40,000 a year). While Jonathan's father routinely supported his college aspirations, Jonathan fell into a cold sweat when he imagined asking his father for money to pay for college. His father did not attend college himself and held multiple jobs at various points of Jonathan's life. While his father would do anything to support his postsecondary choices, Jonathan sensed that his financial contribution remained tenuous.

Last, Jonathan was particularly impacted by a series of troubling encounters with Ms. Holbrook, his pre-calculus teacher. He received an F on the first exam and sought her out for extra help. She agreed to provide supplemental instruction in the mornings before school started. This arrangement required Jonathan's arrival at school a full hour before it started for two days a week.

After six weeks working together, both were startled to find that Jonathan only marginally improved his performance on the second exam. Instead of outright failing the exam, Jonathan received a D. Even more startling, Jonathan found it more difficult to meet with Ms. Holbrook after the second exam. Sensing that she had relinquished the tutoring relationship, Jonathan desperately sought her input on his college search process. He was worried that his current struggles in the course forecasted failure in college.

Jonathan approached Ms. Holbrook after a class session with a list of eight colleges in which he was interested. Ms. Holbrook retrieved the sheet of paper and glanced at it, dropping her head down into her chest, cupping her forehead with her free hand. She removed her glasses and raised her head only to reveal a timid grin. "Jonathan, you know these are really good schools, right? Like, hard to get into. For God's sake, you have an Ivy League university on your list." Jonathan had heard the term Ivy League before but stood confused, as he was unclear how the schools were distinguishable from other institutions. Ms. Holbrook continued in a soft voice,

> Look, I have to be honest, you may want to rethink this list. You're bound to struggle at these schools; you're failing pre-calculus. The students at these colleges went to good high schools. They're enrolled in advanced placement

---

[1] Shock or dismay experienced by the potential buyers of a particular product or service upon discovering its high or increased published price. See Baum and Schwartz (2012) for more information on the phenomenon as it pertains to college tuition prices.

courses . . . and they don't need to show up an hour before school starts for extra help. Have you seen the tuition and fees at these schools? As a matter of efficiency, I'd advise you to only apply to colleges where you stand a good chance of getting admitted. Not that you can't get into these; but your chances aren't good.

She let out a deep sigh and concluded, "Again, I'm just giving you the cold, hard truth." Dejected, Jonathan left this encounter with two important lessons. First, with her brutal "honesty," Ms. Holbrook qualitatively delineated the differences between the "good" students and him, namely, the fact that they could succeed without receiving help. This finding made him particularly averse to asking his teachers for help thereafter. Second, Jonathan thought it would be wiser to concentrate his efforts on activities that might yield the highest return. In this case, applying to less selective colleges might be a better use of his time given the higher likelihood he might have of being admitted. Jonathan could not help but think this was the same approach Ms. Holbrook took to teaching, generally, and the approach she took to helping him with pre-calculus, specifically.

Jonathan eventually applied to seven institutions, two of which were "branch campuses" of "Land-Grant State University," a public system of colleges and universities in the state adjacent to his. He was particularly interested in attending Land-Grant State's flagship campus for several reasons. First, it hosted a highly ranked business school; Jonathan's intended field of study was finance. Second, it was the largest and most prestigious (as measured by academic selectivity) among the twenty-two campuses across the state. Last, Jonathan was familiar with the campus since he had visited the university to participate in a football camp the summer between his sophomore and junior year. Yet still, Ms. Holbrook's advice echoed in his ear; he thought applying to the flagship would be unwise. The branch campuses offered a smattering of four-year degree programs, but overwhelmingly provided two-year options, which facilitated the potential of transfer to the flagship while incurring a significant reduction in cost.

A couple of months after Jonathan submitted his applications, he found himself at home on a cold January evening; he received a call from an admissions officer from Land-Grant State University. The officer called to notify him that he had been offered admission for the fall. Jonathan was relieved; it was the first acceptance offer he had received. Notwithstanding, the officer had a few questions. He was interested in knowing Jonathan's reasons for applying to the branch campuses. Jonathan simply replied, "They seemed like they made sense." The officer informed Jonathan that he was impressed with his application, and the institution wanted to enroll Jonathan in classes at the flagship campus. They were impressed not only with his academic achievement, but with his commitment to community service and the leadership he displayed in his co-curricular activities.

In addition to being captain of the high school's football and track teams, Jonathan was the coordinator of a peer-counseling program at a local elementary school; he started a student organization called Facing Race, which served as an Intergroup Dialogue Program; and he initiated conversations between community organizers and local law enforcement agencies to develop restorative justice approaches, all of which was documented in his letter of recommendations and his personal statement. Last, the admissions officer mentioned that the school planned to award Jonathan a Wells-Evers scholarship, named in honor of the first Black woman and man to graduate from the flagship campus. This conversation expanded Jonathan's collegiate horizons, reinforced in him the value of service and leadership, and advanced his progression toward his life goals. So, too, did the institutional grant; taken together with federal aid (i.e., a Pell Grant and work-study), a scholarship provided by his local civic association, and various on-campus jobs, the financial pieces fell in place, affording Jonathan a prosperous collegiate career from which he graduated with relatively little student loan debt.

ACADEMIC UNDERMATCH

Higher education literature indicates that knowledge about an institution's academic standards, as well as its application process are critical factors in discerning whether a college is a good match for a student (Dukakis, Duong, Ruiz de Valasco, & Henderson, 2014). Increasing evidence indicates that many students, particularly those from poor or low-resourced communities, experience "undermatch" by applying to and enrolling in colleges and universities of lower academic quality than their scholastic record would permit (e.g., Bowen, Chingos, & McPherson, 2009; Hoxby & Avery, 2012; Roderick, Nagaoka, & Coca, 2008; Rodriguez, 2013, 2015). For example, some students who are qualified and prepared to attend a four-year college but end up enrolling in a community college. In other cases, some high-achieving students do not end up enrolling in college at all.

This phenomenon affects not only application and matriculation to college, but also completion. Students are more likely to graduate when the college is the most academically selective postsecondary institution that admits them (Bowen et al., 2009), and many researchers believe that the likelihood of graduating is predicated on the current graduation rate of an institution (Bowen et al., 2009; Roderick et al., 2008).

In the first national study on the topic, 41 percent of students were undermatched, most often those from low-income families graduating from underresourced high schools (Smith, Pender, Howell, & Hurwitz, 2012). Moreover, a 1999 study of high school seniors in North Carolina found that 40 percent of highly qualified students did not enroll in a selective college (Bowen et al., 2009). The situation became widely known as the result of a series of reports by the Consortium on Chicago Schools Research (e.g., Roderick, Coca, & Nagaoka, 2011; Roderick, Nagaoka, & Allensworth, 2006; Roderick et al., 2008; Roderick, Nagaoka, Coca, & Moeller, 2009). They found that more than 60 percent of Chicago Public School graduates who enrolled in college were undermatched. Furthermore, undermatching commonly occurred among students with the "strongest academic credentials"; only 38 percent of students who were qualified for a "very selective" institution enrolled in that college type.

COMMON RATIONALIZATIONS

Education researchers have found that most schools and counselors are ill-equipped to provide accurate and timely information to students and families about their college choices (McDonough, 1997, 2005). In Jonathan's case, his guidance counselor wrote him recommendation letters but acknowledged that she was overwhelmed by the issues facing the other 500 students she served. Hoxby and Turner (2013) found that providing college information to high-achieving, low-income students appears to impact their college choice behaviors: with good advice, more students were likely to apply to and enroll in colleges for which they were a better academic match. However, Black, Cortes, and Lincove (2015) found that undermatching still happens, even when students have more complete information. For example, in the state of Texas, where the top ten percent of high school graduates are guaranteed admissions to a flagship university, the authors found that more information (e.g., about college prices and financial aid) and more transparency (e.g., about exactly what colleges are looking for, outside of GPAs and test scores) alone did not reduce college undermatch (Black et al., 2015).

Less is known about the messages and signals that cause students, particularly Black boys, to feel reticent about applying to selective institutions. Scholars have found that many have negative experiences with high school guidance counselors and teachers, particularly when discussing their postsecondary aspirations (Byndloss & Reid, 2013; Harper & Associates, 2012; McDonough, 2005). For example, a qualitative study focusing on ninety Black male students revealed that their high school guidance counselors advised them not to apply to selective private colleges because they would not be accepted (Harper & Associates, 2012). Nearly all of the students in the study who attended an elite private college noted that they would not have ended up there if they had heeded their guidance counselor's advice.

Rodriguez's quantitative analysis (2013) of nationally representative data revealed Black students, particularly Black males, were uniquely sensitive to encounters with guidance counselors and teachers, particularly regarding college information. Rodriguez (2013) found that Black males were more likely to undermatch the more often they discussed "college information" with teachers and guidance counselors. These trends, taken together, call to question the role educators play in the reluctance many Black boys and men experience in the college application and choice processes.

■ ■ Engaging the Mind ★ Taking Action ★ Inspiring Excellence
A Way Forward

1. DISCUSS THE ELEMENTS OF THE HOLISTIC APPLICATION REVIEW WITH YOUR STUDENTS.

Students should be told that the admissions process at some colleges includes more than a review of the applicant's GPAs and test scores. Educators should continually find ways to promote the notion of holistic review, as many selective and highly selective universities employ such a practice to craft the *right* admissions class. As a result, each applicant is reviewed comprehensively, including a review of an applicant's letters of recommendation, strength of the high school transcript, volunteer or leadership activities, and indicators of grit, determination, and persistence though adversity. Educators should facilitate activities to help students get in the practice of cataloguing and showcasing these facets of their lives. The digital application Raise.Me[2] can help students keep track of their academic achievements and

co-curricular activities. The College Board's Big Future[3] website and the CollegeGo mobile app allows students to list their accomplishments while collecting information about specific colleges that meet their needs. These tools can be shared and employed during class sessions.

2. PLAY THE FINANCIAL AID GAME.

Help students complete the Free Application for Student Financial Aid (FASFA) by talking about the form's purpose, while offering seminars to facilitate application submission. Many institutions of higher education have a NetPrice calculator (cost of attendance after financial aid is considered), and most institutions host a financial aid shopping sheet.[4] Showcasing these digital tools during class can be a useful exercise.

---

[2] See www.RaiseMe.org for more details.

[3] See https://bigfuture.collegeboard.org/college-search# for more details.

[4] See http://www2.ed.gov/policy/highered/guid/aid-offer/index.html for more details.

(Continued)

(Continued)

3. ENGAGE PARENTS, GUARDIANS, AND FAMILIES.

In a follow-up study, Hoxby and Turner (2013) examined the efficacy of interventions that offered students primarily web-based, partially customized information on college application and costs and included paperless waivers for application fees and materials to educate parents about some of the misconceptions they may have about college quality and cost. Materials were sent directly to the students and families rather than to a teacher or counselor. Findings indicated a causal link between students' use of these interventions and their subsequent acceptance and matriculation at selective colleges. Furthermore, freshman grades for these students were on par with their counterparts in a control group that attended less selective institutions with fewer resources, lower graduation rates, and students with lower academic qualifications. Strengthening relationships with parents and guardians is always a good thing, but it can be an especially important step in sharing accurate information or addressing myths.

4. HELP YOUR STUDENT DISCERN "FIT."

Undermatch is distinct from, but complementary with, "fit," which is defined as the alignment between a student's aspirations and a college's experiential dimensions, such as the racial and cultural climate, proximity to home, athletic pedigree, and co-curricular offerings. There are also mission-related dimensions of the college experience such as a college's historical legacy of service, its vocational orientation, or the offering of an immersive religious experience. Students should know that college life is multidimensional; discussing the potential experiences offered at different types of colleges can help students paint a more robust picture of their postsecondary possibilities.

Jonathan ended up dropping out of pre-calculus, but the subject reappeared upon his arrival at Land-Grant State University. He earned a B in business calculus during his first semester on campus and went on to earn a bachelor of science degree in economics. Jonathan's tale is not shared with the goal of artificially directing students to the most selective college possible or steering them away from community colleges. Rather, it is shared with the goal of helping educators confront their implicit biases to avoid imposing misguided expectations on Black boys. Moreover, educators should convey information to Black boys about the full breadth of postsecondary options this country has to offer. Last, educators are responsible for facilitating conversations with students that lead them to a purposeful postsecondary choice, ideally, one that is suited to their professional and life aspirations, while rooted in the needs and realities of their families and communities.

Sometimes White college counselors express concern that telling a Black student they possibly have unforeseen opportunities in the admissions process because of (rather than in spite of) their racial minority status or their economic circumstances could be undermining or objectifying. They don't want to suggest that affirmative action will make it easy to get into college because they know that is untrue. This is an important concern. When students get to college—and throughout the application process—they will likely face accusations that they got there only because of affirmative action, and counsellors don't want to water those seeds of doubt and self-doubt. In an attempt to maintain a colorblind, need-blind relationship, however, teachers and counsellors sometimes avoid delving into some of the very specifics that might help them best support the individual student in front of them.

Focus on having honest conversations that are not marginalizing. If you talk about affirmative action at all, know that there are many misconceptions about affirmative action in its current incarnation. Affirmative action has been banned in at least ten states, including Texas, California, and Michigan (three of the largest states with some of the best public postsecondary education systems in the country). Even in states where the policy is permitted in public settings, administrators feel extremely uneasy and downright oppositional about it.

Introduce resources and information about scholarships, but also contextualize the information within the larger picture of college funding. For example, lots of upper-middle class and affluent White students receive scholarships/admissions advantages (merit-aid, legacy, Scottish Rite, donations, etc.), which, in many cases, are provided as a lever to influence choice. In many cases these types of provisions are not facilitated out of financial need. Because the field of education, and educators specifically, do not talk about these types of support, many students of color, particularly those from low-income backgrounds, likely feel stigmatized if not uncomfortable about receiving scholarships/grants based on income or racial ethnic status (the latter of which are being continually eroding, in both number available and award amounts).

Black boys and their families can't operate out of a position of empowerment if they think they are the only ones receiving a "handout."

In the following vignette, Aaron Abram shares a story from his classroom about watching a White colleague undermine the potential of his students, describing his own efforts to teach them material that holds them to high expectations, even in the face of so much doubt.

Vignette: Nonviolence, Violence, Standing Up

Aaron Abram

Our teaching trio (main teacher and two paraprofessionals) was told that teaching our Special Education for Adolescent Needs (SPAN) students the concept of nonviolence was a waste of time because of their "lack" of comprehension due to the violence of their neighborhoods. The School program leader told us that we would be better off teaching them concrete educational concepts that were "within their reach" as students with Emotional & Behavioral Disorders (EBD). Perhaps she was right. But we interpreted her statements as indicative of a larger disconnect with the lived experiences and capacity of our students. She thought student input, action, and creativity were frivolous. She was a White woman who commuted from the suburbs, with very little experience in this community. Most of our students were Black boys. Because we knew them and we knew where they came from, we felt they would be able to handle it.

We introduced the concept of nonviolence by watching *The Making of the Mahatma*. After the movie, we talked to the students about the movie and what Mahatma Gandhi did to gain independence for his people. Some Black male students instantly said, "I would never let somebody put hands on me and not do anything back," "I would've come through with that 'thumper' (slang for pistol) and let them know," and similar expressions. When the kids began saying these things, the lead teacher in the program had a smug smile, the type that said, "I told you so," because she saw these comments as "unnecessary to the classroom environment/discussion." I noticed the looks of anger directed at this teacher, mainly because they believed she was laughing at them. Instead of seeking compliance and stopping the conversation, members of our group took a creative approach. I replied by saying, "Ok, I understand that this may be the way that some have told you is the best way to handle situations, but *how* would you act in a situation where you couldn't use a weapon? If you were outnumbered and faced with this problem?" I acknowledged their lived experiences, and immediately the conversation took off because they were able to apply their reality to the reality of the historical figures that we watched without judgment. But the students weren't done yet.

Another SPAN classroom had misbehaved, which meant that both classes lost recess for a week. None of the boys in my class were acting out, but for compliance reasons, they were still punished. We had the students line up at the front of the room for lunch. As the two other teachers in the room and I began to talk about how we were going to get the students to the lunch room and back, the students became quiet. Eerily quiet. When we turned to see why, all of the students were sitting down. When asked what they were doing they replied, "We are not going to lunch until you give us recess. We are on a hunger strike like Gandhi and his people."

The program leader stormed back into our room to see why we weren't in the lunch room and began immediately scolding the students for sitting. They began to chant, "Hunger Strike! Hunger Strike! Hunger Strike!" She demanded that we "control" our students and do our jobs; we smiled and let her know that these students were sitting *because* we did our job. We supported our students in exercising their creativity and learning, rather than complying with unjustified discipline and silenced voices. The program leader said, "Fine. You can have your recess, but only tomorrow," to the cheers of our students. As we walked them to the lunch room, they routinely asked each of us if we were proud of them. We let them know that we were. They stood for what was right. They did not get vulgar or violent to get their point across, simply because they understood that they had other options, a concept that previously we were all told they would never be able to conceive.

The number of interracial families is rapidly growing in the United States. Dr. Jennifer Chandler, the mother of a biracial son and author of a research project on working with mothers of multiracial children, addresses the forces that shape behavior in social groups through a model for understanding social norms and how people tend to collude and collide in their interactions. Through the story of "Gloria," Chandler shares how teachers tend to gravitate toward the White parent, the "comfortable" parent, when issues need to be addressed. But by dissecting and exploring social norms, teachers have an opportunity to look at, identify, and discuss the norms operating in their schools as they move forward toward breaking down the barriers school often presents for Black boys.

CHAPTER 34

The Collusion of Social Norms and Working With Interracial Families

Jennifer Chandler

The number of interracial families is increasing across the country (Pew Research Center, 2006; Root, 2001; U.S. Census Bureau, 2012). While every family is unique, White women teachers may have a common set of behaviors they use when interacting with such families. Focusing on how White women teachers interact with interracial families may help reveal larger patterns that deserve attention. This chapter starts with a story that briefly describes one interracial family's decision to move their Black son out of the public school he had attended for years to a very small private all-boys school near their home. Gloria is White, her husband is Black, and they have one biological son and one biological daughter. Gloria told her story as part of a recent study examining the experiences of White mothers across the United States whose sons and daughters are not White (Chandler, 2016).

GLORIA'S STORY

Gloria's son's path to the private all-boys school started many years ago when his first-grade teacher told Gloria to "go ahead and just sign him out because it is just going to frustrate him to take the test" when it was time to test all the first graders for the school district's advanced placement program. Gloria's son took the test and scored the highest in the class. Gloria explained that the "teacher couldn't believe it, and they retested him and he did it again." Gloria and her husband did not put their son in the program because it would mean switching schools, but the experience stuck with Gloria. It was Gloria's first glimpse of what she later referred to as the many ways in which her son "was not treated fairly and not getting a good education" at that school. Gloria and her husband's decision to move their son was not a response to a single incident; rather, it was their choice to escape the accumulation of little things that they had endured year after year.

Recalling other early experiences at her son's elementary school, Gloria remembered the principal who made students sit on the stage at lunch rather than sit at the lunch tables if their teacher reported them for breaking a rule in class. When her son was in fifth grade, Gloria recalled that when she went to the school at lunchtime, "it was all the Black kids sitting on the stage at lunch." Her son was one of those students. He had walked his younger sister to class, and he was in the hallway when he was not supposed to be. That was just one of the many times Gloria remembered her son receiving discipline at the school. Gloria kept the many detention slips that teachers gave her son, and she referred to the practices at the school as "criminalizing a normal behavior" such as drinking water on the bus and reading in the halls. Gloria met with the principal to discuss her concerns and the idea of switching her son to different school. The principal was not supportive and framed the situation as one in which her "son's problems were internal and would follow him wherever" he might go.

Before moving her son to the new school, Gloria described being "very worried that I was going to lose my son" if they had stayed at the old school. Gloria was shocked when she realized that her son's White female teachers were, in effect, expecting her to go along with their view of her Black son. The way that those teachers viewed her son was drastically different than her own view of her son.

Gloria's story is not unique. Recently, I interviewed thirty White mothers whose families are interracial; some of those with Black sons told similar stories (Chandler, 2016). Those mothers, too, described how their sons were not treated fairly and not thriving at their schools. In addition, the White women teachers repeatedly behaved as if they expected the White mothers to hold the same views toward Black boys that the teachers held. And the White women teachers seemed to be missing the opportunities they had to develop entirely new views of Black boys by viewing them through their White mothers' eyes. However, we also know that Gloria and the other White mothers of children of color have experienced things that White moms of only White sons or daughters have not experienced. Some of those White moms of children of color have come to see life through new eyes. They learned, experientially, to recognize that many of the social norms that typify nice White womanhood were not healthy for them nor for their sons and daughters. White women teachers can learn from those mothers.

WHAT ARE SOCIAL NORMS AND WHY DO THEY MATTER?

In this chapter, we are addressing the forces that shape behavior in social groups. Those forces exist in every organization; they are not unique to schools. What are those forces? I invite you to think about the fact that every organization or group has its own "feeling." That feeling is maintained through repeated similar behaviors among the members of the organization. Those repeated similar behaviors in organizations are the social norms of the organization. Everyone is influenced by social norms at the same time we are influencing those around us. Sometimes the social norms of an organization are in line with the written goals and mission of the organization, and sometimes they are not. The social norms of an organization can shift over time depending on many factors.

Many of the social norms we comply with are simply things we do because we have always done things that way. We often do not give our social norms much thought, but when we do, we have an opportunity to examine the larger forces operating. This chapter invites you to look at the social norms regarding race that are practiced by teachers and school staff. Teacher behavior regarding race in schools has been examined recently by a handful of researchers (Lensmire, 2012; Meeks, 2010; Pennington, Brock, & Ndura, 2012; Picower, 2009), but a consolidated list of social norms regarding race as practiced in schools has not been compiled. Analyzing the norms in their school will assist teachers in working with interracial families; the school's set of norms may not be helpful for all families. Analyzing the norms will also help you make changes in your own teaching practices and work collectively with other teachers to make your school a healthy place where Black boys thrive.

Think of Gloria's son, whose White female teacher recommended that Gloria keep her son from participating in the advanced placement test and argued that he would be "frustrated" by it. It might be tempting to think of her behavior as a singular isolated incident, but we know that it is not. It is a norm across the United States for White women teachers to treat their Black boy students this way (Case & Hemmings, 2005; Fasching-Varner, 2012; Gordon, 2005; Lensmire, 2012; Meeks, 2010; Mosley & Rogers, 2011; Pennington et al., 2012; Picower, 2009). In my research with White mothers, teachers' patterns of behaviors opened some of their eyes. For some of the mothers, their experiences had provided years of education about systemic racism, systems of oppression, and racial inequities. For example, Gloria began recognizing a pattern of behaviors (i.e., social norms) at the school that was not healthy for her son, and yet, the teachers practicing those behaviors thought they were helping Black boys like Gloria's son. Gloria knew that her son's teacher cared about her son, and yet that teacher did not have an understanding of how structural and systemic racism functions and impacts Black students in the U. S. public school system so her "care" was trapped in social norms that warped it.

How might teachers be enacting equally harmful norms in your school? Some common norms regarding race enacted by teachers include the following:

- Follow a colorblind approach by actively avoiding the topic of race.

- When planning lessons and making curricular choices, do not consider structural and systemic racism.

- Use a White student as your benchmark. Compare your students of color to this benchmark image and decide they are deficient.

- Pretend the experiences of White people universally apply to all people. Assign your own meanings to the actions of families of color, concluding that they do not care about education.

- Believe that people should stick together based on their race, and therefore that it is more work for a White woman to teach a student of color. In this case, **any** effort invested would be considered going above and beyond and there is no need to educate yourself about structural and systemic racism to be a good White woman teacher.

A MODEL FOR UNDERSTANDING NORMS

How norms function and the common ways in which people interact with them is depicted in the model below. This model refers to all norms. The specific norm that people are interacting with does not matter in this model. The model merely explains how norms function in social groups. There are two interacting sequences in this model. The clockwise movement through the left side of the model perpetuates the dominant norms within a group. The counterclockwise movement on the right contains the counterstories to those dominant norms that press for change to the dominant norms. Starting with the process on the top left people are indoctrinated by existing members of a group when they are newcomers. This process happens with all sorts of groups of people, for example, newborns, incoming students at schools, and new employees. The dominant norms of the group are explained to the newcomers, and the newcomers are expected to learn and conform to those norms. Those explanations rarely use the word *norm*. People often use expressions like "the way we do things" or "what is valued here is." Sometimes, newcomers intentionally do things counter to the dominant social norms of the organization they join because they are trying to bring in new ideas. Long-standing members in the organization treat those new ideas like mistakes and give helpful advice about how to fix the mistakes; they are sanctioning the newcomers for not conforming to the norm. Those sanctions function to keep the newcomers in line with the dominant norms.

FIGURE 34.1   Three Common Ways of Interacting With Social Norms

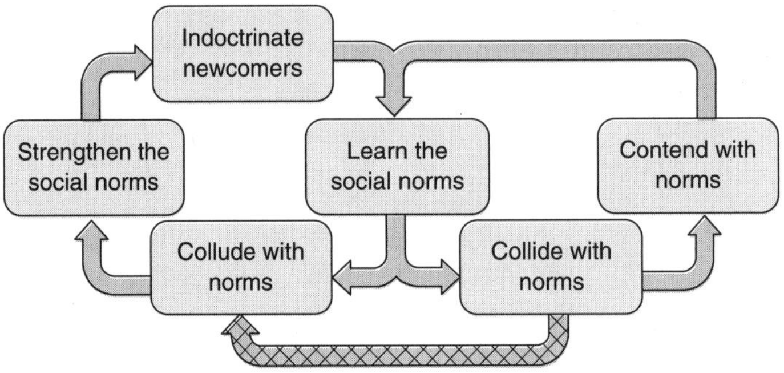

SOURCE: © Jennifer L. S. Chandler, 2016.

Conforming to the norm is what people are doing in the box that is labeled "Collude with norms" in the model. Colluding with a social norm also includes taking a neutral position regarding the norm. Doing nothing either to comply with or to change the norm is a type of collusion. People benefit from colluding with dominant social norms. Sometimes, the only benefit for colluding with a norm is avoiding the sanctions that people impose on people for not colluding. Collusion with norms reinforces them. Thus, they remain the dominant norms. The arrow pointing to the next box on the left, labeled "Strengthen the social norms" in the model, represents this process of reinforcement. Reinforcing the dominant norms then leads to indoctrinating even more newcomers to those norms.

It is important to keep in mind that the idea of collusion we are using here is neither good nor bad. There is no inherent moral value tied to the act of colluding. Even though the word *collusion* may have a negative connotation, in this usage, collusion simply means conforming to the norms. The social norm one is colluding with could be deemed morally good or morally bad, but the model does not judge that. The model simply provides a way for understanding how powerfully norms function in groups and organizations.

Consider when you first joined your school. You acclimated yourself through your observations of teachers modeling social norms. If you saw a White woman teacher directing her attention to the White parent while interacting with an interracial couple whose child is a student at the school, you may not have thought much about it. You simply absorbed it as a norm.

Collusion is the most common way people interact with the dominant norms, but it is not the only way. Sometimes, people actively refuse to collude with the norm, and that is represented in the model by the "Collide with norms" box. Colliding means not going along with behavior that is expected because one does not believe the norm is helpful or healthy. The colliding process moves away from the cycle that keeps that norm in place. Collisions are often filled with emotion: anger, shock, and disbelief are common. Often people become aware of a norm only when they collide with it. Until then, they were perhaps not aware that the norm existed or that they were expected to conform to it.

Consider that the strong emotions you see expressed by the parents of Black boys could be part of their collisions with social norms that are harming their sons. You can use that understanding and shift your perspective in order to see social norms to which you have been oblivious.

Keep in mind that the processes of collusion and collision are going on simultaneously for every norm. Collusion is happening all the time. Collisions are occurring, too, just maybe not as often as collusions. People can collude with one norm sometimes and collide other times. Thousands of norms operate in all social situations. People can collide with a norm and then return to collusion after the initial sting of their collision subsides. That path is depicted as the shaded arrow in the model. Some people, after repeated collisions or after a particularly damaging collision, seek new information to understand their experiences. Gloria did that. After she collided over and over, she began recognizing that dominant norms were operating, and she sought out new information to help her understand what she was experiencing. Some people use their newfound information to begin forming ways to contend with the norms. Contending is a process of engaging with the other side of the model in ways that offer alternative meanings, perspectives, stories, experiences, and realities to disrupt the perpetuation of the dominant norms by pressuring those norms to change. The box labeled "Contend with norms" completes the counterclockwise loop on the right in the model.

White women teachers are encouraged to use this model to help identify and discuss the norms operating in their schools. You can also use the model to determine the ways in which you are participating with those norms.

TABLE 34.1 Suggested Exercise Steps

ACTIVITY	TYPE OF ACTIVITY	TIMEFRAME
1. Read this chapter and document your questions.	Solitary	Week 1
2. Discuss your questions and the model to develop a shared understanding.	Facilitated collective	Week 3
3. Speculate on the norms regarding race operating among teachers in your school.	Solitary	Week 5
4. Discuss those norms to form a common understanding of them. Are they dominant norms? In what ways are teachers participating with them? In what situations are some teachers colluding, colliding, or contending?	Facilitated collective	Week 7
5. Identify norms for replacement and formulate replacement norms.	Facilitated collective	Week 9
6. Implement the replacement norms.	Working with the leadership of the level selected	Ongoing

CONCLUSION

The steps offered in this chapter can be used at any level. They can be used districtwide, schoolwide, within a department, or within a grade; the model can be used by a handful of teachers or a single teacher. The steps are the same. Your personal investment in uncovering the norms that operate in your school will be one of the ways in which you deepen your practice discussing race. Working with your colleagues to identify the norms operating in your school will also allow you to discover the ones you are unconsciously colluding with. Many of the mothers I interviewed went through similar discovery processes. I, too, have discovered, and I continue to uncover, norms that I am colluding with. It is hard and necessary work. That hard work will illuminate possible replacement norms that are healthy for you and your students.

When we think about the success of Black boy students in schools, it requires not only a knowledge of biases and an understanding of each child's experiences of race and gender. It also requires that we know his learning style and preferences and how teaching either facilitates or hinders his learning. How can we modify a classroom to systematically address the individual needs of each student? The following chapter by Brian Johnson offers teachers a practical strategy for organizing their classrooms and their interventions with students in order to design a program that works for that individual student.

CHAPTER 35

What Are We Doing to Support "These" Students to Meet Their Potential?

Strategies for Creating Equitable Classrooms

Brian Johnson

Meet Quincy: Above-average academic skill set, unmotivated, rarely participates, seems socially unsatisfied in school.

Meet Bryce: Average academic skill set, needs one-to-one attention, lacks confidence, afraid to push himself.

Meet Gerald: Average to below-average academic skill set, needs academic support with reading, math is on grade level, recently enrolled at your school, finding it difficult to make friends.

Meet Darryl: Average to below-average academic skill set, struggling with exploring his sexuality, is the victim of ridicule and bullying, easily distracted, parents are having a rough time with his exploration.

Do these student profiles sound familiar?

Unfortunately, the profiles of these students are far from uncommon in today's schools whether they be public, parochial, charter, or private. And this profile is also very much a part of our nation's achievement gap (some call this the "opportunity gap") problem. Schools routinely excuse the underachievement of Black males without questioning whether they are reaching their potential.

As I enter Year 26 of my career as a Black male educator, I've served in all types of schools: I taught for twenty years in a very racially diverse suburban public school, served a year as an administrator in an inner-city charter school, and spent five years as a private school administrator. I approach my job from different perspectives, but I have consistently focused on the achievement gap—sometimes successfully, sometimes not. In this chapter, I will share a program I created to address the gap, called *Equitable Classrooms*.

Equitable Classrooms is a structure that every classroom teacher can use to focus on individual students who are not meeting their potential. It does not have to focus exclusively on Black males—in fact, it's better if Black males are not isolated in the program because that isolation can be academically marginalizing, as if they are the only students who need academic support. This program can aid you in designing an intentional strategy for looking at each of your Black male students as an individual and supporting him to live up to his potential. The steps below can enable you to create an Equitable Classroom program through a systemic approach, whether for a single teacher, team of teachers, or as a school.

THE EQUITABLE CLASSROOMS PROGRAM REQUIRES THE FOLLOWING TEN STEPS:

1. Identify criteria you will use for inclusion in the program.

2. Identify students whom you want to include. Focus on students who are not meeting their potential.

3. Involve parents.

4. Survey the identified students, their parents, and their teachers about their experiences of school, homework, effort, behavior, and achievement.

5. Review the data.

6. Receive the feedback.

7. Create strategies and interventions to address student challenges.

8. Meet weekly with students.

9. Assess your interventions and strategies.

10. Rotate students out of Equitable Classrooms if they are meeting the goals.

1. Identify criteria you will use for inclusion in the program.

Ideally, inclusion in the program will align with the values of your school. Some schools will develop criteria that are based on grades and homework submission, while others will emphasize a more holistic set of criteria. In my school, we tried to focus on students in the middle of the achievement range, who typically do not receive Individualized Education Plan (IEP) resources or giftedness resources. To systematize decisions, baseline criteria might involve: Average to above-average skill set, comparatively low achievement in two or more subjects, social-emotional challenges, and needing one-on-one attention. But I reiterate, you should set your criteria based on your goals for students.

2. Identify students who you want to include. Focus on students who are likely not meeting their potential.

Select students based on the chosen criteria. Something I found helpful was to select students in the beginning who are likely to respond positively to the program because you want to sell the idea. You also want to feel good about what you're doing. As you get better at it, work your way toward students who present more of a challenge. If the students who begin the program have early success, then other teachers and students will see the program as something useful and doable.

3. Involve parents.

Parents need to be notified that their child was selected to be in the program, especially because their involvement will be critical to its success. They may panic that their child is being classified as needing extra help; you should reassure them that the project is simply a way to learn more about the student's perspective so that you can better meet his or her needs. You may even say that your school recognizes it is not meeting the needs of Black students, and that you are trying to get better by getting feedback from Black students and families. While such an admission might be intimidating to make, you would be surprised how much it can help you build trust. Parents are going to want to know why their child was selected as well as the purpose of any surveys. Carefully worded messaging will get most parents on your side from the beginning, thus making your work easier. For those parents who are hesitant, try to get them to understand the program's goal of helping students to be their best selves by getting to know them better and truly understanding what is challenging for them. Also, keep parents informed throughout the program of any strategies or interventions being implemented. Indeed, sharing information allows parents to reinforce your classroom goals at home.

4. Survey the identified students, their parents, and their teachers about their experiences of school, homework, effort, behavior, and achievement.

It's important to acknowledge that the causes of achievement gaps are not limited to the social and emotional experience of Black boys. In addition to income, opportunity, culture, and bias gaps, academic deficits also play a significant role. Throughout my teaching career, the data clearly revealed such deficits, which then had to be understood and addressed. Using data to pinpoint academic deficits is relatively easy, and most schools have plenty of metrics readily available.

To make your use of data more holistic, teachers will need to design survey tools that will measure overall and individual student experience, such as: the quality and depth of teacher-adviser/student relationships; individual effort and attitude toward school; individual classroom experience; and individual treatment by teachers and advisers. These data can reveal issues/problems that teachers and advisers had little to no idea existed and allow them to devise interventions.

The first set of surveys for identified students will provide teachers with a benchmark as to where individual students are social-emotionally and academically. Later surveys should be customized based on previous findings. This practice will allow you to uncover and explore issues specifically related to the child, thus affording you the opportunity to differentiate strategies and interventions. (Note surveys should occur every four to six weeks.)

Surveys can be intimidating for students. Some fear that they can't be completely honest. To mitigate this, you might have another teacher/administrator give the survey. You can also administer it yourself while emphasizing how being honest will assist you in supporting the student. Indeed, surveys are your key to unlocking the information you need to bring about positive change!

5. Review the data.

Learn how to effectively analyze the qualitative and quantitative data you collect. Organize it so it is easy to work with. I recommend using Google Forms, which will direct all your data to Google spreadsheets so that you can see it all at one time. Take notes on it. Be sure to share it with others to gain their insights. Use existing data protocols for guidance. For instance, I recommend *What Do You See in These Data* by Professor Elizabeth City of the Harvard School of Education (youtube.com). I have also found the following protocol useful:

a) What parts of the data (answer) stand out?

b) What do the data tell us—and *not* tell us?

c) What good news is there to celebrate?

d) What problem(s) does the data suggest?

e) Is there enough information to make key conclusions/hypothesis?

f) Identify key conclusions/hypothesis

g) Make recommendations to address the problem(s)

h) Identify resources needed to address the problem(s)

6. Receive feedback.

Honest feedback from students and parents is essential for you to uncover challenges and to develop structures to address issues. Your ability to process and learn from the feedback is equally as important. Adopting a growth mindset will be to your advantage.

7. Create strategies and interventions to address student challenges.

With your data analyzed, begin to create action steps to address student challenges. The key is to think pragmatically: What will best serve this student? While the data will dictate your specific strategies, the following might be useful starting points:

- Consult with others who work or have contact with the student: counselors, teachers, coaches, and parents.

- Think boldly: You may be entering uncharted territory; you're going to make mistakes.

- Don't overthink it: Something as simple as extra tutoring may do the trick.

8. Meet weekly with students.

Strong relationships are essential to gaining your students' trust. It increases their desire to work with you and willingness to dive deeper into their challenges. The research is very clear that relationships count.

Brief weekly meetings (ten to fifteen minutes) allow you to further uncover and explore challenges and issues. It also affords you the chance to create, implement, review, and revise your strategies and goals. Of all the steps for creating Equitable Classrooms, this is probably the most important. It is also the one that some teachers find most challenging for their schedules. Yet what's the point of spending all the time it takes to survey, analyze data, and come up with strategies, if you don't check in with students? Teachers that got the most out of this program all mentioned that this was a crucial aspect.

Some questions and issues to explore during meetings:

a) Talk about nonschool-related topics; show them your interest in them goes beyond school.

b) Set goals.

c) Cocreate strategies/interventions.

d) Discuss recent successes and challenges regarding goals.

9. Assess your interventions and strategies.

Designate time to assess whether what you have created works. How you assess depends on the intervention or strategy. It is also good practice to check in with your students and perhaps their parents, as well as others who work with them, to gain their insight.

10. Rotate students out of equitable classrooms if they are meeting the goals.

Ideally, an educator wants to give students the structures and strategies needed to become independent. In addition, educators want to learn the best ways to instruct individual students. This is also true of Equitable Classrooms. It is meant to provide students with the knowledge and strategies to overcome the challenges that brought them into Equitable Classrooms. It is also meant to better equip teachers to instruct these students. Enrollment in Equitable Classrooms should be fluid. Any number of reasons may result in longer rates of participation for certain Equitable

Classrooms students. These reasons can range from the time it takes for the supports to succeed to the student's development issues.

Things to Consider in Creating Equitable Classrooms Across Grades or Schoolwide

Collect evidence to discover and describe your schools' achievement gap: Are significant numbers of students underperforming academically and/or social emotionally?

- Analyze standardized test scores, report cards, and discipline records to make your case to key players in your school.

- Identify your potential roadblocks to success and people who could hinder your efforts.

- Ensure you have strong backing and support from your administration for the program; have them sign on to the message that this is something important for our students.

- Identify teachers who are hungry and want something different to pilot Equitable Classrooms.

- If you have no backing from your team or administration, try implementing Equitable Classrooms in your own class.

In working to improve Equitable Classrooms over the last several years, I learned a very valuable lesson this current school year. It's important that we don't focus only on academic performance. We need to also hone in on the whole child: the social and emotional aspects of the child. In doing so, you can address important additional issues that impact student achievement, as described in other chapters of this book: for example, teacher cultural competency, stereotype threat, racial stress, and microaggressions. To focus solely on academic performance is not sustainable. Let's not forget that people in general work best for and with people with whom they have an actual relationship.

Equitable Classrooms Bringing About Equity

Maybe the above seems a bit daunting. I am not going to deny that Equitable Classrooms takes significant effort. It adds to your workload. But the payoff is real for teachers and students.

I've seen teachers use Equitable Classrooms to help identify cases of stereotype threat among students of color and mitigate its impact. I've seen an adviser become more emboldened to support a student of color in response to a teacher who was known for poor treatment of students of diverse heritages. I've seen team teachers become more confident in their ability to effectively support a boy exploring his gender identity. I've seen 60 percent of a cohort of Equitable Classrooms students increase their GPAs after one semester. I've had hesitant teachers ultimately argue the school should adopt Equitable Classrooms as part of its school program. And I've had teachers say that Equitable Classrooms helped them become better teachers and more accountable for the success of their students.

Perhaps Equitable Classrooms can eventually be seen as a tool that teachers can use to help bring about an equitable school experience for *all* students. If you are struggling, contact me.

Let's begin creating your own Equitable Classrooms. See the **How To Create Equitable Classrooms** section above for steps to create your own Equitable Classrooms. Start with one student and build from there.

A fundamental premise of this book is our belief—and our experiential knowledge—that most White teachers want to be effective, reliable teachers of their Black boy students. We also realize that this desire often begins as a byproduct of the "savior mentality" cultivated by media and movies in which White teachers literally "save" Black boys from poverty, their communities, their families, and their own self-destructive behaviors (see—or rather don't see—Dangerous Minds or Freedom Writers). We are asking readers to recognize that trope, that hurtful narrative that exists for White women, and to go beyond it, to build relationships with Black boys, their families, and communities from a position of solidarity, rather than dependency and powerlessness. This next vignette by Marvin Pierre describes the harmful impact of the White savior mentality on Black students.

Vignette: Dismantling the "White Savior Mentality"

Marvin Pierre

Historically, teaching young boys of color from urban communities has been no easy task. Across many U.S. cities, young boys of color continue to struggle to attain both academic and social success. As a former administrator of an all-boys school, I have often spent my time dispelling the myths that come with working with young boys of color within our school system. In my six years as administrator, my biggest challenge has been getting my White teachers to not see themselves as "saviors" but rather as a resource to help young men navigate their way through life. One of the first moments that this mindset became evident for me was during summer staff professional development. I would often start with framing the "why" behind our calling to do this work and somewhere in between those responses, a staff member would say that they were here to "save" boys of color from a world that wants them to fail. My response to this statement has always been that educators both White and Black are not asked to "save" the lives of young men of color. Our purpose in their lives is to be a resource that can help them successfully navigate the world that they live in, so that they can save themselves.

White teachers must rely less on the perceptions and pictures that society paints of young boys of color. Children who grow up in challenging communities overcome more obstacles on their way to school than the rest of us do in a lifetime. Students of color, especially boys, don't need a handout or someone to feel sorry for them, they need resources, and that is something all educators can provide. In my role as an administrator, I used my position of influence to educate my White teachers who didn't know how to be a resource to our young boys of color. In my coaching sessions, I stressed three critical things that all teachers, especially White teachers, needed to know when working with boys of color: (1) seek to understand, (2) build authentic relationships, and (3) set high and clear expectations. *Seeking to understand* the story of their students can provide teachers with the insight that helps them know exactly what students need; otherwise, they may make assumptions that all students of color have the same challenges, which only perpetuates the savior mentality. *Building authentic relationships* lets students and families know that the school genuinely cares and that teacher attempts to build relationships are not simply a formal protocol. Last, *set high and clear expectations*. Young boys of color like to be challenged and setting the bar high for them from the start sends the message that teachers believe in their abilities and are invested in their long-term success.

I firmly believe that our educational system must begin to shift the narrative around the White savior mentality that continues to be imbued in many of our White teachers. In doing so, it positions us to help all educators, regardless of race, to be successful in their roles.

So many of the issues that Black boys encounter in education are related to Black cultural styles (verve or Black language) or to their learning preferences as boys, or to teachers' misperceptions of their movements and intentions. In the following chapter, Erica Snowden, teacher and administrator, writes from her experience about how White teachers tend to misidentify and overidentify Black boys for ADHD classification.

CHAPTER 36

Interrupting School Structures

ADD/ADHD Overidentification and How Black Cultural Styles Are Often Confused for ADD

Erica Snowden

Each year teachers wait with excitement to meet their new students. In certain schools, a teacher may be privy to a meeting with the student's previous teacher to talk about the incoming students. The intention of these meetings is to pass on helpful tips about the students: academics, social-emotional characteristics, learning styles, and even family structures. However, they can easily become a purveyor of stereotypes about children in general but especially Black boys.

"So, tell me about Marshawn." "Well, he's such an adorable boy." They always start off with a physical observation, but often go south as the conversation turns to behavior and learning style. "Well . . . Marshawn is really excitable, extremely busy, and loud. He talks all the time. I have to give him redirection several times a day, and he interrupts his peers and the teacher. He just can't concentrate for long periods to complete his work or when he completes it, he can't sit still. I've tried everything." I have heard similar stories often from educators, and trying everything is always the most telling aspect of the story. They often end with Black boys being put on a list for evaluations and later being identified as having Attention Deficit Disorder (ADD) or Attention Deficit and Hyperactivity Disorder (ADHD). Teachers can find themselves moderately diagnosing students through their actions and accommodations before an actual evaluation and diagnosis. This might include decreased academic expectations, behavior charts, frequent check-ins, and close student monitoring.

Unfortunately, this leads to an overabundance of Black boys in special education classes, and although ADHD is not a learning disability, it is classified as a health impairment. Classic observations include hyperactivity, disorganization, and verbal outbursts among others. Where did you learn organization? If your home life is not an organized one, where can you learn to become organized? What is the importance of organization? Why is it optimal to wait for others to finish talking before interjecting? I enjoy visiting my family in Detroit, and our gatherings are not complete if several conversations are not happening simultaneously on high volume! The great part is that we seamlessly transition from each different conversation. I quickly learned that I had to be really loud in order to be heard at home in a family of seven. Where did you learn not to interrupt? It seems that teachers want all students to come in with the same base knowledge, and that doesn't happen for several reasons. Each year, my students create class guidelines, and I always help them to turn "no talking" into "one person speaks at a time." Then we talk about why that is purposeful, helpful, and important. We even practice and act out the opposite. Teachers must willingly and patiently teach these skills and others.

This includes answering the great question: Why? When I showed a student several times how to organize his desk and keep track of pencils, that student became more efficient in his work. I explained to him, if you have a pencil at the ready and immediately start your work, finishing early is probable, which gives you a choice about what do to do when you finish early. How many teachers have engaging activities ready for students who finish work quickly? Think about choice options and incentives available to students who finish work quickly. Are they ditto sheets, mindless games, or challenge activities and strategy games? Do they allow students to be social or further perpetuate quiet and independent work?

Many believe that a quiet class of children who sit around working independently indicates learning. While this can be true, it does not mean that children cannot learn in a classroom bursting with movement, conversation, and collaboration. Children learn and retain more from collaborating with their peers than listening to their teachers (Jacob, 1999). What do you do with that Black boy who can't stop talking? Try research. Find out his passions, what he knows and can teach to others. Coach him on ways to help students learn without giving them the answers, and then set him loose when he finishes his work, or maybe carve out time for him to be the teacher. This is no small notion, but it accomplishes a great deal, in that you simultaneously make a connection to that child by showing interest in him and build his confidence while helping him to harness leadership abilities. Have you ever noticed that students learn games, the rules to those games, and songs from their friends, not teachers? Why can't they learn skills from their classmates?

Therefore, teachers must work to create a counternarrative for teaching Black boys that does not include over diagnosis of ADD/ADHD. One study showed a 70 percent increase in ADHD identification for Black children between 2001 and 2010 (Getahund et al., 2013). These diagnoses start as young as five years old, and Black boys are a part of this epidemic. Think for a moment, how often do you as a teacher sit at your desk? During your last professional development, were you sitting? How long? How did that feel? Were you free to stand in the back of the room or doodle while you listened? As teachers, we move constantly and most always notice restlessness in professional development that confines us to chairs. This is the same thing that we see in Black boys. Flexible seating or standing with boundaries allows boys to work but also releases energy. Students can learn to doodle or complete small tasks while listening. Do you know a student who likes to drum on the table? Why is this considered a distraction and not musicality? Give that child space to express himself through music. Instead of ringing a bell for transitions, have that student drum during transitions. I consider myself a rhythmic and musical person; however, I didn't realize how intricate and complicated drumming was until I had a student who loved to drum. He tried to teach me, and I taught him patience because I was horrible. We have to change our mindset when working with Black boys.

But what happens if the student really has ADHD? This can be tricky, especially when teachers cannot diagnose students and even more so when working with sensitive families. I'm sure that most parents do not hope to have their child diagnosed with ADHD, and this is more of an issue for Black parents. "He's just a normal boy." "All boys are busy." These are comments that I have heard too often. While boys will be boys, symptoms of ADHD must be observed on a consistent basis with clear evidence through notes and regular communication. However, communication is key. When attempting to have these conversations, teachers must be gentle, empathetic, compassionate, prepared, and open to backlash. Preparation includes family-friendly information about ADHD as a learning difference and exhaustive notes that include observations of the child—both Glows and Grows. *Glows* are areas where the child excels and shines, while *Grows* are areas for growth. Teachers should also have evidence of interventions that they've already tried from their personal teacher toolkit. For me, these include behavior charts, personal signals, frequent breaks, flexible seating, constant praise, fidgets, and more.

These initial steps show parents that the teacher has paid close attention to their child, seen the *Light* in their child, and tried several options before coming to the final question of a possible ADHD diagnosis. In these cases, I have even invited parents in to observe their child in the classroom setting. While this seems scary, it can be eye-opening as parents see firsthand how their child behaves in relation to peers. Ask parents what behaviors they see at home. What is their home life like? Does everyone talk loud? Is the family musically inclined? Is the child one of many siblings? Does the student have a sacred, organized, and quiet space for doing homework? What is the student's diet like? Does the child play rough with a family member? Parents can't expect a child to vastly change how they behave at home when they attend school.

Along the same lines, while a child might try really hard to behave, it's not likely that all behaviors will cease to exist around parents. This could include constant moving when other children sit quietly on the rug, blurting out, fidgeting with objects, inattention, or extreme lethargy to name a few. In addition, having administrative support from your school is paramount. Counselors, learning specialists, or support staff should be included in the conversation with parents and serve as experts in student learning. They can validate and strengthen the teacher's observations. Communicating this type of news with learning specialists or support staff shows a team effort and unites the parties involved in a common goal of helping the child to excel.

It is key that verbiage and tone are positive. "I've tried everything, and he hasn't improved" sounds vastly different from: "I've tried several strategies from my teacher toolkit, some more successful than others, and I would be a better teacher if I knew specific strategies that would work for your son." Remind parents that they are not alone and that the end game may not result in a diagnosis. Also, what are the benefits of a diagnosis? A diagnosis takes the blame off the child and puts it on the difference. Often, children are being blamed for something they cannot control. "But isn't a diagnosis a label?" Some may see it that way, but students diagnosed with ADHD can become aware of how they learn best, advocate for those accommodations, and thrive in those circumstances. Share success stories with parents, along with more information and frugal options for testing because finances can create a barrier to testing. Most important, *do not* recommend medication as an option for managing ADHD! Parents already know about medicating children for learning differences, and it scares them. Consider that addictions plague the Black community, and parents are not eager to introduce them to their children. Let them conclude that medication is needed as a last resort.

Black boys are not problems. Behaviors often identified as learning disabilities are simply learning differences. Might they impede learning if not understood and addressed? Absolutely. However, teachers must realize that a diagnosis and a pill are not the answers to everything, especially for Black boys. When a doctor tells you that you have hypertension and may need medication, they might also tell you to try other options first, such as a change in diet, exercise, or meditation. Let's help change the narrative on teaching Black boys. Incorporate flexible seating arrangements and movement in the classroom. Be intentional and teach organization and the reason for it. Help students see themselves in your classroom. This means finding texts that show Black boys as more than enslaved Africans or sports stars. Learn about students' interests and look for ways to honor their gifts and talents, even if they are new to you. Add brain breaks or dance breaks to class routines. This may seem daunting initially. However, when teachers put forth the effort to create a better educational environment for Black boys to succeed, other students will benefit as well.

■ ■ Engaging the Mind ★ Taking Action ★ Inspiring Excellence
Take a Challenge

This is a useful exercise for teachers. Think about your students of color. How many need academic or behavioral support? How does this compare to the overall population of students of color? Take a challenge. During one day, make a tally chart and document each time you redirect a student, then look at the end of the day to see which students receive the most tally marks. Are these the only students exhibiting these behaviors? Do you find yourself watching specific children proactively?

All too often, Black boys are expected to be good in sports, and if they perchance are, it is assumed that this will be their way to a successful future, whether by playing in the major leagues or by using their athletic ability to gain a college degree through a sports scholarship. Most people find it easier to name Black football players, basketball players, or rappers rather than Black scholars, politicians, and inventors. Drs. Eddie Moore Jr. and Frederick Gooding Jr. point out the archetypes that occur in sports for Black boys and call for educators to believe in not only the athletic abilities of their students but also their excellence in cognitive endeavors.

CHAPTER 37

Football, Sports, and Moore

Using School Structures to Get More out of Black Boys

Eddie Moore Jr. and Frederick Gooding Jr.

↾⇀

I was a high school two-sport athlete and college three-sport athlete. I made my reputation and built relationships with my teachers and coaches based on my athletic ability and performances. I went to college because of my interest in athletics and a coach who inspired me and guided me into a college opportunity. I often have to ask, "Where would I be now if not for my athletic ability?" But I also have to ask, "Might I be even further ahead if in addition to football, basketball, and baseball, I had done debate, theater, or music?" The skills I would have learned there—writing, researching, organizing, forming and supporting arguments, and speaking in front of people—were skills I needed but did not have that first year in college. Being involved in a theatrical performance might have introduced me to Shakespeare, Chaucer, or August Wilson, which would have enhanced my knowledge of literature. I love music, and I now have to ask if band might not have forced my brain to work in ways it didn't really like. So much research says music enhances your brain power, and I have to ask, "Was some of my brain left to ferment because I was only tracked into sports?"

Why didn't someone coach me into doing Moore? Streamlining Black boys into athletics has multiple strengths, but streamlining them *only* into athletics has multiple weaknesses. They become pigeon-holed into one archetype, and opportunities begin to close. How many Black boys go to high school and college expecting to "go pro"? And how many graduate and actually do? What has not been as closely examined is the effects of the different types of extracurricular activities. For many Black boys, athletics is seen as a means of escape, a means of social mobility and financial possibilities, and most important, a door to respect among peers. But it can also be "a treadmill to oblivion" (Sabo, Melnick, & Vanfossen, 1993, p. 53). Sports are great, but let's get our Black boys doing Moore. We can't let them fall into the trap, into the archetype that closes doors and limits their abilities. The more opportunities we create, the better the chances of success.

—Eddie Moore Jr.

This chapter aims to raise the consciousness of educators so that they do not underestimate the academic ability of Black boys even if they have athletic ability. When Barack Obama became president of the United States, he brought a whole different possibility to young Black men who thought that the only way they could get ahead in this life was by breaking into the major leagues especially in football, basketball, or baseball. Instead of telling young Black brothers they can get ahead by using their minds, they are encouraged to use their feet and their brawn. For every Frederick Douglass, W.E.B. Dubois, Benjamin Banneker, Elijah McCoy, and Miles Davis, most young Black men can name ten sports figures. To break this stereotype, we need teachers who look at their Black boys and see leaders in all fields, not just on sports fields. To address this idea, we present an analysis of archetypes that present themselves within the realm of sports as they impact not only White women but also the young Black boys who do not see themselves elsewhere in either the curriculum or in the eyes of their educators.

ARCHETYPE ANALYSIS

Many of us are familiar with stereotypes, which can be defined as often negative, broad mischaracterizations of a group of people. Stereotypes are usually quite damaging, particularly in racial contexts. They make it hard to see a person clearly. Even "positive" stereotypes such as being strong are actually negative because they obscure the reality and the complexity of the individual. Perhaps the individual in the stereotyped group is strong, but a stereotype would suggest that strong is all he is. Strength and athleticism are stereotypes of Black boys, and this stereotype has always been linked with a corollary stereotype: being unintelligent. The opposite is true, too. Many people suggest that being smart is a "positive" stereotype of Asian Americans, but it is almost accompanied by the flipside of the stereotype, which is being weak and unathletic. Seemingly "positive" stereotypes almost always have such a corollary. Stereotypes (either seemingly positive or negative) obscure the individual and are especially dangerous in school.

Archetypes are similar, but not the same. Archetypes are common character patterns that, according to Carl Jung (1959), exist in the collective unconscious of people in a society. Usually archetypes occur in literature, such as the evil villain, the wise old woman, the bully, the hero. Archetypical patterns appear benign on the surface but within the aggregate nonetheless contribute to themes of marginalization. According to Jung (1959) a key component of archetypes is that they evoke deep emotions. This may be part of the evocative power of the story of *The Blind Side* (2009), in which a wealthy White family adopts a poor Black teenage boy and facilitates a football career that ends on an NFL team, the Baltimore Ravens. Even though (or perhaps because) it so obviously plays on White savior/Black victim archetypical character patterns, the collective unconscious of society finds satisfaction in the fulfillment of those archetypes. Throughout this piece we use the concept of archetypes to examine common character patterns that exist in sports, waiting—like empty, prelabelled boxes—for Black boys to fill them. There is little doubt that the archetypes listed below in one way or another evoke deep emotions; they also often interfere with the academic achievement so many of our Black boys are capable of obtaining.

Along the fear axis, there are the three archetypes of the Diva, Intellectually Suspect, and the Menace to Society. The Diva is the Black boy who is good in his sport, but the problem is that he "knows" that he is good. This bravura or confidence—qualities we desperately yearn to nurture and develop in White boys and girls—is frowned upon when displayed by Black boys. The Diva offends White-dominated authority structures inasmuch as the Black boy will not "stay in his place." If the Black boy hints at not being humble over his extraordinary accomplishments, then he is chastised and castigated for not being humble and playing the right way. Popular examples include former NFL wideouts Terrell Owens or Chad "Ochocinco" Johnson. All too often, high school coaches improperly label Black players who engage authority as "divas" whereas White males are taught to engage authority at a young age.

The Intellectually Suspect is the Black male athlete who is presumed to be unaware of thinking as an asset and to be unable to appreciate the larger picture. Nowhere is this more manifest than with Black quarterbacks. The presumption is that African Americans are incapable of being quarterbacks because others (predominantly White coaches and owners) do not trust their intellectual capacities. Their brawn on the field is viewed as their best opportunity for success. This is where Black boys' aptitude is shunted because they become stuck in this Intellectually Suspect archetype, and then other identity options become closed off to them. Suddenly participating in school plays or playing in the band are not feasible options because he is only seen as a football prospect.

The next archetype on the fear axis is the Menace to Society where the Black male poses a threat to established White-centered norms and mores. Here the conduct of Black boys is readily and immediately interpreted as a disciplinary matter that must be controlled. Rarely do we see the same amount of effort expended to inquire and investigate "what's wrong" when Black boys exhibit signs of distress. In contrast, White students are treated as people with potential who may be rehabilitated and should not be callously castigated without care and compassion.

Along the fascination axis, the three archetypes are the Buck, Comic Relief, and Model Citizen. With the Buck, the Black athlete is regarded only for physical prowess, and his body is valued at the expense of intellectual or emotional capacities. This archetype is called Buck, harkening back to post-Reconstruction time and the stereotype of Black men, their physical attributes, and their prowess. This archetype is quite dangerous for it is so deceptively alluring. White students and coaches consistently fawn over Black bodies, obsessing about their height and weight and their ability to leverage their bodies for personal White entertainment. In some states, Friday night football is bigger than the latest movie release. Some high school basketball games are truly the hottest ticket in town. Students—White and Black alike—learn that Black bodies and the labor they produce can still be valuable commodities indeed.

The Comic Relief is the sports figure whom everyone loves to laugh at, and not necessarily with. This archetype provides a sense of merriment and distracts from some of the real tensions revolving around Black bodies (e.g., police brutality). Former NFL running back Marshawn Lynch eating Skittles candy before rushing out onto the field to seek another touchdown is such an example. Many delighted White fans gleefully chanted "Feed the Beast!" in merriment over such a display, and many White-dominated high schools devise similar memes or routines around the Black players they hold worthy of being beloved.

Last, the Model Citizen is the mythical Black athlete who is perfect in conduct and speech, never really hinting at or reminding Whites that he is cognizant of his role. This athlete is lauded for simply "playing the game" and for not creating any trouble. The issue with this archetype is that young Black boys are socialized early in life not to question or think critically and are constantly chasing an improbable behavior target, a target that requires an extensive understanding and embodiment of White cultural norms, styles, and language, as well as—in many cases—a denial of self to reach it. One of those cultural norms is colorblindness, the norm not to see or talk about race or racism. Conformity is essential to this archetype.

In sum, when the archetypes are added all together, at an early age and stage, Black boys quickly get the message that as opposed to appearing in the school play, they can perhaps ameliorate the effects and friction of White oppression by proving their worth and value through their body. The archetypes together, created out of White projections of power and control, slant the playing field and make it incredibly challenging for Black boys to explore a substantial existence outside of sports or even a healthy one within it. Limiting Black boys to these archetypes is extremely damaging insofar as Black boys themselves begin to internalize paternalistic messaging that suggests that they must perform the role of Buck or Comic Relief to gain social acceptance from both teachers and student colleagues, especially if they are deemed to be Intellectually Suspect and are not expected to contribute in any other meaningful way outside of their bodies.

Last, when considering what Moore we as a society can do, perhaps teachers can help by educating upcoming generations that there is more to our Black boys than merely figuring out how society can best profit off of or exploit their physical skills. For society to grow, we must similarly grow past the idea that Black bodies are still only skin deep. An untold number of Black intellectuals are never recognized for their excellence or exceptional possibilities. This is a problem, and there is a simple solution. See each child for who he is, what he wants to be, what education can help him strive to be and break the archetypes because no one deserves to be known as only an object of fear or fantasy.

ARCHETYPES

FIGURE 37.1

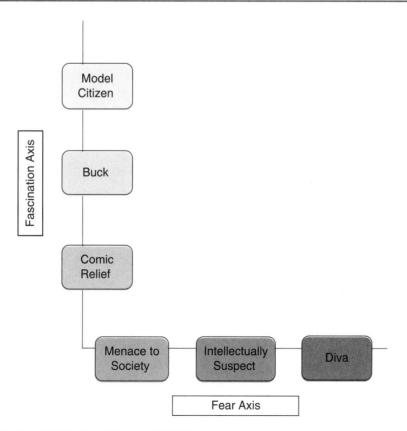

1. Name five Black male student athletes who excelled in athletics as well as the arts.

2. Name Black male athletes who broke the color barrier in football, baseball, basketball, hockey, and tennis.

3. Name five Black entrepreneurs who started as athletes.

PART 6

CONNECTING STUDENT SUCCESS TO SCHOOL STRUCTURES AND CLASSROOM STRATEGIES

As we continue to look at strategies to use in the classroom, we want to support teachers to build a bridge between what they believe and what they do. The following vignette, written by musician and teacher Russell Marsh, asks teachers who march and advocate for Black lives to demonstrate that Black lives matter in their curriculum. In the subsequent chapters, we offer other strategies to support teachers to demonstrate how Black lives matter in their curriculum.

Vignette: How Do Black Lives Matter in Your Curriculum?

Russell Marsh

One day, I was sitting in the cafeteria, and I overheard two teachers talking about attending a Black Lives Matter rally. I was slightly offended by the way they were talking about the rally. It felt as if they were talking about a play date. All I kept saying in my head was "my life is not a trending hashtag!" After hearing their conversation, I felt a disconnect between their actions in the streets and the content that they taught. In previous conversations, these men and I had spoken about how the school has failed black students in many aspects of the school. They both recognized the many privileges they have (white, male, cisgender, heterosexual, middle class and both over six feet tall), and they asked me to hold them accountable so they can be better allies.

I decided to take them up on their request for an accountability partner. I approached them separately and asked them the same question: How do black lives matter in your curriculum? I sat down with the history teacher first. We discussed a brief overview of his curriculum. I asked him if he realized that black people are victims throughout the history curriculum. "You only discuss black people during slavery and the 1960s Civil Rights Movement. How do black lives matter in your curriculum if we're only seen from a deficit model? What are your students taking away from this limited curriculum? What are your students experiencing when they study these units? Where is the balance of story in your curriculum? Where are all the positive contributions?"

Then I sat down with the math teacher, who was also the International Baccalaureate (IB) coordinator and asked him the same question: How do black lives matter in your curriculum? I spoke to him about my frustration teaching a curriculum where European classical music was seen as the highest form of music. Where are all the black people and other people of color? He responded that one question out of the five on the exam asks about "world music." I laughed. I asked him if he realized that most of the world is made up of people of color who are poor, non-Christian women who don't speak English. So how does the global majority get one question for an international music program? He then suggested that I can supplement some music. I reminded him that the exam would stay the same, and that's not fixing the problem. I told him we are paying to miseducate our students.

Before any of us became adults with careers, we were students. The messages in our curriculum leave lasting impressions. Some people don't believe black lives matter because they've never been taught about the many contributions of black lives. You don't have to dig deep to find the many contributions of black Americans. All you need to do is be willing to look. Black excellence has always been here, even under the most inhumane conditions. Again I ask teachers: How do black lives matter in your curriculum?

The following chapter offers an analysis of classroom conflict, as well as strategies for de-escalating conflict. We invited this chapter because we have witnessed the frequent and common escalation of conflict by White teachers with Black students, and we see this type of issue as a result of both unexamined bias and a lack of skills. Drs. Barbara Moore-Williams, Deitra Spence, and Christopher McGinley are veteran administrators and professional developers, who (collectively) have coached thousands of teachers through the work of skill building for teaching across difference. Their experience is evident in their chapter; every word feels relevant to the work of teachers.

CHAPTER 38

Strategies That De-escalate Conflict in the Classroom

Barbara Moore-Williams, Deitra Spence, and Christopher McGinley

Ms. James is a White, female, seventh-grade social studies teacher in a high-poverty, poorly resourced school in the inner city. Semaj, her student, enters the room with loud, harsh words for his friend, Kareem, and Ms. James quickly decides that something may be "brewing." Because she has carefully built a relationship with both boys, one built on mutual trust and understanding, she moves toward them with a calm voice and says,

> We know what to do when we are upset. Let's take a breath (moving with Semaj toward his seat), and when we have our "Temperature of the class" time, we can get help from our classmates to resolve this problem. This is the village, right? I trust you all to do the right thing. (classroom observation by Moore-Williams, 2015)

The story described above is an example of a White female teacher employing a strategy to prevent or de-escalate negative behaviors and attitudes in her classroom. As incidents occur with Black boys, White teachers must first ascertain the causes, including actions that precede the conflict in the classroom. To do this effectively, researching Black boys' needs, aspirations, experiences, and realities becomes critical. If White women teachers understand these aspects, they will choose the appropriate responses or interventions that match the situation and the student. Ms. James used strategies that preserved the dignity of the students. She restated expectations, moved with them rather than directing their movement, and told them that what they were concerned about could be discussed later. White female teachers must design classroom environments that allow self-expression yet promote positive behavior, preserving a modicum of respect and rapport.

DE-ESCALATION STRATEGY: BUILD ON RELATIONSHIPS

Societal vilification of Black males is in part the problem with battles in the classroom. Historically, from slavery until today, Black males in U.S. society have been viewed as dangerous and treated with suspicion until proven otherwise. This pervasive stereotype creeps into classrooms every day. Protecting the dignity of Black boys and building respectful relationships can result in a de-escalation or avoidance of conflict. Students' perceptions of White teachers and teachers' perceptions of Black boys color all interactions, but especially when conflicts arise. White female teachers need to be able to connect and establish authentic relationships with these students to change negative perceptions and implicit bias that students may have of them, often from lived experiences. Teachers have the responsibility to be overt in their "getting to know" activities with the males and actively demonstrate that they value who they are and what interests and motivates them to learn. Part of this process is being open about themselves and help students see them as people who have families, interests, struggles, and celebrations that are very much like their own.

Also important is divulging their own White identity and how that is similar and different than that of their students. Whether or not the attitudes, behaviors, and expectations of White teachers are of a caring nature will have a significant impact on the teacher-student relationship in times of conflict. Teachers who understand that the escalation of conflict can be deterred by relationship building:

1. Use surveys, forums, home visits, and class discussions to learn the culture and personal stories of each student.

2. Use language and posture that is friendly yet demonstrates high expectations.

3. Use proximity in the classroom to demonstrate connectedness.

Successful White female teachers emphasize the importance of a caring classroom facilitator and often demonstrate a maternal presence in schools that is particularly helpful with Black boys. The maternal presence concept is offered by Lisa Delpit (2012), who describes effective teachers of Black students as being "warm demanders" (p. 72), holding students responsible, setting high expectations, and supporting students in mastering new skills. One White teacher who participated in a case study involving middle-school Black boys said that she "spent the first couple of days [of class] getting to know each other, like team building and finding out what people like—music, games, sports, TV, whatever." (Spence, 2002, p. 117). The Black boys in this case study described their experiences with teachers who are mindful of this important role: "Try to get to know us and not just in class. Be there for us when we have problems with other teachers. She goes above and beyond to help" (p. 139).

Relationship building will reduce the need for de-escalation strategies. Knowing each student intimately—their fears, hopes, dreams, which "buttons" to push or not, what turns them off, and what turns them on—is extremely useful in classroom management. Disruptions in classrooms will be minimized because teachers know which experiences, cultural mores, and strategies to remind students to use before, during, and after the incidents. Teaching and reinforcing the social skills required in school, which may not be the same as those Black boys use with their peers outside of school, must be an important part of the curriculum, especially in the beginning of the school year. Social skill development—that is, arguing without being disrespectful, sharing ideas, materials, and space—will greatly reduce the need for intervention in disruptive situations. These skills take time to master and need modeling, reinforcement, and feedback. When teachers create an atmosphere of community in the classroom, disruptions are minimal and often handled skillfully by the students themselves.

DE-ESCALATION STRATEGY: ENGAGE STUDENTS IN MEANINGFUL/RELEVANT WORK

As we consider another proactive approach to the de-escalation of conflict and stress in the classroom, we must understand that Black boys live in a world where they enjoy rich conversations and debate with family and friends daily. They thrive on honing their discourse skills and can be encouraged to use them appropriately in academic and social situations. The males want to be in classrooms where exciting things are happening and they can engage in friendly competition with each other in activities that excite them. Murrell (1999) states: "An important principle for responsive teaching for African American males is that the instructional practices designed to bring about conceptual understanding must be in the organization of **activity settings** in the classroom, not merely classroom discourse" (p. 95).

When students are not fully engaged in creating new ideas and collaboratively solving problems, the teacher may unknowingly create situations where students have many opportunities to interact with each other in nonproductive, competitive situations that lead to conflicts. Black boys can and do learn to work with others with whom they may not have positive relationships, when the activities pique their interest and stretch their imaginations. Teachers who design meaningful group work and speak about the tasks and the students with expectations for success have less need to de-escalate incidents because students are fully engaged. Students know the difference between teachers who see the work and the classroom as "ours" and those who see the work as merely assignments for the students. Terms like "our work", "our classroom" and "the work we need to do" encourage a community feel to the classroom that is paramount to mitigating situations of conflict.

The structure in classrooms for Black boys need to mirror the best of African American community ideals and practices. Individual competition should be downplayed, as it often leads to arguments and negative situations. Effective teachers of Black males encourage them to connect personally as they read, talk, and write about things so that their real-life experiences are legitimized as part of the "official curriculum". Activities that encourage expressive individualism and orality are in tandem with the interactive communication style of African Americans, often referred to as "call-response." Requiring students to speak aloud as they learn gives them opportunities to use their knowledge and voice in a positive manner. One teacher shared the following strategy: "They love to talk aloud. If you want a child to process information, the best way is for them to explain it aloud. Not to themselves quietly, but aloud (Spence, 2002, p. 121).

De-escalation techniques are seldom needed when teachers engage students in the type of learning that goes beyond the typical recall of information, teaches students how to become critical thinkers, and encourages them to reflect on their learning with their peers. One student shared his description of an engaging strategy used in his classroom: "I think the best work I did in that class was a project on the French Revolution. I had to write about the different lifestyles in the three estates and I had to do a rap about it" (Spence, 2002, p. 116).

Interesting activities that require personal engagement leave less time to be "off task." Using their communicative skills (i.e., rap, spoken word) enhances students' social capital, leading to better relationships throughout the classroom.

Teachers must have a repertoire of effective instructional strategies, strive to know and understand the culture of their students, and work to build a classroom culture that embraces and engages rather than controls the learners. A proactive approach to creating this type of environment includes

1. Build relationships with students at the very beginning of the school year and nurture those relationships every day.

2. Use active and engaging communication strategies that allow teachers to hear the students' complete thoughts about the conflict.

3. Be proactive in teaching strategies to include many opportunities for students to work together in meaningful and relevant assignments where their natural penchant for community and solving problems together is an integral part of the day.

In conclusion, excellent communication skills are the key to building cross-cultural relationships and defusing hostile situations. Strategies to de-escalate situations with Black males require serious self-reflection about and knowledge of the Black male culture as well as honing effective culturally responsive teaching skills. This is not something teachers are generally taught in most preservice programs. Of utmost importance is remembering that preserving the dignity of young Black males in a time where they are too often vilified and seen in less than a positive light is a requirement in all situations.

■ ■ Engaging the Mind ★ Taking Action ★ Inspiring Excellence
Phone Call Home

Connecting with Black males and their families on a personal level is imperative for teachers in building positive relationships. A positive phone call, often paired with home visits, builds collateral in the relationship bank. The purpose of this call should be to find out what the caretakers' hopes and dreams are for their children and to learn their story as you share yours. It is not just an interview, it's an exchange. Families will often open up when asked, "Is there any other information that would be useful for me to know as I try to be the best teacher for your child?" The bottom line to empowering families is listening with our ears, instead of our mouths. Initiate a call to the family using the following prompts:

I am delighted to have (name) join our classroom community. I am really looking forward to working with your family to support (name's) learning experiences.

I want to give you two positive things I have learned about your child.

Can you give me two ideas that will help me be a better teacher for your child?

Thank you for taking the time to have this conversation with me so that I can get to know (name) and your family better.

Take notes and use them in future conversations as you design instruction and assignments. Relationships are the key!

Teachers sometimes find it helpful to have something laid out when they go to write lessons: a gentle reminder of a book to add, a push toward thinking a little deeper into the lesson than what is laid out in the pre-formatted curriculum. Teachers' days are so filled with the demands of "do this, test this" that often doing what they know is right takes a back seat to doing what is required. The following chapter by Drs. Marguerite W. Penick-Parks, Suzanne Fondrie, and Omobolade Delano-Oriaran provides a framework educators can use to remind them how to push all their students to a higher level of critical thinking and collaborative experiences. Based on extraordinary ten-year ethnography of Shirley Brice Heath, this chapter explores ways teachers can understand and incorporate the strengths their students bring to school as opposed to the strengths they expect the students to have when they arrive.

CHAPTER 39

Meeting Students Where They Are

Project-Based Learning and Critical Thinking Skills

Marguerite W. Penick-Parks, Suzanne Fondrie, and Omobolade Delano-Oriarian

> *"They can't sit still, they don't raise their hands, they shout out answers and have no idea what phonics are. I can't work with my other students, because the Black boys take up so much of my time trying to keep them quiet. Don't their parents teach them anything?"*

—White teacher from the Midwest

Heard around U.S. classrooms are teachers bemoaning the notion that not all students enter their classroom ready to "do school." The blame often falls on the parents, as opposed to an educational system where expectations are grounded in middle-class White cultural beliefs of what "knowledge" and "behavior" should look like. Some educators are unable to recognize that ways of knowing, literacy events, and how children are raised to communicate vary not only across cultures but also across families and that these variations are typically grounded in privilege, or lack thereof. If students enter school "lagging" in terms of literacy compared with White mainstream teachers' expectations, the gap is viewed as a deficit in the students, in their parents, and in their culture. What needs to be addressed instead of the presumed deficit in students is the disconnect between the pedagogy and the strengths students bring to school. Project-based learning is not new, it is not "inventive," it is not "doing a project"; it is not easy. Instead, it is simply a good pedagogical idea for reaching and teaching to the strengths of all students to increase their academic success and their social skills.

The reality is that 82 percent of teachers are White and 62 percent are White women (Toldson, 2012), and there is very little probability of change in the future. According to Ferguson (2000), teachers' negative perceptions of Black boys often begin as early as kindergarten. Black boys face a triple threat in schools: the opportunity gap, a lack of representation in gifted and advanced classes (Hallett & Venegas, 2011), and overrepresentation in special education and discipline (Kearns, Ford, & Linney, 2005; Togut, 2011). Yet schools continue to implement curricula and practices steeped in eurocentric, hegemonic ideology, practice, and content, which perpetuates the system of privilege while playing lip service to issues of diversity. Without an overhaul—not only of teachers' practice but of attitude, the educational system will continue to give priority to White students through mainstream curriculum and pedagogy. When students arrive at school they bring multiple strengths and have multiple needs, and schools need to foster all skills from the moment they walk through the school doors. One major way to do this is through the ideas of project-based learning, which is grounded in validating the strengths students bring into the classroom and engaging and empowering them to meet and exceed the learning outcomes.

There is strength in multiple "ways of knowing"

Literacy events and "ways of knowing" (Heath, 1983) take on a new meaning when one realizes that current literacy expectations, in reading and writing specifically, are middle-class White expectations. Heath (1983) describes multiple forms of literacy events—ways of knowing—that privilege some and exclude others. The author's analysis of literacy events, ways of talking, ways of knowing, culture, and academic success highlights how schools privilege certain literacy skills and undervalue others. If overall academic success is dependent on academic success within the first three years of school, not only understanding how to teach but also recognizing and valuing the strengths and cultural literacy skills students bring to their first day of preschool is essential for all students to enter a system where they can be successful.

Ways with Words (Heath, 1983) is based on three communities in North Carolina. Maintown students come from homes where they are surrounded by literacy in multiple ways and at all times of day. They enter school knowing how to answer "what" and "why" questions, to sit still and listen, to be creative and participate when asked, and to both construct and deconstruct the knowledge in books. In terms of comparing their skills to Bloom's Taxonomy of Learning, Maintown students (middle class white) arrive in kindergarten with the skills they need to participate at all levels. Roadville students (working class white) come from homes where reading is an event that happens only at bedtime and then not as a participatory activity but as a passive listening event. Roadville students know how to sit quietly and answer "what" questions, and they can deconstruct knowledge from text, but they have rarely been taught how to engage in creative and participatory activities. Because of this background, they tend to be successful at the lower level of Bloom's taxonomy, which requires them to reiterate knowledge as opposed to use it. Trackton students (working class Black) arrive steeped in verbal literacy skills from a community that embraces their ability to out-talk and out-debate one another. Literacy events in Trackton are predominantly oral: storytelling, playing the dozens (engaging in good-natured insults), singing. They can construct knowledge from text, but they cannot decontextualize the information. They tend to arrive thinking and interacting at the upper level of Bloom's taxonomy: thinking outside the box, being creative and engaging, demonstrating skills with "why" questions. However, they are not well prepared for the "what" questions. Moreover, they may not have been taught to adhere to school norms of sitting, waiting, and taking individual turns because their literacy events are interactive. This ethnography describes the racial and class dynamics of one particular geographic region, and could not be generalized to all people of similar racial and class backgrounds across the U.S. The behaviors found in White middle-class Maintown children for example, are not uncommon for Black students in many neighborhoods, while the patterns of behavior in Black working class Trackton students may arise in many different populations, including White populations, in different areas of the country. Even multiple children in one family may actually fall into different groups. However, teachers may recognize patterns in these descriptions that help them better understand students whom they may have previously seen with a deficit lens, and sometimes the patterns might overlap with the racialized and classed patterns exposed in Heath's work.

The conclusion Heath (1983) draws is that the students who are eventually successful in schools are those who arrive already knowing how to do school: the Maintown students. Roadville students do well until about third grade when they become B and C students because they are required to use upper-level critical thinking skills, something they have never been taught to do. And the Trackton students—the Black students in her ethnography—have been labeled unteachable early on. They can't sit still, they won't listen, they blurt out and are argumentative, all before the upper-level and creative critical thinking skills they arrive well versed in are expected, or accepted, by the teachers. Subsequently, they are labeled ED, BD, ADHD; angry, difficult, or loud; and are disciplined and even suspended for interrupting and not remaining quiet, despite the critical and engaging ideas they bring to the lessons. Often, they can't keep up with the formalized curriculum or end up tuning out, all because school is not ready for them, not because they aren't ready for school.

What Heath (1983) reveals is that the literacy skills students often bring to kindergarten are not always congruent with the literacy skills expected by European practices reinforced by White teachers and espoused in the teaching pedagogy. Essential information often left out of teacher education programs is how to be knowledgeable about specific ways of implementing lessons from the very beginning that honor and accentuate multiple literacy skills. Heath (1983) notes that if these changes are not made in Grades K–3, students are essentially lost to the system before they have a chance to enter it.

Instead of blaming the students for this mismatch, this chapter argues the answer lies not in the student but in the pedagogy. Students steeped in critical thinking skills need a curriculum that challenges those skills instead of squelching them. If students become active and engaged participants in their learning, then the academic skills will be seen as essential and relevant. To address many of these issues, educators are turning to the ideas of project-based learning as a means of reaching and teaching all students, even at the kindergarten level, to address and connect with their strengths and to keep them in school.

PROJECT-BASED LEARNING

Project-based learning historically has emerged in a variety of forms, and many of the successful project-based programs can be traced to the educational philosophies of John Dewey. Through the years, additional research has emerged supporting a variety of the important aspects that build on and expand this philosophy. The recent research of Linda Darling-Hammond and John Bransford (2005) supports a framework for thinking about education that is learner centered, knowledge centered, and assessment centered. Educator and author Deborah Meier (2002) says students who are exposed to a framework founded in project-based learning will leave with the knowledge that nothing is more difficult or requires more training than learning to make critical judgements in life.

There is a distinct difference between project-based learning and "doing projects," one that is often misunderstood. When students "do projects," the parameters are set by the teacher and traditionally follow the make and mold of everyone doing the same thing using the same strengths. Examples of doing projects are research assignments outlining specific material, for example, place, leaders, food, and clothes. Then all students put their results into a paper or a PowerPoint or a poster with specific guidelines from the teacher. Project–based learning is a student-centered model that allows students to individually and collaboratively learn through inquiry-based, interest-based projects that add depth and meaning to learning. Project-based learning is grounded in the idea that all students have strengths and weaknesses that need to be nurtured through a variety of learning opportunities. Traditional classrooms tend to highlight the strengths of inductive, analytical learners who benefit from teacher-centered methods. Students who are drawn to the deductive atmosphere of interdisciplinary, whole to part, interactive group learning are often stifled by traditional methods. Project-based learning, when used correctly as a basis for the classroom, blends together the best of both philosophies, allowing for greater success of all students by enhancing their learning opportunities through engagement, creativity, enhanced speaking skills, and personal engagement in learning.

An essential component of project-based learning is the idea of voice and choice. Students are allowed to choose a topic (choice), research or study it, and present their findings in the method of their choice whether it be through art, music, writing, or any other format that highlights the learning they did as a means of reaching the learning outcome of the project (voice). Students have an active voice and role in their learning, with the ability to propose projects that further their curiosity, inquiry, and learning. Self-directed projects give the students ownership of their learning and gives them the opportunity to contribute, the ability to choose and participate in an engaging and challenging environment. As students develop the skills needed to work in a project-based environment, they will move from teacher-directed learning and projects to student-directed learning and projects.

A PEDAGOGY FOR ALL STRENGTHS

Recently we had the opportunity to observe multiple preservice teachers in action. Because of the demographics of our higher education institution (in Wisconsin), all of the students we observed were white and predominately white women. The astonishing take-away was that despite all of the research about student engagement leading to student success, the educational system remains predominantly teacher led and content specific. Despite teacher candidates putting students into "groups," there was no evidence of voice or choice, and little engagement; no lesson observed challenged the students beyond the third level of Bloom's taxonomy, Application. Teacher candidates stood at the front of the room asking lower-level questions. If this is the type of environment where students who crave a stimulating lesson are being taught, then the system is setting them up for failure. The students Heath identifies as members of the Trackton community, Black students for whom literacy events are grounded in participating, challenging, and connecting to personal life events, would have found no place in the classrooms we observed. It is for these reasons we propose project-based learning as a means of engaging students at all levels to enhance their learning. According to the Buck Institute, one of the leading organizations on project-based learning, three of their key components about "why pbl" include: making school more relevant, increasing learning, and creating an environment for promoting educational equity (https://www.bie.org/about/why_pbl).

If students are coming to school with the ability to answer the critical why questions and actively desire to participate in their education, what is the best way to engage them? By standing in the front of the room and talking at them? By requiring rote memorization? By silencing them when they try to ask questions or actively participate? Or by giving them a question and giving them the choice of how they want to research and present it? Why does a book report have to be written as a five-paragraph theme? Why can't it be a song, or a blog, or a PowerPoint or a creative book talk? Learning to read and write comes from wanting to find out information, not from having information expounded at the student. Worksheets, times tables, and phonics taught out of context are just worksheets, times tables, and phonics taught out of context. If all teachers are going to learn to teach to the multiple strengths of their students, they are going to have to change how the classroom functions. They need to come up with innovative and engaging ways to help their students want to learn. This is hard. The teachers we have worked with who have changed to project-based learning, many after fifteen-plus years in the classroom, admit it is the hardest thing they have ever done. They spent years being retrained in grounding their classroom in questions, multiple means of assessment, and engaging inquiry-based pedagogy. They talk about how difficult it was to give up control and learn to trust that education is taking place even when it doesn't look like "traditional" learning. They also say that they would never go back to teaching the way they had been teaching before they turned to project-based learning. They claim all of their students are learning so much more and that each and every day is a completely new adventure for the whole classroom. The research says all students have strengths. It is the school's job to match the pedagogy to the strengths of the child, not the child's job to assimilate to the pedagogy.

And Then . . .

And then, because the question is why stop at project-based learning that is only within the classroom walls, if school is truly going to be meaningful and relevant, then teachers need to make connections to what is happening outside the school walls. Service-learning takes the process one step further and allows students to truly participate in a socially just and equitable environment. Project-based learning talks about place-based learning, which has students leave the classroom walls and learn about their community. Taking place-based learning into true service-learning opportunities will allow students not only to engage in learning but also to become social justice activists. For true service learning to occur, there must be reciprocal learning (Sigmon, 1979), where learning takes place on all sides. Students who arrive at school filled with "why" questions need to be challenged to search for the answers. The ability to answer the "what" will follow when children are curious, engaged, supported, and encouraged and see education as a relevant activity that they engage in with purpose and hope.

■ ■ Engaging the Mind ★ Taking Action ★ Inspiring Excellence

To begin a project-based lesson, first think of a broad question (known as the guiding question) that is open-ended, non-judgmental, and inquiry based. An example might be "What is waste?" Students then engage in inquiry to address the questions. Voice and choice become essential here as students choose what and how they wish to engage in inquiry and how they wish to present their findings. The teacher acts as a guide and a facilitator to assist the students as they search for their answers. Two exemplary resources are listed below, which give step-by-step guides for implementing project-based lessons as well as resources, professional development, and lesson ideas.

Here are two major resources online for project-based learning:

Buck Institute: https://www.bie.org

Edutopia: https://www.edutopia.org

Both of these sites give explicit ideas for how to incorporate project-based learning into your classroom, professional development training opportunities, and rubrics for assessing project-based lessons. Take a look at the websites and choose one lesson you do every year that you believe would truly benefit your Black boys by changing to project-based learning and rewrite the lesson. Reflect on the lesson you taught prior to teaching it as PBL and then reflect on it after you implement PBL. Challenge your students and yourself to be engaging, creative, and personal in the learning process. Build relationships with your parents and your communities as you create the lesson. Engage in all levels of Bloom's taxonomy. Flip your classroom, flip your teaching, and engage your students through both what and why questions.

Read *Black Ants and Buddhists: Thinking Critically and Teaching Differently in the Primary Grades,* by Mary Cowhey, and learn how a second-grade teacher created a socially just classroom that met the needs of all of her students.

Many of the chapters in this book reference the over-recommendation of Black boys for special education and the under-recommendation of Black boys for gifted education, honors, and advanced placement classes. This issue has many parallel problems with academic tracking, which are critical to fixing education for Black boys. When students are tracked into higher-level classes, they usually have access to more experienced teachers, more stimulating curriculum, and, perhaps in part because of the first two items, more engaged peers (Oakes, 2005). The tracks become self-fulfilling, and students who are tracked into lower levels often become disengaged or apathetic. Gifted education tends to engage the mind and the body, drawing kids into an interactive and stimulating curriculum in small groups with highly resourced teachers. Students are given the message repeatedly from multiple adults that they are gifted. It's a setting in which most children would thrive, given the opportunity. Some districts address this issue of disproportionality by eliminating tracking. Some individual parents address this issue by not allowing their children to partake in gifted education, for while it has some educational merits, it is overwhelmingly a tool of racial segregation. While we disapprove of the mainstream practice of gifted education, we acknowledge that such programs are not going anywhere fast. This is a staple of American schooling. As long as your school or district has gifted education, Black boys should be included in it. Intelligence and "giftedness" are distributed throughout the general population, but White and Asian students are overwhelmingly identified for gifted classes. The following chapter will give you tools for identifying and supporting "giftedness" in your Black boy students.

CHAPTER 40

Black Faces and White Spaces

Recognizing and Supporting Black Boys in Gifted Education

**Brian L. Wright, Donna Y. Ford,
and Tarek C. Grantham**

THEY (MY WHITE TEACHERS) . . .

My parents told me I was gifted. They said my parents were wrong. They said gifted education is for more advanced students. They said test scores do not lie.

They told me Columbus discovered America. My father told me civilizations were already here. They said my father was wrong.

They told me that Black people were slaves. My pastor said they were kings and queens, great scientists, mathematicians, writers, musicians, and farmers. They said my pastor was wrong.

When I challenged their opinion, they said I was "overly aggressive" and to stop asking questions.

They said I was "below average" academically. My parents said I was smart and one day I would become a teacher. They (my White teachers) told me to stop using African American Vernacular English. They never stopped to think that they were wrong.

The vignette above captures an example of what happens when teachers in general, and White teachers in particular, are faced with the challenge of recognizing and appreciating what gifted Black children (and other nonmainstream groups) learn in their homes and communities as relevant to school. The vignette also raises important questions: How do teachers recruit and retain more Black boys in gifted education? What are the challenges faced by Black boys in their pursuit of academic success in gifted education? How do we prepare White teachers to recognize, understand, and validate the gifts that Black boys bring to their schooling experience?

The answers to these questions are complex since, for many White female teachers, so few Black boys are in gifted classes, and this may be their first direct and ongoing contact. This reality begs the question: How can you teach a Black boy when you do not know or understand his culture? In response to this important question, we assert that White teachers must first understand that gifted Black boys are expected to learn early how to manage multiple developmental tasks: (1) typical tasks of life course development; (2) developmental tasks associated with being gifted; and (3) tasks that involve negotiating and navigating sources of stress associated with assumptions regarding their race, culture, socioeconomic status, language variation, gender, ability, and disability.

Let's consider Shadeem. He is a tall dark-skinned Black seventh grader who wears his school uniform with shirt hanging out, pants below his waist, and shoes loose and untied; this is no different from other boys across race in his school. He enjoys a huge reputation among his peers because of his lyrical rap combinations and ability to skillfully talk his way out of trouble, which is common among adolescents. He is movement oriented (tactile and kinesthetic) and vervistic (high energy—for a more in-depth reading on verve, see Dr. Darla Scott's chapter on Verve in this book), which teachers find frustrating. Shadeem sometimes turns in his homework late. On quizzes and tests, he gets a combination of high, average, and low scores. Strangely, to some of his teachers, Shadeem gets the correct answers or comes up with the most original responses on the most complex assignments and quiz or test items. When the assignment interests him, he asks lots of questions, but he gets frustrated with simple or simplistic responses, as is common among gifted and advanced students. Instead of noticing that within Shadeem's talk, reasoning, and behavior are cognitive strengths, such as high verbal skills, leadership, interpersonal intelligence, problem solving, and creativity, White teachers are often consumed by what they perceive to be Shadeem's inappropriate dress (Enter: Trayvon Martin), behavior (Enter: Tamir Rice), "hyperactivity," and academic disengagement. Therefore, few teachers would recommend him and many other Black males to be screened for gifted or advanced programs, as has been shown in many studies (Ford, Grantham, & Whiting, 2008a, 2008b; Grissom & Redding, 2016). Black boys are woefully underrepresented in gifted programs, by more than 50 percent; these boys are the least likely to be referred to and participate in gifted education. Such exclusion and stigmatization are, in large part, based on teachers' subjective views and reinforced by society's negative view of Black boys. It can create a self-fulfilling prophecy. Shadeem's gifts and talents go unrecognized when he is viewed (from a deficit perspective) as an underachiever who cares less about trying to conform to the culture of school and more about maintaining his social credibility or "street cred" among his peers (i.e., commanding a level of respect in one's community due to experience in or knowledge of issues, happenings, etc.).

In the fictitious example above, we illustrate further our earlier point that Black boys must manage life as a typical adolescent while also coping with commonly held stereotypes (e.g., troublemaker, bad boy, crime, athletics, academic failure) and misperceptions about them in and outside of school. As in Shadeem's case, Black boys are expected to "toe the line" as they negotiate and navigate often unsubstantiated, unquestioned, and inaccurate thoughts and beliefs about them individually and collectively. Black boys are compared to a White middle-class norm from which they often differ culturally (e.g., verve, movement, orality). As a result, they must work against harmful and detrimental views of who they are and what they are capable of academically and intellectually. This culture of fear, stoked by colorblindness and stereotypes, hampers efforts to meet the social-emotional, cultural, and academic needs of gifted Black boys.

BLACK FACES AND WHITE SPACES

Gifted education programs have long been a White space—overenrolled by White students, taught by White teachers, and protected by White middle-class parents. Historically, advocates for greater numbers of Black faces in gifted and advanced programs have been confronted by White power brokers who view difference as deficit and uphold biased views of intelligence that maintain the White-enrollment status quo (Baldwin, 1987; Ford, 2013; Ford & Grantham, 2003; Frasier, 1987; Hilliard, 1990; Torrance, 1974).

Since 2002, the Office of Civil Rights has collected data on school districts as documented in its Civil Rights Data Collection (see www.ocrdata.ed.gov), and each year, the office finds that Black students are underrepresented in gifted education. For the 2011–2012 school year, which represents the most recent published data, Black boys comprised 9 percent of students enrolled in public schools across the country, but less than 4 percent were identified as gifted. This wide disparity of underrepresentation among Black boys in gifted education, where White middle-class children are overrepresented, is a long-standing problem. Regardless of whether the school enrollment is majority Black or mixed race, Black males' underrepresentation in advanced programs is pervasive because gifted education programs represent a White space in public schools.

Racial steering of White middle-class children into gifted education is supported by narrow definitions of giftedness based primarily on IQ scores and traditional theories of normative development that subvert the promise, potential, and possibility of Black boys being referred to gifted education. As a result, the strengths and cultural assets of Black boys, which tend to manifest in different attitudes, beliefs, values, and practices as captured in the example of Shadeem, go unrecognized and unsupported in gifted education (Ford, 2010, 2013).

BLACK BOYS AND GIFTED EDUCATION

Diversification of the faces and, by extension, the space of gifted education raises two important questions: (1) How do race and culture directly impact students' access to learning opportunities in a racially stratified society? and (2) How can schools and individual teachers structure or limit Black boys' access to gifted education and advanced curricular materials? These and other questions are explored in the remaining sections of this chapter. Sample strategies and resources grounded in equity and excellence are provided to increase Black boys' access to gifted education and to underscore that the tie that binds all students is the desire to be academically successful.

When it comes to gifted Black boys' success in school, teachers' mindset is a crucial internal attitude that significantly shapes students' talent trajectory and teachers' effectiveness in nurturing talent. With this in mind, it is important that White teachers not be bystanders, but rather engage in experiences that both challenge and help them question, wrestle with, and counter fears, stereotypes, and deficit views of Black boys (Grantham, 2011; Wright, Counsell, & Tate, 2015).

White female teachers must build an arsenal of resources to increase the likelihood that gifted Black boys will achieve in school. Trusting relationships with family and community members are key resources. White female teachers must engage Black boys beyond the school walls to build relationships with family members, leaders, and peers who can promote a positive Black male scholar identity (Ford et al., 2008a, 2008b; Wright et al., 2015). Such relationships give White female teachers counternarratives to help reframe their beliefs, expectations, and practices regarding the education and teaching of Black boys. Trusting relationships can be formed when White female teachers:

> *Self-Reflect.* Adopt an attitude of care, engaging in reflective practice, and showing a willingness to tackle personal prejudicial and stereotypical thinking;

doing so will help remove blinders in order to see gifts, talents, and potential in Black boys.

Immerse. Take the necessary steps to immerse themselves in Black communities; the more interaction, including at community and sporting events, the more expectations improve, along with sending a powerful message of commitment.

Collaborate. Focus on open reciprocal home-school communication and engagement; communicate with families about their son's strengths; empower them with information and resources.

Communicate. Seek opportunities to engage in dialogue around racism, discrimination, and economic inequities that still disconnect teachers and Black boys and then take steps in their relationships with Black boys and in curricular plans to have a multicultural and social justice focus.

Get Education and Training. Take formal coursework and professional development in gifted education, creativity, talent development, *and* multicultural education to become culturally competent.

This type of engagement to build trusting relationships can help White female teachers to recognize and support gifted Black boys, resulting in upstander teachers. Grantham (2011) defined an upstander teacher as the opposite of a bystander teacher. Upstander teachers take a stand and engage in proactive roles to address injustices. Upstander teachers are also culturally competent teachers who can see beyond deficit-oriented, segregated mindsets (Grantham, Trotman Scott, & Harmon, 2013) to identify and cultivate the gifts, creativity, and potential of Black boys. As outsiders to the White space of gifted education, Black boys who are identified for such programs often gain access because of teachers who understand and recognize creativity as a form of giftedness. Recognizing students' strengths as suggested in the opening vignette can increase teachers' referrals of Black boys for gifted education. Too many Black boys fail to recognize, understand, and value their own gifts, talents, creativity, and potential, when confronted with the predominantly White teaching force. The impact is clear: academic disengagement, underachievement, low test scores, low graduation rates, high dropout rates, push-out rates, and more that marginalizes them. The waste of gifts and talents is clear and prevalent among Black boys more than any other group of students (Ford, 2010, 2013).

With the above in mind, an important strategy for White female teachers is the practice of engaging Black boys in rigorous culturally relevant academic experiences that recognize and value their intellectual strengths, cultural assets, and capacity to identify problems in their community and to solve them (Grantham,

Hines, Dennis, Solomon, & Anderson, in press). A talent development model is required. Take Shadeem; teachers must recognize that behind his talk, reasoning, and misunderstood behaviors are talents that can be developed and prove useful in academic competitions with peers, where he can productively lead others. This requires involving Black boys in enrichment and afterschool programming, such as a debate team (see http://budl.org/about/) and a Community Problem Solving team, which is part of the Future Problem Solving Program International (see http://www.fpspi.org/cmps.html). Also consider accelerating Shadeem and other gifted Black boys in an online class to explore their scholarly identity while fine-tuning divergent verbal skills, leadership, interpersonal skills, logical reasoning, and creativity abilities to solve meaningful and relevant problems.

To ignore any of these recommendations perpetuates bystander educators and a system of oppression that assaults Black boys' need, right, and capacity to be identified as gifted. Gifted Black boys need upstander educators who proactively confront and debunk prevailing stereotypes of the dangerous, lazy, dishonest, violent, hypermasculine and unintelligent Black boy and who understand and value the contexts and situations where their creativity, brilliance, and passion reside. Only then, will Black boys begin to say, "My White teacher said I am gifted!"

■ ■ Engaging the Mind ★ Taking Action ★ Inspiring Excellence
What Do You See, When You See a Black Boy?

1. Give a Black boy a blank, unlined sheet of paper.

2. Direct him to draw a large box on the sheet of paper to represent a mirror.

3. Ask him to describe what and whom he sees in his reflection.

4. Take a sheet of paper and write down what you see in the student in terms of his promise, potential and possibility. Examine similarities and differences. If either or both drawings focus on perceived deficits rather than strengths, take on the above recommendations to increase his scholarly identity and to change your views of him as a gifted Black boy.

CHAPTER 41

The Book Matters

Using the Color-Coded Bloom-Banks Matrix to Support the Literacy and Engagement of Black Boys

Michelle Trotman Scott, Brian L. Wright, and Donna Y. Ford

"Why Ryheim Does Not Like to Read"

Ryheim, an African American boy, is a rambunctious, imaginative, and intelligent second grader who asks a lot of questions and always has an elaborate story full of intimate, layered details to share during class meetings. Ryheim's almost all-White classmates are captivated by his way with words and always ask him to tell a story. He is a good reader, but he does not like to read. When his White female teacher (Ms. Woods) invites the class to select a book from the classroom library, Ryheim is always the last to choose a book. When he finally selects a book, he retreats to a corner of the classroom, away from the other children and teacher. As usual, his teacher walks around to talk with groups of children about their chosen book. She typically asks them to map out their story (i.e., the setting, character, problem, and solution). Hiding from his teacher, Ryheim is caught daydreaming and talking to his classmates about a trip to the zoo with his dad. When asked by Ms. Woods to tell her about his book, Ryheim, with a sad look and much frustration, asks "how come there ain't no Black boys in these books?"

Too often, Black students, especially Black boys, quickly lose interest in reading. Many complain of finding little relevance in books, and we must take their complaints seriously. When disengaged, they may resort to acting out, which contributes to suspensions, underachievement, and achievement gaps. Of all students, Black boys, including those in PreK–3, are most likely to be suspended. According to the U.S. Department of Education, Black preschool students represent 19 percent of the student enrollment but 45 percent of suspensions (U.S. Department of Education, 2014). Compounding disciplinary issues, Black boys also tend to have lower literacy rates than other students. For example, data from the ongoing Early Childhood Longitudinal Study reports that by age four, children living in poverty have heard 30 million fewer words than their more affluent peers (Hart & Risley, 2011). By fourth grade, gaps in early reading proficiency for children of color, especially Black boys, are significantly below that of White boys (Annie E. Casey Foundation, 2016). We maintain that *aliteracy* is also at work: Black boys *can* read but *won't* read, as with Ryheim. The authors of this chapter assert that until reading instruction is grounded in meaningful texts (e.g., *Jamal's Busy Day* by Hudson, 1991) that build on academic and personal identities toward resiliency inside and outside of school, Black boys will show little interest in reading.

In this short chapter, we share the story of Ryheim, a second grader, who has lost interest in reading like far too many Black boys. The authors adopt the color-coded Bloom-Banks Matrix (Trotman Scott, 2014) that is revised from Ford (2011) to encourage and motivate Ryheim and other Black boys to find a passion for reading. The sample matrix provides guidance for teachers to develop rigorous and culturally relevant curriculum. (See Figure 41.1.) It is one resource for improving achievement, behavior, engagement, and literacy by challenging and engaging Black boys.

There are legitimate concerns about the need to make curriculum and literature relevant for boys, particularly Black boys. Too often, Black boys complain about what is presented in their classes; the material is not interesting or relevant to their lived experiences. If education is not relevant, it becomes meaningless. If there is a school/teacher-student mismatch, learning, academic achievement, and motivation are compromised. More specifically, if the curriculum and literature do not engage Black boys, they may lose interest, begin to fail, and, in many cases, be removed from the classroom (i.e., suspension).

In 1999, Ford and Harris developed the Bloom-Banks Matrix, a two-fold model used to address the need to make learning rigorous and relevant for students. The Matrix blends the best of critical thinking (Bloom, 1956) and multicultural curriculum (Banks, 2009) to provide teachers with a tool to develop lessons that offer rigor with substantive multicultural content. The Bloom-Banks Matrix has been since been revised by Ford (2011) and then color-coded by Trotman Scott (2014). This chapter summarizes the color-coded Matrix and describes how it can be used to increase rigor and relevance in the classroom using the children's book *Jamal's Busy Day* by Hudson (1991).

Engaging Black Boys Using Rigorous Culturally Responsive Curriculum and Literature

Culture-purposed instruction must be implemented to ensure that students are not given a colorblind or culturally assaultive curriculum. Educators must ensure that culturally responsive practices, theories, and research are adopted in all classrooms and honors the kinds of talk and thinking that children use in their everyday lives. When used properly, Ford's (2011) Bloom-Banks Matrix can increase the interest and achievement of Black boys like Ryheim. The Matrix is a unique model that merges rigor and relevance, a win-win situation for all students.

The Bloom-Banks Matrix: An Overview

Bloom's Taxonomy of Educational Objectives provides instructional rigor: critical thinking, creative thinking, and problem solving. When teachers utilize the six-level cognitive domains, they are able to determine Black boys' ability or skills to recall basic and factual information (knowledge/knowing); understand and explain what was learned (comprehension/ understanding); apply and use what was learned (application/applying); form views, predict, and compare-contrast information (analysis/analyzing); study, judge/critique, and support what was taught and learned (evaluation/evaluating); and use what is taught and learned to develop new, original, and/or improved products (synthesis/creating).

Lessons and literature are not rigorous if students are not given the opportunity to think and act accordingly. Curriculum must allow students, and in this case Black boys, to see themselves positively reflected in literature and curriculum. Banks's 2009 four-level model (contributions, additive, transformation, and social action) provides this needed multicultural rigor. At the Contributions Level, lessons focus on cultural artifacts and materials (e.g., food, games, celebrations, fashion, and folklore) in ways that render them superficial. We caution teachers to avoid the "tourist approach" to other people's culture. At the Additive Level, lessons focus on multicultural topics, ideas, and concepts in a safe way and during certain times (e.g., Black History Month). The Transformation Level, unlike the previous two, promotes critical thinking by using multiple and alternative points of view. Teachers infuse multicultural content in all content areas; topics, issues, and themes are richer. The highest level, Social Action, has the goal of empowering students to be change agents, social activists, service minded, and problem solvers. Students are taught and encouraged to make recommendations or act on their ideas (agency).

The Bloom-Banks Matrix (Ford, 2011; Ford & Harris, 1999) combines Bloom's Taxonomy (Bloom, 1956) and Banks's Model (2009) to create a model that reflects the goals, objects, and perspectives of differentiation that encompasses rigor and relevance. The result of the merger is a four-quadrant matrix that consists of twenty-four cells. The lowest cell level is knowledge-contributions and the highest and most rigorous cell is social action-synthesis. As depicted in Figure 41.1, Trotman Scott (2014) color-coded the matrix to conceptualize the differences and characteristics of each quadrant.

Red/Stop = Quadrant 1: Lessons presented in this quadrant are low on both Bloom's Taxonomy and Banks' Multicultural Model. Teachers commonly provide lessons from six cells in this quadrant. However, when lessons are low on Bloom's Taxonomy (knowledge, comprehension, and application) *and* low on Banks' multicultural levels (contributions and additive), it may be not challenging or interesting for Black boys (Ford, 2011; Trotman Scott, 2014).

Yellow/Caution = Quadrant 2: High on Bloom's Taxonomy but low on Banks's multicultural levels. Lessons within this quadrant allow Black boys to use their critical thinking, creativity, and problem-solving skills, but multicultural content is superficial or presented in stereotypical ways. Assignments in this quadrant challenge Black boys cognitively, but substantive multicultural content will be missing. This quadrant is most commonly used when teachers are familiar with Bloom but not Banks (Ford, 2011; Trotman Scott, 2014).

Blue/Guarded = Quadrant 3: Low on Bloom's Taxonomy but high on Banks' multicultural levels. Lesson plans in these six cells allow Black boys to elaborate on events, facts, and characteristics of culturally different groups; this will help them to become more aware and gain additional and meaningful knowledge about different groups, issues, concepts, and themes. Black boys will be given opportunities to view cultural events, concepts, and themes through the lenses and lives of others. However, this quadrant is considered guarded because although social action may take place, it does not require critical thinking and problem solving. When developing lessons, teachers may be familiar with Banks's multicultural model but not with Bloom's Taxonomy (Ford, 2011; Trotman Scott, 2014).

FIGURE 41.1 Color-Coded Bloom-Banks Matrix Applied to *Jamal's Busy Day*

	QUADRANT 1 RED/STOP			QUADRANT 2 YELLOW/CAUTION		
	Knowledge/ Knowing	*Comprehension/ Understanding*	*Application/ Applying*	*Analysis/ Analyzing*	*Evaluation/ Evaluating*	*Synthesis/ Creating*
Contributions	What do Jamal's parents do for a living? What are their jobs?	How does Jamal's day begin?	What are examples of a healthy breakfast? Share a list of food items.	What do Jamal and his mother have in common? What do Jamal and his father have in common?	Interview at least one classmate about his/her career goals.	Create a menu for a healthy breakfast.
Additive	What does an architect do? What does an accountant do? What are their responsibilities?	Why is breakfast important?	Make a timeline showing Jamal's day and compare it to your busy day.	Do you think Jamal will become an accountant or an architect? Make a prediction.	What do you want to be when you grow up? Study/ research the career/ job requirements.	How does Jamal use his imagination about school and work? Think of more examples of how school and work are similar.

	QUADRANT 3 BLUE/GUARDED			QUADRANT 4 GREEN/GO		
	Knowledge/ Knowing	*Comprehension/ Understanding*	*Application/ Applying*	*Analysis/ Analyzing*	*Evaluation/ Evaluating*	*Synthesis/ Creating*
Transformation	What do you like about math?	Why is math important for being an accountant and architect?	Make a Venn diagram of how Jamal compares school to work.	Do you agree with Jamal that school is similar to work? If yes, explain. If no, explain why not.	Interview two teachers about why they became a teacher. What is similar and different?	Create a flyer showing how school and jobs are either similar or different.
Social Action	Read the book to a sister, brother, cousin, or friend.	If you saw a classmate being bullied, what would you do?	Make a list of classroom rules about anti-bullying.	Talk to a sister, brother, cousin, or friend about the importance of doing well in school.	Study the breakfast or lunch menu. Make at least two suggestions to make it healthier.	Create an anti-bullying poster to be placed in the cafeteria use pictures of diverse students.

Adapted from Ford (2011) and Trotman Scott (2014). The authors recommend that teachers be mindful of and sensitive to asking students to talk about the career/job of their parent(s) due to high rates of unemployment in diverse communities. It is important not to embarrass students, which would be culturally insensitive and assaultive.

Green/Go = Quadrant 4: High on Bloom's Taxonomy *and* Banks' Multicultural levels. This quadrant provides Black boys with opportunities to think critically, solve problems, and review a multitude of multicultural topics, issues, and themes. An important characteristic is that students suggest or make recommendations for social change. Lessons in this quadrant are both rigorous *and* relevant. Moreover, Black boys will be able to think and solve problems at the highest levels, while being exposed to content that validates them individually and as a group. This is the ideal quadrant for all students (Ford, 2011; Trotman Scott, 2014).

The Matrix is useful in all educational settings ranging from gifted, mixed-ability, and special education classrooms. When using the Matrix, teachers will be able to teach the same content on differing levels and allow all students, specifically Black boys, to experience meaning and success on a level that meets their individual needs and interests. All students have the right to be educated using rigorous *and* relevant lessons, materials, and literature. In the end, the book really does matter.

The following chapter is written by Marie Michael, a diversity professional who puts the notion of positive racial identity at the center of her work with teachers. Recognizing that teachers need an affirmational approach to race that is consistent with child development, she supports teachers to design curricula and lessons around the vision of supporting positive racial identity development in students. Her chapter introduces teachers to the notion of supporting positive racial identity development, building on the framework of racial identity development that we read earlier in the book by Bentley Edwards, et al. Michael includes in this chapter multiple current and practical recommendations for books and approaches that teachers can use in the classroom.

CHAPTER 42

Books and Curriculum

What to Read With Black Males in Elementary School to Create a Strong Foundation of Positive Racial Identity Development

Marie Michael

Black boys, just like any other babies, are born with positive identities. Years of negative racial socialization, in a society that upholds Whiteness as superior and Blackness and brownness as inferior, can erode their strong sense of self, however. Books, pedagogical strategies, and curricular choices can be used to address this issue, providing African American boys with positive role models and stories that allow them to see and hear reflections of themselves. I call this work supporting the positive racial identity development of African American boys. It includes intentional and continual intervention. One essential component is creating a classroom that, rather than upholding European standards, presents a multiracial reality, where all children can learn about themselves and others. In that classroom, race, and eventually racism and White privilege, can be talked about in intentional and explicit ways. Louise Derman-Sparks and Julie Olsen Edwards (2010) point out that "children's racial identity is shaped from the outside *and . . .* the inside" and "teachers can play a critical role in helping children make sense of the confusing and often emotionally charged messages they receive about who they are" (p. 79). In their classrooms, teachers can work to present a reality where all people, across the color spectrum, are seen as precious, capable, and fully human. To do so, teachers must be intentional in counteracting society's racial norms, providing accurate information and fostering a positive attitude among children about their racial identities (Crumbley, 1999; Derman-Sparks & Olsen Edwards, 2010).

Students need language to talk about aspects of their race and culture. They need to have an understanding that race is complex and at times confusing. It is key they know that others may see them differently than they see themselves. Derman-Sparks and Olsen Edwards note that "racial identity . . . is about how we are treated by society's institutions and by other people *and* about how we come to understand, feel, and live our racial group membership. It is both what other people say about us and what we say about ourselves"(p. 78). As students get older, it is important to teach them the language society uses to identify racial groups and to add more nuance and layers to the conversation. Teachers can begin to help students understand that race is a social construction that has been used to oppress some and to uplift others. In sharing stories and processing students' own experiences, teachers can help them understand the realities of racism and discrimination and learn ways to stand up against unfair treatment.

Since this is a book designed for White female teachers educating Black boys, this chapter will primarily focus on books and resources White teachers can use to support the racial identity development of Black boys, particularly in elementary school, where they are creating the foundation for a child's sense of self. However, because of the need to create a classroom of students who understand their own and other identities, and where they see themselves and each other as fully human, it will also include some resources that will help all students develop language and concepts to begin to understand race and culture and to build the foundation for strong racial identities.

PRESCHOOL AND EARLY ELEMENTARY (PK–SECOND GRADES)

As early as three years old, children notice differences, like skin and eye color, hair color and texture, and physical characteristics. Although they don't understand the sophisticated concept of race, they are constantly internalizing racial cues from their environment and talking about it with others (Tatum, 1997). These are the years when teachers must build a solid foundation of positive racial identity on which children can grow and develop. Rather than being colorblind, ignoring the racial identity of children in the classroom, teachers must instead see and honor each child for who they are and engage students in cocreating a classroom environment where everyone can feel proud of his or her identity.

In PK–K, a key experience is reading books that contain Black characters doing everyday activities, experiencing fun adventures, spending time with family: books that show aspects of Black culture. Books like *Full, Full, Full of Love* and *So Much* by Trish Cooke, *Looking Like Me* by Walter Dean Myers, the Peter series by Ezra Jack Keats, and *Hewitt Anderson's Great Big Life* by Jerdine Nolen are good examples. These books also create an opportunity for students to share their own family stories and experiences with each other, allowing moments to center each child and his or her own experiences. *The Colors of Us* and *Shades of Black* can introduce skin color in a creative and fun way. *Black Is Brown Is Tan* is a rhyming book that illustrates skin color in a biracial family. These books provide a chance to talk about and describe the many shades of skin color.

First and second grade is a good time for all children to learn about different aspects of race and culture and to be taught that it is normal to notice and talk about differences. In *Identity Safe Classrooms*, Dorothy M. Steele and Becki Cohn-Vargas (2013) write, "It is essential that teachers use curricula, materials, and learning tasks that have meaning for all of their students, and that it includes experiences, images and references from the many cultures and lived experiences of the students" (p. 69). *People* by Peter Spier provides countless detailed descriptions of people throughout the world, exploring the great diversity among us. *The Skin You Live In* provides illustrations and creative descriptions of children and adults who have different skin colors. In combination with *The Skin You're In!: The Secrets of Skin*, these books provide an easy entry into a conversation about skin and why we have it, the role of melanin, and what skin does and doesn't tell us about ourselves and each other. Teachers can share current racial terminology and give examples of how it often changes, for instance, the change from colored to black to African American. You can remind children of the range of skin color in one racial group, noting that it isn't always easy to name a person's race just by the way he or she looks, which is why it is important to let people self-identify. After exploring these books, you can ask students to create self-portraits and stories to accompany them, mixing colored pencils or paint colors to find just the right skin tone, choosing clothing, and depicting other items to illustrate important aspects of their culture.

During these early years, it is essential to expose young Black boys to images of themselves and positive Black male role models. Steele and Cohn-Vargas (2013) note that "[s]tudents flourish when they see themselves and the groups they belong to reflected on a daily basis, and so they are not seen as other" (p. 74). Teachers can read books like *Bippity Bop Barbershop,* about a Black boy's trip to the barbershop with his father to get his first haircut. The story introduces the landscape of the Black barber shop, allowing an opportunity to give language to all students about how to describe Black men's hairstyles. Many children will relate to having a first haircut and will enjoy describing their own hair color, texture, and length and naming their hairstyles. This is an opportunity to counteract the notion that there is a "normal" kind of hair. Instead, as one second-grade student at Blake School shared, "everyone has their own normal." *The Jones Family Express* is great for a unit on telling stories about travel adventures. For boys who are athletic, books like *A Nation's Hope: The Story of Boxing Legend Joe Lewis* and *Michael's Golden Rules* offer an opportunity to read about Black male sports legends while also talking about skills, beyond just athleticism, needed to be successful in sports and life. *Take it to the Hoop Magic Johnson* is a poem that is fun to read aloud, and teachers can use it to teach poetic techniques. Teachers can bring Troupe's actual voice and image into the classroom by showing a short video of him reading the poem dramatically. Inviting Black fathers and other men into the class to read these books and others is a great way to expose the whole class to positive Black male role models and counteract negative stereotypes.

Later Elementary (Third to Fifth Grades)

In later elementary grades, children begin to more firmly categorize and create friend groups; as they are exposed to issues of race and culture, teachers can build on the positive racial identity foundation from early years. Continue to give children the language to talk about race, about differences and similarities to normalize these conversations. In addition, "opportunities to reflect on and to share from their personal lives give students the chance to connect with their backgrounds in a positive way that lets them be in control of the information that is disclosed" (Steele & Cohn-Vargas, 2013, p. 75). Using books, activities, and teachable moments that emerge through typical student interaction also allows teachers to model respectful ways to ask questions and listen to other perspectives. Students don't always have to agree with each other. They can listen to each other's stories, learn from them, and begin to practice empathy. "Simple comments from teachers that show they are unbiased and do not tolerate teasing and prejudice go a long way to model acceptance in the classroom" (Steele & Cohn-Vargas, 2013, p. 75). Along with providing opportunities for students to connect with and learn from each other, teachers must also model the kind of mindsets and behaviors they want to instill in their students, creating an environment of mutual trust, respect, and interdependence. The book, *Keep Your Ear on the Ball,* is a great example of what such a classroom looks like. It is a story narrated by an African American boy who, along with his classmates, practices empathy and teamwork as they learn the right way to support their classmate who is blind.

As Black boys get older, continuing to bring authentic and diverse stories, voices, and images of African American boys and men into your classroom is essential. In *Countering the Conspiracy to Destroy Black Boys,* Vol. Jawanza Kunjufu (1990) points out the numerous struggles Black boys contend with around the age of nine. His research shows that during third or fourth grade, they experience a decline in their teachers' expectations. In additionally, teachers no longer see them as "cute and innocent," but instead as "aggressive, hostile, and a discipline problem" (p. 31). The boys experience increasing peer pressure at the same time as declining parent involvement (p. 29). Finally, a "slower maturation rate" (p. 32) and a more active learning style lead them to be diagnosed as hyperactive and disproportionately placed in special education (p. 33). Finally, Kunjufu highlights the negative effects of a shortage of Black male teachers and role models in the school environment (p. 33).

So these years are a time to pay particular attention to Black boys' experiences, to engage parents, and to directly address any bullying or racist behavior among their peers. Teachers can help students develop the skills of "calling in" these behaviors in their peers and standing up for themselves and others. Bringing in African American parents, older boys who are students in the school, or men in the community to partner with children for activities, to read one-on-one, to teach mini-lessons, to share their expertise, or to accompany the class on field trips: All of these activities provide informal modeling and mentorship during a critical time for Black boys. These men and boys can also share their strategies for dealing with stereotypes and discrimination.

Sharing the life and work of an African American man like artist Kadir Nelson is one way to both describe his impressive career and illustrate how Black men tackle injustice in our society. Nelson's books highlight not only the racism evident in history, but also the amazing lives of people who have incredible skills, values, and mindsets, who have achieved social justice not only for themselves, but also for the world at large. He has a number of texts teachers can read aloud or that boys can read on their own. Teachers can share how he, like other authors, will sometimes illustrate the words of a song in a book like *He's Got the Whole World in His Hands. Hewitt Anderson's Great Big Life*, is great to read aloud, a surprising and fun book that will capture students' hearts. Use Nelson's book, *We Are the Ship: The Story of Negro League Baseball,* to introduce the Negro Leagues as part of a unit that illustrates the history and realities of segregation in our country, as well as the unique personalities of the players, along with their creativity and resilience. *Testing the Ice: A True Story About Jackie Robinson* is a powerful metaphor of Robinson's experience integrating baseball and illustrates the kind of courage needed by anyone who is trying to change an unjust system. A video of Nelson reading the book is also available. Adding in a brief story about Branch Rickey, the Brooklyn Dodger's general manager who hired Robinson intentionally to break the color barrier, could illustrate the role of allies, showing how cross-racial courage and collaboration are needed to help people and institutions change.

Other books that offer a way to talk about Black men who were change makers, getting beyond the lone story of Martin Luther King, Jr., would be *Richard Wright and the Library Card, Wind Flyers, John Lewis in the Lead,* and *Let Them Play.* For older boys, *Hand in Hand: Ten Black Men Who Changed America* is a great anthology. Conversations about these books could create an opportunity for students not only to discuss the racism in history and how people dealt with it, but also to make connections to current examples and how they can be agents of change in their own lives. These kinds of dialogues empower Black male students, all students really, so they don't feel like victims or bystanders, and they know they are not alone.

At all times, White female teachers must be willing to take stock of their interactions with Black boys. At different times throughout the year, stop and consider questions like these: How are you working to get to know the boys in your classroom? Are you using culturally responsive pedagogy—making the curriculum relevant and codeswitching appropriately to connect? One exercise that can support this process is creating a folder for each student at the beginning of the year. Use the folder to collect information over time about a student's family life; racial, ethnic, and cultural background (Black boys come from a variety of backgrounds and experiences), and favorite books, music, and activities. Then, refer to the folders when creating lessons and activities to ensure they are relevant to students. Among other strategies, being culturally responsive involves building "bridges of meaningfulness between home and school experiences as well as between academic abstractions and sociocultural realities" (Gay, 2000). Black boys should be able to see themselves and their experiences reflected throughout the school day. They should hear flavors of their language, recognize familiar images and sounds, and make use of their background knowledge. Finally, in my interviews with Black boys and men, they made it clear that teachers should remember that even though boys may share a common racial and cultural identity, each has his own interests, skills, and personality, so teachers must see them as individuals in order to make real and meaningful connections.

Create a folder as suggested above for one African American boy in your class. Include information on the student's family life; racial, ethnic, and cultural background; languages spoken (include Black English as a language, if relevant); and his favorite books, music, and other interests and activities. Then, use this information to revise or design a lesson with this student in mind. Don't tell him what you are doing, but note the impact. As you can, create more student folders and use them to influence lesson and even assessment design. When relevant, let students know how their backgrounds, experiences, and interests are central to your design of the curriculum. Ask them if it makes a difference? And, if it does, how so?

Author's Note: This chapter is also drawn from personal Interviews conducted with Aisosa Edison-Edebor, Sean Groomes, Allen Hill, Tyler Jackson, Aaron Sharper, Mark Robinson, and Chaun Webster in July 2016.

We close with a final chapter that we hope will inspire readers to think big about the future of Black boys. Dion Crushshon, an experienced teacher, writes about the personal logistical and emotional barriers to traveling abroad as a Black man and the rather simple and strategic ways that he navigated around them. In a straightforward, step-by-step manner, Crushshon builds an argument that has incredible potential to liberate and educate, blowing the doors off the box that keeps Black boys local, under-exposed, and left out of international learning opportunities. We encourage teachers especially to take inspiration from this chapter and to think about all the places within the educational community where Black boys do not have a foothold. Find ways to create pathways into those spaces, whether they be study abroad, band, debate, theater, foreign language clubs, poetry journals, yearbook committees, school newspapers, student council, golf, swim team, principal's advisory board, and so on. Use the knowledge you have gained in this book to create spaces for Black boys to have centrality and belonging in every aspect of the school's life and culture.

CHAPTER 43

Global Skills

Beyond the Classroom and the Playground

Dion Crushshon

When I was going through high school, the last thing I ever would have imagined myself doing would be "studying abroad." Getting on an airplane seemed out of reach, and traveling out of the country was out of the question. This was just not something kids from my neighborhood did. It seemed to be in the realm of white tablecloth restaurants, spring break vacations, country club memberships, and skiing in the mountains. The people I knew saw these experiences as the purview of the rich, well beyond the means of our families.

I didn't apply for my first passport until I was into my thirties and had a chance to travel to South Africa with my wife as a part of a sabbatical I received from my school. As far as international travel goes, this was a first for both of us. We were excited and prepared ourselves by reading whatever we could about South Africa before we left. For three memorable weeks, we traveled through this amazing country, spending stretches of time in beautiful and picturesque Cape Town, dense and dramatic Johannesburg, and the desolate yet colorful countryside of Orange Free State, Lesotho, and Swaziland. We drove for hundreds of miles in our rented car, and we passed hundreds of black men and women walking—on streets and in highways—with their left arm held out in the hope that our car, or any car for that matter, would stop to pick them up. Over the course of our trip, we never saw a white person walking, and we never saw a black person driving. We had many observations like this one that bothered and unnerved us. We were made uncomfortable and uncertain.

We had lengthy and animated late-night conversations every evening about race, class, privilege, and identity. We were challenged by our privilege to travel across this country and the power we had to decide to which child we might give a handout or donation. We went to South Africa unprepared for the individual challenges we would experience related to our own complicated identities and incomplete perspectives. We left wanting to learn and know more, not about the history and culture of South Africa, but about our own personal identities and home culture. We felt compelled to explore and examine the cultural framework and societal systems present and in our own lives back at home. Our experience in a foreign country, spent immersed in a similar but vastly different culture, challenged and stretched us in ways that we had not anticipated.

For many young people today, distant lands are more accessible and less foreboding. Air travel is easier and more affordable. Widespread electrification, technological advances, and the introduction of the Internet have allowed people to travel and immerse themselves in various countries and regions without requiring them to ever entirely disconnect from family and friends back at home. Smart-phone cameras and social media apps have made for immediate documenting and sharing of personal travel experiences.

In some friendship circles, it appears as if almost every person has traveled to some foreign country and has captured on camera themselves alongside, astride, or atop some foreign monument or natural wonder. However, in many circles of Black boys, not much has changed from the experience I described from my childhood. International travel still seems out of reach, if not out of the question for many individuals and families. You can imagine the gap in worldliness and global awareness that can result between people living these two very different realities.

Former President of Goucher College and Harvard Professor Sanford Ungar (2016) has argued, "Now that every academic field, profession, and industry has taken on an international dimension, study abroad increasingly appears to be an essential element of success, a requirement to compete in the global marketplace."

A related but disheartening statistic that must be noted is the following: only 5 percent of Americans who study abroad are Black, even though there are now more Black people in higher education than ever before (Tensley, 2015). In my own experience over years of planning and coordinating international travel experiences for high school students, I can attest to the underrepresentation of Black children among the student travelers, particularly Black boys. But an important issue is not only that student travelers are predominantly White, but so are the trip planners, coordinators and leaders, the program representatives, sponsors and recruiters, and the chaperones, guides, and alumni.

So What Does All This Mean And What Can We Do About It?

If we agree about the benefits of international travel and global immersion, and if it is true that these benefits and advantages gained prove valuable as preparation for the professional workplace, then Black boys are missing important opportunities. The experiences they are missing are just what they need to prepare for the evolving professional world. Thus, Black boys are further disadvantaged and behind the educational and experiential curve. It's as if we did not provide Black boys access to technology. And let us not forget, as Brandon Tensley (2015) points out in his article for *The Atlantic,* "These missed opportunities don't just harm individuals—they also rob society of social capital."

When I look closely at the conspicuous absence of Black boys in study and travel abroad programs, a few questions come to mind: (1) What individual, familial, and cultural characteristics prevent Black boys in the United States from engaging in these opportunities? What systemic and structural realities create barriers to access for Black boys? (3) What can White teachers do to increase the involvement of Black boys in international travel and study programming? The remainder of this chapter will be devoted to exploring these three questions.

WHAT INDIVIDUAL, FAMILIAL AND CULTURAL CHARACTERISTICS PREVENT BLACK BOYS FROM ENGAGING IN THESE OPPORTUNITIES?

<u>Skepticism or nonidentification ("That's not something we do.")</u>: Many Black boys are skeptical about the practicality of traveling abroad. For so very long, international travel has largely been seen to belong exclusively to the domain of the White and wealthy—a domain that many Black boys and their parents may likely tune out when such opportunities are presented. When there is a high likelihood that programs will be unaffordable and therefore inaccessible, it makes sense that a child and his parents would want to avoid getting their hopes up, only to have them dashed and would rather ignore the information and deny the possibility than inquire about financial aid and engage in a conversation. Often the knee-jerk response is, "That's not me."

<u>Fear of rejection, discrimination, and hostility:</u> Farai Chideya (2014) points out that "For African Americans, domestic and international travel used to be

filled with significant roadblocks." These might have included substandard traveling conditions that White people were not subjected to, uncertain accommodations, discriminatory treatment, and vulnerability to unprovoked hostility. These realities reinforced a mindset that traveling for Blacks was unduly risky and impractical. However, as times have changed, so has this reality. Black people are everywhere in the world, often to our surprise, and the extent and intensity of racial hostility is not what it once was. Also, Black travelers—just like White travelers—travel with money in their pockets, and we all know, money talks wherever you go. Many Black travelers now speak of the liberation that international travel provides from racial tension and hostility they experience in the United States.

International travel seen as luxury expenditure or extended vacation: Unfortunately, educators and professionals have not done a good job enumerating the benefits of international travel for young people, especially our young Black boys. Too often the journey is billed as one of "self-discovery" or a "moratorium," instead of one with practical short-term benefits and long-term advantages for academic and professional careers, whether it is international relations or the STEM fields. Many colleges and universities are now requiring students to have at least one semester study-abroad experience because they know the long-term benefits for their graduates, which include the expansion of professional networks, the development of global competency skills, a greater understanding of societal systems and paradigms, growing self-confidence and independence, and foreign-language acquisition and fluency.

WHAT SYSTEMIC AND STRUCTURAL REALITIES CREATE BARRIERS TO ACCESS TO INTERNATIONAL TRAVEL FOR BLACK BOYS?

Accessibility/Affordability: Certainly, international travel costs are not to be minimized. It's expensive to get on a flight to London or Ecuador or Kenya. Accommodations and in-country transportation can also add significant costs to any adventure abroad. However, the program funding sources, devoted financial aid dollars, and a philosophy of inclusivity and acceptance of diversity are more present today than ever before. All-White travel groups are still common, but ongoing attempts by providers and school programs to diversify the pool of travelers are in earnest in most places. Still, if young Black boys do not know that programs with scholarships or with diversity goals exist, they will never know to apply. Effective outreach is still lacking, and Black adult models and mentors remain in short supply.

Dearth of Black role models: Seeing someone who looks like you do something you thought was impossible suddenly makes that same thing seem altogether possible. Black boys need to see more Black adult males sharing stories about their international travel experiences. Some prominent Black folks may have traveled extensively or may be fluent in a second or third language or may have lived in a foreign country for an extended period of time, but we would never know about it as it is not something that is often highlighted or mentioned. Black boys need to know there are people who look like them who have gained international travel experience and leveraged it for professional advancement.

Lack of effective outreach: Far too often, schools and programs have announced or promoted international travel opportunities in traditional settings lacking representation of Black boys. A number of other factors may lead to a disconnect between the Black family and the program right from the start. Program leaders, school leaders, and trip leaders:

- Are all White

- Are unfamiliar to Black boys and their parents

- Are uncomfortable or uneasy communicating with Black boys and their parents

- Do not anticipate and understand the culturally specific concerns Black parents might have about the makeup of the specific travel group, the background of the trip leaders, the philosophy of program, or the cultural norms of the destination

WHAT CAN WHITE TEACHERS DO TO INCREASE THE INVOLVEMENT OF BLACK BOYS IN INTERNATIONAL TRAVEL AND STUDY PROGRAMMING?

Provide more information and more representative models: Khyle Eastin, recent graduate of Pomona College, alumni of School Year Abroad (SYA) China, and current Peace Corps Volunteer in rural China, said to me, "underrepresented groups (i.e., Black boys) need to be targeted." He continued,

> Drill home to both students *and* families with less exposure to these opportunities that there are significant benefits career- and education-wise to study-abroad programs—perhaps use examples of successful Black people and comb through their overseas experiences. Also noting and pointing out

that you don't need money for these opportunities—funding exists, and emphasize that.

He is so right.

Anticipate initial or even repeated rejection and skepticism: As stated above, often when Black boys (and sometimes their parents) hear about opportunities for international travel, they immediately think, "Not for me." or "That's not what we do." But teachers must recognize that this immediate rejection is often based on misunderstandings and misassumptions that need to be challenged.

Talk to Black boys: It's sometimes hard to know what might be getting in the way of a child's participation. It may be socioeconomic realities, fear of the unknown, family responsibilities, a focus on athletics, or complicated family dynamics. They may feel that travel abroad is out of reach and assume they would never be accepted to the program. Or, could it be that the type of experience that would most appeal to Black boys has not been offered? We can make some educated guesses about the practical barriers to participation for Black boys, and we can also generally understand resistance and reluctance to participate, but for a particular boy sitting right in front of us, we may never know his reality until we ask. There may be intractable personal or family issues making participation impossible, or there may be easily solvable challenges that can be met with support and guidance of a caring adult.

Build trust with students and parents: When it comes to Black families, White teachers must understand that due to historical subjugation, exclusion, and marginalization, many Black parents have developed what Cornel West (1994, p. 18) called *passionate pessimism* as an approach to working with White people and the system. This means that they are not quick to trust and are sensitive to subtle bias and prejudice. So when a Black parent's child asks for permission to travel to a foreign country or to live with a host family abroad, they might shut the idea down immediately, especially if they are unfamiliar with the adults involved and don't feel they can trust that their child will be afforded the same respect and care as his White counterparts, either by the traveling group, program representatives, trip leaders, chaperones, or the in-country hosts. Extra time taken with Black boys and their parents together can build rapport and trust and head off undue fears and misperceptions while also allowing space for the airing of valid concerns and essential questions.

ACTIVITIES FOR TEACHERS:

(1) Plan a lesson or activity where your students research countries they dream of visiting and then have a way to share what they have learned with the class, including whether their desire to visit has increased or decreased after doing their research.

(2) Plan an activity where your students conduct an interview with one or more outside professionals from organizations that plan travel or study-abroad programs. In the interview the students may inquire about participation rates of Black boys as compared to other groups, and they may also inquire about financial aid programs.

(3) Find a person of color in your network (ideally a Black male) who has traveled abroad and would be willing to share his experiences with students (in person or via internet). Have him connect you to other Black people in his network who have traveled abroad.

Before we complete this book, we have one more substantial contribution. This book focuses on White women and Black boys, for all the reasons that we explain throughout the book. While some of the lessons here are particular to Black boys, many are relevant to Black girls as well. And yet, there are particular issues that Black girls experience—particularly in relation to their White women teachers—that are specific and unique to their racial and gender background. We invited womanist researcher and Executive Director of the Girls Justice League, Dr. Charlotte Jacobs, to reflect on The Guide for White Women Who Teach Black Boys *as a whole, to comment on the aspects of the book that apply to Black girls as well, and then to write about some of the issues that are particular to Black girls that have not been covered here. This is the out-tro to this book and the intro to the one we hope comes next! Stay tuned for forthcoming* The Guide *for White Women Who Teach Black Girls.*

Outtro

Remember, Black Girls Aren't Doing "Just Fine"

Supporting Black Girls in the Classroom

Charlotte E. Jacobs

BRINGING IN THE VOICES OF BLACK GIRLS: A VIGNETTE

For the past five years, I have led various discussion groups for adolescent Black girls, and one of the topics that I ask the girls to reflect on are their experiences with education—their interactions with teachers and administrators, their school curriculum and traditions, and their relationships with their peers. After the girls describe their successes and challenges, and experiences of being both invisible and too visible, I close our time together with points to remind them of their agency and their power. I always ask the girls what they want educators to know about them, and how they think their schools can better support their needs. Here are some of their responses:

What do you wish people in your school knew about Black girls?

- "I wish they had a better understanding of why we hang out together, why we have the opinions about the school that we do, and I wish there were more teachers of color."

- "We are just as capable as a White male."

- "We're not all the same. People in the community (mainly staff) could take the time to get to know each child better."

- "I just want them to understand our feelings and take our thoughts about certain topics regarding race into consideration."

How can your school better support Black girls?

- "I wish that the school would make the topic of not only race, but any controversial topic more open for discussion."

- "Be understanding of what we go through."

- "Seeing more Black female faces in presentations, textbooks, powerpoints, books. Talking about more topics in classrooms so other students can recognize that seeing a Black face is just as normal as seeing a White face. Integration in all aspects is key!"

- "People need to be aware and conscious of microaggressions and not making assumptions based on skin color."

In reading through the narratives, classroom portraits, and recommendations for supporting Black boys in the classroom in *The Guide for White Women Who Teach Black Boys*, I was struck by how many of the themes that emerged from the chapters could also be applied to Black girls. Among the classroom realities that Black boys and girls share are: the need for teachers to reflect on their mindsets and biases about the capabilities of their students; the phenomenon of a "zero margin for error," both inside and outside of the classroom; and invisibility in the curriculum. Yet, research and practice-based conversations about Black girls' educational experiences, trajectories, and outcomes still remain on the margins of focused policy work, programming, and pedagogical practices.

As a former Black girl and now Black woman who works with Black girls in both research and practitioner arenas, it is clear to me that we can no longer continue to focus exclusively on supporting Black boys at the expense of Black girls' well-being. Recent reports such as *Unlocking Opportunity for African American Girls* (National Women's Law Center [NWLC], 2014) and *Black Girls Matter: Pushed Out, Overpoliced, and Underprotected* (African American Policy Forum [AAPF], 2015), and books such as *Pushout: The Criminalization of Black Girls in Schools* (Morris, 2016) highlight how a lack of focused data and attention on Black girls is causing educators to overlook how girls are increasingly becoming targets of excessive school disciplinary policies, sexual abuse, and violence and how they lack access to quality mental health services. Consider the 2015 video of a sixteen-year-old Black girl being slammed to the ground by a school resource officer while in class at Spring Valley High School in South Carolina and the 2014 incident in which Kiera Wilmot was arrested and threatened with school expulsion after her science project accidentally exploded (the charges were later dropped and she was allowed back in school). These events demonstrate the need for researchers, policymakers, and educators alike to focus more attention on Black girls' experiences in school.

This chapter will first explore how the idea that Black girls are "doing fine" in schools is a perpetual myth that distracts us from examining the actual state of Black girls in the U.S. education system. Next, the chapter reviews how the racial and gender socialization of Black girls often translates into a clash of norms and expectations, once they enter the classroom. Last, this chapter will close with recommendations of how White teachers, and schools more broadly, can support the education and development of Black girls.

Debunking the "Doing Fine" Myth: The State of Black Girls in U.S. Education

Like Black boys, Black girls are assigned a status in the U.S. education system that is complex, nuanced, and often overshadowed by an assumption that Black girls are "doing okay" because overall trends in their academic achievement and outcomes outpace those of their Black male peers. It is true that Black girls are enrolling in higher education programs and institutions at higher rates than all other subpopulations of students (NWLC, 2014) and that they are more likely to aspire to be leaders and to rate themselves more highly on leadership skills and ability compared to White girls (NWLC, 2014). Yet, when the educational attainment of Black girls is compared to other female populations, data in almost all states show that the high school graduation rate for Black girls is significantly lower than that of White girls and the national average for all girls (Editorial Projects in Education, 2010) and that Black girls are "retained" or "held back" a grade at a rate of 21 percent, which is twice as high as the proportion of girls overall (Ross et al., 2012). In addition, Black girls who pursue a postsecondary degree are less likely to enroll in four-year higher education institutions, and they have lower completion rates than other girl populations who enroll (National Center for Education Statistics [NCES], 2006).

The discrepancy between the comparatively high rate of Black girls enrolling in higher education institutions but then not attaining a degree speaks to a faulty pipeline issue in the K–12 arena: Black girls are graduating from high school but are not ready for college or careers. Many Black girls are attending the same schools and live in the same neighborhoods as the Black boys who are the focus of this book. Like Black boys, Black girls are less likely to have access to quality instruction and curricula that will prepare them for postsecondary education and high-earning careers (NWLC, 2014). In fact, according to National Assessment of Educational Progress [NAEP] 2013 data, 63 percent of Black girls attending U.S. high schools scored "below Basic" in math, and 39 percent scored "below Basic" in reading. In addition, Black girls who attend schools that disproportionately serve students of color have less access to higher-level math and science courses and are often taught by teachers who are unqualified (NWLC, 2014).

Another growing trend concerning Black girls in the K–12 arena is their growing presence in the school-to-prison pipeline due to zero-tolerance discipline policies in schools and schools' increased use of punitive rather than restorative responses to address situations of conflict (AAPF, 2015; Evans-Winters, 2017; Morris, 2016). According to the U.S. Department of Education's civil rights data for 2012–13, the suspension rate of Black girls is six times the suspension rate of White girls, higher than any other subpopulation of girls, and higher than the suspension rates of White, Asian, and Latino boys. Even though Black girls are 16 percent of the total U.S. female student population, they represent nearly one-third of all female school-based arrests and more than one-third of all girls referred to law enforcement (Morris, 2016). One way in which the school-to-prison pipeline functions differently for Black girls in comparison to Black boys is that Black girls are often targets of sexual harassment and bullying while at school (AAPF, 2015; NWLC, 2014). The zero-tolerance discipline policies and the failure of schools to intervene effectively on Black girls' behalf places Black girls in situations where they have to either endure the harassment or risk harsh disciplinary measures when they choose to defend themselves (AAPF, 2015).

The effects of schools' increased harsh disciplinary tactics leads to what Morris (2016) describes as a criminalization of Black girls and a phenomenon where Black girls are "pushed out" of school rather than "dropping out." The term "push-out" focuses on how school practices, policies, and systems can work to undermine the success of Black girls in schools by endorsing either a hypervigilance of Black girls' behavior and bodies, rendering them completely invisible in daily school life, or neglecting the realities of Black girls' lives outside of school, such as having family caretaking responsibilities or jobs. As a result, Black girls can feel disconnected and unsupported in school, which could lead to their decision to leave school in hopes of finding social, emotional, and financial support in other places and spaces. Black girls are not "dropping out" of school, but rather the lack of school support and attention pushes them out (AAPF, 2015; Morris, 2016).

The consequences of Black girls not having access to quality education, as well as their experience of pushout, can lead to what the *Unlocking Opportunity for African*

American Girls (NWLC, 2014) report termed the "School-to-Poverty Pathway" where they found that more than 40 percent of Black women twenty-five years of age or older without a high school diploma were living in poverty, compared to 29 percent who had a high school diploma and 8.7 percent who had a bachelor's degree or higher.

NAVIGATING THE CONTRADICTIONS: BLACK GIRL SOCIALIZATION AT HOME AND IN SCHOOL

Research on the school-to-prison pipeline and school pushout as it relates to Black girls finds that a large contributing factor to disciplinary action that could lead to suspension, expulsion, and being pushed out of school among Black girls is a result of teachers and administrators misreading the communication styles, behaviors, and emotions of Black girls (AAPF, 2015; Evans-Winters, 2017; Morris, 2016; NWLC, 2014). Scholars have found that often educators wrongly believe that Black girls need more social correction than other student subpopulations, and therefore their behaviors and actions often fall under intense scrutiny because they do not reflect accepted institutional norms, which usually stem from a White normative frame (AAPF, 2015; Evans-Winters & Esposito, 2010; Fordham, 1993; Gibson, 2015; Morris, 2007). Growing research on Black girls' experiences in school shows that Black girls are often viewed by their teachers and administrators as loud, unruly, disrespectful, and unmanageable, when often the situation was that Black girls were attempting to express their opinions and needs.

The disconnect between the dominant norms in school—that girls are expected to be quiet, respectful, and docile and to defer to authority—and Black girls' contrary behaviors speaks to the contrasting ways in which Black girls are socialized at home compared to socialization at school. Socialization can be defined as "the acquisition and reproduction of ways of being in the world" (Arrington & Stevenson, 2012, citing Pelissier, 1991, p. 81). Taking this definition into account, what most Black girls experience when they attend school is a clash between what their parents (particularly their mothers) have taught them about how to navigate the world as a Black girl and what their schools value as important in preparing them to be successful students.

Black girls learn at an early age that they live in a world that was not made for them. Society tells them that their identities of race, gender, and often class intersect to exclude them from what is valued in society: They are not boys, they do not meet White feminine beauty standards of having straight hair, light skin, and thin figures, and their class status could also place them outside of middle-class norms (Hill, 2002; Jones, 2015; Ward, 1990). In response to their "othered" status, parents often socialize their Black daughters to take on what Belgrave (2009) refers to as "androgynous" gender roles and beliefs, meaning that they possess both high masculine beliefs (being "independent, assertive, willing to take risks, a leader, and decisive" (p. 18)) and high feminine beliefs (being "emotional, attentive, caring, cooperative, and helpful" (p. 18). This androgynous gender-role identity of Black girls is advantageous: Black girls who have this type of gender role identity tend to have higher self-esteem, a higher sense of ethnic identity, and are less likely to participate in risky drug use and sexual behaviors (Belgrave, 2009).

Ward (1996) argues that Black parenting is inherently a "political act" and that "addressing racism and sexism in an open and forthright manner is essential to building psychological health in African American children" (p. 93). Ward's research with Black girls reveals that many Black parents have intentional conversations with their daughters to teach them to resist the prevalent negative stereotypes associated with being Black and female. One resistance strategy that Ward describes is how Black mothers engage in "truth telling" with their daughters: "The intent of the 'harsh critique' is 'to tell it like it is', to dismantle futile idealism, unmask illusions, and ultimately strengthen character" (p. 94). Some girls describe this truth telling as having a particular "attitude," which is "a way of forcefully expressing themselves. While it may be considered inappropriate, ineffective, or rude at times, such confident articulations force people to listen and take their thoughts and feelings seriously" (Way, 1998, p. 89).

Other research highlights the contradictory messages that Black girls receive from their parents: They are taught to be strong, assertive, hard-working, and key contributors to their community, yet they are also taught the importance of being nurturing and the need to be respectful of and submissive to White authority to succeed in life (Hill, 2002). Morris (2016) points out how the contradictory nature of these messages creates a situation where Black girls are required to "participate in identity politics that marginalize them or place them into polarizing categories: they are either 'good' girls or 'ghetto' girls who behave in ways that exacerbate stereotypes about Black femininity" (p. 10).

Because Black girls often embody androgynous gender-role beliefs, their behaviors in school often do not conform to traditional gender expectations and norms, which may cause teachers and administrators to respond more harshly to what they perceive as negative behaviors (Morris, 2016). In his study on the experiences of Black girls in school, Morris (2007) found that teachers described Black girls' behavior as "loud, defiant, and precocious"; Black girls were more likely to be reprimanded for their "unladylike" behavior compared to their White and Latina peers. Morris (2007) also found that Black girls' willingness to speak up and question school policies and practices also led teachers and administrators in their school to view them as constant threats to authority. Morris (2016) points out how this perspective of viewing Black girls as "irate," "insubordinate," "disrespectful," "uncooperative," or "uncontrollable" fails to appreciate that Black girls are actually using their voices to critically analyze and respond to encounters of injustice, discrimination, and oppression. Instead of being seen as leaders and thinkers, Black girls often receive negative feedback from teachers when they voice their opinions in the classroom. Researchers have found that this constant policing of their behaviors can lead Black girls to silence themselves or disengage from school (Fordham, 1991; Grant, 1992).

WHAT WHITE TEACHERS AND SCHOOLS CAN DO TO SUPPORT BLACK GIRLS

- **Support the achievements and contributions of your Black girl students.** Findings from the *Black Girls Matter* report (AAPF, 2015) indicate that Black girls tend to distance themselves from school in terms of motivation and engagement if they feel that they are being overlooked or undervalued in the classroom. Because Black girls are less likely to get attention in the classroom compared to other peer groups, it is important that teachers monitor their classroom practices to ensure that Black girls have an equal opportunity to participate in discussions and activities and that their achievements receive supportive recognition by teachers and peers alike.

- **Support the visibility of Black girls in the curriculum.** Research shows that students are more likely to be engaged and motivated in the classroom when the material is relevant to their own experiences (Emdin, 2016; Ladson-Billings, 2009, 2014). It is important to bring books and materials into the classroom that feature Black girls and women in leading and nonstereotypical roles. Too often in school curricula, Black girls and women are either absent, have minimal roles, or are limited to the canonical figures of Harriet Tubman, Rosa Parks, and Marian Anderson. As an example, in 2016, eleven-year-old Marley Dias led a #1000blackgirlbooks campaign (http://grassrootscommunityfoundation .org/1000-black-girl-books-resource-guide/) to collect books that had Black girls as the main characters because she was tired of reading about "White boys and their dogs." For Black girls, being able to see themselves in the curriculum from a positive and strengths-based perspective can contribute to a positive development of their self-esteem and self-image.

- **Listen to Black girls talk about their experiences in school.** To better understand how to support Black girls' development and educational needs, educators need to make space for Black girls to reflect on and critique their experiences. Much of the recent educational research that focuses on the status of Black girls in education places Black girls in the position of experts about their experiences (AAPF, 2015; Evans-Winters, 2017; Gibson, 2016). By taking the stance that Black girls are experts of their own lived experiences, educators can open the door to understand what Black girls find confusing or frustrating about their experiences, as well as what they love about being students.

- **Adopt an intersectional approach in the classroom and in school.** When working with Black girls a key goal for educators is to take the time to reflect on their own biases and assumptions to avoid playing into and reinforcing stereotypes that surround Black girls. Educators need to approach understanding and interacting with Black girls by using an intersectional lens. This means understanding that while each Black girl brings her own unique identity and personality to school each day, the presence of structural racism, sexism, classism, and heterosexism also dictates that all Black girls will share some common experiences in school. To support Black girls, educators, practitioners, and administrators need to interrogate how school practices, policies, and traditions reinforce dominant messages that continue to marginalize Black girls.

The aim of this chapter was to illustrate how, when searching for ways to make schools more equitable and inclusive spaces, the educational experiences of Black girls cannot be overlooked. Black girls often attend the same schools and live in the same neighborhoods as their Black male counterparts, leading to common experiences of low-quality education, biased assumptions and stereotypes from teachers and administrators, and invisibility in the curriculum. However, this chapter also points out how Black girls' intersecting identities of race, gender, and class lead to experiences in school that also differ from those of Black boys. Encounters with sexual harassment and the policing of Black girls' bodies and behaviors to push them to fit into a White feminine mold are unique to Black girls' experiences in school. That being said, educators can work to support Black girls by recognizing and supporting the strengths they bring with them to the classroom. Black girls' assertiveness, confidence, and leadership abilities are all traits that schools should seek to nurture so that Black girls can continue to develop as the strong, resilient, and brilliant individuals that they are.

Video Resources

In this section you will find QR links to accompanying video clips, arranged by chapter numbers or vignette titles. You may also access the videos at http://resources.corwin.com/WWBBGuide.

Introduction *What's Love Got to Do With It?*

 We're All in It Together Chapter 1. Ready To Make A Difference, The Old-Fashioned Way

Vignette: Raisins in the Sun: White Teacher as a Force of Nature Buffering the Radiation of Racial Retaliation *Being the Voice for the Dominant Society*

 Push Us Past Our Comfort Zone Chapter 2. The State of the White Woman Teacher

Vignette: Two Black Boys *With Black Teachers the Results Are Different*

 The Work Is Forever Chapter 4. Understanding Unconscious Bias As One More Tool In The Committed White Teacher's Equity Toolkit

(Continued)

(Continued)

Chapter 5. White Female Teachers And Black Boys: Right Teachers And (Mis)Understood Boys		*No Preparation, Just High Stakes*
	I'm Not Who I Thought I Was Going to Be as a Teacher	Chapter 6. White Racial Identity Development
Chapter 7. What if being called "racist" is the beginning, not the end, of the conversation?		*Competence Matters*
	Lifelong Learning Is Key	Chapter 8. What does it mean to be a White teacher?
Chapter 9. Respecting Black Boys And Their History		*Don't Be Afraid*
	Cs Aren't Better	Chapter 17. White Privilege and Black Excellence: Two Terms I've been "Afraid of for Much of My Life
Vignette: I Had a Right		*I Knew From Other People He Was a Troublemaker*
	There Are Different Kinds of Oppression	Chapter 18. Black Boys And Their Racial Identity: Learning How They Fit Into Society and in Your Classroom

Chapter 19. Teaching Black Boys During Childhood: A Counternarrative And Considerations

Inviting in the Whole Student

Pathologizing Black Boys

Chapter 21. The N!gga(er) In Me

Chapter 23. White Teachers and the Power To Transform: Early Childhood Educators and the Potential for Lasting Harm

It's Going to Take All of Us to Change the Reality

How Can I Be an Advocate for a Black Queer Boy

Chapter 24. Learn About Us Before You Teach (About) Us: Queer Black Boys

Chapter 9. Respecting Black Boys and Their History

I Was Taught Egypt Was Not a Part of Africa

People Want to Be Seen, to Be Validated

Chapter 10. "I Can Switch My Language, But I Can't Switch My Skin": What Teachers Must Understand About Linguistic Racism

Chapter 11. Identity Safety as an Antidote to Stereotype Threat

These Kids Are Exceptional

Understand the Culture of Black Children

Chapter 12. The Science Behind Psychological Verve and What It Means for Black Students

(Continued)

(Continued)

 Chapter 13. The Visit

#FearofBlackness

 Expectations and Building Community

Chapter 14. Rewriting the Narrative

Chapter 15. "Don't Lean—*Jump* In": The Fierce Urgency to Confront, Dismantle, and (Re)Write the Historical Narrative of Black Boys in Educational Institutions

 How Is This Inequity So Present?

 Don't Be a Stranger

Chapter 26. Helping Amazing Black Boys Become Amazing Black Men

Chapter 27. Connecting With Black Students and Parents: Equal Vision

 Communicate Respect

 He Has to Live With It Every Day, Every Moment

Vignette: Being a Black Mom of Black Boys

Chapter 28. Activating Inclusiveness

 Teacher and Student Connections Matter

 Community in the Classrooms

Chapter 29. Belief, Pedagogy, And Practice: Strategies for Building Powerful Classroom Communities

Vignette: The Symbolic Teacher

 You've Got to Investigate You

My Kids Conformed

Chapter 30. Ruminations From the Intersections of a #Blackmommyactivist

Chapter 31. Find Freedom in the Classroom: A Love Letter to My Babies' Teachers

 Listen to Young People, the Whole Dynamic Can Change

 High Expectations

Chapter 32. Start Out Firm

Chapter 33. A Parable of Academic Misgivings: The Educator's Role in Addressing College Undermatch

 Love Reflect Grow Repeat

 Hanging Demographics

Chapter 34. The Collusion of Social Norms and Working With Interracial Families

Chapter 35. What Are We Doing to Support "These" Students to Meet Their Potential?

 It Takes Leaving the Classroom

 They Just Aren't Being Nurtured the Way That They Should

Chapter 36. ADD/ADHD Overidentification and How Black Cultural Styles Are Often Confused for ADD

Chapter 38. Strategies That De-Escalate Conflict in the Classroom

 Everyday, All Day

(Continued)

(Continued)

 It's Important to Understand Systemic Racism

Chapter 43. Global Skills: Beyond the Classroom and the Playground

Outtro: Remember, Black Girls Aren't Doing "Just Fine": Supporting Black Girls in the Classroom

 Looking at Black Kids Differently Than White Kids

THE GUIDE FOR WHITE WOMEN WHO TEACH BLACK BOYS

References

FRONT MATTER

FOREWORD 1

Cross, W. E. (1991). *Shades of black: Diversity in African-American identity.* Philadelphia: Temple University Press.

Duncan, G. A. (2002). Beyond love: A critical race ethnography of the schooling of adolescent black males. *Equity and Excellence in Education, 35*(2), 131–143.

Hilliard, A. G. (1995). *The maroon within us: Selected essays on African American community socialization.* Baltimore, MD: Black Classic Press.

Singleton, G. E. (2015). *Courageous conversations about race: A field guide for achieving equity in schools.* Thousand Oaks, CA: Corwin.

INTRODUCTION

American Association of Colleges for Teacher Education. (2013). The changing teacher preparation profession: A report from AACTE's Professional Education Data System (PEDS). Washington, D.C.: Author.

Burgstahler, S. (2015). *Equal access: Universal design of instruction.* Seattle: University of Washington. http://www.washington.edu/doit/equal-access-universal-design-instruction. Accessed on June 11, 2017.

Ferguson, A. A. (2000). *Bad Boys: Public schools in the making of Black masculinity.* Ann Arbor: University of Michigan Press.

Goldring, R., Gray, L., & Bitterman, A. (2013). *Characteristics of public and private elementary and secondary school teachers in the United States: Results from the 2011–12 schools and staffing survey* (NCES 2013-314). U.S. Department of Education. Washington, DC: National Center for Education Statistics. Retrieved September 25, 2015, from http://nces.ed.gov/pubsearch

Harper, S. R. (2015). Black male college achievers and resistant responses to racist stereotypes at predominantly White colleges and universities. *Harvard Educational Review, 85*(4), 646–674.

Kena, G., Musu-Gillette, L., Robinson, J., Wang, X., Rathbun, A., Zhang, J., Wilkinson-Flicker, S., Barmer, A., & Dunlop Velez, E. (2015). *The condition of education 2015* (NCES 2015–144). U.S. Department of Education, National Center for Education Statistics. Washington, DC. Retrieved September 25, 2015, from http://nces.ed.gov/pubsearch

Kimmel, M. S. (2000). *"What about the boys?" What the current debates tell us and don't tell us about boys in school.* Wellsley, MA: Centers for Research on Women.

Lopez, I. H. (1997). *White by law: The legal construction of race.* New York: NYU Press.

Schott Foundation. (2010). *Yes we can: The Schott 50 state report on public education and Black males.* Retrieved September 25, 2015, from Black Boys Report: http://blackboysreport .org/bbreport.pdfhttp://blackboysreport.org/bbreport.pdf

Stevenson, H.C. (2013). *Promoting Racial LIteracy in Schools.* New York: Teachers College Press

Toldson, I. (2012). *Show me the numbers: Do black kids have problems in schools because so few teachers look like them?* Retrieved October 3, 2015, from http://www.theroot.com/ articles/culture/2012/10/how_race_matters_in_the_classroom.2.htmlhttp://www.theroot .com/articles/culture/2012/10/how_race_matters_in_the_classroom.2.html

U.S. Bureau of Labor. (2011, August). *Women in the labor force: A data book.* (Report No. 1034). Retrieved September 25, 2015, from Bureau of Labor Statistics. Online via GPO Access: http:// www.bls.gov/cps/wlf-databook-2011.pdf http://www.bls.gov/cps/wlf-databook-2011.pdf

PART I

CHAPTER 2

Albert Shanker Institute. (2014). *The state of diversity in education: Selected findings.* Washington DC: Author.

Broughman, S., Goldring, R., Gray, L., & Bitterman, A. (2013). *Characteristics of public and private elementary and secondary school teachers in the United States: Results from the 2011–12 schools and staffing survey.* Washington, DC: National Center for Educational Statistics.

Carpenter-Ford, A., & Sassi, K. (2014). Authority in cross-racial teaching and learning (re)considering the transferability of warm demander approaches. *Urban Education. 49*(1), 39–74.

Christensen, Linda. (2000). *Reading, writing, and rising up.* Milwaukee, WI: Rethinking Schools.

Emdin, C. (2016). *For white folks who teach in the hood and the rest of y'all too: Reality pedagogy and urban education.* Boston, MA: Beacon Press.

Papageorge, N., Gershenson, S., & Holt, S. B. (2016). Who believes in me? The effect of student-teacher demographic match on teacher expectations. *Economics of Education Review, 52,* 209–224.

Pica, R. (2014, February 3). Can white educators successfully teach black boys? *The Huffington Post.*

Woods, L. (2010). *Black male students in the minds of white female teachers: A phenomenological examination of how white female teachers construct their attitudes about black male students.* Retrieved from ProQuest Digital Dissertations. (3448621)

Zamora, K. (2016, May 16). Teacher of the year breaks the mold. *Minneapolis Star and Tribune.*

CHAPTER 3

Digest of Education Statistics. (2012). *Fall 2001 and Spring 2007 through Spring 2012, Graduation Rates component* (This table was prepared November 2012.). Washington, DC: U.S. Department of Education, National Center for Education Statistics, Integrated Postsecondary Education Data System (IPEDS).

Harris, F., III, Bensimon, E. M., & Bishop, R. (2010). The Equity Scorecard: A process for building institutional capacity to educate young men of color. In C. Edley, Jr. & J. Ruiz de Velasco (Eds.), *Changing places: How communities will improve the health of boys of color* (pp. 277–308). Berkeley: University of California Press.

National Assessment of Educational Progress. (2013). *2013 Mathematics and Reading Assessment.* Washington, DC: National Center for Education Statistics.

Schott Foundation. (2012). *The urgency of now: The Schott 50 state report on public education and Black males.* Cambridge, MA: Author.

U.S. Department of Education. (2009). *2003-04 beginning postsecondary students longitudinal study, second follow-up* (BPS:04/09) (Computation by NCES PowerStats on 7/31/2014). Washington, DC: National Center for Education Statistics.

White House. (2014). *My Brother's Keeper.* Retrieved June 2, 2014, from: http://www.whitehouse .gov/my-brothers-keeper

Chapter 4

Biernat, M., & Manis, M. (1994). Shifting standards and stereotype-based judgments. *Journal of Personality and Social Psychology, 66*(1), 5–20.

Comaford, C. (2016, June 25). How to work with unconscious bias in your organization. *Forbes.com.* Retrieved from https://www.forbes.com/sites/christinecomaford/2016/06/25/how-leaders-bust-unconscious-biases-in-business/#1e84e9822c66

Devine, P. (1989). Stereotypes and prejudice: Their automatic and controlled components. *Journal of Personality and Social Psychology, 56*(1), 5–18.

Dixon, T. L., & Linz, D. (2000). Overrepresentation and underrepresentation of African Americans and Latinos as lawbreakers on television news. *Journal of Communication, 50*(2), 131–154.

Fort, D. C., & Varney, H. L. (1989). How students see scientists: Mostly male, mostly white, and mostly benevolent. *Science & Children, 26*(8), 8–13.

Gillam, W. S., Maupin, A. N., Reyes, C. R., Accavitti, M., & Shic, F. (2016, September 28). *Do early educators' implicit biases regarding sex and race relate to behavior expectations and recommendations of preschool expulsions and suspensions?* (Yale University Child Study Center Research Brief). New Haven, CT: Yale University. Retrieved from http://ziglercenter.yale.edu/publications/ Preschool%20Implicit%20Bias%20Policy%20Brief_final _9_26_276766_5379.pdf

Goff, P. A., Jackson, M. C., Allison, B., Di Leone, L., Culotta, C. M., & DiTomasso, N. A. (2014). The essence of innocence: Consequences of dehumanizing Black children. *Journal of Personality and Social Psychology, 106*(4), 526–545.

Green, A. R., Carney, D. R., Pallin, D. J., Ngo, L .H., Raymond, K. L., Iezzoni, L. I., & Banaji, M. R. (2007). Implicit bias among physicians and its prediction of thrombolysis decisions for black and white patients. *Society of General Internal Medicine, 22*(9), 1231–1238.

Kang, J. (2009, August). *Implicit bias: A primer for courts.* Williamsburg, VA: National Center for State Courts. Retrieved from http://www.americanbar.org/content/dam/aba/migrated/ sections/criminaljustice/PublicDocuments/unit_3_kang.authcheckdam.pdf

Neal, L. V. I., McCray, A. D., Webb-Johnson, G., & Bridgest, S. T. (2003). The effects of African American movement styles on teachers' perceptions and reactions. *The Journal of Special Education, 37(1), 49–57.*

Rachlinski, J. J., & Johnson, S. L. (2009). Does unconscious racial bias affect trial judges? *Notre Dame Law Review, 84*(3), 1195–1246.

Reeves, A. N. (2014). *Written in black & white: exploring confirmation bias in racialized perceptions of writing skills.* Chicago: Nextions Yellow Paper Series. Retrieved from http://www.nextions.com/wp-content/files_mf/14468226472014040114WritteninBlackandWhiteYPS.pdf

Rudd, T. (2014, February). *Racial disproportionality in school discipline implicit bias is heavily implicated* (Kirwan Institute Issue Brief). Columbus: The Ohio State University. Retrieved from http://kirwaninstitute.osu.edu/wp-content/uploads/2014/02/racial-disproportionality-schools-02.pdf

Staats, C. (2015, Winter). Understanding implicit bias: What educators should know. *American Educator, Winter,* pp. 29–43.

Steele, C. M., & Aronson, J. (1995). Stereotype threat and the intellectual performance of African Americans. *Journal of Personality and Social Psychology, 69*(5), 797–811.

Sue, D. W., Capodilupo, C. M., Torino, G. C., Bucceri, J. M., Holder, A. M., Nadal, K. L., & Esquilin, M. (2007). Racial microaggressions in everyday life: Implications for clinical practice. *American Psychologist, 62*(4), 271–286.

Todd, A. R., Bodenhausen, G. V., Richeson, J. A., & Galinsky, A. D. (2011). Perspective taking combats automatic expressions of racial bias. *Journal of Personality and Social Psychology, 100(6),* 1027–1042.

Todd, A. R. Thiem, K. C., & Neel, R. (2016). Does seeing faces of young black boys facilitate the identification of threatening stimuli? *Psychological Science, 27, 384–393.*

Toppo, G. (2016, September 28). Study: Teachers' 'implicit bias' starts in preschool. *USA Today.com.* Retrieved from https://www.usatoday.com/story/news/2016/09/28/study-teachers-implicit-bias-starts-preschool/91179538/

U.S. Department of Education, Office of Civil Rights (2014, March). Civil rights data collection. *Data snapshot: School discipline* (Issues Brief No. 1). Retrieved from http://ocrdata.ed.gov/Downloads/CRDC-School-Discipline-Snapshot.pdf

CHAPTER 5

Deiro, J. A. (1994). *What teachers do to nurture bonding with students.* Unpublished doctoral dissertation, University of Washington, Seattle, WA.

Delpit, L. (1988). The silenced dialogue: Power and pedagogy in educating other people's children. *Harvard Educational Review, 58*(3), 280–299.

Du Bois, W., & Edwards, B. H. (2008). *The souls of black folk.* Oxford, UK: Oxford University Press.

Fordham, S., & Ogbu, J. U. (1986). Black students' school success: Coping with the "burden of 'acting white'". *The Urban Review, 18*(3), 176–206.

Howard, T. C. (2001). Telling their side of the story: African-American students' perceptions of culturally relevant teaching. *The Urban Review, 33*(2), 131–149.

Ladson-Billings, G. (1994). *The dreamkeepers: Successful teachers of African American students.* San Francisco, CA: Jossey-Bass, Inc. A Wiley Company.

Lee, C. D. (2005). The state of knowledge about the education of African Americans. *Black education: A transformative research and action agenda for the new century* (pp. 45–72). Mahwah,NJ: Lawrence Erlbaum.

Slaughter-Defoe, D. T., & Carlson, K. G. (1996). Young African American and Latino children in high-poverty urban schools: How they perceive school climate. *Journal of Negro Education, 65,* 60–70.

West, C. (2004). *Democracy matters: Winning the fight against imperialism.* New York: Penguin Books.

Chapter 6

Helms, J. (2007). *A race is a nice thing to have*. Hanover: Microtraining Associates.

hooks, b. (1995). *Killing rage: Ending racism*. New York: Henry Holt.

King, M. L. (1956). Facing the challenge of a new age. *The Phylon Quarterly, 18*(1), 25–34.

Tatum, B. D. (2003). *Why are all the Black kids sitting together in the cafeteria?* New York: Basic Books.

Chapter 7

DiAngelo, R. (2011). White fragility. *International Journal of Critical Pedagogy. 3*(3), 54–70.

Dovidio, J., Gaertner, S. L., Ufkes, E. G., Saguy, T., & Pearson, A. R. (2016). Included but invisible? Subtle bias, common identity, and the darker side of "we." *Social Issues and Policy Review, 10*(1), 6–46.

Frankenberg, R. (1993). *White women, race matters: The social construction of Whiteness*. Minneapolis: University of Minnesota Press.

Gonzalez, N., Moll, L. C., & Amanti, C. (Eds.). (2005). *Funds of knowledge: Theorizing practices in households, communities, and classrooms*. New York: Routledge.

Gorski, P. (2013). *Reaching and teaching students in poverty*. New York: Teachers College Press.

Helms, J. (1992). A race is a nice thing to have: *A guide to being a White person or understanding the White persons in your life*. Topeka, KA: Content Communications.

McIntosh, P. (1998). *White privilege and male privilege: A personal account of coming to see correspondences through work in women's studies*. Wellesley, MA: Center for Research on Women.

McIntyre, A. (1997). *Making meaning of Whiteness*. Albany: State University of New York Press.

Palmer, P. (1998). *The courage to teach*. San Francisco: Jossey-Bass.

Stevenson, H. (2013). *Promoting racial literacy in schools*. New York: Teachers College Press.

REFERENCES FOR TRANSITION PIECES

Bartoli, E., Michael, A., Bentley-Edwards, K. L., Stevenson, H. C., Shor, R. E., & McClain, S. E. (2016). Training for colour-blindness: White racial socialization. *Whiteness and Education, 1*(2), 1–12).

Hamm, J. V. (2001). Barriers and bridges to positive cross-ethnic relations: African American and White parent socialization beliefs and practices. *Youth and Society, 33*, 62–98.

Sue, D.W. (2006). The invisible whiteness of being: Whiteness, white supremacy, white privilege, and racism. In M. G. Constantine & D. W. Sue (Eds.), *Addressing racism: Facilitating cultural competence in mental health and educational settings* (pp. 15–30). Hoboken, NJ: Wiley and Sons.

Part 2

Chapter 9

Browder, A. (2007). *Nile Valley contributions to civilization*. Washington, DC: Institute of Karmic Guidance.

Carson, C. (1987). *Eyes on the prize: America's civil rights years: A reader and guide*. New York: Penguin Books.

Kunjufu, J. (1983). *Countering the conspiracy to destroy Black boys* (1st ed.). Chicago: Afro-Am Pub.

Kunjufu, J. (2005). *Keeping Black boys out of special education* (1st ed.). Chicago: African American Images.

Kunjufu, J. (2007). *Raising Black boys* (1st ed.). Chicago: African American Images.

Kunjufu, J. (2010). *Reducing the Black male dropout rate.* Chicago: African American Images.

Kunjufu, J. (2011). *Understanding Black male learning styles.* Chicago: African American Images.

Kunjufu, J. (2013). *Changing school culture for Black males.* Chicago Heights, IL: African American Images.

James, G. (1992). *Stolen legacy: Greek philosophy is stolen Egyptian philosophy* (First Africa World Press ed.). Trenton, NJ: Africa World Press, Inc.

Van Sertima, I. (1976). *They came before Columbus* (First ed.). New York: Random House.

Williams, C. (1987). *The destruction of Black civilization: Great issues of a race from 4500 B.C. to 2000 A.D.* (Rev. ed.). Chicago: Third World Press.

Yardley, J. (1931). *Before the Mayflower.* New York: Doubleday, Doran.

CHAPTER 10

Alim, H. S., Rickford, J. R., & Ball, A. (2016). *Raciolinguistics: How language shapes our ideas about race.* New York: Oxford University Press.

Alim, H. S., & Smitherman, G. (2012). *Articulate while Black: Barack Obama, language, and race in the U.S.* New York: Oxford University Press.

Baker-Bell, A. (2013). "I never really knew the history behind African American language": Critical language pedagogy in an Advanced Placement English language arts class. In K. C. Turner & D. Ives (Eds.), Social justice approaches to African American language and literacy practices [Special issue]. *Equity & Excellence in Education, 46*(3), 355–370.

Charity Hudley, M., & Mallinson, C. (2014). *We do language: English language variation in the secondary English classroom.* New York: Teachers College Press.

CEE Executive Committee. (2009). Conference on English Education Position Statement: Supporting Linguistically and Culturally Diverse Learners in English Education. Retrieved from NCTE.org.

Flores, N., & Rosa, J. (2015). Undoing appropriateness: Raciolinguistic ideologies and language diversity in education. *Harvard Educational Review, 85*(2), 149–171. doi:10.17763/0017-8055.85.2.149

Green, L. (2004). African American English. In E. Finegan & J. Rickford (Eds.), *Language in the USA: Themes for the twenty-first century.* Cambridge, UK: Cambridge University Press.

Haddix, M. (2015). *Cultivating racial and linguistic diversity in literacy teacher education: Teachers like me.* New York & Urbana, IL: Routledge & National Council of Teachers of English.

Johnson, L. L., Jackson, J., Stovall, D., & Baszile, D. T. (2017). "Loving blackness to death": (Re)Imagining ELA classrooms in a time of racial chaos. *English Journal.* In press.

Kynard, C. (2013). Vernacular insurrections: Black protest, and the new century in composition-literacies studies. Albany: SUNY Press.

Lippi-Green, R. (2012). English with an accent: Language, ideology, and discrimination in the United States. New York: Routledge.

Martinez, D. (2017). Imagining a language of solidarity for Black and Latinx youth in English language arts classrooms. *English Education, 49*(2), 179–196.

Paris, D. (2016). "It was a Black city": African American language in California's changing urban schools and communities. In H. S. Alim, J. R. Rickford, & A. Ball (Eds.), *Raciolinguistics: How language shapes our ideas about race.* New York: Oxford University Press.

Pimentel, C. (2011). The color of language: The racialized educational trajectory of an emerging bilingual student. *Journal of Latinos and Education, 10*(4), 335–353.

Rickford, J. R. (1997). Suite for ebony and phonics. *Discover magazine.* Retrieved from http://discovermagazine.com/1997/dec/suiteforebonyand1292

Rickford, J. R. (2002). *How linguists approach the study of language and dialect.* Unpublished manuscript, Department of Linguistics, Stanford University, Stanford, CA.

Smitherman, G. (2006). *Word from the mother: Language and African Americans.* New York: Routledge.

Young, V. A., Barrett, R., Young-Rivera, Y., & Lovejoy, K. (2014). *Other people's English: Code-meshing, code-switching, and African American literacy.* New York: Teacher's College Press.

Wheeler, R. S., & Swords, R. (2006). *Code-switching: Teaching standard English in urban classrooms.* Urbana, IL: NCTE.

Wheeler. R. S., & Swords, R. (2010). *Code-switching lessons: Grammar strategies for linguistically diverse writers.* Portsmouth, NH: Firsthand Heinemann.

Williams, B. (2013). Students' "write" to their own language: Teaching the African American verbal tradition as a rhetorically effective writing skill. In K. C. Turner & D. Ives (Eds.), Social justice approaches to African American language and literacy practices [Special issue]. *Equity & Excellence in Education, 46*(3), 411–427.

CHAPTER 11

Cohen, G. L., & Steele, C. M. (2002). A barrier of mistrust: How stereotypes affect cross-race mentoring. In J. Aronson (Ed.) *Improving academic achievement: Impact of psychological factors on education* (pp. 305–331). Oxford, UK: Academic Press.

Cohen, G. L., Steele, C. M., & Ross, L. D. (1999). The mentor's dilemma: Providing critical feedback across the racial divide. *Personality and Social Psychology Bulletin, 25,* 1302–1318.

Gutiérrez, K., & Rogoff, B. (2003). Cultural ways of learning: Individual traits or repertoires of practice. *Educational Researcher, 32*(5), 19–25. doi:10.3102/0013189X032005019

Hammond, Z. (2015). *Culturally responsive teaching and the brain, promoting authentic engagement and rigor among culturally and linguistically diverse students.* Thousand Oaks, CA: Corwin.

Ladson-Billings, G. (1999). Just what is critical race theory, and what's it doing in a nice field like education? In L. Parker, D. Deyhele, & S. Villenas (Eds.), *Race is. Race isn't: Critical race theory and qualitative studies in education* (pp. 7–30). Boulder, CO: Westview Press.

Markus, H. R., Steele, C. M., & Steele, D. M. (2000). Colorblindness as a barrier to inclusion: Assimilation and nonimmigrant minorities. *Daedalus, 129*(4), 233–259.

National Education Association. (2011). *Race against time: Educating Black boys.* Retrieved from http://www.nea.org/assets/docs/educatingblackboys11rev.pdf

Steele, C. M. (1999). *Secrets of the SAT* Frontline Interview *(para. 33).* Public Broadcasting System. Retrieved from http://www.pbs.org/wgbh/pages/frontline/shows/sats/interviews/steele.html

Steele, C. M. (2010). *Whistling Vivaldi: How stereotypes affect us and what we can do.* New York: W. W. Norton.

Steele, C. M., & Aronson, J. (1995). Stereotype threat and the intellectual test performance of African-Americans. *Journal of Personality and Social Psychology, 69,* 797–811.

Steele, D. M., & Cohn-Vargas, B. (2013). *Identity safe classrooms: Places to belong and learn.* Thousand Oaks, CA: Corwin.

Stroessner, S., & Good, C. (2009). *What is stereotype threat?* Retrieved from http://reducingstereo typethreat.org/definition.html

CHAPTER 12

Allen, B. (1987). *Differential effects of low and high sensate stimulation and movement affordance on the learning of Black and White working-class children* (Unpublished doctoral dissertation). Howard University, Washington, DC.

Bailey, C. (2001). The role of task variability and home contextual factors in the academic performance and task motivation of African American elementary school children. *Journal of Negro Education, 70*(1–2), 84–95.

Bailey, C. (1998). *Facilitating effects of physical stimulation on the academically relevant task performance and motivation of African American and European-American school children* (Unpublished doctoral dissertation). Howard University, Washington, DC.

Boykin, A. W. (1994). Afrocultural expression and its implications for school. In E. Hollins, J. King, & W. Hayman (Eds.), *Teaching diverse populations: Formulating a knowledge base* (pp. 243–274). Albany: State University of New York Press.

Boykin, A. W. (1986). The triple quandary and the schooling of Afro-American children. In U. Neisser (Ed.), *The school achievement of minority children* (pp. 57–92). Hillsdale, NJ: Erlbaum.

Boykin, A. W. (1983). The academic performance of Afro-American children. In J. T. Spence (Ed.), *Achievement and achievement motives: Psychological and sociological approach* (pp. 350–381). San Francisco, CA: Freeman.

Boykin, A. W. (1982). Task variability and the performance of Black and White schoolchildren: Vervistic explorations. *Journal of Black Studies, 12,* 469–485.

Boykin, A. W. (1979). Psychological/behavioral verve: Some theoretical explorations and empirical manifestations. In A. W. Boykin, A. J. Franklin, & J. F. Yates (Eds.), *Research directions of Black psychologists* (pp.). New York: Russell Sage.

Boykin, A. W., & Allen, B. A. (1988). Rhythmic-movement facilitation of learning in working-class Afro-American children. *Journal of Genetic Psychology, 149*(3), 335–347.

Boykin, A. W., & Bailey, C. (2000, April). *The role of cultural factors in school relevant cognitive functioning: Synthesis of findings on cultural context, cultural orientations, and individual differences* (Technical Report No. 42). Washington, DC: Author.

Boykin, A. W., & Noguera, P. (2011). *Creating the opportunity to learn: Moving from research to practice to close the achievement gap.* Alexandria, VA: ASCD.

Bullard, C. (1987). *Task persistence of educationally successful and educationally at-risk fourth grade African American boys* (Unpublished master's thesis). Howard University, Washington, DC.

Ellison, C.M., Boykin, A. W., Towns, D. P., & Stokes, A. (2000, May). *Classroom cultural ecology: The dynamics of classroom life in schools serving low-income African American children* (ERIC Number: ED442886). Washington, DC: Center for Research on the Education of Students Placed at Risk.

Erwin, H. E., Abel, M. G., Beighle, A., & Beets, M.W. (2011). Promoting children's health through physically active math classes: A pilot study. *Health Promotion Practice, 12*(2), 244–251.

Griffin, A. (2004). *The effect of vervistic instructional strategies on academic engagement, immediate and long-term comprehension* (Unpublished master's thesis). Howard University, Washington, DC.

Gregory, A., & Thompson, A. R. (2010). African American high school students and variability in behavior across classrooms. *Journal of Community Psychology, 38*(3), 386–402.

Hart, L. (1987). *The relationship between home, environmental, child attribute and school related factors for working class Afro-American children* (Unpublished master's thesis). Howard University, Washington, DC.

Martin, R., & Murtagh, E.M. (2015). An intervention to improve the physical activity levels of children: Design and rationale of the 'Active Classrooms' cluster randomized controlled trial. *Contemporary Clinical Trials, 41*, 180–191.

Pas, E. T., Larson, K. E., Reinke, W. M., Herman, K. C., & Bradshaw, C. P. (2016). Implementation and acceptability of an adapted classroom check-up coaching model to promote culturally responsive classroom management. *Education and Treatment of Children, 39*(4), 467–492.

Rohrer, D., Dedrick, R. F., & Stershic, S. (2015). Interleaved practice improves mathematics learning. *Journal of Educational Psychology, 107*(3), 900–908.

Sana, F., Yan, V. X., & Kim, J. A. (2016). Study sequence matters for the inductive learning of cognitive concepts. *Journal of Educational Psychology, 109*(1), 84–98.

Scott, D. M. (2006). *The impact of background stimulation and variability on academically relevant outcomes for low income African American students* (Unpublished doctoral dissertation). Howard University, Washington, DC.

Tuck, K., & Boykin, A. W. (1989). Task performance and receptiveness to variability in Black and White low-income children. In A. Harrison (Ed.), *The eleventh conference on empirical research in Black psychology*. Washington, DC: NIMH Publications.

Tyler, K. M., Boykin, A. W., Miller, O. A., & Hurley, E. (2006). Cultural values in the home and school experiences of low-income African-American students. *Social Psychology of Education, 9*(4), 363–380.

Walton, S. (1994). *Verve effects: The influence of cultural attributes, task variability and background stimulation on the task performance of African American schoolchildren* (Unpublished master's thesis). Howard University, Washington, DC.

Walton, S. (1998). *Verve effects: The influence of cultural attributes, task variability, and background stimulation on task performance of African-American and European-American schoolchildren* (Unpublished doctoral dissertation). Howard University, Washington, DC.

CHAPTER 13

Bourdieu, P. (2001). *Masculine domination* (R. Nice, Trans.). Stanford, CA: Stanford University Press.

Dumas, M. J. (2016). Against the dark: Antiblackness in education policy and discourse. *Theory Into Practice, 55*(1), 11–19.

Entman, R. M., & Rojecki, A. (2001). *The black image in the white mind: Media and race in America.* Chicago: University of Chicago Press.

Henry, K. L., & Warren, C. A. (2017). The evidence of things *not* seen? Race, pedagogies of discipline, and White women teachers. In S. D. Hancock & C. A. Warren (Eds.), *White women's work: Examining the intersectionality of teaching, identity, and race* (pp. 177–199). Charlotte, NC: Information Age Publishing.

Howard, T. C. (2008). Who really cares? The disenfranchisement of African American males in preK–12 schools: A critical race theory perspective. *Teachers College Record, 110*(5), 954–985.

Howard, T. C. (2014). *Why race and culture matter in schools.* New York: Teachers College Press.

Jackson, I., Sealey-Ruiz, Y., & Watson, W. (2014). Reciprocal love: Mentoring Black and Latino males through an ethos of care. *Urban Education*, *49*(4), 394–417.

Neal, L. V. I., McCray, A. D., Webb-Johnson, G., & Bridgest, S. T. (2003). The effects of African American movement styles on teachers' perceptions and reactions. *Journal of Special Education*, *37*(1), 49–57.

Noguera, P. A. (2003). Schools, prisons, and social implications of punishment: Rethinking disciplinary practices. *Theory Into Practice*, *42*(4), 341–350.

Powell, T. (2014, July 24). *My son has been suspended five times. He's 3*. Retrieved January 08, 2017, from https://www.washingtonpost.com/posteverything/wp/2014/07/24/my-son-has-been-suspended-five-times-hes-3/?utm_term=.857b09517e01

Warren, C. A. (2014). Towards a pedagogy for the application of empathy in culturally diverse classrooms. *The Urban Review*, *46*(3), 395–419.

Warren, C. A., & Lessner, S. (2014). "Who has family business?" Exploring the role of empathy in student-teacher interactions. *Perspectives on Urban Education*, *11*(2), 122–131.

Watson, W., Sealey-Ruiz, Y., & Jackson, I. (2014). Daring to care: The role of culturally relevant care in mentoring Black and Latino male high school students. *Race Ethnicity and Education*, 1–23.

Waytz, A., Hoffman, K. M., & Trawalter, S. (2015). A superhumanization bias in Whites' perceptions of Blacks. *Social Psychological and Personality Science*, *6*(3), 352–359.

CHAPTER 14

Comer, J. P. (2004). *Leave no child behind: Preparing today's youth for tomorrow's world*. New Haven, CT: Yale University Press.

Ferguson, R. F. (2008). Helping students of color meet high standards. In M. Pollock (Ed.), *Everyday anti-racism*. New York: The New Press.

Stevenson, B. (2014). *Just mercy: A story of justice and redemption*. New York: Spiegel & Grau.

VIGNETTE REFERENCES

Cleaver, E. (1968). *Soul on ice*. New York: Dell.

CHAPTER 15

Delpit, L. D. (1995). *Other people's children: Cultural conflict in the classroom*. New York: New Press.

Foucault, M. (1979). *Discipline and punish: The birth of the prison*. New York: Vintage Books.

King, M. L. (1967). *Beyond Vietnam: A time to break silence*. Speech given at Riverside Church on April 5, 1967, New York City. Retrieved from http://www.hartford-hwp.com/archives/45a/058.html

Little, S. D. (2005). *"Death at the hands of persons known": Victimage rhetoric and the 1922 Dyer anti-lynching bill* (Doctoral Dissertation). Indiana University.

Steele, C. M., & Aronson, J. (1995). Stereotype threat and the intellectual test-performance of African-Americans. *Journal of Personality and Social Psychology*, *69*(5), 797–811.

PART 3

CHAPTER 18

Cross, W. E., Jr. (1991). *Shades of black: Diversity in African American identity*. Philadelphia: Temple University Press.

Cross, W. E., Jr. (1995). The psychology of nigrescence: Revising the Cross model. In J. G. Ponterotto, J. M. Casas, L. A. Suzuki, & C. M. Alexander (Eds.), *Handbook of multicultural counseling* (pp. 93–122). Thousand Oaks, CA: Sage.

Sellers, R. M., Smith, M. A., Shelton, J. N., Rowley, S. A., & Chavous, T. M. (1998). Multidimensional model of racial identity: A reconceptualization of African American racial identity. *Personality and Social Psychology Review, 2*(1), 18–39.

CHAPTER 19

Dumas M., & Nelson, J. (2016). (Re)imagining Black boyhood: Toward a critical framework for educational research. *Harvard Educational Review, 86*(1), 27–47.

Ferguson, A. (2000). *Bad boys: Public schools and the making of Black masculinity*. Ann Arbor: University of Michigan Press.

Mooney, C. G. (2013). *Theories of childhood: An introduction to Dewey, Montessori, Erikson, Piaget, and Vygotsky* (2nd ed.). St. Paul, MN: Red Leaf Press.

Nelson, J. (2016). Relational teaching with Black boys: Strategies for learning at a single-sex middle school for boys of color. *Teachers College Record, 118,* 1–30.

Reichert, M., & Hawley, R. (2010). *Reaching boys, teaching boys: Strategies that work*. San Francisco, CA: Jossey-Bass.

Reichert, M., & Hawley, R. (2014). *I can learn from you: Boys as relational learners*. Cambridge, MA: Harvard Education Press.

Reichert, M., & Nelson, J. (in press). I Want to Learn From You: Relational strategies to engage boys in schooling. In N. Way, A. Ali, C. Gilligan, & P. Noguera (Eds.), *The crisis of connection: Causes, consequences, and solutions*. New York: New York University Press.

Wood, R. (2010). *Yardsticks: Children in the classroom ages 4–14*. Turners Falls, MA: Northeastern Foundation for Children, Inc.

CHAPTER 20

Johnson, L. (2002). "My eyes have been opened": White teachers and racial awareness. *Journal of Teacher Education, 53*(2), 153–167.

Ladson-Billings, G. (2000). Fighting for our lives: Preparing teachers to teach African American students. *Journal of Teacher Education, 51*(3), 206–214.

Milner, H.R. (2015). *Rac(e)ing to class: Confronting poverty and race in schools and classrooms*. Cambridge, MA: Harvard Education Press.

Skiba, R. J., Michael, R. S., Nardo, A. C., & Peterson, R. L. (2002). The color of discipline: Sources of racial and gender disproportionality in school punishment. *The Urban Review, 34*(4), 317–342.

Chapter 22

Clifton, L. (1993). "Won't you celebrate with me," *Book of Light*. Reprinted by permission of Copper Canyon Press. Retrieved from https://www.poetryfoundation.org/resources/learning/core-poems/detail/50974https://www.poetryfoundation.org/resources/learning/core-poems/detail/50974

GLSEN, Gay, Lesbian and Straight Education Network. (2015). *National School Climate Survey*. Retrieved from https://www.glsen.org/article/2015-national-school-climate-surveyhttps://www.glsen.org/article/2015-national-school-climate-survey

REFERENCES FOR VIGNETTE

Burdge, H., Licona, A. C., Hyemingway, Z. T. (2014). LGBTQ youth of color: Discipline disparities, school push-out, and the school-to-prison pipeline. San Francisco, CA: Gay-Straight Alliance Network and Tucson, AZ: Crossroads Collaborative at the University of Arizona.

Degruy, J., Kjellstrand, J. M., Briggs, H. E., & Brennan, E. M. (2012). Racial respect and racial socialization as protective factors for African American male youth. *Journal of Black Psychology, 38*(4), 395–420.

Grossman, A. H., Haney, A. P., Edwards, P., Alessi, E. J., Ardon, M., & Howell, T. J. (2009). Lesbian, gay, bisexual and transgender youth talk about experiencing and coping with school violence: A qualitative study. *Journal of LGBT Youth, 6*(1), 24–46. doi:10.1080/19361650802379748

Harrison-Quintana, J., Lettman-Hicks, S., & Grant, J. (2009). *Injustice at every turn: A look at Black respondents in the National Transgender Discrimination Survey*. Washington, DC: National Gay and Lesbian Task Force.

Chapter 23

Bentley-Edwards, K. L., Thomas, D. E., & Stevenson, H. C. (2013). Raising consciousness: Promoting healthy coping among African American boys at school. In *Handbook of culturally responsive school mental health* (pp. 121–133). New York: Springer.

Gilliam, W. S. (2005). *Prekindergarteners left behind: Expulsion rates in state prekindergarten systems*. New York: Foundation for Child Development.

Monroe, C. R. (2005). Why are "bad boys" always Black? Causes of disproportionality in school discipline and recommendations for change. *The Clearing House: A Journal of Educational Strategies, Issues and Ideas, 79*(1), 45–50.

Townsend, B. L. (2000). The disproportionate discipline of African American learners: Reducing school suspensions and expulsions. *Exceptional Children, 66*(3), 381–391.

Chapter 25

Anderson, J., (1988). *The education of Blacks in the South, 1860–1935*. Chapel Hill: University of North Carolina Press.

Feistritzer, C. E. (2011). *Profile of teachers in the U.S. 2011*. New York: National Center for Education Information.

Green, R. L., White, G., & Green, K. K. (2012). The expectations factors in Black male achievement: Creating a foundation for education equity. In *A call for change: Providing solutions for Black male achievement* (pp. 140–173). Boston, MA. Houghton Mifflin Harcourt.

Garrison-Wade, D., & Lewis, C. (2006). Tips for school principals and teachers: Helping black student achieve. In J. Landsman & C. W. Lewis (Eds.), *White teachers/diverse classrooms: A guide to building inclusive schools, promoting high expectations, and eliminating racism* (pp. 150–161). Sterling, VA: Stylus.

Lewis, C. W. (2006). African American male teachers in public schools: An examination of three urban school districts. *Teacher's College Record, 108*(2), 224–245.

Lewis, C. W. (2013). Black male teachers' path to U.S. K–12 classrooms: Framing the national discussion. In C. W. Lewis & I. A. Toldson (Eds.), *Black male teachers: Diversifying the United States' teacher workforce* (pp. 3–14). Bingley, UK: Emerald Group.

Lynn, M. (2006). Education for the community: Exploring the culturally relevant practices of Black male teachers. *Teacher's College Record, 108*(12), 2497–2522.

National Center for Education Statistics. (2013). "Public School Teacher Data File," 1987–88 through 2011–12. Retrieved from http://nces.ed.gov/programs/digest/d13/tables/dt13_209.10.asp

Toldson, I.A. (2013). Race matters in the classroom. In C. W. Lewis & I. A. Toldson (Eds.), *Black male teachers: Diversifying the United States' teacher workforce* (pp. 15–21). Bingley, UK: Emerald Group.

TRANSITIONS IN PART III

Emdin, C. (2016, August 27). Why black men quit teaching. *New York Times*.

Cassidy, E. F., & Stevenson, H. C. (2005). They wear the mask: Hypermasculinity and hypervulnerability among African American males in an urban remedial disciplinary school context. *Journal of Aggression, Maltreatment, and Trauma, 11*(4), 53–74.

PART 4

CHAPTER 26

Gladwell, M. (2005). *Blink: The power of thinking without thinking.* New York: Little, Brown.

Kunjufu, J. (2002). *Black students. Middle class teachers.* Sarasota, FL: First Edition, Tenth Printing.

Kunjufu, J. (2005). *Keeping black boys out of special education.* Sarasota, FL: First Edition, Tenth Printing.

Kunjufu, J. (2013). *Changing school culture for black boys.* Sarasota, FL: First Edition, Tenth Printing.

Okonofua, J. A., & Eberhardt, J. L. (2015). Two strikes race and the disciplining of young students. *Psychological Science, 26*(5), 617–624.

Tatum, B. D. (1997). *Why are all the black kids sitting together in the cafeteria?: And other conversations about race.* New York: Basic Books.

CHAPTER 28

Howard, G. R. (2006). *We can't teach what we don't know: White teachers, multiracial schools* (2nd ed.) New York: Teachers College Press.

Reichert, M., & Hawley, A. (2014). *I can learn from you: Boys as relational learners.* Cambridge, MA. Harvard Education Press.

Stevenson, H. (2014). *Promoting racial literacy in schools: Differences that make a difference.* New York: Teachers College Press.

Strand, P., Smith, R. G., Cotman, T., Robinson, C., Swaoim, M., & Crawley, A. (2011). *Gaining on the gap: Changing hearts, minds, and practice.* Lanham, MD: Rowman & Littlefield in partnership with the American Association of School Administrators.

Style, E. (1996). Curriculum as window & mirror. *Social Science Record, 35–38.*

Webb-Johnson, G. (2002). Are schools ready for Joshua? Dimensions of African-American culture among students identified as having behavioral/emotional disorders. *International Journal of Qualitative Studies in Education, 15*(6), 653–671.

CHAPTER 29

Believe to Achieve [Interview by national urban alliance for effective education]. (2008, March 28).

Comer, J. P. (2005). Child and adolescent development: The critical missing focus in school reform. *Phi Delta Kappan, 86*(10), 757–763.

Jackson, Y. (2011). *The pedagogy of confidence: Inspiring high intellectual performance in urban schools.* New York: Teachers College Press.

Kunjufu, J. (2011). *Understanding black male learning styles.* Chicago: African American Images.

National Urban Alliance. (2008, November 17). *Reuven Feuerstein, addresses NUA National Conference* [Video file]. Retrieved from https://www.youtube.com/watch?v=uXopVpQwivY

Kristinsdóttir, S. B. (2008, October 21). *Reuven Feuerstein.* Retrieved October 31, 2016, from http://mennta.hi.is/starfsfolk/solrunb/feuerst.htm

Steinberg, B. (2011). Dr. Reuven Feuerstein on why intelligence is modifiable. *Brain World Magazine,* p. 30.

Steinberg, M. P., Allensworth, E., & Johnson, D. W. (2011). *Student and teacher safety in Chicago public schools: The roles of community context and school social organization.* Chicago: Consortium on Chicago School Research.

CHAPTER 30

Arki, S. J. (2016). Teachers as activists: Using a black, feminist pedagogy to prevent classroom bullying. In A. Osanloo, C. Reed, & J. Schwartz (Eds.), *Creating and negotiating collaborative spaces for socially-just anti-bullying interventions for K–12 schools* (pp. 241–256). Charlotte, NC: Information Age Publishing.

Collins, P. H. (1986). Learning from the outsider within: The sociological significance of black feminist thought. *Social Problems, 33*(6, Special Theory Issue), S14–S32.

Love, B. (2014). "I see Trayvon Martin": What teachers can learn from the tragic death of a young black male. *The Urban Review, 46*(2), 292–306. doi:10.1007/s11256-013-0260-7

Nieto, S., & Bode, P. (2012). *Affirming diversity: The sociopolitical context of multicultural education* (6th ed.). Boston: Pearson Education.

Whitehead, K. W. (2016). [(2015) Excerpts from the Diary of a #BlackMommyActivist.] https://kayewisewhitehead.com/

REFERENCE FOR VIGNETTE

Chua, A. (2011). *Battle hymn of the tiger mom.* New York: Penguin Press.

Chapter 31

Hill, M. L. (2016). *Nobody: Casualties of America's war on the vulnerable, from Ferguson to Flint and beyond.* New York: Atria Books.

Ferguson, A. A. (2001). *Bad boys: Public schools in the making of black masculinity.* Ann Arbor: University of Michigan Press.

Foucault, M. (1977). *Discipline and punish* (A. Sheridan, Trans). New York: Vintage, 1979).

Part 5

Chapter 32

Bottiani, J. H., Bradshaw, C. P., & Mendelson, T. (2016). A multilevel examination of racial disparities in high school discipline: Black and White adolescents' perceived equity, school belonging, and adjustment problems. *Journal of Educational Psychology, 109*(4), 532–545.

Dotterweich, J. (2006). *Positive youth development resource manual.* Binghamton, NY: ACT for Youth Upstate Center of Excellence.

Morris, M. (2016). *Pushout: The criminalization of Black girls in schools.* New York: The New Press.

Chapter 33

Baum, S., & Schwartz, S. (2012). *Is college affordable? In search of a meaningful definition.* Washington, DC: The Institute for Higher Education Policy.

Black, S. E., Cortes, K. E., & Lincove, J. A. (2015). Academic undermatching of high-achieving minority students: Evidence from race-neutral and holistic admissions policies. *American Economic Review, 105*(5), 604–610.

Bowen, W. G., Chingos, M. M., & McPherson, M. S. (2009). *Crossing the finish line: Completing college at America's public universities.* Princeton, NJ: Princeton University Press.

Byndloss, D. C., & Reid, C. (2013). *Promoting college match for low-income students: Lessons for practitioners.* New York: MDRC.

Dukakis, K., Duong, N., Ruiz de Valasco, J., & Henderson, J. (2014). *College access and completion among boys and young men of color: Literature review of promising practices.* Palo Alto, CA: John W. Gardner Center for Youth and Their Communities.

Harper, S. R., & Associates. (2012). *Succeeding in the city: A report from the New York City Black and Latino male high school achievement study.* Philadelphia: University of Pennsylvania, Center for the Study of Race and Equity in Education.

Hoxby, C., & Avery, C. (2012). *The missing "one-offs": The hidden supply of high-achieving, low-income students* (NBER Working Paper No. 18586). Retrieved from National Bureau of Economic Research website: http://www.nber.org/papers/w18586

Hoxby, C., & Turner, S. (2013). *Expanding college opportunities for high-achieving, low-income students* (SIEPR Discussion Paper no. 12-014). Retrieved from Stanford Institute for Economic Policy Research website: http://siepr.stanford.edu/research/publications/expanding-college-opportunities-high-achieving-low-income-students

McDonough, P. M. (1997). *Choosing colleges: How social class and schools structure opportunity.* Albany: State University of New York Press.

McDonough, P. M. (2005). *Counseling and college counseling in America's high schools.* Alexandria, VA: National Association for College Admission Counseling.

Roderick, M., Coca, V., & Nagaoka, J. (2011). Potholes on the road to college: High school effects in shaping urban students' participation in college application, four-year college enrollment, and college match. *Sociology of Education, 84,* 178–211.

Roderick, M., Nagaoka, J., & Allensworth, E. (2006). *From high school to the future: A first look at Chicago public school graduates' college enrollment, college preparation, and graduation from four-year colleges.* Chicago: Consortium on College School Research.

Roderick, M., Nagaoka, J., & Coca, V. (2008). *From high school to the future: Potholes on the road to college.* Chicago: Consortium on College School Research.

Roderick, M., Nagaoka, J., Coca, V., & Moeller, E. (2009). *From high school to the future: Making hard work pay off.* Chicago: Consortium on College School Research.

Rodriguez, A. (2013). *Unpacking the blackbox* (Unpublished dissertation). University of Pennsylvania, ProQuest.

Rodriguez, A. (2015). Tradeoffs and limitations: Understanding the estimation of college undermatch. *Research in Higher Education, 56*(6), 566–594.

Smith, J., Pender, M., Howell, J., & Hurwitz, M. (2012). *A review of the causes and consequences of students' postsecondary choices.* New York: The College Board Advocacy & Policy Center.

CHAPTER 34

Case, K. A., & Hemmings, A. (2005). Distancing strategies: White women preservice teachers and antiracist curriculum. *Urban Education, 40*(6), 606–626.

Chandler, J. L. (2016). *Colluding, colliding, and contending with norms of Whiteness.* Charlotte, NC: Information Age Publishing.

Fasching-Varner, K. (2012). *Working through Whiteness: Examining White racial identity and profession with pre-service teachers.* Lanham, MD: Lexington Books.

Gordon, J. (2005). White on White: Researcher reflexivity and the logics of privilege in White schools undertaking reform. *The Urban Review, 37*(4), 279–301.

Lensmire, A. (2012). *White urban teachers: Stories of fear, violence, and desire.* Lanham, MD: Rowman & Littlefield Education.

Meeks, M. A. (2010). *Racial microaggressions by secondary school teachers against students of color* (Doctoral dissertation). Retrieved from http://hdl.handle.net/10518/3522

Mosley, M., & Rogers, R. (2011). Inhabiting the "tragic gap": Preservice teachers practicing racial literacy. *Teaching Education, 22*(3), 303–324.

Pennington, J. L., Brock, C. H., & Ndura, E. (2012). Unraveling the threads of White teachers' conceptions of caring: Repositioning White privilege. *Urban Education, 47*(4), 743–775.

Pew Research Center. (2006). *Guess who's coming to dinner: 22% of Americans have a relative in a mixed-race marriage.* Washington, DC: Author.

Picower, B. (2009). The unexamined Whiteness of teaching: How White teachers maintain and enact dominant racial ideologies. *Race Ethnicity and Education, 12*(2), 197–215.

Root, M. P. (2001). *Love's revolution: Interracial marriage.* Philadelphia: Temple University Press.

U.S. Census Bureau. (2012, December 12). *U.S. Census Bureau projections show a slower growing, older, more diverse nation a half century from now.* Retrieved from United States Census Bureau - Newsroom Archive: https://www.census.gov/newsroom/releases/archives/population/cb12-243.html

Chapter 36

Jacob, E. (1999). *Cooperative learning in context.* New York: State University of New York Press.

Getahun, D., Jacobsen, S. J., Fassett, M. J., Chen, W., Demissie, K., & Rhoads, G. G. (2013). Recent trends in childhood Attention-Deficit/Hyperactivity Disorder. *JAMA Pediatrics, 167*(3), 282–288.

Chapter 37

Bourne, T. M., Smith, M., & Stoff, E. (Producers) & Hancock, J. L. & Lewis, M. (Writers). (2009). *The Blind Side.* Los Angeles: Warner Brothers Studio.

Jung, C. G. (1959). *The archetypes and the collective unconscious* (R.F.C. Hull, Trans.). New York: Routledge &Kegan Hall.

Sabo, D. F., Melnick, M. J., & Vanfossen, B. E. (1993). High school athletic participation and post-secondary educational and occupational mobility: A focus on race and gender. *Sociology of Sport Journal, 10,* 44–56.

Part 6

Chapter 38

Delpit, L. (2012). *Multiplication is for white people: Raising expectations for other people's children.* New York: The New Press.

Murrell, P. (1999). Responsive teaching for African American male adolescents in society and schools. In V. Polite & J. Davis (Eds.), *African-American males in school and society: Practices and policies for effective education.* New York: Teachers College Press.

Spence, D. (2002). *The efficacy of the pedagogical practices of white teachers in relation to the experiences of African-American students in middle level schools.* Unpublished doctoral dissertation, Temple University, Philadelphia, PA.

Chapter 39

Cowhey, M. (2006). *Black ants and Buddhists: Thinking critically and teaching differently in the primary grades.* Portland, ME: Stenhouse.

Darling-Hammond, L., & Bransford, J. (Eds.). (2005). *Preparing teachers for a changing world: What teachers should learn and be able to do.* San Francisco: Jossey-Bass.

Ferguson, A. A. (2000). *Bad boys: Public schools in the making of masculinity.* Ann Arbor: University of Michigan Press.

Hallett, R. E., & Venegas, K. M. (2011). Is increased access enough? Advanced Placement courses, quality, and success in low-income urban schools. *Journal for the Education of the Gifted, 34*(3), 468–487.

Heath, S. B. (1983). *Ways with words: Language, life, and work in communities and classrooms.* Cambridge, UK: Cambridge University Press.

Kearns, T., Ford, L., & Linney, J. A. (2005). African American student representation in special education programs. *Journal of Negro Education, 74*(4), 297–310.

Meier, D. (2002). *The power of their ideas: Lessons to America from a small school in Harlem*. Boston: Beacon Press.

Oakes, J. (2005). *Keeping track:How schools structure inequality*. (2nd ed.). New Haven, CT: Yale University Press.

Sigmon, R.L. (1979). Service-learning: Three principles. *ACTION, 8*(1), 9–11.

Togut, T. D. (2011). The gestalt of the school-to-prison pipeline: The duality of overrepresentation of minorities in special education and racial disparity in school discipline on minorities. *American University Journal of Gender, Social Policy, and Law, 20*(1), 163–181.

Toldson, I. (2012). *Show me the numbers: Do black kids have problems in schools because so few teachers look like them?* Retrieved October 3, 2015 from http://www.theroot.com/articles/culture/2012/10/how_race_matters_in_the_classroom.2.html

Chapter 40

Baldwin, A. Y. (1987). I'm Black but look at me, I am also gifted. *Gifted Child Quarterly, 31,*180–185.

Ford, D. Y. (2010). *Reversing underachievement among gifted Black students* (2nd ed.). Waco, TX: Prufrock Press.

Ford, D. Y. (2013). Multicultural issues: Gifted underrepresentation and prejudice—Learning from Allport and Merton. *Gifted Child Today, 36*(1), 62–67. doi: 10 1177/1076217512465285

Ford, D. Y., & Grantham, T. C. (2003). Providing access for gifted culturally diverse students: From deficit to dynamic thinking. *Theory Into Practice, 42*, 217–225.

Ford, D. Y., Grantham, T. C., & Whiting, G. W. (2008a). Another look at the achievement gap. *Urban Education, 43*, 216–239.

Ford, D. Y., Grantham, T. C., & Whiting, G. W. (2008b). Culturally and linguistically diverse students in gifted education: Recruitment and retention issues. *Exceptional Children, 74*(3), 289–308.

Frasier, M. M. (1987). The identification of gifted Black students: Developing new perspectives. *Journal for the Education of the Gifted, 10*, 155–180.

Grantham, T. C. (2011). New directions for gifted Black males suffering from bystander effects: A call for upstanders. *Roeper Review: A Journal on Gifted Education, 33*, 263–272.

Grantham, T. C., Hines, M., Dennis, A., Solomon, M., & Anderson, B. (in press). Developing cultural competence in gifted and advanced students using community problem solving. In J. L. Davis & J. L. Moore III (Eds.), *Gifted children of color around the world, advances in race and ethnicity in education* (Vol. 3). United Kingdom: Emerald Group Publishing Limited.

Grantham, T. C., Trotman Scott, M., & Harmon, D. (Eds.). (2013). *Young, triumphant, and Black: Overcoming segregated minds in desegregated schools*. Waco, TX: Prufrock Press.

Grissom, J. A., & Redding, C. (2016). Discretion and disproportionality explaining the underrepresentation of high-achieving students of color in gifted programs. *AERA Open, 2*(1), 1–25. doi: 10.1177/2332858415622175

Hilliard, A. G. III. (1990). Back to Binet: The case against the use of IQ tests in the schools. *Contemporary Education, 61*, 184–189.

Torrance, E. P. (1974). Differences are not deficits. *Teachers College Record*, 75, 471–487.

U.S. Department of Education Office for Civil Rights. (2011-12). Retrieved from www.ocrdata.ed.gov.

Wright, B. L., Counsell, S. L., & Tate, S. L. (2015). We're many members, but one body: Fostering a healthy self-identity and agency in African American boys. *Young Children, 70*(3), 24–31.

CHAPTER 41

Annie E. Casey Foundation. (2016). *Early warning! Why reading by the end of third grade matters.* Retrieved from http://www.aecf.org/resources/early-warning-why-reading-by-end-of-third-grade-matters/

Banks, J. M. (2009). *Teaching strategies for ethnic studies* (8th ed.). New York: Allyn & Bacon.

Bloom, B. (Ed.). (1956). *Taxonomy of educational objectives. Handbook I: Cognitive domain.* New York: Wiley.

Ford, D.Y. (2011). *Multicultural gifted education* (2nd ed.). Waco, TX: Prufrock Press.

Ford, D. Y., & Harris III, J. J. (1999). *Multicultural gifted education.* New York: Teachers College Press.

Hart, B., & Risley, T. R. (2011). *The early catastrophe.* Retrieved from https://www.aft.org/sites/default/files/periodicals/TheEarlyCatastrophe.pdf

Hudson, W. (1991). *Jamal's busy day.* East Orange, NJ: Just Us Books.

Trotman Scott, M. (2014). Using the Bloom-Banks matrix to develop multicultural differentiated instruction for gifted students. *Gifted Child Today 37*(3), 163–168.

U.S. Department of Education. (2014). *2013-2014 Civil Rights Data Collection: A First Glance. Office for Civil Rights.* Retrieved from https://www2.ed.gov/about/offices/list/ocr/docs/2013-14-first-look.pdf

CHAPTER 42

Crumbley, J. (1999). Seven tasks for parents: Developing positive racial identity. *Adoptive Families,* September/October. Retrieved August 20, 2016, from: http://www.nacac.org/postadopt/transracial_identity.html

Derman-Sparks, L., & Olsen Edwards, J. (2010). *Anti-bias education for young children and ourselves.* Washington, DC: National Association for the Education of Young Children.

Gay, G. (2000). *Culturally responsive teaching: Theory, research, and practice.* New York: Teachers College Press.

Kunjufu, J. (1990). *Countering the conspiracy to destroy black boys* (Vol. 3). Chicago: African American Images.

Steele, D. M., & Cohn-Vargas, B. (2013). *Identity safe classrooms: Places to belong and learn.* Thousand Oaks, CA: Corwin.

Tatum, B. (1997). *Why are all the Black kids sitting together in the cafeteria?* New York: Basic Books.

CHAPTER 43

Chideya, F. (2014, January 3). Traveling while Black. *New York Times.*

Tensley, B. (2015, March). What's keeping Black students from studying abroad? *The Atlantic.*

Ungar, S. J. (2016, March/April). The study abroad solution: How to open the American mind. *Foreign Affairs.*

West, C. (1994). *Race matters.* New York: Vintage Books.

CHAPTER 44

African American Policy Forum & Center for Intersectionality and Social Policy Studies (AAPF). (2015). *Black girls matter: Pushed out, overpoliced, and underprotected.* New York.

Retrieved from http://static1.squarespace.com/static/53f20d90e4b0b80451158d8c/t/54dcc1ece 4b001c03e323448/1423753708557/AAPF_BlackGirlsMatterReport.pdf

Arrington, E. G., & Stevenson, H. C. (2012). "More than what we read in books": Black student perspectives on independent schools. In D. T. Slaughter-Defoe, H. C. Stevenson, E. G. Arrington, and D. J. Johnson (Eds.) *Black educational choice: Assessing the private and public alternatives to traditional K–12 public schools* (pp. 78–90). Santa Barbara, CA: Praeger.

Belgrave, F. Z. (2009). *African American girls: Reframing perceptions and changing experiences*. Richmond, VA: Springer.

Editorial Projects in Education. (2010). *Education Counts database using Editorial Projects in Education, Research Center, Custom Table Builder*. Retrieved from http://www.edcounts.org/ createtable/step1.php

Emdin, C. (2016). *For white folks who teach in the hood. . . and the rest of y'all too: Reality Pedagogy and Urban Education*. Boston: Beacon Press.

Evans-Winters, V. E. (2017). Flipping the script: The dangerous bodies of girls of color. *Cultural Studies↔Critical Methodologies*, 1532708616684867.

Evans-Winters, V. E., & Esposito, J. (2010). Other people's daughters: Critical race feminism and black girls' education. *Educational Foundations*, *24*(1), 11–24.

Fordham, S. (1991). Racelessness in private schools: Should we deconstruct the racial and cultural identity of African-American adolescents?. *Teachers College Record*, *92*(3), 470–484.

Fordham, S. (1993). "Those loud black girls": (Black) women, silence, and gender "passing" in the academy. *Anthropology & Education Quarterly*, *24*(1), 3–32.

Gibson, G.A. (2015). Education vs. schooling: Black adolescent females fight for an education in the 21st century. In C. F. Collins (Ed.) *Black girls and adolescents: Facing the challenges* (pp. 199–210). Santa Barbara, CA: Praeger.

Grant, L. (1992). Race and the schooling of young girls. *Education and Gender Equality*, 91–113.

Hill, S. A. (2002). Teaching and doing gender in African American families. *Sex Roles*, *47*(11–12), 493–506.

Jones, J. J. (2015). The mis-education of black girls: Learning in a white system. In C. F. Collins (Ed.) *Black girls and adolescents: Facing the challenges* (pp. 269–286). Santa Barbara, CA: Praeger.

Ladson-Billings, G. (2009). *The dreamkeepers: Successful teachers of African American children*. Hoboken, NJ: John Wiley & Sons.

Ladson-Billings, G. (2014). Culturally relevant pedagogy 2.0: aka the remix. *Harvard Educational Review*, *84*(1), 74–84.

Morris, E. W. (2007). "Ladies" or "loudies"? Perceptions and experiences of black girls in classrooms. *Youth & Society*, *38*(4), 490–515.

Morris, M. (2016). *Pushout: The criminalization of Black girls in schools*. New York: The New Press.

National Women's Law Center (NWLC) and NAACP Legal Defense and Educational Fund. (2014). *Unlocking opportunity for African-American girls: A call to action for educational equity*. Washington, DC. Retrieved from http://www.naacpldf.org/files/publications/Unlocking%20Opportunity%20for%20African%20American%20Girls_0.pdf

National Assessment of Educational Progress (NAEP). (2013). *Reading and mathematics assessments*. Retrieved from http://nces.ed.gov/nationsreportcard/naepdata/

National Center for Education Statistics (NCES). (2006). *Graduation rates of first-time, full-time bachelor's degree-seeking students at 4-year postsecondary institutions, by race/ethnicity, time to completion, sex, and control of institution: Selected cohort entry years, 1996 through 2006*. Retrieved from http://nces.ed.gov/programs/digest/d13/tables/dt13_326.10.asp

Ross, T., Kena, G., Rathbun, A., KewalRamani,A., Zhang, J., Kristapovich, P., & Manning, E. (2012). *Gaps in access and persistence study*. Retrieved from http://nces.ed.gov/pubs2012/2012046.pdf

U.S. Department of Civil Rights Data Collection (2014). Data snapshot: School discipline (Issue Brief No. 1, 3). Retrieved from http://ocrdata.ed.gov/Downloads/CRDC-School-Discipline-Snapshot.pdf

Ward, J. V. (1990). *The skin we're in: Teaching our children to be emotionally strong, socially smart, spiritually connected.* New York: The Free Press.

Ward, J. V. (1996). Raising resisters: The role of truth telling in the psychological development of African American girls. In B. J. Ross Leadbetter & N. Way (Eds.), *Urban girls: Resisting stereotypes, creating identities* (pp. 85–99). New York: New York University.

Way, N. (1998). *Everyday courage: The lives and stories of urban teenagers.* New York: NYU Press.

Index

Curriculum
  books and, 363–369
  culturally responsive literature and, 358
  global skills, 370–376
  history, 92–93, 258
  partnerships, 45–46
  role in inclusiveness, 258

Davis, Jordan, 104
Davis, Miles, 328
Deaf Black students, 184–186
Deafness, 184–186
De-escalation of classroom conflicts, 336–340
Deficit perspective, 35, 144–147
DeGeneres, Ellen, 222
De Gruy, Joy, 202, 249
Deiro, J. A., 64
Delpit, Lisa, 62, 144, 338
Deming, W. Edward, 42
Derman-Sparks, Louise, 363
Diallo, Amadou, 191
Dias, Marley, 383
Dickinson, Emily, 202
Die Nigger Die: A Political Autobiography, 202
Discipline, school, 3–4, 128–129
  and adopting data tracking systems and
    scorecards to identify schools with
    disproportionately high suspension and
    special education placement rates, 46–47
  assumptions about "good" student behavior
    and, 33–34
  harsher on Black boys, 129–131
  school-to-prison track and, 279–285
  starting out firm with, 290–293
Disintegration phase, 68–69
Dissociation, 206
Diversity
  within Blackness, 173–174
  cultivated as resource for identity safety, 114–115
  vs. multiculturalism, 77
Douglass, Frederick, 93, 328
Dovidio, John, 77
DuBois, W. E. B., 240, 328
Dunbar, Paul Laurence, 240

Early-alert systems, 49–50
Early childhood education, 213–216
Eastin, Khyle, 374
Eberhardt, J. L., 237
Edwards, Jordan, 104
Edwards, Julie Olsen, 363
Effective openness, 64
Emdin, Christopher, 37
Empathy, 117
Encounters, 170

Engagement of Black boys
  of students in meaningful/relevant work,
    338–340
  using the color-coded Bloom-Banks matrix to
    support literacy and, 356–362
Equality *vs.* equity, 77, 194
Equalization of student status, 115
Equal vision, 248
Equitable classrooms, 312–313
  bringing about equity, 318–319
  program steps, 313–318
  things to consider in creating, 318
Equity
  vs. equality, 77, 194
  pedagogy, 77
  plans, 45
Everyday Anti-racism, 138
Expectations of intelligence and academic
    performance, 58, 75
Expertise, student, 36, 115

Faulkner, William, 74–75
Fears
  of Black males, White people and, 4–5, 34, 57
  of parents of Black boys, 239–241
Federally designated minority-serving
    institutions, 51–52
Feedback, wise, 117
Ferguson, Ann, 282, 283, 343
Ferguson, Robert, 138
Ferrell, Jonathon, 192
Feuerstein, Reuven, 262, 263
*Fine Dessert: Four Centuries, Four Families, One
    Delicious Treat, A*, 288
Ford, D. Y., 357–358
Fordham, S., 62
*For White Folks Who Teach in the Hood and the
    Rest of Y'all Too*, 37
Frost, Robert, 202
Full, Full, Full of Love, 365

Gaslighting, 206
Gates, WIllie, 28
Gender
  disaggregated student right-to-know data by
    race/ethnicity within, 50
  intersectionality of race, poverty, and, 191–194
  preferences, 36–37
  self-study of student experiences and outcomes
    with data disaggregated by race within, 51
  sexism, 33
Gifted education, Black boys in, 350–355
Gillam, Walter, 56, 62
Gladwell, Malcolm, 241
Global skills, 370–376

A SAGE Publishing Company

Helping educators make the greatest impact

CORWIN HAS ONE MISSION: to enhance education through intentional professional learning.

We build long-term relationships with our authors, educators, clients, and associations who partner with us to develop and continuously improve the best evidence-based practices that establish and support lifelong learning.

Solutions you want. Experts you trust. Results you need.